LANtastic Made Easy

Tom Rugg

Osborne **McGraw-Hill**

Berkeley New York St. Louis San Francisco
Auckland Bogotá Hamburg London Madrid
Mexico City Milan Montreal New Delhi Panama City
Paris São Paulo Singapore Sydney
Tokyo Toronto

Osborne **McGraw-Hill**
2600 Tenth Street
Berkeley, California 94710
U.S.A.

For information on translations or book distributors outside of the U.S.A., please write to Osborne **McGraw-Hill** at the above address.

LANtastic Made Easy

1234567890 DOC 998765432

ISBN 0-07-881804-4

Publisher

Kenna S. Wood

Acquisitions Editor

Jeffrey M. Pepper

Associate Editor

Emily Rader

Project Editors

Madhu Prasher
Kelly Barr

Technical Editor

Werner Feibel

Copy Editor

Ann Krueger Spivack

Proofreader

Linda Medoff

Indexer

Lynn Brown

Computer Designer

Jani Beckwith

Illustrator

Susie C. Kim

Cover Design

Bay Graphics Design, Inc.

Contents

Acknowledgments .... *xiii*
Introduction .... *xv*

1 LAN Background **1**
LAN History 2
The LAN Today 3
LAN Components 4
Physical LAN Topologies: Bus, Star, and Ring 7
LAN Signaling Methods: Ethernet, Token Ring, and ARCnet 10
Other Connectivity Methods 14
Sneakernet 15
Print Buffers 15
Serial and Parallel Port Connectors 16
Multiuser Operating Systems 17

2 LANtastic Uses **19**
Knowing the Terminology 19
Workstations Versus Engineering Workstations 21
How People Use LANtastic Today 21
Shared Printers 23

Shared Data Space 24
Shared Database Applications 25
Shared Software 34
Shared CD-ROM Disk Drives 37
Shared Modems 40
Some Real-World LANtastic Users 40
Case 1: A Small Law Firm 40
Case 2: A Food Processing Company 41
Case 3: A Yacht Chartering Company 41
Case 4: A Small Insurance Office 41
Case 5: A Software Development Company 42
Case 6: A Magazine Publisher 42
Case 7: A Retail Business 42

3 The LANtastic Product Line **43**
Ethernet LAN Products 43
LANtastic Ethernet Starter Kits 44
Other Ethernet Products and Components 47
2Mbps LAN Products 52
Voice Products 55
Software Products 57

4 Planning for LANtastic **59**
Why Bother Planning? 60
Analyze Your Needs 62
Situations Inappropriate for LANtastic 62
LANtastic in a Novell World 64
Workgroup Needs and Wants 65
Remember Your Objectives 65
Checklists 83
Inappropriate Situations for LANtastic 83
Clarify Objectives 84
Preparing to Choose and Install a LAN 84

5 Installing and Testing LANtastic **87**
Quick Installation 88
Quick Hardware Installation 89

Quick Software Installation for a Server 90
Default Settings and Default Values 91
Quick Software Installation for a Workstation 94
A Chapter Overview 95
Detailed Hardware Installation 96
Installation from a Starter Kit and LANtastic Components 97
Installation of Independent Hardware 107
Detailed Software Installation for a Server 109
LANtastic/AI Installation 111
The LANtastic/AI Network Adapter 117
Detailed Software Installation for a Workstation 122
Starting and Testing LANtastic 125
Starting LANtastic 125
Testing LANtastic 130
Installing LANtastic Z 134
Installing LANtastic Z Hardware 134
Installing LANtastic Z Software 134
Starting LANtastic Z 135
Testing LANtastic Z 135

6 Sharing Primary Resources: Disks, Printers, and E-Mail 137
Shared Hard Disks 138
The NET Menu 138
Commands at the DOS Prompt 148
Shared Printers 150
Printer Redirection from the NET Menu 151
Printer Redirection from the DOS Prompt 154
Printer Queue Control 154
Shared Printer Products 159
Electronic Mail 163
Setting Up E-Mail 163
Using E-Mail 164

7	**Sharing Other Resources: CD-ROMs, Modems, and Other Devices**	**173**
	Sharing CD-ROM Disk Drives	174
	Installing a CD-ROM Disk Drive	177
	Accessing a CD-ROM Drive	184
	CD-ROM Disk Drive Products	186
	Sharing Modems and Other Two-Way Serial Devices	187
	What ArtiCom Does	188
	Installing ArtiCom	189
	Running ArtiCom	193
	Other Modem-Sharing Products	198
	Using a Tape Backup System	199
	Tape Backup Strategies	201
	Using Tape Systems with LANtastic	203
	Tape Backup Suppliers	205
	Attaching Portable Computers	206
	Artisoft Central Station	206
	Portable LAN Adapters	211
8	**The Artisoft Sounding Board**	**215**
	Installation	217
	Hardware Installation	217
	Software Installation	218
	Starting the Software	219
	Testing the Sounding Board	220
	HTEST: The Handset Test	220
	LTEST: The Line-In and Line-Out Test	220
	SAY: Play a Prerecorded Message	221
	RECORD: Create and Play Your Own Message	221
	Using Voice Chat	222
	Using LANtastic Voice E-Mail	225
9	**Troubleshooting**	**231**
	General Troubleshooting	232
	Start with the Obvious	232

Run LANCHECK 235
Isolate the Problem 235
Specific Problems 238
Single Computer Lockup 238
Inability to Communicate 240
Corrupt Disk Files 242
UPS Systems 244
Other Problems 245

10 **LANtastic Security** **249**
Controlled Logins 250
Establishing User Accounts 252
Access Control Lists 261
Access Rights 262
Limited Server Resource Offerings 267
Audit Trails 271
Protecting NET_MGR 273

11 **LAN Administration** **275**
LAN Security 277
Data Backup 277
Server Disk Space 278
Computer Viruses 279
Physical Security Measures 284
User Support 284
Configuration Management 285
LAN Optimization 286

12 **LANtastic and Windows** **287**
Single-User Windows Configuration 289
Installation of Single-User Configuration 289
Using the Single-User Configuration 295
Multiuser Windows Configuration 296
LANtastic for Windows 296
Installation of LANtastic for Windows 297
Using LANtastic for Windows 297

13 **LANtastic Optimization** 303
Optimization Methodology 304
Possible Benchmarks 306
Optimizing for Speed 308
LANcache 309
ALONE 318
DOS Parameters 320
Server Parameters 323
Parameters on Other LANtastic Programs 327
Other Speed Tips 328
Optimizing RAM Usage 331
LANtastic and DOS Parameters 332
Upper Memory Usage 334
Optimizing Disk Space Usage 334
Highlights 335

14 **LANtastic Software Reference** 337
The General Command Format 338
Common Parameters 339
The /help Parameter (/help or /?) 339
The /remove Parameter 339
The /verbose Parameter 340
The @filename Parameter 340
AEX 340
Format 340
Parameters 341
AILANBIO 342
Format 342
Parameters 342
ALONE 344
Format 344
Parameters 345
LANCACHE 345
Format 345
Parameters 345
LANCHECK 347
Format 347

Parameters 348
LANPUP 348
Format 348
Parameters 348
NET 349
Format 349
Parameters 349
NET_MGR 369
Format 370
Parameters 370
REDIR 374
Format 374
Parameters 374
SERVER 375
Format 375
Parameters 375
UPS 378
Format 378
Parameters 378

A Sample Startup Files 381
A "Typical" Configuration 382
AUTOEXEC.BAT for a Server or Workstation 382
CONFIG.SYS for a Server 382
STARTNET.BAT for a Server Named TOM 383
CONFIG.SYS for a Workstation 383
STARTNET.BAT for a Workstation Named LESLIE 383
A Troubleshooting Configuration 383
CONFIG.SYS for a Server 384
STARTNET.BAT for a Server Named TOM 384
CONFIG.SYS for a Workstation 385
STARTNET.BAT for a Workstation Named LESLIE 385
A High-Performance LAN Server Configuration 385

CONFIG.SYS for a Server That Runs LANcache 385
STARTNET.BAT for a Server Named TOM 386
A "Minimum RAM" Configuration 386
CONFIG.SYS for a Server 387
STARTNET.BAT for a Server Named TOM 387
CONFIG.SYS for a Workstation 387
STARTNET.BAT for a Workstation Named LESLIE 387
A DOS 5 Extended Memory Configuration 388
CONFIG.SYS for a Server 389
STARTNET.BAT for a Server Named TOM 389
CONFIG.SYS for a Workstation 389
STARTNET.BAT for a Workstation Named LESLIE 390

B LANtastic Support Sources 391
Artisoft Support 391
Artisoft Voice Telephone Support 393
Artisoft Fax Support 393
Artisoft BBS Support 393
Artisoft Support on CompuServe 394
Artisoft Dealers 394
Other Support Sources 395
Catalog Vendors 395
Contact the Author 396
LANtastic Software from the Author 396

Glossary 397

Index 411

Acknowledgments

Many people contributed in varying ways and degrees to make this book possible. My thanks go:

To everyone at Artisoft, the creators of LANtastic. My particular thanks to Nora Tangeman, Joe Waldygo, Mimi Ho, Adrian King, Rick Roth, and Chris Lagemann for their open-minded approach of providing assistance without making any attempt to influence the content of this book. Artisoft's commitment to quality is evident in their hardware, software, customer support, and dealer support, and this book was a joy to write as a result.

To everyone at or associated with Osborne/McGraw-Hill, publishers of this book, for their support and assistance during the course of this project. Special thanks to Jeff Pepper, Emily Rader, Werner Feibel, Madhu Prasher, Kelly Barr, Ann Krueger Spivack, and Jani Beckwith.

To Nick Anis for planting the seed that grew into this book, to Tom and Bonnie Herron for providing open access to office equipment, to CMS Enhancements in Irvine, California, for providing an excellent test computer, and to Phil Mourey, Myles Matsuoka, Ray Smith, Jim Holmes, John Hannan, and countless others for helping me learn about LANs over the years.

To numerous LANtastic dealers, consultants, and users, who endured my questions and provided helpful answers about LANtastic hardware, software, applications, and troubleshooting. Among them are Mark Schiffman (Hi-Tech Resources, Tarzana, CA), Wayne Chen (Teltron, Thousand Oaks, CA),

Dave Jolley (Apogee Computer Systems, Panorama City, CA), Frank Fuller (WSC Company, Elk Grove, IL), Robert Laszko, Sr. and Robert Laszko, Jr. (Data Management Systems, Fallbrook, CA), Al Margolis (The Software Engineering Store, San Francisco, CA), and Technical Computer Services, Fort Lauderdale, FL.

And finally, extra special thanks to Phil Feldman, my coauthor and collaborator on so many books in the past, to my wife Leslie, who is my coauthor and collaborator on my most important production (our daughter Whitney), and to my parents, Jim and Annette Rugg, who coauthored and collaborated on me.

Introduction

Local area networks (LANs) are a hot topic in today's computer world. Hundreds of thousands of small LANs have been installed in the past two years, and many people are confused by them. Before you go any farther in this book, here's a one-minute explanation of what a LAN is and why you might want one.

A LAN is an assortment of hardware and software components that connects your workgroup's PCs together. Once a LAN connects your PCs, you can all use the same laser printer, you can copy files to and from a shared hard disk to eliminate the need to carry floppy disks around, you can all access the same database files (name and address lists, inventory files, or whatever), you can coordinate your appointment calendars, and you can communicate using electronic mail, among other things.

LANtastic consists of hardware and software. The hardware is basically a LAN card that you install in each IBM-compatible PC, plus cables to connect them together. The software is the LANtastic network operating system, which is several programs that run on your PC so it will know how to interact with the other PCs and do the things mentioned in the previous paragraph. You can buy the hardware either from Artisoft (makers of LANtastic) along with the software, or from other manufacturers that sell compatible equipment.

Other LANs are available, but LANtastic has become the market leader in small LANs for several reasons:

- LANtastic's cost is low for small groups, especially groups with 30 computers or less. Users can easily spend less than $250 per computer, and it's possible to spend less than $200. (Many competitors cost much more.)
- LANtastic is easy to install and use, not nearly as complicated as most competitors. Yet LANtastic has all the features needed to provide access to shared data and computer devices—either unrestrained access for everyone or limited access if you prefer.
- LANtastic is compact and efficient. It uses very little RAM (PC memory) and moves data between PCs plenty fast for nearly any group's needs.
- LANtastic is reliable and is backed up by a company that has shown a commitment to quality and support.

As a result of these facts, LANtastic has collected dozens of awards from computer trade magazines for Product of the Year and design excellence. Over 60,000 LANtastic LANs are running today, most of them connecting between 2 and 12 computers. Most are installed by ordinary PC users who have no great technical experience.

This book's purpose is to explain in simple terms what a LAN is, what you can do with a LANtastic LAN, and how to plan for, buy, install, and exploit a LANtastic LAN.

About This Book

This book assumes you know nothing about LANs and not necessarily very much about personal computers. As the book title indicates, the goal of the book is to explain LANtastic in a way that is "made easy" for you. The explanations are no more technical than necessary. The approach is practical—the explanations are aimed at the pragmatic reader who wants to get to the bottom line: How do I do this and what good can it do me? If you are looking for detailed explanations of a LAN's electronic circuitry and software design algorithms, go buy another book. Instead, this book explains in straightforward terms the practical aspects of planning, installing, and using a LANtastic LAN in a small workgroup.

The typical reader of this book is someone who has worked at least a little with PCs as a user yet is not a computer expert. If you can run a word processor or a spreadsheet program to create simple documents, you have all the background you need. There are two categories of readers for this book:

- *People who are considering a LAN* If you think your office or workgroup might benefit from connecting its PCs together, this book explains how to decide. In particular, the first five chapters take you through the basics of how LANs work, what you can do with a LAN, what LANtastic products are available, and how to plan and install a LANtastic LAN. Later chapters show how to share devices and use special features of LANtastic. You can read any or all of these chapters to see how a LANtastic LAN would fit in your group.
- *People already using a LAN* If you already use LANtastic, this book shows you capabilities you may not know about, with step-by-step instructions. You can share CD-ROM disk drives and modems, exchange voice messages, and use tape backup systems, for example. What's more, if your LAN does not use LANtastic's software, this book shows what you might gain by switching to it. Even if you use some other hardware (Novell, 3Com, Western Digital, and others), you can run the LANtastic software and gain productivity because of its ease of use. You might be surprised to learn how many offices have given up on Novell NetWare 2.x or 3.x due to their complexity.

This book provides you with answers to the following questions:

- What is a LAN? What different types are there? In general terms, how do they work?
- What can I do with a LANtastic LAN? What is its practical benefit to a workgroup? How does it change what I already do with my PCs?
- How should I plan for and buy a LANtastic LAN?

- How do I install and test a LANtastic LAN? Do I need professional help or can I do it myself?
- How do I share disk space and printers? What other devices can I share and why might I want to?
- What do I do if something goes wrong? Can I troubleshoot problems myself or do I have to call in experts? Who do I call?
- How do I implement LAN security if I don't want everyone in the group to have access to all disk files?
- What kind of day-to-day administration does the LAN need?
- What steps can I take to make the LAN process user requests faster?

How This Book Is Organized

This book's chapters can be grouped into four sections. The first section includes chapters 1 through 4 and explains background and planning. Chapter 1 explains what a LAN is and briefly how it works. This chapter doesn't go into a lot of technical depth, but if it's still more than you want, skim it and go on to Chapter 2. Chapter 2 explains what you can do with a LANtastic LAN. A good subtitle might be "What's in it for me? Why should I care about LANtastic or any LAN?" Chapter 3 presents the LANtastic product line, complete with list prices at the time this was written, to help you understand your alternatives and the costs involved. Finally, Chapter 4 explains how to plan for LANtastic, both to decide if LANtastic is right for you and to figure out the preparations you must make in your workgroup's environment.

The second section covers LANtastic installation and consists of Chapter 5. This chapter takes you through the hardware and software installation process in detail, and shows you how to test for success afterward.

The book's third section is chapters 6 through 13, which explain how to use and maximize LANtastic. Chapter 6 explains the fundamental sharing that most users do: disk drives, printers, and electronic mail. Chapter 7 discusses other types of sharing: CD-ROM drives, tape backup systems, modems, and attachment of portable computers. Chapter 8 explains a unique feature of LANtastic, voice communication using the Artisoft Sounding

Board option. The important topic of troubleshooting is covered in Chapter 9, which explains what to do if something goes wrong. Chapters 10 and 11 go into the duties of a LAN administrator. Chapter 10 covers how a LAN administrator implements security to prevent outsiders (or insiders) from accessing private data, and Chapter 11 goes through all the administrative actions that someone occasionally needs to take to assure a productive LAN. Chapter 12 explains how to use LANtastic with Microsoft Windows, and Chapter 13 explains LANtastic optimization—how to make the LAN run better (which usually means faster).

Finally, the fourth section of the book is Chapter 14, which is a summary of all the commands and parameters you can use with all the LANtastic programs. You won't ever need most of these, but the material is listed alphabetically in one place in case you do.

The book also has two appendixes and a glossary. Appendix A provides sample startup files for your PC and LANtastic. Appendix B explains how to get help or more information about LANtastic, including several ways to contact Artisoft's Technical Support Group and how to contact the author.

A Word From the Author

This is an independent book. I don't work for Artisoft (which makes LANtastic), and I'm not a reseller of Artisoft products. I get none of your money when you buy these products, whether from Artisoft or other vendors. This means you get in this book my own version of unbiased explanations and recommendations. Of course, I have biases, but they're not biases that put money in my pocket if I convince you to buy a particular product. My goal is to make this book understandable and clear, so you can make the right decisions about whether a LANtastic LAN is right for you, and how to plan, buy, install, and use LANtastic.

Let me state one of my biases right now: I like LANtastic. A lot. I have worked with other LANs and know how complicated, confusing, and expensive they can be. Artisoft has done an outstanding job in designing LANtastic to avoid these problems. If you want to find a simple and effective way to connect a few PCs together, give LANtastic a good look. I don't think you'll be sorry.

If something in this book is unclear or if you disagree with my advice, let me know. You can reach me either through this book's publisher, Osborne/McGraw-Hill, or at the address shown in Appendix B.

Conventions Used in This Book

The conventions in this book are simple and similar to the conventions you may have seen in other books and manuals.

- **Boldface** text indicates commands that you should type from the keyboard, for example "type **net**," or "enter the command **cd\dos**." While commands that you enter are shown in this book in lowercase letters, you can enter them as capital letters if you like.
- Special keyboard keys that you are asked to press are printed in lozenges, or boxes, like this: ENTER, ESC, INS, DEL, and F1.
- Keystroke combinations are shown using lozenges connected by hyphens. They indicate you should press both (or all three) keys simultaneously. For example, "Press CTRL-ALT-DEL to reboot" means to hold down CTRL while pressing ALT and DEL all at the same time. "Press CTRL-BREAK" means to hold down CTRL and then press BREAK.

1

LAN Background

To understand whether or not LANtastic will help you, and to be able to fully utilize it once you install it, you need some background in LAN history, concepts, terminology, and other fundamentals. This chapter gives you that background. Don't worry, it won't feel like a history class; you'll get just enough background so you'll understand why LANs of *any* kind exist and how the hardware and software components fit together to form a LANtastic LAN.

If you're incredibly impatient and supremely confident in your LAN background, you can skip ahead to Chapter 5 and learn how to install and start running LANtastic within an hour. Unless you feel completely comfortable with LAN concepts, the uses of a LAN, and how to plan a LAN installation, it will probably be most helpful to read the earlier chapters first. These early chapters (especially Chapter 3) will also tell you what's available in the LANtastic product line.

LAN History

In the beginning there was the mainframe computer. Between 1950 and 1980, just about the only way to do any computing was to submit a deck of punch cards to your company's central computer installation and wait for someone to process your computing request. If you were lucky, you got your results (printed output) returned to you within a few hours. If you needed a lot of computing resources, such as several tape drives, or if the computer center was backlogged with high priority work, you had to wait overnight or several days for your results. These mainframe computers typically cost between $1 million and $5 million for the computer itself, and another $1 million to $5 million for tape and disk drive equipment. Such expensive and complicated resources were tightly controlled by the data processing departments of large organizations. If you wanted computer work done, you followed their rules and waited your turn.

In the early 1980s, personal computers began to make their presence known. (Some early models existed in the mid-1970s, but the 1981 announcement of the IBM PC really started the rapid spread of personal computers.) All you had to do was to convince your boss to come up with $2 thousand to $5 thousand and you could buy your own computer. By the mid-1980s, millions of IBM PCs (and IBM-compatible models from companies such as Compaq) were installed and running word processing, spreadsheets, database managers, and presentation graphics programs.

The computers and software weren't quite as sophisticated as today's versions, but they worked pretty well; after a bit of training most PC users were happily productive with their PCs and programs. With their own computers, most workers could do small-scale computer work without relying on the whims of the corporate data processing gurus.

The word *personal* in personal computer was particularly appropriate during this period. You as a PC user had your own personal data on your own personal computer. The PCs of your associates were all separate entities, often called *stand-alone* computers, that for the most part did not interact with your PC. Of course, someone else could send you computer information by copying the data files onto floppy disks and carrying or mailing them to you, but that was about the extent of interconnectivity between PCs.

Some bright, forward-looking companies saw the need to connect all those stand-alone computers. (Actually, they had earlier realized the potential in connecting mainframes and minicomputers, and simply adapted the techniques to PCs.) They saw that PC users would soon want to be able to do the following:

- To quickly and simply make data files such as word processing documents or spreadsheet files available to all the PCs in a work group, without the bother and delay of passing floppy disks around.
- To somehow allow the many PCs in a work group to use the same database files simultaneously so that everyone would have access to the same, up-to-date information.
- To give everyone access to a small number of expensive peripheral devices such as laser printers, color printers, plotters, and high-speed modems, without the need to buy one of these devices for every single PC.

These companies designed *local area networks* (LANs) to address these needs. Early LANs used *proprietary designs*, which meant that you had to buy all your hardware and software from the LAN manufacturer. As time went on, customers demanded standards before they would buy a LAN. As a result, more companies offered products that worked on a variety of LANs, which caused the prices for many of the hardware and software components to drop.

The LAN Today

Today's LAN is made up of a number of hardware and software components that are physically connected together and send electronic signals and messages back and forth. This section briefly explains what these components are, how they are physically connected, and how they send signals and messages.

LAN Components

Today's LANs are constructed with hardware and software components that interact together to perform the three connectivity functions: making data files available to each PC in a work group; allowing many PCs to use the same file simultaneously; and giving every PC access to peripherals.

The hardware components in simple LANS are LAN cards, LAN cables, connectors, and terminators. The software components are the network operating system, the application software, and the LAN utility software. The following sections cover each of these.

The LAN Card The LAN card is the PC add-on card that you install in an available PC card slot to connect the PC to the LAN. Some LAN cards use 8-bit data paths, which means that 8 bits of data (a byte) move at a time between the LAN card and the computer's processor. Others use 16-bit data paths and therefore move twice as much data at once. A LAN card can be referred to by various names: *LAN adapter card, network interface card (NIC),* or *network interface unit (NIU).* Since the simplest name is LAN card, that's what this book will use.

Figure 1-1 shows a photograph of the most common LANtastic LAN card, the LANtastic AE-2 Ethernet adapter. Different LAN cards have different ways of sending signals to other LAN cards. The most common types are Ethernet, token ring, and ARCnet, all of which are explained shortly.

LAN Cables LAN cables connect the LAN cards together. Because the LAN cards are installed in PCs, the cables connect the PCs together. Many types of cable are used. The most common two types are *thin coaxial cable* (variously called *thin co-ax, thin Ethernet, cheapernet,* or *thin net*), which is similar to the cable used for cable-TV, and *unshielded twisted-pair cable* (*UTP,* or just *twisted pair*), which is used in some parts of telephone wiring networks. The specific types of thin coaxial cable used are called RG58 A/U and RG58 C/U and have 50 ohm impedance. The unshielded twisted-pair cable is actually two twisted pairs, and therefore often called *dual twisted-pair (DTP).* Standard types are AT&T 104, 205, or 315, or Belden 1227A. This is *not* the same as flat telephone extension cable, often called *silver satin.* Figure 1-2 shows what thin co-ax and twisted-pair cabling look like. A new development called the *wireless LAN* communicates between LAN cards without cables. Instead, either radio or infrared signals carry information between computers.

Figure 1-1. ***The LANtastic AE-2 Ethernet adapter***

Figure 1-2. ***Thin coaxial cable and unshielded twisted-pair cable***

Thin coaxial cable

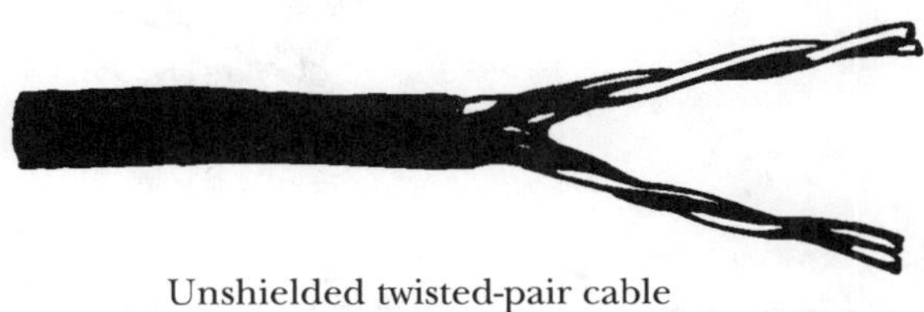

Unshielded twisted-pair cable

Connectors At the end of each cable is some type of connector that must plug into a matching socket on the LAN card. The standard for thin co-ax cable is a *BNC connector* (a bayonet-type connector that you insert and twist in place), and twisted-pair cable uses *RJ-45 modular plugs* and jacks, which look like oversize telephone modular plugs. You can buy cables with connectors already attached, or you can buy bulk cable and install connectors yourself. Figure 1-3 shows a T-type BNC connector, which permits two different BNC connectors to attach to the same device. The T arrangement allows the LAN cards to be daisy-chained together, from one PC to the next. That is, PC number one connects to one side of PC number two's T connector, and the other side of PC number two's T connects to PC number three, which in turn connects to number four, and so on.

Terminators Some LAN designs (notably those that use thin coaxial cable) require a special attachment at each end of the daisy chain of cables so that the electrical signals don't misbehave when they reach the end. Think of a terminator as a dead-end plug that marks the end of the LAN.

Figure 1-3. *T-type BNC connector*

The Network Operating System (NOS) Sometimes called the *LAN operating system* or the *network software,* this is the software that allows your PC to interact with other PCs on the LAN. Your MS DOS software doesn't have all the necessary capabilities to talk to another PC on a LAN. The NOS has this added intelligence. Artisoft's network operating system is called LANtastic. (Novell's system is called NetWare, Microsoft's is called LAN Manager, and Banyan's is called VINES.)

Application Software Most "regular" application software products, such as word processors, spreadsheets, or database managers, work just fine on a LAN. You can use the software to get at shared disk files on the LAN just as you would access disk files on your own hard disk. Other products need special LAN versions to work properly, or to be able to fully utilize the LAN environment, or to satisfy manufacturer licensing restrictions. One new category of application software, called *groupware,* was specifically designed to work on a LAN and allow a group of people to be more productive. Chapter 2 explores application software in more depth.

LAN Utility Software Special utility programs help you do your job in a LAN environment, just as special utilities help you use your PC in a non-LAN environment. These programs help you make backup copies of shared disk drives, monitor LAN activity, administer user names and passwords, and help with many other functions. Sometimes these utilities come with the network operating system and sometimes you have to buy them separately.

Physical LAN Topologies: Bus, Star, and Ring

Now that you have an idea of what components make up a LAN, an obvious question will occur to anyone who ever bought a toy with the dreaded words "some assembly required" printed on the box. "How do you connect these things together?"

Each computer or other device connected to the LAN is called a *node,* or sometimes a *station.* The way individual nodes are physically connected together is called the LAN's *topology.* Three topologies, bus, star, and ring, shown in Figure 1-4, are popular today.

Figure 1-4. The bus, star, and ring topologies

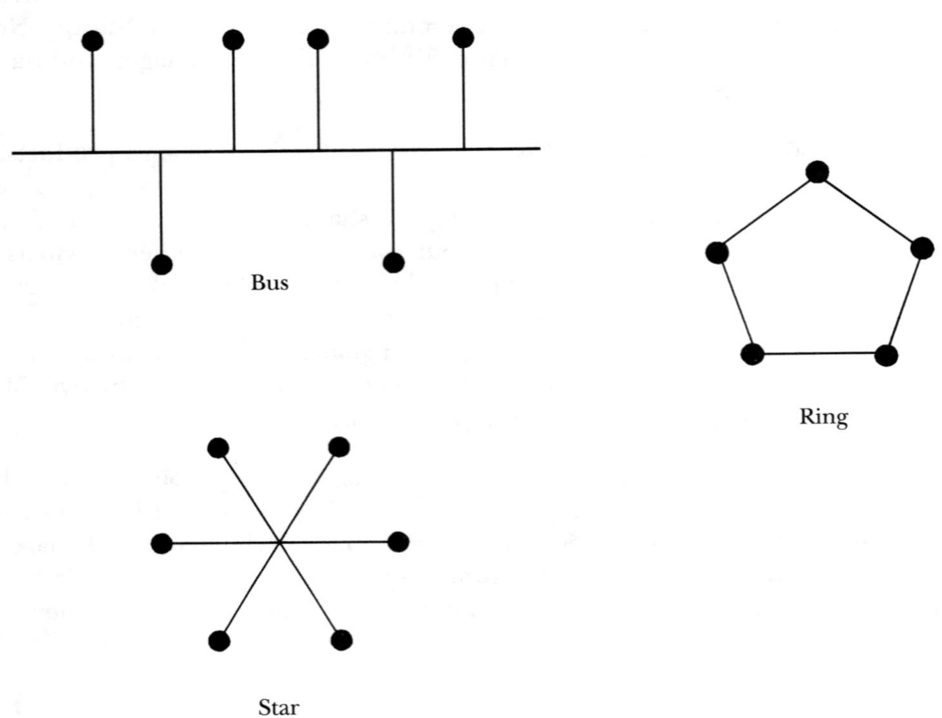

Bus Topology

The simplest and most common topology is the *bus*. The bus, in effect, is one long cable to which all nodes attach. The LANtastic LAN that is based on thin coaxial cable uses a bus topology. In reality, thin co-ax LANs do not use a single long cable. Instead, each node is connected to the next with a separate cable. However, these cables all connect end-to-end by use of the

BNC T-type connectors on the LAN cards, so the effect is the same as having one long cable.

In a bus topology LAN, a node that sends a message out to another node really broadcasts the message to everyone on the LAN. Nodes are programmed to ignore any message not addressed to them.

If any cable between two nodes is broken or disconnected, all nodes may be unable to communicate over the LAN. In some cases, nodes on either of the two separated sections can continue communicating with others on the same section, but because the sections each lack a terminator the chances of the whole LAN going down are high. Sometimes finding the point of failure is difficult for a bus LAN, but if you are reasonably careful where you route the cables, failures caused by damaged cables are pretty rare.

Star Topology

The *star* topology has a central *hub* to which all nodes are connected. The cable that connects a node to the hub is actually a pair of cables that form a loop between the hub and node, so no terminator is needed. LANtastic's 10BASE-T twisted-pair LAN uses the star topology.

The simplest star topology has one hub and some number of nodes connected to it, typically between 2 and 16. More complicated designs use a hierarchy of hubs, in which each hub connects not only to PC nodes, but also to one or more other hubs, which in turn connect to others. This topology with multiple hubs is called a *tree.* (Actually, purists will insist that the star topology is really not a separate topology in itself, but instead is a special case of a tree. They're right, but star is the more commonly used name, and LANtastic 10BASE-T twisted-pair LANs are usually small, single-hub LANs in a star topology.)

The star, or hub-based, topology has some advantages over a bus topology:

- If the cable between a node and its hub fails, only that node loses its ability to communicate over the LAN. None of the other nodes is affected.
- Current standards call for the use of unshielded twisted-pair cable, which is less expensive per foot than thin coaxial cable.
- Some buildings are prewired with extra twisted-pair cable and wall sockets, making LAN installation easy.,

Unfortunately, disadvantages compensate for these advantages:

- Even though a single cable failure affects only one node, if the hub itself fails for some reason, all the nodes connected to it fail, too.
- A cable failure of a cable that connects two hubs will cut off communication between any two nodes on the different hubs.
- The star topology requires the purchase of the hub, which more than overrides the cost advantages of less expensive cable.
- Unshielded twisted-pair cable is more susceptible than thin co-ax to electrical interference from other equipment with strong electrical or magnetic fields. In most office environments this is not a problem, but in some cases the result can be less reliability.

Ring Topology

The ring topology physically connects all nodes in a big circle, again avoiding the need for terminators. Of course, in real life the shape formed by the cable is seldom close to being a circle. It is, however, a closed loop, and all nodes are connected to exactly two other nodes.

Technical reasons lead to data transfer rates that are potentially a little higher in a ring topology, as well as the capability to attach more devices together before needing additional equipment to boost the signal strength. However, the electronics required on the LAN card to support ring designs result in higher cost. Artisoft makes no LANtastic products that are based on a ring topology.

LAN Signaling Methods: Ethernet, Token Ring, and ARCnet

Deciding the LAN topology is a big step in figuring out how to make the PCs on a LAN communicate, but it's only a beginning. Even though the method of physical connection is established, the logical communication process is not.

Consider a parallel situation with the telephone system that connects your home to virtually every other home in your neighborhood. When the phone company installs a telephone cable leading to your home, that is only the beginning of communications. Many other issues have to be decided, either by the designers of the phone system or by you, the phone user.

First everyone needs a unique phone number. You have to know the phone numbers of others, and they need to know yours. When you call someone, you have to determine what to do if no one is home, or if that person is already using the phone. You may even have to decide what language you are going to speak and how fast to talk, and what to do if you both try to talk at the same time. Rather than stretch the telephone and LAN analogy too far, let's just say that communication is not a simple process, either over telephones or using a LAN. Deciding on solutions to all the possible problems that might crop up takes time and effort.

Similar problems have been dealt with in LAN design. Standards are established so that everyone knows the answers to these problems and can manufacture products accordingly.

Most LAN products adhere to standards adopted by the Institute of Electrical and Electronics Engineers (IEEE). These standards are fully described, numbered, and published so that any manufacturer can design products that comply and will therefore work when connected to other standard products. The names and numbers of these standards are thrown around a lot, so the following sections briefly explain the most common ones.

IEEE 802.3: Ethernet

By far the most popular types of LAN follow one of the standards called *Ethernet.* These standards fall under IEEE's definitions labeled 802.3. Within the Ethernet family are several particular specifications, the most widely used of which are commonly called thick Ethernet, thin Ethernet, and twisted-pair hub. (Separate sections will cover each type shortly.)

A problem that all these standards must solve is contention for the shared LAN communications channel. How does the LAN handle the situation when two or more nodes want to send a message on the LAN at the same time? The LAN is only a single communications channel—only one message can be in transit at any point in time. Somehow, one node must send its message and the other nodes must wait. Each LAN standard uses some well-defined *access method* that spells out exactly how each node accesses the LAN.

All 802.3 standards use an access method called *carrier sense multiple access with collision detection (CSMA/CD).* The CSMA portion of this imposing-looking name means that before any node tries to use the LAN, it must first sense (listen) whether the LAN is already in use. If so, the node must wait. If the node senses that no one is using the channel, it can go ahead and send its message. That method sounds fine, but what if two nodes both listen, hear that the channel is available, and try to transmit at the same time? The result is a *collision* of the two messages.

That's where collision detection comes into play. The electronic circuitry of each LAN card detects that a collision occurs, and that therefore the message is not successfully sent. Both nodes wait and try again. To reduce the chances of a second collision, each node picks a random length of time to wait before retrying.

The CSMA/CD access method works well, especially if the LAN is lightly loaded with message traffic. The busier the traffic load, the higher the chance of multiple collisions before messages are successfully sent. In practice, CSMA/CD works well and is simple and cheap to implement electronically.

All of the 802.3 standards use CSMA/CD, but each has its own cable and electrical specifications.

10BASE5: Thick Ethernet The original type of Ethernet LAN is now called thick Ethernet, because it uses a thick, inflexible, coaxial cable as the main backbone. Not many new LANs use thick Ethernet, due to the higher cost of its components and the fact that it's awkward to install and maintain. The other two 802.3 standards are much more dominant in the marketplace. Several Artisoft LANtastic cards support thick Ethernet cable as well as thin Ethernet, but very few customers use it.

10BASE2: Thin Ethernet Thin Ethernet uses BNC T connectors and RG58 coaxial cable, a thin, flexible 50-ohm cable that is widely available. The name 10BASE2 describes the key attributes of thin Ethernet other than the cable type itself: 10 megabits per second, baseband signals, and 200 meters maximum segment length.

Baseband means that the cable is used for one communications channel. (A more technical way to say this is that the cable's bandwidth is entirely taken up by one signal.) Another method, called *broadband*, modulates a radio frequency signal and permits multiple communications channels on the same cable, but requires extra circuitry and results in more expense. LANtastic products use baseband signaling.

A group of nodes daisy-chained together is called a *segment*. The total cable length of a segment cannot exceed 185 meters (well, that's roughly the 200 meters in the 10BASE2 name), which is about 607 feet. Also, a segment can have no more than 30 nodes attached.

What if you need more than 30 nodes or more than 607 feet? Several solutions are possible. The simplest is to add a device called a *repeater*, which amplifies and regenerates the LAN signals. A repeater can connect two segments of 30 nodes each. You can use multiple repeaters, up to a total of four segments. Other solutions to exceed the 30-node and 607-foot limits are discussed in Chapter 4.

10BASE-T: Twisted-Pair Hub 10BASE-T is based on a star topology using a *hub* (like the center of a bicycle wheel) and connection to nodes using unshielded twisted-pair cable. (The T in 10BASE-T is for twisted pair.) The maximum cable distance between the hub (sometimes called a *concentrator*) and each node is 100 meters (328 feet). Hubs can be connected together, but the maximum number of hubs allowable between two nodes is four.

Even though advertisements often claim that 10BASE-T uses "ordinary telephone wire" and "modular plugs," this does not mean you can use common, flat phone cable, often called "silver satin" or the small modular plugs on ordinary telephones. The cable must meet 10BASE-T specifications, such as AT&T 104, 205, or 315, or Belden 1227A, and the modular plugs are really large RJ45 connectors.

IEEE 802.5: Token Ring

Another family of LAN products is called 802.5, or *token ring*. In spite of its name, token ring uses a star physical topology, not a ring. The token ring name comes from the logical way that nodes interact on the LAN.

Instead of each node waiting for a clear channel before it sends a message, a token ring LAN follows a more orderly method. A special message called a *free token* is passed from one node to the next in an agreed-upon sequence (a logical ring, you might say). A node that wants to transmit a message waits for its turn to get the free token, and then changes it to a *busy token*. The node transmits the busy token, followed by the message it wants to send. Other nodes see there is no free token available, so they wait before trying to transmit their own messages. The node that sent the message eventually receives back the busy token, which it can now change into a free token, and the process starts over.

Token ring LANs are a bit more predictable in their response time under heavy loads, but cost more to implement. IBM has been the biggest proponent of token ring. Token ring LANs are not nearly as widely accepted as Ethernet LANs, primarily due to higher cost and the fact that Ethernet was established first in the marketplace. Artisoft does not sell any token ring products at this time.

ARCnet

ARCnet is not an IEEE-accepted standard, but has been around for so long that it is a de facto standard. The ARC in the name stands for Attached Resource Computing, an architecture developed originally by Datapoint. ARCnet is slow (2.5 megabits per second), but cheap. You can buy ARCnet LAN cards at lower prices than any other kind.

ARCnet uses a physical star topology, originally with connection to a hub by RG62 coaxial cable. More recent products also support a bus-type topology using unshielded twisted-pair cable or thin co-ax. ARCnet's access method is a token-passing scheme, but it differs from the 802.5 standard. Each node is assigned a station number and waits for its number to be called before transmitting.

Because of ARCnet's slow speed and unofficial status, it is generally not a good choice for a new LAN. With modern PCs and hard disk drives becoming increasingly fast at sending and receiving data, a 2.5 megabit per second LAN just isn't a good long-term investment.

Other Connectivity Methods

Chapter 2 explains how people use LANs in general and LANtastic in particular. Before you read that, you ought to have some idea about the alternatives for connecting PCs and sharing resources *without* using a LAN. These methods have more limitations than LANs do, but some of them are a little less expensive, a little simpler, or both.

Sneakernet

Get ready. You're about to undergo a rite of passage by learning the Sneakernet joke. You can't claim to have any significant LAN exposure unless you know the Sneakernet joke.

As you saw earlier in this chapter, one of the most popular LAN card types follows the standard called Ethernet. If you don't have a LAN (Ethernet or another kind), and you want to share data with fellow PC users, how do you do it? You simply copy files to floppy disks, put on your sneakers, and run around to the other users and pass out floppy disks. This not-so-high-tech system has been dubbed *Sneakernet.* Some people who think they're clever like to joke that a company that has no LAN performs data distribution using a Sneakernet network. In fact, some of these people like to use this joke over and over until no one can stand to hear it again. Many of them sell LANs for a living.

There. Now you've heard it, too. If you're lucky, you won't hear it more than fifteen thousand times a year.

Print Buffers

In some offices, the first critical resource that users discover they want to share is a high-cost printer, usually a laser printer. The boss doesn't want to spend the money to install a separate laser printer on every PC, but everyone occasionally needs to use one.

The cheap, but annoying, solution is to attach the laser printer to one PC only. Then, anyone else who needs to print laser-quality output takes a floppy disk over to the laser printer PC and prints from there. This frustrates everyone. The person who does the printing would rather print directly from his or her own PC, rather than walk over to another PC and ask to use it for a few minutes. The person who normally uses the laser printer PC would rather not be interrupted so often by other people who need to borrow the PC.

The more expensive, but less annoying, solution is to buy a print buffer that allows connection of more than one PC to the printer. A typical model has connections for up to five PCs and one printer. Each PC is cabled to the print buffer, and the print buffer connects to the shared printer. The print buffer has its own memory—anywhere from 64K to a couple of megabytes is common—and all five users can simultaneously send printed output to the printer. The buffer stores everyone's print data, and sends each PC's printed output in turn to the printer.

A print buffer is not a bad solution for an office that needs to share only a printer, but has no need for the other advantages a LAN offers (discussed in Chapter 2). A low-cost LAN such as LANtastic isn't much more expensive than a good-quality print buffer, but has *much* more capability. Prices vary, but most print buffers cost $90 to $150 per PC to connect to a single printer, not counting the cost of the printer. Many companies make print buffers. These are just a few of them:

- ASP Computer Products, 160 San Gabriel Drive, Sunnyvale, CA 94086, 800-445-6190
- Black Box Corporation, P.O. Box 12800, Pittsburgh, PA 15241, 412-746-5530
- Comspec Communications, 74 Wingold Avenue, Toronto, ON, Canada, M6B 1P5, 416-785-3553
- Digital Products, 108 Water Street, Watertown, MA 02172, 800-243-2333
- Fifth Generation Systems, 10049 N. Reiger Road, Baton Rouge, LA 70809, 800-873-4384

Serial and Parallel Port Connectors

A number of products are on the market to connect two or more computers together using cables between the serial or parallel ports. Some of these products were originally created to allow data exchange between two PCs that do not have the same type of floppy disk drives. This comes up most frequently for a desktop system with only 5.25-inch drives and a laptop system with only 3.5-inch drives.

Most such products use what is called a *null modem cable* to connect the two serial ports (and/or a special cable to connect the two parallel ports), and software that runs on both PCs. The software displays a menu on each PC, and you select which files you want copied to the other PC. Leading products in this category are LapLink (from Traveling Software, 18702 N. Creek Parkway, Bothell, WA 98011, 800-343-8080) and Brooklyn Bridge (from Fifth Generation Systems, 10049 N. Reiger Road, Baton Rouge, LA 70809, 800-873-4384). Data is transferred through the serial ports at up to 115,200 bits per second, which usually means about 10,000 bytes per second or less. The parallel ports can move data faster, perhaps two to three times as fast.

Other vendors sell what is sometimes called a *zero-slot LAN.* This also connects serial or parallel ports, but instead of running special file-transfer software on each PC, you run software that is similar or identical to a full-fledged network operating system. Artisoft sells such a product, called LANtastic Z, which can connect 2 PCs (see chapters 3 and 4). Other vendors have products that can connect as many as 16 PCs. Because data is transferred so much slower through serial or parallel ports than is possible using a LAN card, these "LANs" are not satisfactory for many uses, especially if they are hooked up to more than 2 PCs.

Multiuser Operating Systems

Another approach to connecting PCs without buying a LAN is to use one of your PCs as a little mainframe computer, more or less, and then connect your other PCs to it. If you run a multiuser operating system on a PC, that's essentially what you are doing.

A multiuser operating system, unlike MS DOS, is designed to talk to many different users at once. Examples are Unix, Xenix, Citrix Multiuser, and DRMultiuser DOS. Install one of these on your most powerful PC and connect your other PCs to it. They will either emulate a dumb terminal to the main PC and can upload and download files, or will run other special software to enable communication. (A dumb terminal is a simple video screen and keyboard that can't run programs like a PC can—it just sends data between the dumb terminal and the attached computer.) Needless to say, this type of approach is much more complicated than the comparatively simple MS DOS world, and is outside the scope of this book. In many cases, you still need a LAN to connect the computers. If not, some other wiring scheme is needed.

2

LANtastic Uses

Chapter 1 gave you some background on what a LAN is, but you might find yourself asking a couple of questions: "Why should I care? What can I actually *do* with a LAN?" Fair enough. So far you have not seen much about the practical aspects of LANtastic or any other particular LAN. Broad statements about communication between PCs and sharing hard disks and peripheral devices are fine, but they don't explain LANtastic's capabilities. This chapter gives you specific details about what you can do with LANtastic, along with particulars about what applications you can use, and some short descriptions of what several real-life computer users do with LANtastic. Chapters 6 and 7 give more details about sharing hardware.

Knowing the Terminology

First, make sure you're clear on the terminology. In general, any PC connected to a LAN is called a *node* or *station.* A PC that makes its resources (hard disk, printer, or other devices) available to other nodes is called a *server,* or sometimes a *file server* or *print server* if the server is specialized. A PC that uses the resources of a server is called a *workstation* or sometimes a *client.* Someone sits at the keyboard of a workstation and performs work—word processing or whatever. On the other hand, a server PC can be unattended while it makes its hard disk available to workstation users. So, a LAN with four computers might be configured as one server and three workstations, for a total of four nodes.

However, LANtastic allows the same PC to act as *both* a server and a workstation. Such a server is called a *nondedicated server.* This means that you can sit at a server PC and use the workstation portion of it to perform your word processing at the same time that other PCs use the server portion's hard disk and printer. A network operating system that allows this combination of server and workstation functionality is often called a *peer-to-peer network.* This ability of LANtastic to use one PC as both a server and workstation translates into cost savings—you don't have to buy a separate server computer. A four-computer network can have one server and *four* workstations, because one computer serves both functions. On the other hand, a NOS that requires a server to do nothing else but act as a *dedicated server* is often called a *client-server network.* Novell's 2.*x* and 3.*x* versions of NetWare are examples.

People who use LANtastic often talk about a computer being a server or a workstation. ("My LAN has five workstations and two servers.") Either type of computer is a "regular" PC. What makes computers servers and workstations is that they are connected to the LAN using a LAN card and cable, and they run the parts of the LANtastic NOS software to make the PCs act as servers or workstations. Some people expect a server or a workstation to be some special kind of computer. As Chapter 4 explains, there are reasons why a server PC often needs to have a faster processor or larger, faster disk drive than other PCs. However, there is no absolute need for this. With a compact, efficient NOS such as LANtastic, an ordinary 8088- or 80286-based PC with a small hard disk and MS DOS can be perfectly adequate as a server or workstation in many cases.

Workstations Versus Engineering Workstations

A LAN workstation is just a normal personal computer with a LAN card, cables, and LAN software added. Confusion about this is common, largely due to a special type of computer called an *engineering workstation,* which is a high-speed desktop computer, typically with sophisticated graphics capabilities, that is used by engineers to design circuits and other products. Major brand names of engineering workstations are Sun and Apollo. In engineering contexts and advertisements, an engineering workstation sometimes is simply called a workstation. Don't be confused. A typical LAN workstation is *not* the same thing. It's simply a regular PC connected to a LAN.

How People Use LANtastic Today

This section looks at the most popular uses of LANtastic today, and functions as an overview for the rest of this chapter. The next few sections explain the uses mentioned here much more thoroughly.

Many other LANs also can perform some or all of these functions. However, LANtastic attractively combines low cost, low RAM usage, a full set of features, and simple, reliable installation and usage. As a result, LANtastic is the market leader in low-cost LANs for small workgroups with IBM-compatible PCs. (A *workgroup* is a loose term for a group of people who work together. The group might consist of several people in a small office, a dozen people in one department of a large company, or an entire company of 50 people. Usually all workgroup members are located close together, but sometimes some are at remote locations.)

Shared Printers For many people, the reason to buy LANtastic comes right after they buy an expensive laser printer in a workgroup that has several PCs. Everyone wants to use the laser printer. If you install LANtastic, you can attach a printer (or several) to one PC's parallel printer ports LPT1, LPT2, or LPT3, or its serial ports COM1 and COM2. Then all other PCs connected to the LAN can enter simple commands to redirect their printer output over the LAN to the shared printer. The result? You need to buy only one expensive printer for the workgroup, but everyone can use the printer as if it were his or her own–without disturbing the person who uses the PC with the laser printer physically attached.

Shared Disk Space The most compelling reason to use LANtastic, or any LAN, is to share disk space. Without a LAN, you exchange disk data by copying files to floppy disks and passing them around. (No, I won't repeat the Sneakernet joke here.) With LANtastic, you can make all, or some, of a server's disk space available to the other LAN stations (or only to the users you select). You might want to set up a shared hard disk on a LAN for three reasons: to provide a shared data space for general usage, to run shared database applications, or to share software. These reasons are listed here separately:

- *Shared Data Space* Think of a shared data space as simply a community disk drive that everyone can use. The LAN software gives everyone the ability to use this shared drive just like a local hard disk. Each person can copy files to and from a server's shared disk. As a result, the files are available to everyone.
- *Shared Database Applications* A *database* is a collection of information organized for some particular purpose, such as a mailing list or a parts inventory. Popular database software, such as dBASE, Paradox, FoxBASE, and Q&A, gives you the capability to manage a database by adding, changing, and deleting data, searching through the data, sorting the data, and printing reports. If you use a LAN, you can put a database on the shared disk drive and everyone can access the same information at once. Other specialized software products manage specialized databases for you. Examples are electronic mail, group appointment calendars, conference room schedulers, and specialized accounting software.

- *Shared Software* Without a LAN, you have to install software products (word processors, spreadsheets, and so on) on each separate PC. With a LAN, you can still run software the same way if you like, but many software products have the option of installation on a server instead of every workstation. Then each workstation user can run the software from the shared disk. This usually does *not* mean you can save a lot of money by buying only one copy. (See the explanation in the longer "Shared Software" section later in the chapter.) However, if you use a central server copy, then you don't have to install separate copies on every PC and you can be sure that everyone uses the same software version.

Shared CD-ROM Drives A CD-ROM (compact disk, read-only memory) disk drive is a special disk drive much like an audio CD player, except that it stores computer data. A wide range of reference material has recently become available on CD-ROMs. Using LANtastic, you can install one CD-ROM drive and everyone can access the reference data, such as encyclopedias, newspaper archives, dictionaries, telephone directories, and specialized databases.

Shared Modems Rather than install a separate modem and telephone line to each PC in your workgroup, you can install one high-speed modem (or several) on one PC and let everyone share it. Modem sharing is not a standard feature of LANtastic, but you can buy an add-on software product called ArtiCom from Artisoft, or other products from other companies, to add this capability.

All LANs share printers and disk space; only some share CD-ROM drives and modems. LANtastic shares them all, does it simply, and uses less RAM than other LANs. The next several sections expand upon the brief explanations just given.

Shared Printers

Many LANtastic customers start off by looking for a way to share a printer among two or three PCs. They learn that the cost to share printers using LANtastic is similar to the cost of buying a good print buffer product that accomplishes the same goal. When they find out that LANtastic also provides the additional LAN capabilities (listed in this chapter), they think, "Why not go with LANtastic? If we do decide to use LANtastic's other features, we come out ahead. Even if we don't, we still can do the printer sharing we need at roughly the same cost." Chapter 6 explains the printer sharing process in detail.

Once you have a LAN installed, the extra expense of a high-cost laser or color printer is much less painful because the cost is spread over all users. An $1800 printer used by six people costs the same as six $300 printers. You can create beautifully printed text and graphics at high speed with your shared part of the $1800 printer. Forever after you will be dissatisfied with the print quality and speed of any $300 printer (or even a $600 printer). But even if you add a shared laser printer, workstations can continue to use their existing individual printers on their PCs just as before. They can choose to use the shared printer only when they prefer. However, once most users learn how easily they can use the shared laser printer with LANtastic, the individual dot matrix printers begin gathering dust.

Shared Data Space

A server's shared data space can quickly become a huge time-saver in a workgroup. Here's a short explanation of how it works.

A user at a workstation enters the LANtastic command called NET. This brings up a menu screen from which the user selects the server's hard disk as a *virtual disk drive* to add to the workstation. As the name implies, a virtual disk drive is not a real hard disk on the workstation computer. Instead, the LAN software "fools" DOS on the workstation into believing it has an additional hard disk. If the workstation user has a PC with a hard disk called C, this command assigns another name, such as L (or whatever you like), to the virtual disk drive. From then on, the workstation user can access this L drive just like another hard disk on the workstation PC. From the user's perspective, the L drive is the server's hard disk. For example, the DOS command COPY C:MYFILE.DOC L: would copy the file MYFILE.DOC from a workstation's C hard disk to the shared L drive.

Rather than use the DOS COPY command, you can load and save files using application programs. With WordPerfect, Microsoft Word, Lotus 1-2-3, or nearly any other product, you can load your file from the L drive instead of the C drive, do your work as usual, and then save your updated file back out to the L drive. The application program acts as if you really have an L drive because the LANtastic software and DOS work together to create that illusion. Because LANtastic knows you assigned the L drive to the server disk, it redirects the input and output operations across the LAN to the server's disk. This ingenious approach is simple and permits nearly all application software to work with LANtastic.

The shared disk drive available to each user need not be the server's entire hard disk drive. You can set up shared disk space to offer only specific subdirectories to users. You can even restrict specific users from updating files on the shared disk. The degree of restriction is up to you. Chapter 6 explains the hard disk sharing process in detail, and Chapter 10 explains how to set up limited access.

Shared Database Applications

Most workgroups can justify the cost of installing a LANtastic network solely from the previous two uses, printer sharing and shared data space. Shared database applications are a step more complicated, but can offer great benefits to many workgroups.

As covered earlier, a database is a collection of information organized for some particular purpose. Most workgroups deal with some kind of information that would add to everyone's productivity if it were instantly available to all. The database might contain customer or supplier names and addresses, or the status of orders in process, or summaries of recently published research information, or almost anything else. Some workgroup members need to update the information in a database–adding, changing, or deleting portions when new information becomes available. Other people might need only to search (or query) the database occasionally to find current information. The main advantage of a shared database on a LAN is that everyone can access the same, current information right when they need it.

Several options exist to implement databases in a LAN environment, depending on your needs, abilities, and budget. The methods listed here are fully explained in the sections that follow.

- Buy a specialized database application product, if one exists that satisfies your particular needs.
- Buy a groupware software product, if one satisfies your needs.
- Buy a general-purpose database management system (DBMS) and design your own database.
- Hire a consultant to create a database application to suit your needs, using a general-purpose database management system.
- Hire a consultant to write programs in a non-DBMS language to meet your needs.

Of course, you can use any of these options (except buying a groupware software product) even if you don't have a LAN. With a LAN, the difference is that everyone connected can access the data at once. Without a LAN, the data is on a single PC and is available to other workgroup members only after a time delay, either to copy the data to floppy disks (and distribute to others) or to print reports that others can read. And without a LAN, only one person can update the data, or else an awkward coordination process is needed to merge everyone's updates together.

Let's look at each of these five options more closely to see how you can implement shared databases in a LANtastic environment.

Option 1: A Specialized Database Application

Software developers have created specialized database products to satisfy many common needs. If your needs match one of the products available, buy that product. Of course, you need to verify that the product is compatible with LANtastic. Fortunately, most database products that work with any LAN also work with LANtastic.

Sometimes these products are categorized as *vertical market software*. This means that the products were created not to appeal to a broad market that includes many categories of users, but instead were designed for specialized categories of users. Examples of these categories are accountants, salespeople, attorneys, and video rental store owners.

Here are some examples of needs for which vendors have created specialized database application products.

- *Accounting* This category has the most products, because every business needs to do at least some accounting. Some products handle all types of accounting and financial reporting; others specialize in certain aspects only. LAN versions of accounting products keep track of accounting records in files on a server's hard disk so everyone with a need can access the information.
- *Contact Management* This new software category has recently crystallized. Many business people, especially salespeople, need to keep track of everyone they contact over the phone and by mail. Contact management products monitor the status of these contacts and display reminders when follow-up calls are needed. These products can also dial your phone, print form letters and mailing labels, and display monthly calendars, among many other capabilities.
- *Forms Design* You can create business forms for use by others in your company or elsewhere.
- *Retail Store Management* Specialized products assist store managers in keeping track of details regarding inventory, employees, and other aspects of the business. Examples are video rental stores, equipment rental stores, and restaurants.
- *Real Estate Management* These products help agents and brokers keeps track of clients, properties, commissions, and other details.
- *Time and Billing* Many service-oriented businesses, such as law firms, engineering firms, and contracting firms, need to keep track of how much time everyone spends working for each client. These products monitor the time spent, print bills, and track payments.

A huge number of specialized database application products are currently on the market. The following software products are provided here either because Artisoft lists them as compatible with LANtastic, the manufacturer claims the product is LANtastic-compatible, or users report the product runs successfully. To be sure of no problems with the latest version, check the most recent LANtastic compatibility list (see Appendix B for how to obtain it) or contact the software manufacturer.

Accounting

Product	Manufacturer
Accpac Plus	Computer Associates
Act 2 Plus	Cougar Mountain Software
BusinessWorks	Manzanita Software Systems
Champion Accounting Software	Champion Business Systems
Client Write-Up	CertiFLEX Systems
DacEasy Network Accounting	DacEasy
Great Plains Accounting	Great Plains Software
Macola Accounting	Macola, Inc.
Peachtree Network Accounting	Peachtree Software
RealWorld Accounting	RealWorld Corp.

Contact Management

Product	Manufacturer
Action Plus	Action Plus Software
Contact Plus LAN	Contact Plus Corp.
Diamond Prospector	Diamond Data Management
GoldMine	Elan Software

Specialties

Product	Manufacturer
Agency Manager	Analysis & Information Services
Automobile Dealership Manager	Zeus Concepts
Broker's Ally	Scherrer Resources
Broker's Notebook	American Financial Systems
Construction Management	Yardi Systems
Decision Pad	Apian Software
EasyFlow	Haventree Software
Excalibur Premier Time Billing	Armor Systems
Formtool	BLOC Development
Key Autoservice	Daniels Associates
MediSoft Advanced Multiuser	The Computer Place
Modular Restaurant System	Genlor Systems
Parcel Shipping System	Aristo Computers
Portfolio Manager	Plaid Brothers Software
Profit-Maker F&I	Pryor Systems
Property Management	Yardi Systems
Prospect Tracking System	HMS Computer Company

Specialties

Product	Manufacturer
Real-t-Pro	REAL-E-DATA Inc.
Realty Ally	Scherrer Resources
Sales Ally	Scherrer Resources

Option 2: Groupware

Sometimes called *network productivity software, groupware* refers to software that is designed to make an entire workgroup of any type more productive. These products are useful for broader categories of workgroups than the specialized database applications. Almost any workgroup can benefit from groupware. This software must run on a LAN to give all group members access to the shared information. Before LANs, groupware didn't exist.

Groupware products that currently are popular contain some or all of the following capabilities:

- *Electronic Mail* Often called *e-mail,* electronic mail sends typed messages back and forth between group members. The messages are stored on a shared disk, and software on each workstation permits each user to write, edit, send, receive, and save messages. LANtastic has a simple built-in e-mail capability, but groupware e-mail capabilities are more sophisticated. Some products permit you to send messages to distribution lists, to attach files to messages, or to receive notification as soon as the recipient reads your message. An extremely small group in a single room may see no need for e-mail. The larger the group and the more geographically spread apart, the greater the benefits.
- *Group Calendaring* For many workgroups, the biggest challenge faced each week is how to set up meetings that everyone can attend. A group calendaring product keeps track of everyone's schedule and displays a choice of meeting times for which everyone's schedule shows free time. Of course, everyone has to actually enter all appointments, trips, and vacation time into the calendar for this to work.

- *Resource Scheduling* Some groupware products allow you to schedule usage of *any* shared resource. Examples are conference rooms, overhead projectors, and company cars. Anyone who wants to use the shared resource enters the date and time needed. Anyone else who subsequently looks at the schedule can see the dates and times still available.
- *Utilities* Many groupware products have the kinds of capabilities available in desktop organizer programs such as SideKick. Examples of capabilities are a calculator, a simple notebook/database, a phone list, a file manager, a menu front-end to DOS, and a text editor.

Here are some of the leading groupware products on the market today:

- *WordPerfect Office LAN* (from WordPerfect Corporation, 1555 N. Technology Way, Orem, UT 84057, 801-225-5000). This is the groupware market leader, with over 300,000 users, counting both LAN and non-LAN versions. This product is not just for users of the WordPerfect word processor, but they learn it especially quickly because the commands are similar. It includes e-mail, group calendaring, and several utilities. The list price is $495 for up to five users, or $1495 for up to 20 users. WordPerfect also sells a product called WordPerfect Connections ($495 additional) to link your LAN e-mail to outside users.
- *Right Hand Man II* (from Futurus Inc., 3131 North I-10 Service Road, Suite 401, Metairie, LA 70002, 800-327-8296, 504-837-1554). Created by a small company and adapted well to LANtastic, Right Hand Man II includes e-mail, group calendaring, and modem sharing. Many utility functions are provided including a database, a phone message center, a to-do list, a Cardex index card database, a file manager, a calculator, and control of LAN print queues. The cost is $195 for one user, $495 for five users, and $1995 for 25 users.
- *Enterprise* (from Chronos Software Inc., 555 De Haro Street, Suite 240, San Francisco, CA 94107, 800-777-7907). Enterprise performs e-mail, group calendaring, and resource scheduling. Utilities include to-do lists, a project manager, and card file databases. Chronos claims Enterprise is so easy to learn that no training is necessary.

The list price is $695 for the first six users, and then either $495 for additions of five users or $1495 for additions of 20 users.

- *Office Works* (from Data Access Corporation, 14000 S.W. 119th Avenue, Miami, FL 33186, 305-238-0012). This product has e-mail, group calendaring, telephone messaging, and a name and address list.
- *SuperTime* (from SuperTime Inc., 2025 Sheppard Avenue E., Suite 2206, Willowdale, Ontario, Canada M2J 1V7, 800-565-3288, 416-499-3288). SuperTime has e-mail, group calendaring, project management, a message center, a contact directory, an in/out board to track employees, and an innovative reference and conversion library feature. The price is $695 for four users, $995 for eight users, $1695 for 16 users, and $2495 for 25 users.

Option 3: A General-Purpose DBMS

A general-purpose *database management system* (DBMS) is the first thing most people think of when they hear the phrase "database software." Because keeping track of organized lists of data is such a good use of computers, these database products were developed so you can keep track of anything you choose.

If no specialized database application exists to accomplish what your workgroup needs, and no groupware product seems to do the job, the next option to consider is designing your own database applications using a general-purpose DBMS.

Designing a DBMS-based application is not simple. You can do it, but some products will intimidate you with their thick stacks of manuals. Other products are much simpler, although often at the expense of having fewer capabilities. To use any DBMS, however, you need to define exactly what you want to accomplish.

Imagine that you are going to keep track of names and addresses on 3-by-5-inch index cards. (In fact, to learn how to use a DBMS, a good choice for the first application you design would be one that you already maintain using index cards, a Rolodex, or some other manual method of storing information.)

You might decide to put the name on the top line of the card, for easy visibility. Then put the street address on the second line, and the city, state, and ZIP code on the third line. That seems easy enough. Oh, you might want to add the person's phone number, too, of course. Actually, two phone numbers, in case the person has a fax machine. No, wait. Three phone numbers, in case you know both the business and home phone numbers. Hey, what about the name of the person's business? Better add that, too. And job title. In fact, when you enter the person's name on the top line, you should show the last name first, so it's easy to alphabetize the cards. Maybe put the last name in red, too. And also....

Well, you get the idea. Most databases start off sounding simple and quickly become more complicated. To implement a database application, you need to make all these design decisions at the start, and use a product that is flexible enough so you can easily make changes. You *will* make changes.

Dozens of general-purpose DBMS products are on the market. Most of them can work on shared databases using LANtastic. The following list gives short descriptions of some of the leading products (each of which supports shared disk usage or has a special LAN version available).

- *dBASE III Plus and dBASE IV* From Borland International (formerly sold by Ashton-Tate, which merged with Borland), the dBASE family has long been the market leader in full-featured database products. Recent software problems, financial difficulties, and intense competition have shrunk its market share.
- *FoxBASE+ and FoxPro* From Fox Software, FoxBASE+ and FoxPro were originally "clone" competitors to dBASE with additional advantages. (The main advantage was that you could run your dBASE programs using FoxBASE, and you could distribute the programs to other users without buying the expensive dBASE for each user.) Most recent published evaluations show FoxPro version 2.0 to be faster than all competitors. That may change by the time you read this.
- *Clipper* From Nantucket, Clipper also started off as a dBASE clone and developed into a unique product.
- *Paradox* From Borland International (which sold Paradox before the merger with Ashton-Tate, and still sells it), Paradox makes better use of available RAM than most other products. Most users find Paradox easier to use than either dBASE product.

- *Q&A* From Symantec Corporation, Q&A is possibly the easiest to use of the big-name database products. Q&A allows you to search databases using English language questions instead of a programming language. Q&A also includes an integrated word processor with mail merge capability. Q&A cannot perform some functions that a fully relational database can, but most users don't need those capabilities anyway.
- *R:BASE* From Microrim, Inc., R:BASE has a nice graphics-style interface of overlaying menus. R:BASE is well designed overall and positioned to respond easily to one-time "ad hoc" inquiries into databases.

Option 4: A DBMS Application from a Consultant

If you have ever picked up one of the 1000-page dBASE books available in bookstores, you may decide you don't want to plow through it all in order to figure out how to design a database application. Some database products are simpler than others, but any DBMS has to be somewhat complex in order to give you all the capabilities you might need.

If you don't want to spend your time becoming a database expert, you can hire someone who is. Free-lance consultants work for $20 to $100 per hour. Be sure the one you hire provides references of satisfied customers, and check out the references. Be sure the consultant is experienced with the products you will use—the database product and LANtastic, too, if possible. Make sure both you and the consultant clearly understand *exactly* what you need. Put it all in writing and keep a copy with the consultant's signature. Get a firm limit to how many hours the project will take, or agree to a total price for the job instead. Be sure you fully test the application when it is ready. Get clear, written documentation before you sign off the job as satisfactorily completed. Be sure you get everything you need to give the job to another consultant in case the first one disappears or proves to be unacceptable when future changes are necessary.

Check with your local computer store for the names of database consultants. You can also look in computer publications, business publications, and local newspaper advertisements. A local computer club might also be a source of references.

Option 5: Consultant-Developed Non-DBMS Programs

Sometimes a consultant will tell you, "What you need isn't a DBMS application. You need some custom-written programs that I can write for you in C (or Pascal or BASIC or some other computer language)."

Maybe this is true and maybe it isn't. If you aren't a computer expert, you can't be sure. Maybe this consultant hasn't worked with any database products, but fancies himself (or herself) a crackerjack C programmer and has no other work available. Or maybe a custom-written program or two in a conventional programming language really is the best approach. How can you find out?

Unfortunately, you can't. You are in the same position if you know nothing about cars and are told by a mechanic that your car needs a complete engine overhaul.

However, you can do a few things to increase your confidence (about the computer consultant, not your car). First, ask for an explanation about why you need custom programs. Ask questions about everything you don't understand. Don't be afraid to repeat questions if you don't understand the answers! If the consultant can't or won't explain it to your satisfaction, say thank you and walk away. Try another consultant. Even if you do get a plausible explanation, try another consultant. See if explanations from both of them match. Maybe your application really doesn't suit itself to a DBMS product. If so, their reasons should be very similar.

And if you decide to go ahead and hire a consultant to write custom programs for you in a conventional language, insist on the safeguards mentioned before, but even more so. Programmers are notorious for underestimating the complexity of programs they write. Also, new programs are notorious for not working properly until after a long, painful, and expensive debugging process. Beware.

Shared Software

In a workgroup with no LAN, you install software such as a word processor or spreadsheet on each PC separately. To stay legal, you need to buy a copy for each PC.

When you have a LAN in the workgroup, nothing needs to change. You can still install software on each individual PC. To use the LAN, you can copy data files to the shared drive, as explained previously under the "Shared Data Space" section.

Some software products, however, are available in a special LAN edition (or network edition or server edition—names vary). To use one of these products, you install the LAN/server edition on a server. Then other users can run the software by accessing the server copy instead of their own hard disks. For some of these products, you need to install a separate workstation edition (or node edition) of the product on each workstation that will use the product on the server.

Different software manufacturers design these products to work in different ways. One method is for the server copy to keep track of how many users are simultaneously running the program. If the number of simultaneous users reaches five (or whatever number the manufacturer picks), no more users can join in. To permit six users at once, you have to buy another "five-user pack" and install it on the server. Then you can have up to ten users at once.

Another method limits the number of users through a "workstation edition" approach. Once again, you install the main software on the server. Then you buy a workstation edition of the software to install on each workstation that will *ever* use the product—not necessarily simultaneously with other node users. Any number of users can use the server edition at once, as long as each one has installed a workstation edition.

Software that manufacturers don't make available in LAN editions work differently. For some products, the software can be installed on a server, but legal restrictions call for each user to buy a copy. The software doesn't restrict the number of users, but instead the manufacturer relies on your honesty to buy a separate copy for each workstation that will run the product. Often the main motivation for users to buy all these copies, other than honesty and fear of prosecution, is to provide each user with reference manuals and telephone support in case of a problem.

Other non-LAN software products fail to share their own program files properly if used illegally. That is, if you and Ed both try to run a copy of the same software from a server, the software fails because it was designed assuming it would run on a single PC with a hard disk no other user can access. For example, the software may create a temporary file in its disk directory in order to store data that won't fit in RAM at the moment. Let's say the program calls this file TEMP.RAM. If you and Ed both run the program from the server, the program will try to create two copies of this file in the same directory on the server. Either the program will fail due to the duplicate filenames, or you and Ed will find your data corrupted because your files overlaid each other. This is just an example. Many other things can go wrong.

In any event, the lesson is to follow the legal restrictions and use software the way it was intended. If you don't, either you may destroy data or your company may get raided for software piracy.

Fortunately, many software manufacturers make pricing attractive for LAN versions of their software. Let's say a stand-alone version of a word processor costs $300. The vendor might sell a LAN server edition for $500, plus $100 for each workstation edition. Simple arithmetic shows that you break even for two users, and you come out increasingly ahead for each additional user. Another approach might be to sell a server edition that supports up to three simultaneous users for $900. In this case, you break even for three users. If you have five users, but no more than three ever use the word processor at once, you come out ahead because you have to pay for only three, not five.

An important point to keep in mind is that software manufacturers do not all have the same LAN policies and they design their software differently. Pricing options and licensing restrictions vary widely and change frequently. Check with the manufacturer to be sure of the current state of affairs.

Fortunately, nearly all major applications software can coexist with a LAN. Even if you can't share the software from a server, you can at least run the regular single-user version of the software at the same time the LAN software runs on your PC. This coexistence wasn't always possible with some early versions of applications software. The following lists some major software products for which either Artisoft has confirmed that a recent version is compatible with LANtastic, or users report successfully running with LANtastic. In some cases old versions may not be fully compatible. Also, some of the products have special LAN versions.

Product	**Manufacturer**
AutoCAD	Autodesk, Inc.
Automenu	Magee Enterprises
Back-It 4 LAN	Gazelle
cc:Mail	Lotus Development
EMM386 (part of MS DOS 5)	Microsoft

Product	**Manufacturer**
Fastback Plus	Fifth Generation Systems
Freelance Graphics	Lotus Development
Generic CADD	Autodesk Retail Products
Harvard Graphics	Software Publishing
Lotus 1-2-3	Lotus Development
Microsoft Word	Microsoft
Microsoft Word for Windows	Microsoft
Microsoft Works	Microsoft
Norton Utilities	Symantec
PageMaker	Aldus
PC Tools Deluxe	Central Point
PC-Write	QuickSoft
PFS First Choice	Software Publishing
PFS Professional Write	Software Publishing
PKZIP	PKWare
Procomm	Datastorm Technology
QDOS LAN	Gazelle
QEMM	Quarterdeck Office Systems
Quattro Pro	Borland International
SideKick	Borland International
Stacker	Stac Electronics
386Max	Qualitas
Time Line	Symantec
Ventura Publisher	Ventura/Xerox
Volkswriter	Volkswriter
WordPerfect	WordPerfect Corp.
WordPerfect Library	WordPerfect Corp.
WordStar	WordStar International
XTreePro	XTree Company

Shared CD-ROM Disk Drives

Not many LANtastic users have yet begun sharing CD-ROM disk drives using their LANs, but every day more discover the amazing capabilities of

CD-ROM. Most other LAN operating systems do not have the ability to share CD-ROM drives, but LANtastic provides it at no extra charge.

A CD-ROM disk looks exactly like an audio CD disk, the kind that has put vinyl record albums on the endangered species list. One of these CD-ROM disks can hold over 600 million bytes of information. The data is available for reading only. You can't write new data on a CD-ROM disk—only the CD-ROM disk manufacturer can. In large quantities, CD-ROM disks can be manufactured for a few dollars apiece. (Costs to buy them are much higher because the manufacturer has to go through a lot of work and expense to acquire the data to distribute on the disks.) The disk drives that read CD-ROM disks have dropped in price, and are now available for under $400. Together, this all means that a manufacturer can send you a disk with a huge amount of data on it much more economically than by using floppy disks, and you can buy a CD-ROM drive to read the data at a reasonable price. If several people can share usage of the CD-ROM data and disk drive over a LAN, the price per user drops even lower.

One of the big benefits of reference material on CD-ROM disks is they are designed to be searched in many ways. In a CD-ROM encyclopedia, for example, you are not limited to looking up entries by the main heading, such as "almonds." You can enter a command to search the encyclopedia for any article that even *mentions* almonds, not just the main entry. Similarly, an archive of newspaper articles allows searching for virtually any word in any article, not just the headlines or main topics. These capabilities permit research that would be completely impractical if you were limited to printed reference material.

What kind of data is now sold on CD-ROM disks? The list is long and rapidly lengthening. Here are a few examples:

- *Microsoft Bookshelf Reference Library* The Bookshelf Reference Library from Microsoft contains many reference books you can search in ways you can't search conventional books. It includes a dictionary, an almanac, a ZIP code directory, a thesaurus, a book of quotations, sample forms and letters, and other reference material.

- *Newspaper Archives* Major newspapers such as the *Los Angeles Times* and the *Washington Post* are available in newspaper archives. Six months or a year of articles are on one CD-ROM disk.
- *Telephone Lists* Two CD-ROM disks contain 90 million names, addresses, ZIP codes, and phone numbers. Other products contain specialized lists.
- *Business Databases* A long list of business databases exists, including ones with information about trademarks, corporate affiliations, small business administration, Standard & Poor's information, and business associations.
- *Medical Databases* Dozens of medical database CD-ROMs are available, including ones specializing in biotechnology, cancer research, family practice, internal medicine, nursing, nutritional analysis, pharmaceuticals, and many other areas. Collections of medical journals are also available on CD-ROM.
- *Government Databases* Census data, agricultural statistics, county and city statistics, the Federal Register, meteorological data, the CIA World Factbook, and many other collections are offered on government databases.
- *Computer Select* This database contains details about nearly all computer hardware and software products offered for sale, plus abstracts or complete articles from dozens of computer publications in the past year.
- *Justis Weekly Law Reports* This compilation offers important Supreme Court decisions and other significant legal developments.

Each CD-ROM disk has its own search software. Most of these programs are compatible with LANtastic in such a way that any workstation can access the CD-ROM data on a server. However, some programs are not compatible. Check with Artisoft or the CD-ROM manufacturer to be sure. Some manufacturers do not yet offer LAN versions or have not established LAN prices. Also, be aware that CD-ROM drives are much slower than hard disks. If too many users try to access the same CD-ROM drive at once, everyone gets extremely slow response.

Shared Modems

Software products are available from Artisoft and other companies to provide the capability of any LANtastic workstation accessing a modem on any other workstation. Chapter 4 briefly discusses the economic trade-offs involved in modem sharing. Because 2400 bit per second (bps) modems are so inexpensive (some are about $50), the demand for modem sharing is not very strong. The cost is not high to install a 2400 bps modem in every computer.

Higher-speed modems, such as 9600 bps models, might be worth sharing in some cases, but their prices have dropped greatly also. The main economy in modem sharing usually comes if a reduction in the number of associated phone lines is also possible, or if every user in a workgroup badly needs to use a modem only once in a while, and not all at the same time.

Some Real-World LANtastic Users

This section briefly describes an assortment of workgroups and companies that use LANtastic in their everyday work. The list is a fairly wide cross section, to give you an idea of LANtastic's diverse capabilities.

Case 1: A Small Law Firm

A small law office has one attorney and one secretary. Each has a 386/33 PC. They bought the LANtastic 10BASE-T Starter Kit (explained in Chapter 3) to connect the two PCs. Both PCs are configured as servers to enable either to access the other's hard disk. The office has a shared laser printer that is located next to the secretary's desk. They run WordPerfect under Windows—the attorney writes documents, and the secretary retrieves the document files and then edits and prints them.

Case 2: A Food Processing Company

A food processing company has a thin Ethernet LANtastic network that connects six computers and uses LANtastic AE-2 LAN cards (specific LANtastic products, such as the AE-2, are presented in Chapter 3). The server is a 386/25 PC with a 200 megabyte IDE disk drive. The other five computers are 80286-based models that have no hard disks and act as workstations. Each workstation boots from a floppy disk and then accesses the server's hard disk via the LAN. The server is dedicated entirely to server functions and runs ALONE to maximize performance. (ALONE is covered in Chapter 13.) The primary use of the LAN is to run a Paradox database application that enables people at all workstations to keep track of inventory and work in process.

Case 3: A Yacht Chartering Company

A yacht chartering company uses LANtastic on a thin Ethernet LAN to connect eight computers. Some computers use LANtastic AE-2 cards, and others use Western Digital Ethernet cards. A 386 computer with an 80 megabyte hard disk is defined as a nondedicated server for sharing disk files. An 80286 computer has three printers connected and acts as a nondedicated server for these devices only, not disk files. One printer is a Hewlett-Packard LaserJet, and the other two are dot-matrix printers that print invoices and other forms that require an impact printer to produce carbons. The other six computers are 80286 models. The main application schedules yacht charters using Lotus 1-2-3 spreadsheets that someone in the company developed. The other main application is word processing. The company also has a remote location with one computer that runs LANtastic Z to access the server over telephone lines at 9600 bps.

Case 4: A Small Insurance Office

A small insurance office has two AT-compatible 80286 computers connected between their serial ports using LANtastic Z. A laser printer is attached to one of the computers, configured as a server, for access by both. The main application is WordPerfect. Both users save all document files on the server's hard disk.

Case 5: A Software Development Company

A software development company's sales department has an assortment of eight PCs, ranging from 386SX/16 models up to 386/25 models, connected to a 10BASE-T LANtastic network. The hub is a D-Link DE-812TP, which has room for up to 12 node connections. The seven workstation nodes use AE-1/T cards and the server uses an AE-2/T card. The main application is the Action Plus contact management program, with which telemarketers monitor sales leads and send out form letters. Two HP LaserJet printers are shared on the LAN—a model III with letterhead stationery and a model IIP with plain paper.

Case 6: A Magazine Publisher

A magazine publisher uses a thin Ethernet LANtastic LAN with AE-2 cards primarily to run Word for Windows. They have a total of nine nodes. A 386/33 PC is the only server. The eight workstations are mostly 386SX computers, used by writers and editors.

Case 7: A Retail Business

A retail computer business runs a computer bulletin board system (BBS). Six computers are linked using LANtastic with AE-2 cards and thin Ethernet. Three computers are nondedicated servers and three are workstations. Each computer has its own U.S. Robotics modem. As many as six people can dial into the BBS at once to access all of the publicly available server files. One server has a NEC CDR-72 CD-ROM drive, which holds a CD-ROM disk that has over 500 megabytes of shareware software.

3

The LANtastic Product Line

This chapter surveys the LANtastic product line. Don't think of this chapter as one long Artisoft advertisement. (Remember, this is an independent book and Artisoft has no control over its contents.) Instead, consider this chapter an explanation of the building blocks you can use to construct your LANtastic LAN. Once you see what the building blocks are you can move on to the next chapter, which explains how to set your objectives and plan your LAN purchase and installation.

Prices shown here are list prices unless otherwise indicated. Like other computer hardware and software, large discounts (usually about 30 percent) are available from many dealers, especially through mail order. Remember that prices and specifications can change at any time.

Ethernet LAN Products

Artisoft makes two different families of LAN products: the Ethernet family and the 2Mbps (megabits per second) family. This section covers the

Ethernet family, which transmits data over the LAN at 10 megabits per second and adheres to IEEE 802.3 standards.

LANtastic Ethernet Starter Kits

Artisoft's LAN starter kits contain all the hardware and software you need to construct a two-node LAN. The two LAN cards (one of which you install in each PC), cable, terminators, LANtastic network operating system, and manuals are all included. If you need to install, say, a five-node LAN, the simplest way is to buy a LAN starter kit plus three more LAN cards and three more cables of the same type. Installation is pretty easy; at software installation time you decide which computers to use as servers and which to use as workstations. (Chapter 5 explains installation of the network operating system software.)

Your biggest jobs are to figure out which kind of adapter card and cable you want, how long the cables should be, and how to route the cables between the PCs. Information in this chapter and the next should help you answer these questions.

The Ethernet starter kits use standard 802.3-compliant Ethernet LAN cards, cables, and connectors. The various models follow different 802.3 standards. The best-selling starter kit uses the AE-2 card and thin coaxial cable.

LANtastic AE-2 Ethernet Starter Kit (ISA): $699 This starter kit includes the following, which are shown in Figure 3-1:

- Two 16-bit AE-2 Ethernet LAN cards (for the ISA bus, which stands for *industry standard architecture,* and means the standard IBM-AT compatible 16-bit bus). The cards will work in either 16-bit or 8-bit PC expansion slots, and comply with the IEEE 802.3 10BASE2 standard ("thin Ethernet"). These LAN cards are compatible with Novell's NE2000 driver software, which means you can decide later to switch to Novell's NetWare NOS without buying new hardware. Instead of thin co-ax, the AE-2 card can be connected to thick coaxial cable, such as Belden 9880, which allows up to 100 nodes on a segment and maximum cable length of 500 meters (10BASE5), but requires an external transceiver and uses 15-pin connectors called db15 AUX connectors. Each AE-2 card contains 16K of buffer RAM, which can be upgraded (for $50) to 64K to improve performance. Optionally the AE-2 can be configured to run in a diskless workstation (a PC with no disk drives) by adding a ROM (read-only memory) chip for $60.

- One 25-foot thin coaxial cable (type RG58 A/U) with BNC connectors on both ends.
- Two BNC T connectors for attachment to the rear of the two LAN cards.
- Two terminators.
- The LANtastic network operating system (NOS) software, which supports from 2 to 300 nodes in any combination of servers and workstations. The software runs under MS DOS or Windows, and allows sharing of server disk drives, printers, and CD ROM drives. An electronic mail (e-mail) capability is included, which allows LAN users to send messages back and forth. Security features provide methods to restrict who can access the LAN's servers and which files these users can read, update, or delete.
- Manuals explaining the LANtastic NOS and the AE-2 LAN cards.

Figure 3-1. *The LANtastic AE-2 Ethernet Starter Kit (ISA)*

If you want to create a LAN to connect two XT or AT-type PCs (AT-type includes 386 and 486 models) that are no more than about 15 feet apart, this kit has all you need. Currently you can purchase the kit through discount outlets for under $500. If you have PC-compatible computers (not PS/2 computers that use Micro Channel cards), the AE-2 starter kit is the simplest, and probably the best, way to start a LANtastic LAN that will work well for most purposes.

You'll need to buy an extra AE-2 or AE-3 LAN card and an extra length of thin coaxial cable for each computer after the first two. Artisoft has various lengths of thin co-ax with BNC connectors: 25 feet for $16, 50 feet for $28, and 100 feet for $40. See Chapter 4 for more discussion about which LAN card and cable type suit you best, and information to determine the cable length you need.

LANtastic AE-2 Ethernet Starter Kit (Micro Channel): $899 This is the same as the ISA version of the AE-2 kit, but the two LAN cards fit in IBM's PS/2 Micro Channel computers. Be aware that some PS/2 computers (mostly the lower numbered models) do *not* use the Micro Channel card type, but instead use the old AT-type, or ISA, cards. (Thanks for the confusion, IBM.) Note the extra price you pay for add-on cards if you have Micro Channel computers. (Thanks again, IBM.) Figure 3-2 shows the contents of this starter kit.

LANtastic AE-3 Ethernet Starter Kit (ISA): $799 This kit is the same as the AE-2 ISA Starter Kit, except the two LAN cards are the AE-3 model. The AE-3 card allows connection of either thin coaxial cable, thick coaxial cable (with external transceivers), or unshielded twisted-pair cable but is otherwise the same as the AE-2 card. Like the AE-2 kit, this kit comes with a 25-foot thin coaxial cable with BNC T connectors. If you buy this kit, you have the flexibility of switching to either unshielded twisted-pair cabling or even thick co-ax cabling later without buying new LAN cards. Or, if your office building already has appropriate twisted-pair wiring installed, you can use these cards and eliminate the need to install new cables. Like the AE-2 card, the AE-3 is compatible with Novell's NE2000 standard and can be upgraded to 64K of RAM or to work in a diskless workstation.

Figure 3-2. *The LANtastic AE-2 Ethernet Starter Kit (Micro Channel)*

LANtastic 10BASE-T Starter Kit: $899 The 10BASE-T Starter Kit is the same as the AE-2 ISA kit, except:

- The two LAN cards are AE-1/T 8-bit Ethernet cards for the ISA bus.
- The cabling is unshielded twisted-pair with RJ45 connectors.
- The kit includes a Peer-Hub 10BASE-T Concentrator.

This kit is meant to be a starting point for a low-cost 10BASE-T LAN. This starter kit costs more than some other kits, but that's because it includes the hub hardware. The next three workstations you add each require only an AE-1/T card (or an AE-3 card, if you prefer), plus twisted-pair cable.

Other Ethernet Products and Components

These Ethernet products are not starter kits, although some of them are included as parts in the starter kits. They are either add-on products to extend your Ethernet LAN to more users, or components that upgrade Ethernet products.

LANtastic AE-2 Ethernet Adapter (ISA): $299 This is the added card you need for each thin Ethernet node beyond the first two that you set up using the AE-2 Starter Kit. While the full price is $299, discount sources offer it for about $200. Figure 1-1 in Chapter 1 shows the AE-2 card.

You install this LAN card in a PC and connect it to another PC with an additional thin coaxial cable. Cable length restrictions and limitations on the number of nodes in the LAN can be a problem if the number of nodes exceeds 30 *or* the total LAN cable length exceeds 607 feet (185 meters). See Chapter 4 for details.

As mentioned previously in the section on the AE-2 Starter Kit, the AE-2 can instead connect to a thick Ethernet LAN, but requires an external IEEE 802.3-compliant transceiver to do so.

LANtastic AE-2 Ethernet Adapter (Micro Channel): $399 Use this card to extend a thin coaxial Ethernet LAN to a Micro Channel PS/2 computer. The same restrictions apply as for the ISA version of the AE-2.

LANtastic AE-3 Ethernet Adapter (ISA): $349 Use this card to extend a thin coaxial, thick coaxial, or twisted-pair LAN to another PC that uses the PC/AT (ISA) bus. Figure 3-3 shows the AE-3 adapter.

LANtastic AE-2/T 16-Bit Ethernet Adapter: $299 For a 10BASE-T twisted-pair Ethernet LAN, use this card in each PC (ISA bus only), and connect them to an Artisoft Peer-Hub 10BASE-T Concentrator or any other standard 10BASE-T hub. If your office already has the right kind of extra unshielded (or shielded) dual twisted-pair cable leading to each PC, you avoid cabling expense and trouble. In addition, this card supports connection to thick Ethernet, in case you need that flexibility. Like the AE-2 card, the AE-2/T is a 16-bit card with 16K of RAM, it is NE2000 compatible, and you can buy options to upgrade to 64K of RAM or configure for a diskless workstation. Figure 3-4 shows the AE-2/T Ethernet adapter.

LANtastic 8-Bit AE-1/T 10BASE-T Ethernet Adapter: $199 For a low-cost Ethernet LAN, use this card in each PC (ISA bus only), and connect them to the Peer-Hub 10BASE-T Concentrator or any other standard 10BASE-T hub.

Figure 3-3. *The LANtastic AE-3 Ethernet Adapter (ISA)*

Figure 3-4. *The LANtastic AE-2/T Ethernet Adapter*

This card transfers only eight bits at a time, and therefore has slightly lower throughput than 16-bit cards. (Not 50 percent less, however. Probably closer to 10-20 percent.) The AE-1/T has 8K of on-board buffer RAM and is compatible with Novell's NE1000. Figure 3-5 shows the AE-1/T 10BASE-T Ethernet adapter.

Artisoft Peer-Hub 10BASE-T Concentrator: $399 The Peer-Hub Concentrator is a card that you install in an ISA PC slot (8- or 16-bit). Up to five other PCs with 10BASE-T LAN cards (AE-1/T, AE-2/T, or AE-3) connect to external RJ45 sockets using unshielded dual twisted-pair cable and modular RJ45 plugs. The Peer-Hub also has three internal connectors, for attachment to other Artisoft products. One can connect to an AE-1/T, AE-2/T, or AE-3 card in the same PC without using one of the five external sockets, so you can have up to six nodes connected. Another lets you connect the 10BASE-T hub to a thin or thick Ethernet LAN through use of the Peer-Hub AUI Interface Kit. The third internal connector provides a way to connect the Peer-Hub Con-

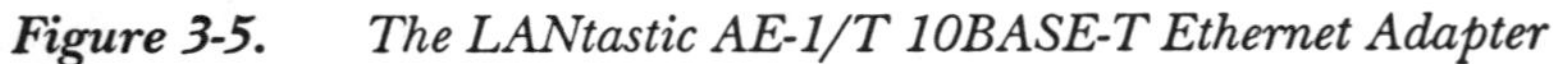

Figure 3-5. *The LANtastic AE-1/T 10BASE-T Ethernet Adapter*

centrator to another Peer-Hub Concentrator, up to a maximum of four in one host PC. Figure 3-6 shows the Peer-Hub card.

Peer-Hub AUI Interface Kit: $399 This is the kit just mentioned that enables connection of a thin or thick Ethernet LAN segment to a 10BASE-T Ethernet LAN hub. The kit includes: a modified AE-3 adapter card, an AUI interface cable, two transformer chips to install in the Peer-Hub Concentrator, and instruction manuals.

Artisoft Central Station Connectivity Processor: $595 Central Station provides a convenient way to attach portable PCs or peripheral devices to a thin Ethernet or 10BASE-T LAN. Central Station has a parallel printer port, two 9-pin serial ports, an auxiliary port, and a PC port with a five-foot cable. The PC port is a special parallel port for attaching a portable computer to your LAN. Software and an instruction manual are also included. Figure 3-7 shows the Central Station connectivity processor.

Figure 3-6. *The Artisoft Peer-Hub 10BASE-T Concentrator*

Figure 3-7. *The Artisoft Central Station connectivity processor*

2Mbps LAN Products

This section covers Artisoft's proprietary 2Mbps products. Proprietary means that Artisoft developed the 2Mbps LAN card to meet its own internal design goals, and it does not adhere to IEEE 802.3 or ARCnet standards. The 2Mbps products are less expensive than the Ethernet 10 Mbps products, but because they are nonstandard you are largely limited to Artisoft as your source for add-on products. If you decide later to switch to Novell's NetWare NOS, for example, you throw away your LANtastic 2Mbps cards and start from scratch.

The 2Mbps LAN cards transfer data more slowly than the 10 Mbps Ethernet cards. This seems like an incredibly obvious thing to say, but in reality a lot of complexity lurks beneath its surface. Users and Artisoft both report that a LANtastic 10 Mbps LAN typically moves data over the LAN about two or three times as fast as a LANtastic 2Mbps LAN. The reasons why the difference isn't a more obvious five times as fast are many and complex: hardware design differences, buffer size differences, software driver differences, differences in the PCs in which the cards are installed, and benchmark measurement differences.

Because the 2Mbps products are nonstandard and significantly slower than the Ethernet products, most users are better off using the Ethernet products. However, if you need to set up a very small LAN and find yourself forced into saving every possible dollar in the short term, then consider a LANtastic 2Mbps LAN. If you need to expand the LAN later to add more users or accommodate a heavier workload, you may find that your only choice is to dump the 2Mbps LAN cards and cables, and buy an entirely new Ethernet LAN.

3

LANtastic 2Mbps Starter Kit (ISA): $499 Like the other LAN starter kits, this one contains everything mentioned under the AE-2 starter kit, except this one contains two of Artisoft's proprietary 2Mbps LAN cards, and the connecting cable is a 15-foot dual twisted-pair cable. The 2Mbps cards each have 32K of RAM and an extra processor on the card. (The LANtastic Ethernet cards use the host computer's processor instead.) The on-card processor runs at a clock speed of 10 megahertz–faster than early IBM PC/XT and AT computers. In addition, Artisoft's implementation of NetBIOS software (part of the low-level LAN operating system) is loaded in the LAN card's RAM and executed by the on-card processor. The results of this LAN card design are that less RAM is used on the PC by LAN software, and faster LAN data movement occurs on slow PCs when compared with LAN cards without an on-card processor.

Cable lengths can total as much as 1500 feet using Artisoft's dual twisted-pair cable, but only up to 300 feet using AT&T telephone-grade dual twisted-pair 24-gauge cable. A network can contain up to 32 nodes. Using the LANtastic 2Mbps Hub, a network can contain up to 300 nodes. Because of this adapter's limited speed, however, a 2Mbps LAN is best suited to a small number of nodes. Even though the 2Mbps card does not conform to IEEE LAN standards, it runs NetBIOS software and uses standard MS DOS redirection. This means that application software will work if it is compatible with NetBIOS, and most regular MS DOS software should work with it. See Chapter 2 for details. Figure 3-8 shows the 2Mbps Starter Kit.

LANtastic 2Mbps Starter Kit (Micro Channel): $699 This kit is the PS/2 Micro Channel version of the 2Mbps Starter Kit. It contains the same

Figure 3-8. *The LANtastic 2Mbps Starter Kit (ISA)*

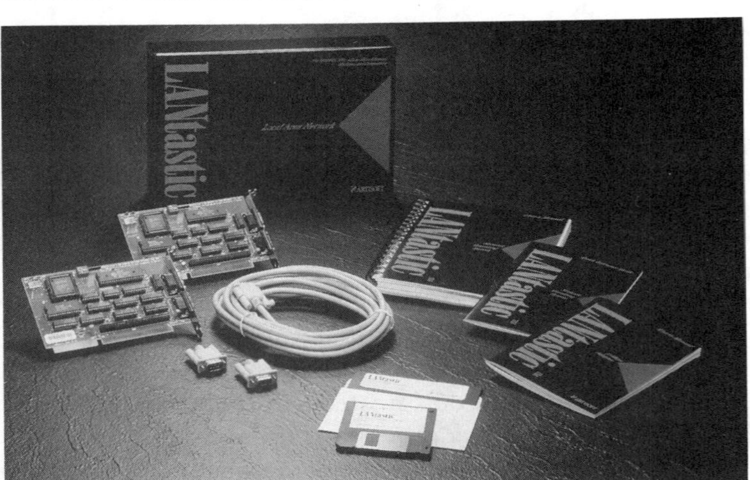

ingredients as the ISA version, except the two 2Mbps cards fit the Micro Channel bus.

LANtastic 2Mbps Adapter (ISA): $199 This is the 2Mbps add-on card for PC compatibles. Use the starter kit for the first two nodes, then this card for the third and beyond. Figure 3-9 shows the 2Mbps adapter for the ISA bus.

LANtastic 2Mbps Adapter (Micro Channel): $299 This is the 2Mbps add-on card for PS/2 Micro Channel computers.

LANtastic 2Mbps Hub: $495 This hub permits more than 32 nodes to connect to a LANtastic 2Mbps LAN. This is *not* the same as the Ethernet Peer-Hub product. In some cases, a LANtastic 2Mbps Hub installation kit ($208) may also be required.

Figure 3-9. *The LANtastic 2Mbps Adapter (ISA)*

Voice Products

In addition to the two LAN product families, Artisoft makes several voice-related products. Most of these products work with or without a LAN.

Artisoft Sounding Board Adapter (ISA): $99 The Sounding Board was previously called the LANtastic Voice Adapter. It includes a telephone handset, an 8-bit PC expansion card for the ISA bus, software, and an instruction manual. The card also has audio in and out jacks for connection to a stereo system or tape recorder. The Sounding Board converts sounds to and from digital data that you can store on disk. The LANtastic NOS supports voice communications as part of its electronic mail. This means two LAN users who each have a Sounding Board can exchange voice messages as well as text e-mail messages. Figure 3-10 shows the Sounding Board, which is covered in depth in Chapter 8. A Micro Channel version of the Sounding Board is also available for $199.

ArtiScribe Digital Dictation Starter Kit (ISA): $499 This kit is designed for an executive and a secretary. It includes two Sounding Board adapters (ISA bus), one telephone handset, one telephone headset (for the secretary), ArtiScribe Station Software for two stations, and instruction manuals. The executive dictates memos and letters at his or her LAN node, and the secretary transcribes them at his or hers. This kit is also available in a Micro Channel version for $699. The ArtiScribe Station Software is available separately for $149, and the headset for $99.

Figure 3-10. *The Artisoft Sounding Board Adapter (ISA)*

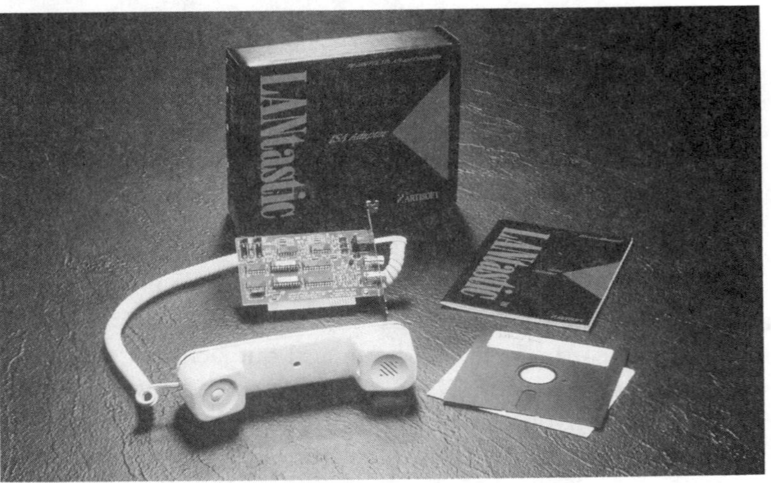

Software Products

These software products work with a LAN, but are not limited to just the Ethernet or 2Mbps product families. As a result, they are listed here as a separate group of products.

3

LANtastic/AI: $99 LANtastic/AI is the adapter independent version of the LANtastic NOS. If you already have LAN cards and cables, or you prefer to buy them from someone other than Artisoft, you can buy LANtastic/AI for each node and run LANtastic's network operating system. An unlimited-use license on one network (well, a maximum of 300 users) is also available for $2499, which is a better deal if you plan more than 25 users. Software drivers are included for an ever-increasing number of popular Ethernet and ARCnet LAN cards that conform to NetBIOS standards. Compatible LAN card models are available from Western Digital, 3Com, ACCTON, Novell, CNet, Shureman, Tiara, Xircom, Standard Microsystems, Thomas Conrad, Datatech Enterprises, and Tandy. Check with Artisoft (see Appendix B) for a current list of specific models.

LANtastic Z Two Station Kit: $125 LANtastic Z is sometimes called a *zero-slot LAN*. This means it connects two computers together and runs LAN software, but does not use a PC card slot to connect the computers. Instead, LANtastic Z comes with two cables to give you a choice of how to connect the computers—either through their parallel ports or their serial ports. This approach is especially useful to connect a portable computer, which does not have standard expansion slots, to a desktop computer. Once connected, you can use the LANtastic Z software to exchange data files or the portable computer can use the desktop's printer. In addition, you can connect the computers using modems and telephone lines. LANtastic Z runs the same LANtastic NOS used by the full-fledged LAN products, but transfers data much more slowly because of the limited capabilities of the serial and parallel ports. Copies of the software on both 5.25-inch and 3.5-inch floppy disks are included.

Another use of LANtastic Z is to experiment with LAN software at a bargain price before deciding to buy a complete LAN. LANtastic Z is also the least expensive way to connect two nearby desktop computers and have them dynamically share the same printer. LANtastic Z connects two computers only; some other zero-slot LANs connect more than two.

LANtastic for Windows: $299 LANtastic runs under Microsoft Windows without this software, but LANtastic for Windows provides a Windows interface of pull-down menus, icons, and on-line help. The price is per network, not per user. See Chapter 12 for details about running LANtastic in a Windows environment.

The Network Eye: $199 The Network Eye (TNE) allows you to sit at one node on a LANtastic LAN (or other NetBIOS-based LAN) and monitor what other nodes are doing. You can actually look at what is on the screen of other LAN users, keeping track of up to 32 at once. This isn't meant for industrial espionage purposes, but instead to enable a network administrator to monitor and assist users who have problems. The administrator can even update the user's AUTOEXEC.BAT or CONFIG.SYS files without going to the user's computer. The price shown is per network, not per user. Chapter 9 explains more about The Network Eye.

ArtiCom Modem Sharing Software: $399 ArtiCom works on any NetBIOS LAN, including LANtastic, to provide users the capability of sharing modems and other COM port devices over the LAN. Using ArtiCom, you can install one 9600 bps modem and telephone line on any LAN station (server or workstation) and then any user on the LAN can use the modem to connect to a remote computer. An ArtiCom server can have up to four shared modems. You can create a *modem pool*, which means users can request the next available modem in the group rather than a specific one that might be in use. Other serial devices that require bidirectional communication, such as fax cards and certain plotters, can also be shared. The price is per network, not per user. See Chapter 7 for details about sharing modems and other devices.

4

Planning for LANtastic

Will a LAN help your workgroup? Should you choose LANtastic? Which products should you buy, and where should you buy them? How should you plan the installation? While these are broad questions without precise answers, this chapter helps prepare you for setting up LANtastic. The previous chapters gave you an understanding of how LANs work, what you can use them for, and what kind of products Artisoft sells. This chapter goes into more detail about how to analyze your specific needs and determine how LANtastic can address them.

Of course, if your workgroup is typical and uses only a handful of MS-DOS-based PCs (let's say two through six or so) located physically close together, and you can afford to spend about $250 per PC to connect them experimentally, and you hate planning, here's a quick answer. (The answer has a good chance of being the same answer this chapter leads you to.) Buy the LANtastic AE-2 Ethernet Starter Kit for the first two computers, plus an extra AE-2 LAN card and a thin coaxial cable with BNC connectors for each additional computer. Be sure you get ISA bus cards for ISA bus computers, and Micro Channel cards for PS/2 Micro Channel computers. If 25-foot cables aren't long enough, buy longer cables. Buy it all from a local Artisoft dealer or a mail-order company, depending on which you are more comfortable with.

But if any of these conditions is not true, the planning process outlined in this chapter will build your confidence that the LANtastic configuration you choose will fit your needs. So for those of you who have more than a handful of PCs, or who have PCs that are not all close together, or who don't shell out money without doing enough planning to feel comfortable everything will work the way you expect, this chapter is for you.

Why Bother Planning?

Suppose you are responsible for recommending or approving a LAN decision in your workgroup. (Your workgroup might consist of a 2-person office, a 15-person group in a large company, or an entire small to medium-sized company.) Ideally, you should perform a detailed and objective analysis of exactly what you need before you buy anything.

In fact, you *should* have created a long-range plan years ago, and updated it every year, before you bought any "office automation" equipment of *any* kind—computers, fax machines, copiers, typewriters, telephone equipment, or almost anything with a power cord on it. This plan should have analyzed your current workload and equipment along with immediate expectations and plans for the next year or more. How many people perform various kinds of work right now and what equipment do they use? How will their work change in the near and far term, and what equipment will they need then? How many new people will be added? How will their work tie in with what others are now doing and will do in the future? What kinds of communications take place between group members, as well as between the group and the outside world?

Of course, you didn't make any such plan. Neither did anyone else. Or if they did, they'll tell you they couldn't get the information they needed to do it right, or they faced an unreasonable deadline, or the boss said not to include something that should have been included, or something unexpected has cropped up since, and so the plan is worthless.

To make a perfect plan for any kind of office automation, whether for a LAN or otherwise, you need the following:

- Perfect knowledge about what functions your workgroup performs now and exactly how each member uses each office automation product
- Perfect knowledge about what functions your workgroup will perform in the future and what each member's needs will be
- Perfect knowledge about what products will be offered in the future and how well they will meet those needs
- Perfect knowledge about what budget restrictions will be imposed on your workgroup in the future
- Perfect knowledge about technical issues and standards, both present and future
- Infinite time and resources to analyze this knowledge and create the plan
- Sufficient time to finish and implement your plan before its recommendations become obsolete due to unforeseen changes

Of course, all these things are impossible. Even if you allow for reasonable limitations, such as substituting the words "fairly good knowledge" for "perfect knowledge" in this list, most workgroups don't have the luxury to spend much time and thought on long-range planning. For many workgroups, long-range planning now means occasionally taking a few minutes over coffee to think about the next month or two. Ideally this planning should take much more time and effort and be directed toward next year and the years after, but in real-life business situations this type of planning is usually accorded low-priority status.

So what should you do? Give up and do no planning?

No, of course not. You have to recognize the limitations of planning, and your own limitations in making those plans. For something like a new LAN for your workgroup, even a little rough planning is far better than no planning at all. Your workgroup is similar to some other workgroups, but far different from others. You need a LAN that fits *your* needs.

You also need a plan that fits your available planning resources. If you have a small office with simple computing and communication needs, a simple plan is fine. If you have a larger office, or an office that needs to link somehow to other offices, or ambitious intentions for "computerizing the office," you need to pay more attention to planning. Of course, you can always bypass planning and later pay the price when things don't work out the way you expected. As a rule, each hour of planning time reduces 10 or even 100 hours you will later spend to fix problems that a good plan would have avoided. A good plan is good business.

Analyze Your Needs

A good way to plan is to analyze your needs alongside the available solutions that can satisfy those needs. If you find solutions that fit your needs, both now and in the future, you can simply plan to acquire and implement those solutions. This is a LANtastic book, so let's look at typical needs that a LANtastic LAN can satisfy.

Situations Inappropriate for LANtastic

First, look at some easy questions. If your answer is "yes" to any of these questions, LANtastic is probably not for you (unless some new products have been introduced since this book's creation):

- *Is your workgroup currently using computers other than MS-DOS-based IBM PC compatibles?* LANtastic currently is not offered for the Apple Macintosh computer. (Options exist to connect LANtastic between PC compatibles and Macs, so don't rule out LANtastic if your workgroup has a few Macs mixed in. See the discussion later in this chapter on MACLAN Connect in the "Macintosh Connection" section.) Also, LANtastic is not currently available for the OS/2 or Unix operating systems. LANtastic was designed to connect PC-compatible computers that run MS-DOS (or its twin, IBM's PC DOS), or MS-DOS with Microsoft Windows.
- *Does your workgroup's LAN need to connect to a different type of LAN?* Some other popular LAN network operating systems are Novell's

NetWare (versions 3.*x*, 2.*x*, and Lite), Microsoft's LAN Manager (and the similar IBM LAN Server), and Banyan's VINES. If you just need a modem connection between one or more of your PCs and a PC on a non-LANtastic LAN, that's not a problem. But if you need your LANtastic LAN and the other LAN to connect together into one large logical LAN, this is presently possible only to a limited degree and isn't easy. Connecting LANs of the same type is your best bet. The best reason to buy Novell NetWare for a small workgroup is because you expect you will soon need to link it to an already existing NetWare LAN in another part of your company. See the box "LANtastic in a Novell World" for more information on connecting LANtastic to a Novell LAN.

4

- *Is there a particular hardware or software product you now use that is incompatible with LANtastic?* Most products you run on a stand-alone PC will work with LANtastic, but some may not. Check to be sure. Other chapters in this book discuss many popular products (see Chapter 2 for software, chapters 6 and 7 for hardware). For the latest information, check with the support sources listed in Appendix B.
- *Do you need to connect a large number of PCs?* LANtastic is best suited for small to medium-sized LANs. To connect more than 30 PCs, a LANtastic LAN gets more complicated and you should carefully consider whether LANtastic is your best choice. If you need to connect more than 60 to 100, you should definitely look at alternatives that were designed for large numbers of users. Yes, LANtastic allows for up to 300 PC connections, but that doesn't mean a 300-PC LANtastic LAN is your best choice. LAN performance and administration might be a problem. The typical LANtastic LAN connects from 2 to 20 PCs. More than 50 is rare. If you need to connect more than 30 PCs, read this chapter to understand the issues and then contact a LAN consultant to discuss alternatives.
- *In the near future, will any of the items on this list apply to your workgroup?* Don't buy a LANtastic LAN today if in six months you will run into one of these problems. Or if you buy now anyway, have your conversion plans in place.

LANtastic in a Novell World

Novell's NetWare, versions 3.*x* and 2.*x*, is the dominant LAN operating system today for medium to large LANs. Novell's recent product, NetWare Lite, is positioned to compete in the small, peer-to-peer LAN market, where LANtastic is king. The jury is still out, but early reviews indicate that the first NetWare Lite release falls short of LANtastic in features, performance, and reliability.

However, the realities of LAN life are that NetWare (3.*x* and 2.*x*) runs on many LANs, perhaps including some in other offices of your organization. As a result, many prospective LANtastic buyers face two questions:

- Can I link my LANtastic LAN to a Novell LAN (now or in the future)?
- What if my whole organization someday decides to standardize on NetWare? Does that mean I'll have to throw away my LANtastic equipment and start over?

At the time of this writing, the answer to the first question is a limited yes. Artisoft sells no NetWare connectivity products, but some other companies claim to. One product is called LANspan/NBP, from IMC Networks Corporation (16931 Milliken Avenue, Irvine, CA 92714, 714-724-1070). IMC says you can install two LAN cards in a LANtastic server PC—one to connect to the LANtastic LAN and one to connect to the NetWare LAN. (The NetWare connection has to use an IMC LAN card.) This way the PC can access data on both LANs and provide a common shared disk that both LANs can access. Artisoft is certainly interested in providing some such connectivity solution also, so ask them about new product announcements to connect to NetWare if you have this concern.

The second question has an easier answer. If you buy Artisoft's Ethernet LAN cards (models AE-1/T, AE-2, AE-3 and their variants), you can switch later to NetWare without buying any new LAN cards or cable. All the AE-*x* cards are compatible with either the NE2000 or NE1000 Novell specification for NetWare. Some models require you to move a jumper connection on the card, which is easy to do (you see how to in Chapter 5). This compatibility means you can buy LANtastic today and then decide to switch to NetWare tomorrow without any penalty (other than needing a whole lot of training to understand NetWare). All you need to buy is the NetWare software.

Workgroup Needs and Wants

Not all workgroups are the same. When you analyze your workgroup needs, some characteristics of your particular workgroup are critical to deciding how to implement a LAN. Some of these have just been mentioned. This section lists these critical characteristics, along with some comments about how to use LANtastic to address each characteristic. Note that some characteristics relate directly to technical considerations of one LAN type versus another. Other characteristics relate instead to how your workgroup functions and the work habits of the people in it. As you read this section, you should find you are making decisions about which LANtastic options you need and what actions you need to take to get ready for LANtastic. Write down these decisions and actions!

Number and Types of PCs

How many PCs do you need to connect, both now and in the future, and what kinds are they? Are they older 8088 and 80286-based computers, or are they newer 386 and 486 models? Are they all desktop computers, or are some of them portables? Do all the computers have older, smaller hard disks, or do some or all have large ones? How much memory (RAM) does each have? Does every PC run DOS version 3.1, 3.3, or later? Are any PCs so old that ROM BIOS upgrades might be needed before running LANtastic? These questions are discussed in this section.

Remember Your Objectives

Keep in mind the overriding question you should continually ask yourself: What do I want the LAN to do? After reading Chapters 1 and 2, you should have a good idea of how you want to use the LAN. Is your objective to eliminate a floppy disk Sneakernet and instead copy files to and from a shared disk drive? To simply share a printer? To run a single shared database application? To use electronic mail? A general desire to keep up with the Joneses and try a little of all this to improve group communication and productivity?

Keep your objectives clearly in mind as you go through this process. If you are not yet clear on your objectives, try to crystallize them while you read this chapter. Your goal is to use LANtastic to help you reach your objectives as simply, conveniently, and inexpensively as possible.

Make a list of all the computers you want to connect together using LANtastic, showing PC attributes along with who uses each computer. Leave room for a few extra columns of information that you will need to add shortly. For a five-person office with four computers, the list would look like Table 4-1.

Who List who uses the computer. Computers most often are used by only one person, or primarily by one person. Show the primary user first. If other people sometimes use the computer, show their names. Notice that in this example, every user conveniently has a unique name. Your real-world office may require last initials, last names, nicknames, or some other way to be sure you uniquely identify each person and computer. Also, if a computer is dedicated to a certain function and is shared by many users, you might instead want to list that function, such as "Graphics" or "Remote Access." The point here is to identify each computer unambiguously and show who uses it. If nothing else seems right, assign a number or name to each computer right now and identify each one that way during planning. This name will probably become the machine name you assign to the computer during LANtastic software installation in Chapter 5.

PC Type Under the "PC Type" column, show the most important aspect of what type of PC each is. You might want to be more specific than the example and show the exact processor and clock speed, such as "8088 (4.77 MHz)", "80286 (8 MHz)", and so on. The processor types and speeds can influence your LANtastic adapter card decision.

If your LAN will connect older PCs (mostly 8088 processors at 4.77 megahertz, as in the original IBM PC and XT), the LANtastic 2Mbps adapter cards may be a reasonable choice. As discussed previously, the 2Mbps cards

Table 4-1. *An Initial PC Attribute List for LAN Planning*

	Who	**PC Type**	**Hard Disk**	**RAM**
1.	Carl	XT	10MB	640K
2.	Jane	AT	30MB	640K
3.	Ed, Al	386SX	40MB	1MB
4.	Bob	386/33	80MB	2MB

are much slower than Ethernet cards and don't adhere to IEEE 802.3 or other standards. However, they are also somewhat less expensive, and each card contains an on-board processor rather than relying on your PC's processor. The result is that an older PC or XT computer doesn't get as bogged down processing LAN traffic as it does if the PC uses an Ethernet LAN card.

The other problem with 2Mbps LAN adapters is that you can't mix them on the same LANtastic LAN (or other LAN) with Ethernet LAN cards. So, you can't start with 2Mbps LAN cards and then add Ethernet cards to the LAN when you add newer, faster computers. If you expect to expand your LAN this way (and most people will), get the Ethernet cards to begin with.

Hard Disk and RAM This computer attribute list is also the starting point for your planning decisions about which computers will act as servers on the LAN. LANtastic gives you the option of setting up *dedicated servers*, which make resources available to other LAN computers and do nothing else, or *nondedicated servers*, which you can use as workstations at the same time. Most LANtastic users prefer not to set up dedicated servers, choosing instead to have a server PC also available for workstation usage. The main advantage to setting up a dedicated server is that it can perform its server duties faster—workstations that transfer data to and from a dedicated server get faster response.

What does all this have to do with hard disk and RAM? A small LAN typically uses only one computer as a server, and the best choice is usually the fastest computer with the largest hard disk drive and the most RAM. Depending on your planned use for the LAN, you may decide to set up more than one PC as a server. You might want two servers, so one can take over for the other in case of failure. You might want all PCs to act as servers, at least some of the time, so a tape backup unit on one workstation can make backup copies of everybody's hard disks.

This is one advantage of a peer-to-peer LAN such as LANtastic—any PC can be turned into a server, even just once in a while. When a PC is a server, its hard disk and other peripherals are available for access by other PCs on the LAN. If you want, of course, you can restrict access to only specified users.

In some cases, you will not want a single-server LAN to use the fastest computer as the server. If the fastest computer doesn't have the largest or fastest hard disk, the computer with the biggest or fastest hard disk might be a better server. Or, if someone needs the fastest computer to run a critical application (perhaps a computer-aided design or desktop publishing program), you may not want to further burden that computer with the server workload. Use the next-to-fastest computer for a server. Of course, if you don't expect the people on your LAN to move a lot of data back and forth on the server's hard disk, even the slowest PC might be the best server. You need to know exactly how you will use the LAN to make these decisions accurately. Before you install the LAN, you *won't* know exactly, so make your best guess.

Fortunately, all these things can be changed later if necessary. You can start using one particular computer for a server and then add another or switch to another later. LANtastic makes this process easy, as you will see in Chapters 5 and 6. (The same can't be said about most other network operating systems.) In addition, you can always upgrade some or all computers later to add more RAM or disk space.

So even though your knowledge isn't complete, you have to start somewhere, so begin by thinking about which PCs will act as servers. Mark them on your PC attribute list, or add another computer that you need to buy, if appropriate. Also mark any PC that you think you will want to upgrade with more RAM or a bigger or faster hard disk.

Portable Computers If you sometimes attach portable computers to the LAN, show them on the list. Add a column to show them as portables, or say so under PC Type. Some users carry laptop computers home to burn the midnight oil, and then want to attach them to the LAN at work the next day to copy files to the shared disk drive. To do this, you need one of the following:

- A portable LAN adapter (such as the Xircom Pocket Ethernet Adapter, explained in Chapter 7).
- Artisoft Central Station (see chapters 3 and 7).
- LANtastic Z, a separate Artisoft product that can connect a portable computer and a LAN computer using either the serial or parallel ports or phone lines using modems. Chapter 5 has details.
- Other laptop file transfer products such as LapLink or Brooklyn Bridge, as explained in Chapter 1.

The first two approaches require an Ethernet LAN and use the parallel port to connect the portable computer to the LAN. Using Central Station is less disruptive to the LAN because it can stay permanently attached to the

LAN cable. LANtastic Z or laptop file transfer products work with either Ethernet or 2Mbps LANs and are the least expensive methods, typically costing under $100.

DOS Version What version of DOS is installed on each PC? LANtastic requires version 3.1 or higher, and version 3.2 is not recommended by Artisoft due to a LAN-related bug. If you find computers that still run DOS 2.1 or 3.2, include in your plan the need to upgrade to a newer DOS version. Add a column headed "DOS Version" to your list. If a PC that needs upgrading has an 80286 or higher processor and also has over 640K of RAM, DOS 5 is worth having. DOS 5 can use RAM above the 640K address mark for some DOS and LAN functions. The result is more usable RAM in the limited DOS 640K address space. LANtastic does not use nearly as much RAM as some other LAN operating systems from the DOS 640K space, but the additional amount you recover using DOS 5 might be necessary to run some application programs.

ROM BIOS If you have some older PCs in the workgroup, check to see the date of the ROM BIOS. The ROM BIOS (read-only memory, basic input/output system) is a chip inside the PC that contains some elementary programming to make the PC work. For some manufacturers, older ROM BIOS chips may be incompatible with LAN requirements. Check with the manufacturer or Artisoft if a PC has ROM BIOS older than 1986. You might need to buy a newer ROM BIOS chip, either from the PC's manufacturer or from an independent vendor. If local computer stores don't sell ROM BIOS upgrades, try Upgrades Etc. (206-881-8294 or 818-992-3365) or major mail-order companies. Cost ranges from $30 to $100. The date and manufacturer of the ROM BIOS is displayed for some versions when you boot the system. For others, use a utility such as SYSINFO (system information, sometimes called SI) in Norton Utilities or PC Tools to display the ROM BIOS date. You may want to add a "ROM BIOS" column to your list and show the dates.

Available Card Slots Each desktop computer you connect to the LAN will need an available card slot inside for the LAN card. (You could connect them using the parallel port, but data access is much slower and the hardware costs more than regular LAN cards.) If you have any doubt, check each PC to be sure an available card slot exists. Either 8-bit or 16-bit slots will work, although performance is a little slower using 8-bit slots. If you like, add a "Card Slot" column to your PC attribute list so you don't forget. For each computer, either show the number available, or just indicate yes or no.

Macintosh Connection If your office has one or more Macintosh computers in addition to PC compatibles, determine what you plan to do. Your choices are as follows:

- Consider the PCs and Macs as separate worlds and don't try to exchange data between them.
- Use various non-LAN connectivity options, such as converting floppy-disk files to ASCII in a format readable by the other computer type.
- Get MACLAN Connect from Miramar Systems, Inc. (201 N. Salsipuedes, Suite 204, Santa Barbara, CA 93103, 805-966-2432). This software product turns a LANtastic workstation into a *gateway* (a connection between two unlike networks) between a Mac LAN and a LANtastic LAN. You also need to buy a second LAN card for the workstation, in addition to the LANtastic card. The second card must be one of MACLAN's supported cards, which includes a list of LocalTalk, EtherTalk, and TokenTalk cards. The MACLAN software turns the PC into a dedicated gateway through which workstations on a Mac LAN can use Appleshare workstation to access LANtastic servers. You can also link the two LANs' electronic mail systems, such as cc:Mail, Microsoft Mail, and WordPerfect Office, among others. List prices for one to four Mac users are $495 for file sharing and mail, or $695 to add printer sharing also. Prices for unlimited users (with a practical limit of about 35) are $995 for file sharing and mail, or $1495 to add printer sharing. MACLAN is a dedicated gateway, which means the PC with both LAN cards cannot also be used as a server or workstation. Development is under way for a Windows version that will permit the gateway PC to be nondedicated so it can also act as a workstation.
- Get another type of LAN, such as Novell Netware 3.*x*, that supports both computer types. These other LAN types have much higher software costs than LANtastic and far greater complexity. To make

sure this approach is necessary, ask Artisoft if recent product announcements support Mac connections.

Total LAN Connections Finally, if the total number of computers you plan to attach to the LAN is greater than 30 (or 21 for 10BASE-T), plan on one of the following configurations:

- For thin Ethernet, install two LAN cards (or more—up to four LANtastic cards are allowed) in a server PC. Connect one thin Ethernet LAN segment of up to 30 PCs to one card and another segment to the other. This way up to 58 other PCs can all access the same server—29 on each segment. If you need more servers, put two cards in a second server; up to 58 nodes can access both servers. Each segment's PCs are isolated from the other segment's PCs except for the double-LAN-card servers they share. In effect, you make two separate LANs that share a limited number of servers.
- For thin Ethernet, buy a repeater to connect two segments of up to 29 PCs each. (The repeater counts as a node toward the 30-node limit per segment.) This connects up to 58 computers into one large logical LAN. All computers have access to all others—you can make any PC a server for all other computers to use. The drawback is that repeaters are expensive. Plan to spend at least $800 to connect two segments. A multiport repeater, which connects more than two segments, costs correspondingly more. Thin Ethernet permits connection of up to four segments, so you can connect up to 116 nodes in one big LANtastic LAN.
- For 10BASE-T, buy concentrator hubs that permit connection of more PCs. Most of these hubs are much more expensive than the Artisoft Peer-Hub Concentrator, but price competition is beginning to lower costs overall. When using Artisoft Peer-Hubs you're limited to 21 computers on the network, based on a configuration in which you install four Peer-Hubs in one computer that also has a LAN card, and you connect each Peer-Hub to five external nodes. You can connect just over 30 computers in a more complicated unbalanced configuration, but you're better off using other hubs.

Other companies sell hubs that can support almost any size LAN you need. Some hubs are designed for you to insert expansion cards in slots, and each card can accommodate 8, 10, 12, or 16 nodes. Other stand-alone hubs support 8, 12, or more nodes each, and you can daisy-chain the hubs into a tree topology. As long as the hub product complies with IEEE 802.3 10BASE-T standards, it should work.

Many manufacturers make such hubs, including Black Box, Thomas Conrad, and Tiara Computer Systems. As with anything, of course, some manufacturers produce higher quality products than others. Prices per node vary widely—most cost between $100 and $300. This added cost is why 10BASE-T is rarely less expensive than thin Ethernet.

For the LANtastic 2Mbps adapters, shame on you if you are even considering a LAN with 30 or more nodes. You haven't been paying attention. But seriously, folks, unless you are severely restricted in your current budget, you expect no future growth, you know all users will use the LAN only extremely infrequently, and you are willing to risk throwing it all away if performance is inadequate, don't use 2Mbps adapters in a LAN anywhere close to this size.

Any of these alternatives adds to your cost, most of them greatly. You should talk to a LAN consultant (another added cost) to consider these and other alternatives if you expect the total number of workstations and servers to exceed 30 with thin Ethernet or 21 with 10BASE-T.

Number and Types of Shared Peripherals

Now take your PC attribute list and expand it by adding important peripheral devices that might be appropriate to share over LANtastic. Start with devices currently installed, and then add planned future devices. The most common peripheral device is a printer, and one of LANtastic's biggest advantages is letting everyone share the same laser (or other) printers. Other devices are modems, plotters, and CD-ROM disk drives. (Each of these is explained in the following sections.)

Tape backup devices cannot be shared when attached to a LANtastic server, but put them on the list. You can use a tape backup drive that is attached to a workstation to back up disk files that are on servers. There's generally no need to list input devices, such as mice, digitizers, and scanners. Input devices don't often work out as shared devices.

Table 4-2 shows a sample PC attribute list that is expanded to show peripheral devices. You may have also added columns to your list for other items previously covered, such as DOS Version, ROM BIOS, and Card Slots.

Printers The peripherals column shows you who uses what devices so you can explore the possibilities for sharing them. A printer is the most common peripheral. In the example shown, the LaserJet printer is the obvious candidate for everyone to share. You might also want to share the Epson 286 printer, or else leave it as an unshared device for use on one PC only.

Talk to all users to find out how they use their printers. In most workgroups, once people find out how easily they can get fast, clear laser printer output over the LAN, they abandon their own personal dot matrix printers.

But beware! A personal printer is an emotional issue to many people. If you, the LAN planner, tell members of the workgroup they are going to lose their precious personal printers and instead start sharing a printer on this mysterious new LAN, you might cause panic. If not panic, count at least on ruffled feathers. The smoothest transition often occurs by allowing people

Table 4-2. An Expanded PC Attribute List for LAN Planning

	Who	PC Type	Hard Disk	RAM	Peripherals
1.	Carl	XT	10MB	640K	Epson FX-80
2.	Jane	AT	30MB	640K	Epson 286, 1200 bps modem
3.	Ed, Al	386SX	40MB	1MB	HP LaserJet II, 2400 bps modem
4.	Bob	386/33	80MB	2MB	No printer, 2400 bps modem

continued use of personal printers as well as shared laser printers. A few months after the LAN is installed, when they see how they use the laser exclusively, they won't mind giving up personal printers. Some will even demand their old printers' removal in order to recover some additional office space where these personal printers sit idle.

Modems Modems in a LANtastic environment can be used in several ways.

- *As if the LAN were not there* You can use a modem from a LAN workstation in the same way you would without the LAN. Install the modem in a PC, connect it to a phone line, and run your communications software as if the LAN were not there. The modem isn't used through the LAN or by other LAN users; it's only used by the person working on the PC in which the modem is installed.
- *Remote access to the LAN using LANtastic Z* If you buy the LANtastic Z product in addition to the LANtastic LAN, you can use a computer in a remote location to connect over a phone line to your LANtastic LAN. The remote computer and the LAN PC both need modems to accomplish this, of course. Using LANtastic Z and the modem-telephone link, the remote PC can use the LAN's resources (shared disk, shared printers, and so on) just as if it were directly connected to the LAN. The only difference is that data movement is *much* slower. If both PCs use 2400 bps modems, for example, data will move at about 200 characters (bytes) per second. Two fast computers on a 10 Mbps Ethernet LAN can transfer data over a thousand times as fast. LANs are fast; modems are slow.
- *Shared modems on the LAN* Everyone on the LAN can use one or more shared modems through the LANtastic LAN, rather than installing a modem in each PC. Unless you have a real need for high-speed 9600 bps modems, modem sharing may not be cost-effective. Costs have dropped so much for 2400 bps modems that the only cost savings for sharing them comes from reducing the number of telephone lines the workgroup requires. Chapter 7 explains how modem sharing works, but generally you won't save money compared with giving each PC user a personal 2400 bps internal modem for $50 or so. Higher cost modems that either have extra flexibility, features, or transfer data at higher speed cost more

and change the cost comparison. To share a modem on the LAN you need to buy ArtiCom or other modem-sharing software that is compatible with LANtastic. Modem sharing is not a standard feature of LANtastic.

Plotters Plotters have characteristics both of printers and, amazingly enough, modems. Even though a plotter is basically a special type of printer because it produces printed output, some plotters require two-way communication with the computer. As a result, a plotter may use a serial port and require LAN software that treats it like a modem. Artisoft's ArtiCom software (or independent products from other vendors) performs this function, as explained in Chapter 7. For planning purposes, if you want to share a plotter, find out if it needs two-way communication or if it is an output-only device. If two-way, plan also to acquire ArtiCom or another suitable product. Some serial printers also have this two-way requirement.

CD-ROM Disk Drives CD-ROM drives are an exciting new technology that appear destined for widespread use. Chapter 2 explained some CD-ROM applications and databases you might want to consider for your workgroup. LANtastic has built-in CD-ROM sharing capability. If you want to share a CD-ROM drive over LANtastic, be sure to add the cost of the CD-ROM drive. No extra hardware is necessary in order to work with LANtastic. In most cases, no extra software is needed either, except whatever application titles you want. Details are in Chapter 7.

Locations of Computers and Printers

Computer and printer physical locations are a critical consideration in LAN planning. Cables must connect these devices together, and in some offices adding new cables causes major problems. Even without a LAN your office may already be the proud possessors of numerous jumbles of wiring that resemble bowls of spaghetti. PCs require so many power and data cables between the system units, monitors, printers, modems, and other devices that wiring messes are inevitable. But at least those messes are localized, usually to a series of Bermuda-triangle areas between each PC, printer, and power outlet.

The LAN's installation adds another level of cable connection—between different offices. Instead of a local jumble that you can push under each desk, now the jumbles are connected together. Even worse, some people in the office constantly want to rearrange furniture and computer locations. If rearrangements happen often, the LAN cables have to connect to a moving target. If at all possible, get each person in the workgroup to agree to a *permanent* (or as permanent as possible) location for his or her PC. The time for PC movement is *before* you do LAN planning, not after.

Even if your office has no cable jumbles, the soon-to-be installed LAN cables present new problems. These cables have to be put somewhere, and many offices are not designed with LANs in mind.

What are the best ways to deal with the problems of connecting LAN cables? The answers are many and varied. Every LAN consultant has a favorite solution or two, depending on the office environment, the user needs, and personal bias. The answers can significantly affect cable choices. The following list shows the possibilities, roughly in the order of frequency these "plans" are encountered in most offices.

- *Let the chips (cables) fall where they may (must)* Connect the computers using thin Ethernet or 10BASE-T and tuck the cables (and external hubs, if necessary for 10BASE-T) into whatever spaces look available and relatively safe. Cables might need routing through ceiling tiles, under carpeting, through walls, or whatever the office layout dictates. The biggest concern is to avoid having cables out where they will be tripped on, stepped on, rolled over by chairs, or damaged by other contact. Make sure no cables run under carpeting or across aisles or other walkways without protection. Otherwise count on two bad things: lawsuits from people who trip, and LAN downtime from damaged cables.
- *Use existing conduit* Modern offices are designed to handle cabling to various office locations, whether for the electrical system, the phone system, or other wiring systems. Often the conduit through which these cables run has room for additional cables. In some cases completely unused spare conduit is available. As long as the conduit leads to the specific locations you require, you can install well-protected cables without too much difficulty. Be aware that routing cables through conduit often requires much longer cables than the line-of-sight distance between two computers. Depending on the conduit layout, 10BASE-T might be more appropriate to install than

thin Ethernet due to cable length restrictions. For a small number of PCs, either method should be feasible.

- *Use existing cabling* Some office buildings, especially newer ones, were designed to accommodate computer cabling. Such offices may already have extra thin coaxial cable or unshielded twisted-pair cable routed to all offices, complete with convenient plugs and jacks. If existing cable meets LANtastic specifications, you can save a lot of time, trouble, and money by using it. Along with preexisting cabling, such office buildings often have wiring closets in which you can install external 10BASE-T hubs, if that is your choice. Check with the building engineer, contractor, or architect to determine the locations of wiring closets and the specifications of the cable that was installed. Get *precise* specifications! Don't accept a broad answer like, "It's good cable. You'll have no problems with it." Compare the building's cable specifications with the specifications for each type of cable in Chapter 1. For the latest information, contact Artisoft and ask for their current cabling specifications document. See Appendix B for details.
- *Install a wireless LAN* Chapter 1 mentioned wireless LANs. If you are willing to pay a lot more and risk the dangers of using technology that isn't as mature as cable-based LANs, you can eliminate cabling problems. Motorola's Altair system has received good reviews, and several other vendors now offer wireless LAN systems.

The Floor Plan To get a handle on the scope of your cabling needs, make a drawing of your office layout with the locations of planned LAN-connected PCs marked. (This process may not be necessary for a three-computer LAN, but for larger LANs it can be a lifesaver.) If possible, use the actual blueprint for your floor plan. Make a rough sketch of your own if a formal floor plan isn't available. Show all offices, closets, and walls, as well as major furniture such as desks, file cabinets, and computer tables. Obviously, a blueprint that already shows electrical and other conduit is the best starting point if one is available.

If you plan to share peripheral devices, mark their most likely locations also. A shared printer, usually a laser printer, is important in most work groups. When you plan its location keep in mind that a shared printer generates a lot of foot traffic when people walk by to pick up printed output. Also, a printer needs care and feeding–someone needs to refill paper trays and check for paper jams. The best printer location is central to all its users, for easy access, and near someone who can tend to it occasionally. The foot traffic can be disrupting in the area immediately adjacent to the printer, so placing a busy shared printer inside someone's office does not usually work out well. The shared printer must be attached either to a server PC or to a Central Station device; make sure that your printer cable is long enough to reach from one of these devices to the printer. Measure ahead of time so if you need a longer cable, you won't have to rush out and buy it on installation day.

Now study the sketch and determine how to connect cables between computers. Unless you have already decided between thin Ethernet and 10BASE-T, draw different colored lines for each one. Use existing cables or available conduit if possible. If necessary just let the cable fall where it must.

Thin Ethernet Cable Planning A thin Ethernet LAN is easier to design than a 10BASE-T LAN, and in most cases is less expensive. However, 10BASE-T is sometimes easier to cable in a given office environment. To plan cabling for thin Ethernet, play "connect the dots" on your floor plan. In this case, the dots are the PCs you want to connect to the LAN. Thin Ethernet is a bus topology, so you connect the PCs in one long jagged line. Each PC connects to exactly two other PCs, except the PCs at each end, which each connect to only one other. You have to decide on the connection sequence. The best sequence is the one that is both easiest for you to physically cable and the least expensive.

Start by drawing connection lines from one end of the sequence to the other in the longest dimension of your office. For example, if the office layout is short and wide, try connecting the PC at the far left to the next one to its right. Continue across the floor plan until you get to the PC farthest to the right. If instead your floor plan is narrow but tall, start at the top and proceed to the bottom. Once you have all the PCs connected in your drawing, you have created one possible cabling scheme.

Is this the *best* possible cabling sequence? Unless you have only two or three computers, probably not. The important question is whether or not your first scheme is an *acceptable* one. What makes a scheme acceptable? Really only two factors: there must be a way to actually run a cable between each connected PC, and the total length of cable must not exceed LANtastic specifications (185 meters, or 607 feet). Note that the total length of the lines you have drawn is not the important factor here. What matters are real cable lengths. If you will route the cables through conduit or up through ceiling tiles or down through false floors, how long must the cables actually be?

If you are working with a good floor plan, you can make close estimates from your drawing. Redraw the lines and show the paths you expect the cables to take. Add the up and down distances for the portions that turn up through the ceiling or turn down under or along the floor. Then add at least five feet extra as "slop" to be sure a small curve or two doesn't leave you a foot short. Ten feet extra is even safer. If you need to allow users the freedom to move PCs around in their offices, be sure to provide plenty of extra cable length. Of course, if you use cables that are way too long, you add to the cable jumble problem and also increase your chances of exceeding the maximum allowed total cable length at some point, if not immediately.

Next go to the planned LAN area itself with your drawing in hand. Verify that each cable can really run where you drew it. Modify your drawing as necessary. See if changing the connection sequence simplifies the cabling. For example, two of the PCs might be extremely close together but have a major obstacle between them—something like a bank vault, a walk-in freezer, or an elevator shaft. Rather than connect the two PCs directly, cabling might be easier if you connect from the first PC to a third PC that is off to the side of the obstacle and then connect from there to the second PC. Follow the cabling path of least resistance. To check cable lengths you can cut lengths of string or rope to common cable lengths (15, 25, 50, and 100 feet) and try them out.

10BASE-T Cable and Hub Planning In general, 10BASE-T cabling and LAN cards succeed better than thin Ethernet in offices where PCs are spread out or perhaps rearranged often. Thin Ethernet is best where the PCs are close together and don't move very often. The definitions of "spread out" and "close together" are fuzzy, so a large gray area exists between the two extremes.

For 10BASE-T, you need to pick one or more tentative hub locations before you look at cable paths. If you use Artisoft's Peer-Hub Concentrators, you will install them in a computer, so mark which computer will contain hubs. This computer must be turned on whenever anyone uses the LAN, so it's usually best to pick a server. Next show cable connections to each PC. If you use other standard IEEE 802.3 10BASE-T hub products, you might install them in closets or in wall cabinets. These other hubs may allow connection of more computers but chances are they will be much more expensive. Each Artisoft Peer-Hub Concentrator can support up to five other computers that have 10BASE-T cards, plus one card internally in the same computer as the Peer-Hub card. This means the first Peer-Hub card normally supports up to six computers, counting the one in which it is installed. If you install a second Peer-Hub card in that PC, it supports up to five more PCs. Add to your drawing a set of colored lines (use a different color than you used for the thin Ethernet lines) that show how the hub connects to each PC.

As you did for thin Ethernet, now go to the workgroup area and determine exactly where the cables will be located. Allow extra length if necessary due to conduit routes or up and down runs through ceilings and floors. Again, allow five or ten extra feet to be safe. Providing extra cable length is less of a problem for 10BASE-T because the maximum length of 100 meters applies to each connection between hub and computer, not the total length of all cables. Change your drawing if necessary to reflect the actual cable locations you select.

Because unshielded twisted-pair cables are less resistant to electromagnetic interference than thin coaxial cable, 10BASE-T LANs require more careful planning. Try to avoid installation of UTP cables near large electric motors, air conditioners, and other potential electronic hazards. Even telephones and fluorescent lights produce potentially harmful electromagnetic fields. If these exposures cannot be avoided, consider using shielded twisted-pair wiring in these areas to reduce the risk. In any event, test the LAN's reliability carefully after installation.

The Office Environment

Consider the office environment for your workgroup when you make your LAN plans. The quality of your electrical supply is a fundamental question. Can you expect frequent power failures, brownouts, or electrical surges? Inexpensive electrical surge suppressors and filters are well worth the cost as a first means of protection. Most commercially provided power is not pure and regular; so for less than $20 you can buy a six- or eight-outlet surge suppressor/filter to reduce the chances of your PC being damaged by irregularities. Whether you have a LAN or not, you should have this protection. When you install a LAN, the need for these safeguards is even stronger due to your increased investment.

If your workgroup is often hit by power failures or your planned usage of the LAN and its computers is especially critical, consider an uninterruptable power system (UPS). Find out first if your building has UPS already installed in some or all areas. If not, investigate small UPS products for your workgroup. A UPS product can keep your computers running for a few minutes (or longer) after a power failure, allowing you to perform a few critical tasks and shut your workstations and servers down gracefully. LANtastic supports many UPS products. See Chapter 9 for details.

Other environmental hazards exist in most office environments. As long as you are planning for a LAN, this is a good time to look at your exposure to other risks, such as excessive dust, water leakage, inadequate building security, and anything else that might cause damage to your LAN, computers, data, and other valuables.

Sources of LAN Equipment

As you saw in Chapter 3, Artisoft sells a wide range of products in the LANtastic family. Other companies manufacture compatible products you may also choose to buy. In either case, you can purchase from local Artisoft dealers, from local consultants, or from mail-order dealers. How do you decide?

Much of the answer to this question depends on what makes you comfortable. Some people love to buy via mail order to get the lowest prices, others wouldn't touch it. Some people want a technical expert to configure and install everything, others want to learn how it works and do it themselves. You undoubtedly have formed a preference already, but this section gives a little more information that may help clarify your options.

A small, simple, LANtastic AE-2 Ethernet Starter Kit is really not hard to buy, install, and run. The rest of this book will help you along the way. If you have a small workgroup for which the LAN installation will not present major problems (as described in this chapter), you can undoubtedly buy the equipment and connect it together yourself. Shop around for the best price and try it. If you can't make it work, *then* you can call an Artisoft dealer or consultant to help you out.

If your LAN needs are more complicated, and you aren't comfortable taking on a bigger project yourself, bring in someone with expertise. Artisoft has "Five Star" dealers all around the country who have experience with these matters. To contact Artisoft for the name of your nearest dealer, see Appendix B.

You might be attracted to the idea of buying the LAN cards and cable from one source (at a low price), and then installing LANtastic software separately. This approach can work just fine, but of course is a little more complicated than getting everything from Artisoft. Again, if you are comfortable with this approach, do your homework and go ahead. If you want to play it safe, get everything from one source. You have to buy a copy of the AI (adapter independent) version of LANtastic for each non-Artisoft LAN card you buy.

Applications Required and Desired

For many people, this issue comes first. You install a LAN to solve problems for your workgroup, as Chapter 2 discusses. If your LAN objectives are simply to share printers and to copy files to and from a shared disk, you may not care about special LAN applications.

If you *do* want to use either special LAN applications (such as e-mail or resource schedulers) or LAN versions of word processors, spreadsheets, or databases, itemize your needs. The LAN hardware, LAN NOS, and application software work together to give users the capabilities to perform these functions. Analyze your problems to see how the LAN and the application software will solve them.

Have you picked the application software yet? If not, study the alternatives and verify LANtastic compatibility. Analyze who in the group does what, and how and why and when. Be open minded to new ways to do things, but recognize that many people don't adapt well to change. Talk to actual users of candidate products to be sure the products really do what you need and that advertiser claims are accurate.

Review Chapter 2 to see what your options are. Determine what fits your workgroup best, and make plans to acquire and use these products.

Unless you plan a large LAN (let's say over 20 users) where everyone pushes a lot of data across the LAN, such as constant database searching, 10 Mbps Ethernet LANs should have plenty of capacity for your needs. Other components, particularly server PCs and their hard disks, may be stretched to their maximum capacities, but the LAN's speed itself is almost never the constraining factor. However, if you use the 2Mbps LAN adapters, or 2.5Mbps ARCnet cards, LAN throughput might be a problem.

Keep in mind that a LAN, along with its servers and server peripherals, is a shared resource. Any time people have to share things, conflicts are possible and problems can arise. Try to plan in advance exactly who is going to use what and how often. Be prepared to expand your resources (hard disk size, server speed, number of shared printers, and so on) if necessary. The more critical the applications you share on the LAN, the more critical that you plan accurately.

Administration Issues

Because a LAN is a shared resource, someone must occasionally perform some administration functions. Chapter 11 covers LAN administration in detail. For now, the important point is to select your LAN administrator (or LAN manager, LAN guru, or whatever title you like) as soon as possible. (Since you are reading this, odds are high that it will be *you*.) If the administrator is involved in the planning process, chances increase that LAN administration will run smoothly.

Your Available Budget

The budget may override all other LAN planning issues. You can survive with LANtastic Z if you have only two computers to connect and your budget is $100. Use 2Mbps cards if you have more computers and are desperately short on cash. Use AE-2 Ethernet cards with thin coax if you can spend a bit more. For lowest cost 10BASE-T use AE-1/T cards. Use AE-3 cards with thin Ethernet cables or UTP if you can spend more and are willing to pay for the flexibility of being able to switch to the other cabling type later if necessary.

Checklists

This section summarizes the information given in this chapter. Refer to the earlier sections for full explanations about what each item means.

Inappropriate Situations for LANtastic

If any of these situations apply to your workgroup, LANtastic is probably not the best choice for you. Look at options other than LANtastic if you

- Need to use PCs other than MS-DOS-based IBM compatibles
- Need to connect a LANtastic LAN to a different LAN type

- Need to use incompatible hardware or software products
- Need to connect more than 60 computers
- Plan to do any of the above in the near future

Clarify Objectives

List the objectives for your workgroup's LAN. Your list will probably include items like these:

Shared disk space
Shared printers
Shared database applications
Workgroup productivity applications, such as electronic mail, resource scheduling, calendaring, and others
Shared modems
Shared plotters
Shared CD-ROM drives
Other ____________________

Preparing to Choose and Install a LAN

The following summarizes the steps you'll take to prepare for, choose, and install a LANtastic LAN:

1. List all desktop PCs with specifications and who uses each.
2. List portable PCs that have LAN connectivity needs.
3. Determine local and remote connectivity methods to use for portable PCs.
4. Check that all PCs use MS-DOS 3.1 or higher.
5. Check that all PCs use ROM BIOS dated 1986 or later.
6. Check that all PCs have available card slots for LAN cards.
7. Determine if Macintosh connection is needed and decide on the best way to accomplish the connection.

8. Determine the total number of PCs to connect to LAN. If over 30 (thin Ethernet) or over 21 (10BASE-T), determine how to configure.
9. List each peripheral device attached to any of the PCs.

   Printers
   Modems
   Plotters
   CD-ROM
   Other ____________________

10. Determine if additional software is needed for modems, printers, or plotters.
11. Obtain or sketch a floor plan.
12. Identify the locations of all PCs.
13. Determine the locations of shared printers and plotters.
14. Update your floor plan with sketched tentative cable positions between PCs, both for thin Ethernet and 10BASE-T.
15. Verify that cables can run in the locations sketched. Revise floor plan if necessary.
16. Determine cable lengths (double-check by running string to all cable locations and measuring it) and verify that cable complies with limitations.
17. Choose between thin Ethernet, 10BASE-T, and Artisoft proprietary 2Mbps LAN cards and cables.
18. Evaluate the office environment for necessary changes. Especially watch for these potential problems:

    The need for electrical surge suppressors and filters
    The need for UPS
    Dust or water in the building, security weaknesses, and other hazards

19. Determine the source for obtaining LAN equipment and decide who will install and test the LAN.
20. Determine which application software you need.

21. Verify that the LAN configuration will adequately support the application software and usage expected.
22. Choose a LAN administrator and start his/her involvement in the planning process.
23. Begin plans to train users on LAN usage and policies.
24. Verify that the available budget can accommodate the purchases needed. Revise plans if necessary.
25. Get approval to spend the money.
26. Order the hardware and software needed.
27. Install hardware and software.
28. Test hardware and software.
29. Begin using LANtastic to satisfy your objectives.
30. Throw a post-installation party.

5

Installing and Testing LANtastic

In the first four chapters you learned a lot about LANs and LANtastic—from introductory concepts up through planning your installation. In this chapter you finally get your hands dirty (but only figuratively, unless you have a filthy computer). This chapter covers how to install, start, and test the LANtastic hardware and software.

The first part of the chapter shows you how to perform a "quick installation" of LANtastic. Don't assume you should actually *follow* these quick instructions, especially the first time you install LANtastic. Instead, read through them for an overview of the process. Afterward, perform your first installation using the three "Detailed Installation" sections that follow on hardware, server software, and workstation software. But, if you are impatient and daring, the Quick Installation instructions cover the most common situations and are usually sufficient. You can install the LAN hardware and software on two computers, a server and a workstation, within 30 minutes in many cases. However, you can avoid problems if you take a more leisurely approach and read the details as you go. You'll also learn more about how LANtastic works. The choice is yours.

Both sets of instructions assume you want to install a LANtastic thin Ethernet LAN with AE-2 LAN cards and version 4.1 of the LANtastic NOS software. The AE-2 is the most popular LAN card, and version 4.1 is the current software (as of this writing). However, notes in the "Detailed Hardware Installation" section explain differences in installing other LAN cards (whether from Artisoft or another manufacturer) or other cabling. A separate section at the end of this chapter covers installing LANtastic Z.

One more clarification: The installation process consists of inserting a LAN card in each PC, connecting the cables, and preparing the LAN software to run from each PC's hard disk. Installation does *not* actually start the communication process between computers. After installation you have to *start* LANtastic in order to share resources or communicate. When you finish the installation process, the "Starting and Testing LANtastic" section of this chapter explains how to start LANtastic and verify that everything is working.

And a final point, before you begin: Don't be afraid. These long lists of details may seem intimidating at first glance. However, each step is quite simple. Read each step carefully and you will see that you can, if you choose, easily install the hardware and software yourself for a small LANtastic LAN. But, if the idea of removing a computer's cover to install a card is just too frightening to even consider, then by all means have someone else install the hardware. If you don't know which floppy disk drive is called A and which is B (and don't want to learn), then have someone install the software, too. This chapter shows you the process so you can decide.

Quick Installation

Here is the short version of instructions for installing the LANtastic hardware and software, using the LANtastic AE-2 Ethernet Starter Kit. Assume the computers all have 80286, 386, or 486 processors and hard disks, and use MS DOS 3.1, 3.3, or later versions, without Microsoft Windows. If you need more explanation for any step, or you want to install something other than the AE-2 Starter Kit on the types of computers listed, refer to one of the "Detailed Installation" sections later in this chapter. If you want to run LANtastic under Windows, read this chapter and then see Chapter 12.

Quick Hardware Installation

These instructions briefly explain how to install the LANtastic hardware:

1. Verify that the default settings for the AE-2 card do not conflict with other devices in each PC. (See the box, "Default Settings and Default Values.") For a typical PC with no unusual peripherals installed, the default settings for IRQ and IOBASE should be fine. See the "Detailed Hardware Installation" section if you need an explanation. For an 8088-based computer (such as the original IBM PC or PC/XT), the default IRQ setting needs to be changed. Refer to the *LANtastic AE-2 Ethernet Adapter User's Manual* or the "Detailed Hardware Installation" section later in this chapter. For any computer with unusual add-on cards or an unusual configuration, review these settings.

Note

If the LAN doesn't work when you first test it, a conflict between hardware settings is a likely cause.

2. Turn off power to each computer and remove the cover. To be safe, disconnect each power cord, also.
3. Carefully install an AE-2 card in each PC, just like you would install any expansion card. Take normal precautions: discharge static electricity buildup in your body first and handle the card by its edges. Use a 16-bit expansion slot, if available. (The AE-2 card also will work in an 8-bit slot, but will not transfer data quite as fast.) You may need to remove the BNC T connector from the card first (if it is attached) in order to fit the card's rear connector through the opening in the back of the computer.
4. Attach (or reattach) the BNC T connector to the rear of the AE-2 card (so it protrudes out the back of the computer).
5. Reinstall the computer cover.

6. Attach thin coaxial cables to connect the PCs. You can rotate the BNC T connector carefully in order to route the cables in the directions you choose.
7. Route the cables to safe, protected locations between the computers. Install protection if necessary. This is the step in which professional help might best serve you–installing cables in walls, under floors, or wherever your office layout dictates.
8. Attach terminators to the unused sides of the BNC T connectors at each end of the daisy chain of cables.
9. Reattach the PC power cords.
10. Turn on the power for each computer. Verify that the computer still works as before. Until you install and start the LAN software, you should notice no difference in computer operation.

Quick Software Installation for a Server

You saw in Chapter 2 that a LAN node that shares its resources (hard disk, printer, CD-ROM drive) with other nodes is called a server. You want to designate at least one computer on your LANtastic LAN as a server. You may want two, or even all of your nodes to be servers. These steps briefly outline the software installation process for a server:

1. At the present time, the LANtastic software comes with an installation program on a floppy disk labeled "LANtastic NETWORK OPERATING SYSTEM Ethernet." Both a 5.25-inch and a 3.5-inch disk are supplied. Make a working copy of the appropriate size disk and insert it into the A drive on the PC you will use as a server. (The same disk installs software for either a server or a workstation. Remember that a server also can act as a workstation, but a workstation is only a workstation–it cannot offer a shared hard disk or printer to other workstations.)

Default Settings and Default Values

These instructions, and many other computer-related instructions, refer to *default settings* or *default values* or just *defaults*. These terms (generally used interchangeably) refer to a selection you make "by default" if you don't override or change the selection. In other words, you give tacit approval to the existing choice unless you take an action to change it.

For example, on the AE-2 card at the present time, the default value for the IRQ selection is 15. (The "Detailed Hardware Installation" section explains IRQs; don't worry about what IRQs are right now.) This means that unless you change the IRQ setting by moving a little connector called a jumper (more about jumpers later in this chapter), you choose to use IRQ 15 by default.

Similarly, when you run the INSTALL program, some settings are immediately listed on the screen. You can change them, but if you don't, you accept these values by default.

Some people are disturbed by this terminology. Maybe they have deep-seated fears about defaulting on a loan or some other negative connotation of "default." Don't lose any sleep over accepting a default value. It's only a convenience for you, to make it easy for you to select a common choice. Just make sure the value is what you want.

2. Read through the README.DOC file on the floppy disk to be sure no recent information from Artisoft requires you to change your installation procedure. Use the DOS TYPE command or any file browser or editor program.
3. Type **a:install** and press (ENTER).
4. Read the directions the INSTALL program displays on each screen and respond to each prompt it presents you. Accept a default value

if it's appropriate for you. If a default is not appropriate, press (ENTER). In some cases pressing (ENTER) causes INSTALL to toggle (switch back and forth) between alternate selections. In other cases, (ENTER) presents a submenu of choices or prompts you to type in your own entry. Hints appear at the top of the screen. Explanations for each option follow in the two "Detailed Software Installation" sections later in this chapter. When you've responded to a prompt to your satisfaction, use the cursor keys to move to the next choice.

5. Type a unique name in the Machine Name field. The maximum length is 15 characters. Don't use embedded blank spaces. Best choices: the primary user's name (LES, TOM-R, JOHNF) or a server number (SERVER1, SERVER2, and so on). Other possibilities: a department name (SALES, ACCOUNTING1) or a computer description (AST286, TELTRON120MB). Be sure the name is unique! Don't try to have two computers named JOHN.
6. In the Machine Type field change the default Workstation to Server.
7. Accept the default Installation Directory and Network Startup Batch File names.
8. Be sure the Network Adapter Installed and Adapter Drivers to Install selections match your LAN card model. Change the selections if necessary.
9. Highlight the CONFIG.SYS parameters option and press (ENTER). Look at INSTALL's suggested changes. Unless you have a good reason not to, accept the changes by pressing (ESC) and type **yes** to accept. Most importantly, the LASTDRIVE parameter must specify a letter higher than the server's highest lettered hard disk (that is, at least D if the computer has a C hard disk). You will usually enter **Z** if you want this server to access another server's shared hard disk. Also, FILES and FCBS must be large enough for the workload this computer will handle. If you don't allow INSTALL to update CONFIG.SYS, be sure to update it yourself.
10. Accept the default (None) for Printer Connections. If you prefer, you can type a printer port number (such as **LPT1**), a server name,

and a resource name. This printer refers to a shared printer that this server will access, even if the printer is attached to this server. (This will be explained further later in this chapter and in Chapter 6.) Surprisingly, if a server has a printer it offers to other nodes, the server must also access the printer using the LAN.

11. Accept the default (None) for Disk Drive Connections. This connection refers to a disk drive on another server. Specifying None means that this server will not automatically set up a connection to another server's hard disk when you start the LAN software. This topic is also covered fully in Chapter 6.
12. Set the Install Default Resources option to YES and INSTALL will configure this server so that when started it automatically offers several resources to workstations. The resources are the server's A floppy disk drive, B floppy disk drive (if present), C hard disk drive, printer attached to LPT1, electronic mail access, and a group user account called * (asterisk). This choice permits any user to have access to all of these server resources. If you select NO, then you have to take steps to offer these or other resources yourself. Chapters 6 and 10 explain how to offer these resources if you select NO, and how to limit access to them if you select YES.
13. Accept the default name for the Control Directory.
14. Press (ENTER) when you highlight the bottom line, which says Perform Installation. This tells the INSTALL program to take the actions necessary to make this computer a server. These actions include creating subdirectories, copying files from the installation disk to the server's hard disk, modifying CONFIG.SYS (unless you said not to), and creating a STARTNET.BAT file that allows you to start LANtastic using the specifications you chose. Note that this Perform Installation step does not actually *start* the LANtastic software–it only installs the software. You need to reboot the computer to make CONFIG.SYS changes active, and then run STARTNET.BAT to start the LAN software. Details are in the "Starting and Testing LANtastic" section near the end of this chapter.

Quick Software Installation for a Workstation

Remember from Chapter 2 that a LAN node that makes use of a server's shared resources (hard disk, printer, CD-ROM drive), but does not provide resources to other nodes is called a workstation. These steps briefly outline the software installation process for a workstation:

1. Insert the same LANtastic installation disk (or copy the installation disk to the appropriate size disk if necessary) into the A floppy disk drive on the PC you will use as a workstation.
2. Verify that no README.DOC information applies to workstation installation.
3. Type **a:install** and press ENTER.
4. As before, read the directions the INSTALL program displays on each screen and respond to each prompt it presents you.
5. Type a unique name in the Machine Name field. The maximum length is 15 characters. Don't use embedded blank spaces. For a workstation, the best choice generally is the primary user's name. Be sure the name does not duplicate another workstation or server name.
6. Accept the default Workstation in the Machine Type field.
7. Accept the default Installation Directory and Network Startup Batch File names.
8. Be sure the Network Adapter Installed and Adapter Drivers to Install selections match your LAN card model. Change the selections if necessary.
9. Highlight the CONFIG.SYS parameters option and press ENTER. Look at INSTALL's suggested changes. Unless you have a good reason not to, accept the changes by pressing ESC and typing **yes** to accept. The LASTDRIVE parameter must specify a letter higher (meaning toward the back of the alphabet) than the workstation's highest lettered hard disk (usually C) if you want this workstation to access a shared hard disk. If you don't allow INSTALL to update CONFIG.SYS, be sure to update it yourself.

10. Accept the default (None) for Printer Connections. You can make this workstation automatically access a server's shared printer at startup by typing a virtual printer port number (**LPT2** is good if this workstation has a real printer on LPT1), server name, and resource name. For the sake of simplicity, don't do this now; follow the procedure in Chapter 6 to set up shared printers.
11. Accept the default (None) for Disk Drive Connections. As with Printer Connections, you can instead use this option to automatically connect to a server's hard disk whenever you start the LAN software. Read the Chapter 6 section on sharing hard disks. After reading that you can, if you like, reinstall the software to automatically make a disk drive connection, or you can just edit the STARTNET.BAT file yourself.
12. Highlight the bottom line, which says Perform Installation, and press ENTER to tell INSTALL to install the workstation software.

A Chapter Overview

The rest of this chapter digs deeper into the steps necessary to install LANtastic hardware and software. The options you face and the choices you take are examined in more depth than in the previous section.

First, so you don't get lost in the details that follow, read this overview of what the remainder of this chapter covers. To install a LAN, you need to take four steps:

1. *Install the hardware.* Think of this hardware installation step as similar to having a telephone and connecting cable installed in your home.

   Hardware for all LANtastic LAN types (except LANtastic Z) consists of a LAN card in each PC and connecting cables. For some LAN types, hardware also includes terminators or hubs. For any PC, but especially a PC on a LAN, you should use protected, clean electrical power. Chapters 4 and 9 discuss the need for surge suppressors and power filters, and explain the benefits you get by using UPS power.

2. *Install the software.* This step is similar to what the phone company does in their office to tell their equipment how to connect electronically to your home and your type of service.

   The LANtastic network operating system (NOS) must be installed on each PC you connect to the LAN. During each installation, you select whether the PC acts as a server or a workstation.

3. *Start the LAN software.* Just as you can't call anyone on your telephone until you pick up the receiver and hear a dial tone, you can't use the LAN until you start the LAN software.

   Each PC must execute commands to activate the LAN software that was installed. You can make a PC take this step automatically each time someone turns on the PC, or you can require a separate action by the PC user.

4. *Test the LAN.* With a telephone, this step is the same as dialing a friend, getting an answer, and talking back and forth to verify you both can hear each other clearly.

   Once the LAN is installed and the LAN software is running, you can type commands to verify that the LAN is working correctly.

Detailed Hardware Installation

This section explains the details of installing the hardware from a LANtastic AE-2 Ethernet Starter Kit, and notes what you must do differently if you install something other than LANtastic AE-2 Ethernet LAN cards and thin Ethernet cables. You can get LAN hardware from many sources and in many configurations. Three general approaches are possible:

- *A LANtastic Starter Kit, plus LANtastic components* The simplest way to buy hardware for a LANtastic LAN is to buy one of Artisoft's LANtastic Starter Kits. With a starter kit you can be sure all the proper components are included for the first two computers. If you want to connect more than two computers, buy additional LAN cards and cables from Artisoft. You won't need more LANtastic NOS software, because the Starter Kit includes software that runs on up to 300 nodes, as long as the nodes all use LANtastic hardware.

- *LANtastic software and independent components* You don't have to buy any hardware from Artisoft. You can choose to buy other manufacturers' LAN cards, cables, connectors, terminators, hubs, repeaters, and any other hardware you need. However, you will need to buy the LANtastic/AI (adapter independent) version of the LANtastic network operating system for each node in order to run LANtastic software on the LAN.
- *A combination of the two* You can mix the two approaches in countless ways. One way is to buy a Starter Kit for the first two stations, then buy low-cost independent LAN cards and LANtastic/AI for additional nodes. Another way is to buy a Starter Kit plus all the LANtastic LAN cards you need, but use cable that is prewired in the building.

So, when you install hardware, you can get it from two sources: Artisoft and other companies. The first part of this section examines hardware installation issues if you buy Artisoft's LANtastic hardware; the second part of the section looks at hardware installation if you buy independent hardware.

Installation from a Starter Kit and LANtastic Components

Artisoft sells different Starter Kit models, listed in Chapter 3. This section explains how to install the LANtastic AE-2 Ethernet Starter Kit, and notes differences for other Starter Kits. Each Starter Kit contains two LAN cards. If you need to install a LAN with more than two nodes, buy extra LANtastic LAN cards and cable for each additional PC and perform the installation as explained here for the first two cards.

As you will see, the other two LANtastic Starter Kits (AE-3 and 10BASE-T) are similar. The AE-3 card is almost identical to the AE-2 when you use it with the thin Ethernet supplied in the Starter Kit. The 10BASE-T Kit includes AE-1/T LAN cards, which have only two settings to check, and also includes a Peer-Hub 10BASE-T Concentrator. The Micro Channel versions of LANtastic LAN cards are easiest to configure—the card configuration is automatic. That's your compensation for the higher purchase price.

This chapter will not discuss details of the LANtastic 2Mbps Adapter. Almost no new LAN installations use the 2Mbps card due to its slower performance and proprietary design. The marketplace clearly has chosen Ethernet (either thin Ethernet or 10BASE-T) as the platform for LANtastic LANs. Both varieties provide higher performance, adherence to standards, and only slightly higher price. However, the 2Mbps Adapter installation process is similar to the process explained here. Refer to the manuals provided with the 2Mbps Adapter or Starter Kit for details of switch settings.

Verify Card Settings

Artisoft's LANtastic LAN cards arrive with certain options set on them. These settings are called the default settings, meaning that you get these settings by default if you take no action. In most cases the default settings are exactly what you want. However, some situations call for different settings. Also, to be sure of no mistakes you should examine each LAN card to verify that the factory correctly set the defaults and no one has changed them. For both reasons, you should review the following explanations with your LAN cards in front of you.

LANtastic's LAN cards make use of tiny double-slot devices called *jumpers* to set options. A jumper is rectangularly shaped, about the size of a pea (if the pea were squashed into a rectangular prism). Jumpers form a connection between two protruding *pins,* which are pairs of prong-like wires that occupy areas on the card called W1, W2, and so on. You select different card settings by sliding the jumper off one pin pair and onto another. You can grab a jumper with your fingers or needle-nosed pliers (carefully) and pull it away from the card. Then attach the jumper to any pin pair by carefully pushing it onto the pins. Compare your newly attached jumper with other jumpers on the card to be sure you properly aligned it and pushed it down all the way.

Caution

Don't damage a LAN card when you handle it. Touch a grounded piece of metal to discharge your body's static electricity buildup before you touch the card. Handle the card by the edges–don't touch the delicate chips. When you move jumpers, put the card on one of the sheets of packing foam that protected the card in the box.

The following list explains each jumper setting on the AE-2 card. In most cases, the default settings are exactly what you want. Go through the list in sequence to verify your cards are properly configured. The LANtastic AE-3 and AE-1/T cards (as noted) are similar, but in some cases use different jumper area numbers. For example, the W1 area on the AE-1/T card is *not* the interrupt selection area; W2 is.

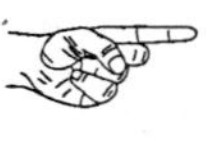

Tip

Before you change a jumper setting, write down both the original setting and the new setting. This information may be useful later if you need to reconfigure the LAN card or get technical assistance. To avoid losing a loose scrap of paper, jot the information in this book's margin or in the user's manual for the LAN card.

1. *W1, interrupt selection* (The default setting is 15.) This jumper setting selects the *interrupt request* (IRQ) line the LAN card uses to communicate with the computer's processor. The LAN card often needs the processor to take action on its behalf, and it notifies the processor with an IRQ. The processor interrupts its other work, takes the action, and resumes work. An IRQ line is the communications channel by which this "shoulder tap" occurs. Other hardware devices in the computer use IRQs, too.

   If two devices try to use the same IRQ number, a conflict causes unpredictable results such as one or both devices not working properly or the computer hanging up and refusing to respond. You need to be sure your LAN card's IRQ number is not used by some other device in your computer. The default value of 15 is seldom used by any other device. Note that IRQ 15 exists only on AT-class computers (that is, those with 80286, 386, or 486 processors). If you install the card in an XT-class computer (with an 8088 or 8086 processor), you must change from the default setting of 15 to another available IRQ. An XT's IRQs go up only to 7. Try IRQ 3 if the XT has no COM2 port (or the port is disabled), or IRQ 4 if there is no COM1 port, or IRQ2. Be aware that a bus mouse, sound card, or other device might use any IRQ, so check the device's manual. On an AT-class computer if IRQ 15 is not available, use IRQ 10. If you change the IRQ from 15 to something else, you also have to use the IRQ parameter to tell the AEX software, as mentioned later in this chapter in the "Starting and Testing LANtastic" section.

- *AE-3 Differences* None.

- *AE-1/T Differences* W2 specifies the interrupt selection. Choices and considerations are the same.

2. *W2 and W3, DMA channel selection* (The default setting is disabled.) The AE-2 driver software doesn't use DMA (direct memory access) channels–another way of communicating inside the computer. If you use this card on another LAN with other driver software, you might change W2 and W3. For LANtastic, leave these jumpers in the default position.

   - *AE-3 Differences* None.
   - *AE-1/T Differences* No DMA channel selection option is available.

3. *W4, I/O port address selection* (The default setting is 300H.) The I/O ports provide a means for the processor and peripheral devices (such as LAN cards) to send data back and forth. Devices must not use the same I/O port address numbers. The AE-2 card uses a series of I/O port addresses starting with a base address number called an *IOBASE*. The addresses are by convention specified in hexadecimal, which is what the H in 300H stands for. The AE-2 needs 32 addresses (that's 20H), so the default 300H uses up the address range from 300H to 31FH. If you use another device that requires these addresses, change to addresses that are not used. The two jumpers on W4 pin sets A and B specify an IOBASE of 300H. A and C specify 320H, B and D specify 340H, and C and D specify 360H. Don't use 320H on an XT; the XT's hard disk controller uses I/O port addresses in that range. Don't use 360H on an XT or AT if the computer has a second parallel printer port (LPT2). If you change from the default value, you also must use the IOBASE parameter to tell AEX of the change.

   - *AE-3 Differences* None.
   - *AE-1/T Differences* W1 specifies the I/O port address selection. Choices and considerations are the same, except the AE-1/T uses only 24 addresses, not 32.

4. *W5, Ethernet type selection* (The default setting is standard thin Ethernet.) Jumper the bottom pins for the default "C-NET"

(cheapernet, or thin Ethernet). To switch to the original Ethernet (thick Ethernet), jumper the top pins labeled "E-NET" (standard thick Ethernet). Note that to use the thick Ethernet setting, you must use thick Ethernet cable and external transceivers.

- *AE-3 Differences* The AE-3 uses W9 to choose between C-NET (the default) and E-NET. To use thin Ethernet, also set W10 to AUI (the default), not TPI (twisted pair). Both these jumper areas are located near the large square chip—W10 is to its right and W9 is below it. To use thick Ethernet, set W9 to E-NET and leave W10 set to AUI. To use twisted-pair cable, set W9 to the E-NET position and set W10 to TPI.
- *AE-1/T Differences* Does not apply; twisted pair is the only cable supported.

5. *W6, boot ROM enable and address selection* (The default setting is disabled.) A diskless workstation is a computer with no floppy or hard disks. To boot a diskless workstation, the computer needs to get the boot information somewhere other than a disk drive. Enable this option and the card will use a 16K ROM chip (available from Artisoft for you to install on the AE-2 card) that provides instructions to load the diskless computer's LAN software. The other jumper positions tell the card which address range this ROM chip should occupy. See the AE-2 manual for the complete list.

   - *AE-3 Differences* Same as the AE-2, except W6 has additional jumper settings. The AE-3 supports either 8K, 16K, or 32K boot ROM chips. A Novell boot ROM requires you to jumper the 8K pins, other 16K ROMs require you to jumper the 16K pins, and an Artisoft ROM requires neither. The pins marked "UV" must be jumpered if the ROM comes from a source other than Artisoft (such as Novell or other companies). As with the AE-2, the AE-3 manual explains jumper settings for the ROM chip's address range.
   - *AE-1/T Differences* Does not apply; the AE-1/T does not support diskless workstations.

6. *W7, thin Ethernet segment length selection* (The default setting is standard thin Ethernet length.) Jumper the bottom pins for the default 802.3 standard thin Ethernet segment length (maximum 185 meters, or 607 feet). To switch to an extended segment length option of up to 300 meters (984 feet), jumper the top pins together. In this extended mode, you are limited to a single segment of up to 300 meters—no repeaters are permitted to connect other cable segments. Also, all LAN cards on the segment must be Artisoft cards that are switched to this extended-segment setting. If you use this extended mode, you violate IEEE 802.3 standards. If your nodes are too far apart to fit within the 185-meter limit, this extended mode selection may be your simplest choice to make the LAN work.

   - *AE-3 Differences* None.
   - *AE-1/T Differences* Does not apply; the AE-1/T does not support thin Ethernet or an extension to the 10BASE-T cable length limit.

7. *W8, nonstandard bus selection* (The default setting is standard.) The A-B position indicates standard. Change to the B-C position (nonstandard) for certain computers with nonstandard bus timing. Examples are the Toshiba 5200 laptop computer and certain 386 computers that use an early chip set from Chips and Technologies. For these nonstandard bus-timing computers, the computer will hang up when you try to run the LANtastic driver software unless you set this jumper to indicate a nonstandard bus.

   - *AE-3 Differences* None.
   - *AE-1/T Differences* This selection is not available.

8. *W9, 16-bit enable selection* (The default setting is 16-bit mode.) The AE-2 card automatically senses if you install it in an 8-bit or a 16-bit PC slot. Put this jumper in the 8-bit position and the card will operate in 8-bit mode even if you install it in a 16-bit slot. The reason you might want to do this is to avoid a conflict with another device, such as certain VGA video cards when they operate in 16-bit mode. Switching the VGA card to 8-bit mode may also solve the problem. These conflicts are rare.

- *AE-3 Differences* The AE-3 uses an unlabeled jumper area tightly squeezed between W4 and W5 for this selection. The pins are marked "8" and "16" and work the same way.
- *AE-1/T Differences* Does not apply; the AE-1/T operates in 8-bit mode only.

9. *W10, NE2000 emulation mode* (The default setting is AE-2 mode.) Put this jumper in the N (Novell NE2000) position and the LAN card emulates a Novell NE2000-specification LAN card. This permits you to use the card on a Novell LAN if you wish. If you upgrade the card to 64K of RAM, only 16K is used in Novell mode.
   - *AE-3 Differences* None, except W5 is used for this selection.
   - *AE-1/T Differences* The AE-1/T is compatible with the Novell NE1000 (not NE2000) specification. No jumper is necessary to switch between Novell and Artisoft compatibility.

Power Off and Remove the Cover

Before you work on a computer, turn the power switch off (also turn off attached devices such as video monitors) and then disconnect the power cable. This step protects both you and the computer. Once the power is off, remove the computer's cover to gain access to the inside. Check the computer's *Guide to Operation* (or similarly titled hardware reference manual) for details. Most computers have from two to six screws on the back. Five is a common number. Many computers also have additional screws on the back that you should *not* remove. Check your manual to avoid a mistake. Once you remove the screws, different computer models have covers that remove by sliding to the front, sliding to the back, lifting up, or a combination of movements. Carefully remove the cover (don't snag any internal cables) and put it out of your way for the moment. Don't lose the screws.

Choose a Slot and Install the LAN Card

Choose an expansion slot for the LAN card. In most computers, any slot will work. In AT-class computers, slots are either 8-bit or 16-bit. (XT-class computers have 8-bit slots only.) You'll notice that 8-bit slots are shorter than 16-bit slots; the slot into which you insert the card's edge connector is shorter while the overall length of the space for the card is usually the same. Some computers have one or two slots that have room only for short expansion cards, usually called *half-cards*. These short spaces may use either 8-bit or 16-bit slots (look at the edge connector slot), but are usually 8-bit. Some 386 and 486 computers also have one or two 32-bit slots, which are even longer. Special cards are required for 32-bit slots. Check your hardware manual if you have any doubt about which ones are 8- or 16-bit slots.

To install a 16-bit card such as an AE-2 or an AE-3, you should use a 16-bit slot. The cards work in 8-bit slots too, but if put in a 16-bit slot they don't transfer data between the card and the processor quite as fast. (The speed between the card and the LAN is 10 Mbps either way.) Artisoft's 16-bit cards automatically sense if they are installed in 8-bit slots and work properly anyway; some other 16-bit cards *require* a 16-bit slot or they won't work. An 8-bit card will work in either slot size, but you might as well put it in an 8-bit slot in case you later need all 16-bit slots for other 16-bit cards.

If your computer has lots of slots available, pick one that has some space around it. Don't squeeze all the expansion cards close together. Spread them out to give yourself easier access to each one, in case you need to remove one or change a jumper. Another advantage to spreading out expansion cards is that cables coming from the back of the computer have some room between them, reducing knuckle scrapes and profanity. Also, spreading apart your cards provides each with more air space, which reduces the chance of damage from overheating.

The AE-2 and AE-3 cards may be factory assembled with the BNC T connector attached to the back edge. If so, you probably need to remove it before you install the card in the computer. Grab the ridged ring around the T connector and make a one-quarter turn counterclockwise. This loosens the connector so you can slide it off the card. The AE-1/T card has no protruding connector, just a socket for an RJ45 plug.

Each expansion slot has a back plate that seals the rear of the computer. For your selected slot, remove the screw that holds the back plate in place and remove the back plate. Save the plate in case you remove the card some day, unless you have accumulated a large supply. Some people use them as letter openers. Keep the screw handy to attach the LAN card you install.

Insert the LAN card into the slot. Hold the card by the top of its chrome mounting bracket with one hand and on the opposite edge with the other. Gently move the card downward toward the slot. Watch that the edge connector fits properly into the card slot on the computer motherboard.

When the card is in place, push downward on the top edge and mounting bracket until the card clunks into place. (It doesn't quite click, snap, or slide, it clunks.) Don't force it! If necessary, rock back and forth slightly by pressing on the top's front and back ends. When properly seated in the slot, the card stays firmly in place and the screw hole on the computer's top back edge aligns with the notch on the card's mounting bracket. Use the same screw you removed along with the back plate to attach the mounting bracket to the computer.

Attach the BNC T Connector

Reattach the BNC T connector to the rear of the AE-2 or AE-3 card. (If you plan to use twisted-pair cable with the AE-3 card, you don't need to attach the BNC T connector; save it for possible future use.) Attach it by aligning the T connector's slotted openings with the pins on the card connector. Push the T connector on and twist the ridged ring a quarter turn clockwise. The BNC T connector clicks into place (not a clunk this time) and protrudes out the rear of the computer.

Reattach the Computer Cover

Reattach the computer cover and replace the screws to hold the cover in place. Be careful not to snag any internal computer cables when you replace the cover.

Attach Cables

Your office layout might cause you to decide to do the next step, to route and protect your cables, before this step. In some cases you can manipulate the cables better if they are not attached to anything. In other instances, it makes more sense to attach the cables to the cards and then move the spans of cable to your planned locations. Do whatever is best for your office environment.

Caution

This is a good place to remind you once more to be absolutely sure you have the right cables for the LAN cards you selected. Just any old thin coaxial cable is not good enough for a reliable thin Ethernet LAN.

Double-check that the cables meet Artisoft's specifications. For thin Ethernet, the characters "RG58 A/U" or "RG58 C/U" should be printed on the cable itself. Don't accept RG58/U or RG58. Some vendors will try to tell you there's no difference. Go to another vendor. Use the same cable type from the same manufacturer throughout the LAN. The larger your LAN, the more important this is. Be sure your total cable length does not exceed the 185-meter (607 feet) maximum for a segment.

Similarly, for twisted-pair cable be sure to comply with Artisoft's current specifications. If you have the slightest doubt, contact Artisoft to be sure. See Appendix B for more information on how to contact Artisoft. At the moment, acceptable 10BASE-T cable is either Artisoft's UTP (unshielded twisted-pair) cable, AT&T's 104, 205, or 315 cable, or Belden's 1227A cable. The maximum segment length is 100 meters (328 feet) between each LAN card and its hub. Set up and configure the hub the way the hub manufacturer recommends. If your hub is the Artisoft Peer-Hub Concentrator, follow the directions in the accompanying *Artisoft Peer-Hub Adapter User's Manual.*

For a thin Ethernet LAN, you can rotate each computer's BNC T connector to route the one or two cables you attach in whatever directions work best. Don't turn the ridged ring; turn the crossbar part of the T. Attach the cables and click the BNC connectors into place.

For a 10BASE-T LAN, insert an RJ45 plug that is at one end of a cable into the LAN card's RJ45 socket until it clicks into place. Connect the RJ45 plug at the other end of the cable to an RJ45 socket on a hub or concentrator.

Route and Protect Cables

Chapter 4 discussed the need to route cables to avoid damage and accidental tripping. Follow the steps outlined there. If you need professional help, get it.

Attach Terminators

AE-2 or AE-3 cards that use thin Ethernet require a terminator at each end of the daisy chain of thin coaxial cables. A terminator has a BNC connector on one end. The other end can appear in various shapes, usually either flat or with a short rod sticking out. Two terminators come with each thin Ethernet Starter Kit from Artisoft. No matter how many computers you connect in the middle, the daisy chain of cables has exactly two ends. Put a terminator on each end. A 10BASE-T LAN uses no terminators—each cable between a LAN card and a hub is actually a loop (dual twisted-pair), not a two-ended cable.

Reattach Power Cords

Attach the power cords back to each computer and power source. This is also a good time to verify each computer gets to its power source through a surge suppressor and filter. If not, you risk a fried computer (and LAN card) in the event of a power fluctuation. Chapters 4 and 9 give you more information about surge suppressors and power filters.

Turn Computers On

Turn each computer's power on, one at a time. Verify that each computer still works as before. Until you install and start the LAN software, you should notice no difference in computer operation. Simply installing the LAN card and cable shouldn't change anything unless the card has a severe problem. The most likely possibility is that the LAN card isn't properly seated in its card slot. If you installed 10BASE-T cards and cable, you can check cable integrity at this point. Be sure the hub/concentrator is powered on and configured per manufacturer's specifications. Look next to the RJ45 socket on the AE-1/T or AE-3 card for a small green LED (*light emitting diode,* a small light). If this light glows, the cable connection between the LAN card and hub is good. If not, you may have a broken cable, a broken connector, miswired connectors (the wires in the cable don't go to the right pins on the connectors), or a power problem on the LAN card or hub.

Installation of Independent Hardware

If you buy independent hardware instead of LANtastic products, the process remains nearly the same as the process just covered. The biggest difference lurks in that large "Verify Card Settings" section that explains all the options on LANtastic LAN cards. Other LAN cards have different sets of options, and LANtastic cards are far more flexible than most. Especially if you choose low-cost cards, you will find that most don't allow the range of IRQ choices or IOBASE choices of LANtastic's, not to mention all the other options such as expandability to 64K of RAM.

The burden is on you to determine if other LAN cards offer the features and compatibility you need. As long as you verify that the cards you choose have compatible driver software as part of the LANtastic/AI product, you should at least be able to make the LAN work. Remember that you need to buy a copy of LANtastic/AI for each non-LANtastic LAN card, which usually offsets your cost savings from the other cards.

Another big concern if you buy independent hardware is to be sure you buy all the necessary components, and that the components all work together properly. Doing so is not difficult, but be sure you don't overlook anything or make a wrong assumption. Be sure that

- you use cable that meets specifications
- you can return the LAN cards if they prove unsatisfactory
- you buy terminators for thin Ethernet
- your 10BASE-T hub meets IEEE 802.3 specifications and has enough ports for the number of nodes you plan
- you buy from vendors who guarantee satisfaction and have a track record of stability

Finally, perhaps your biggest worry is what happens if you buy all the parts, put everything together, and you can't get the LAN to work. Unless you hire a single consulting firm to buy and install everything, and it stands behind its work, you may soon learn the true meaning of passing the buck. Each supplier will claim its products work fine, and your problem must be that one of the other guys sold you some bad equipment. The advantage of getting everything from a single source is you can go to that source and say, "Look, you sold me all this stuff, so *you* caused my problem. Fix it!"

Fortunately, this problem isn't very likely if you exercise a little care to be sure all parts meet specifications and are compatible with LANtastic. Read Chapter 9 on troubleshooting to see how you can isolate any problems you encounter. If all else fails, or you don't want to take the time yourself to fix a problem, you can call the nearest Artisoft dealer or an independent consultant who has worked with LANtastic. You may spend some extra money, but you should be up and running quickly.

Detailed Software Installation for a Server

Once you install the LAN hardware, you can turn your attention to the LAN software. You'll recall that a LAN node that shares its resources (most frequently a hard disk and printer) with other nodes is called a server. You want to designate at least one computer on your LANtastic LAN to be a server. You may want two servers, so one can quickly take over if the other fails, or to spread the workload between two computers. Some people choose to make all of their nodes servers, which enables anyone to access resources on any other computer. There are two main disadvantages to this: first, a server uses about 30K more RAM and second, everyone has access to a server's hard disk unless you take steps to prevent access. Some users don't want everyone prowling through their disks.

After reading Chapters 2 and 4, you should have a good idea about how you will use your LAN and which computers will need to act as servers. If you have not previously made your decision, now is the time. If you can't decide, make all computers servers during the software installation process. You can easily change them later to act only as workstations.

The following steps correspond with the steps already explained briefly in the "Quick Installation" section of this chapter. This time more detailed explanations are provided for the server software installation options. To simplify the process, these installation instructions configure a straightforward server that takes reasonable default choices.

Once you install server and workstation software for all nodes, you can start the LAN and run some simple tests. If everything works fine, you can either keep the configuration as it already is, or you can make changes to fit your particular needs. Chapters 6, 7, and 10 cover the most likely customizing changes you might want to implement. This approach lets you verify that you have installed the LAN hardware and software properly, plus get some experience using the LAN. If problems arise during later changes, you will know the cause was not a mistake in your initial installation.

Make an Installation Disk

Currently, the LANtastic software comes on a floppy disk labeled "LANtastic NETWORK OPERATING SYSTEM Ethernet." Both a 5.25-inch and a 3.5-inch disk are supplied, so you can use whichever fits your system. On the disk you choose are all the programs and information you need to run LANtastic, both for a server and a workstation. Just to be safe, make a copy of the original LANtastic disk (or both disks, if you will use both sizes on different computers) and work from the copy instead of the original. Use the DOS DISKCOPY command or some other disk copy program. We'll call this working copy your installation disk.

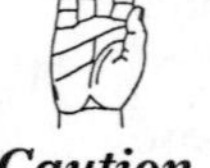

Caution

Artisoft might change at any time the way it distributes the LANtastic software or the way you should install it; if the instructions that come with LANtastic contradict the instructions shown here, follow Artisoft's revised instructions.

Insert your installation disk into the A floppy disk drive on a PC you will use as a server. You can use the B drive if you prefer, but examples here will assume you use the A drive.

Review README.DOC

If Artisoft made changes (or found problems) too late to include in the LANtastic manuals, they explain them in a file called README.DOC. This file might also include tips to help you avoid making mistakes during installation or usage of LANtastic. Scan this file and look for anything that might relate to the installation process. Most of the information will probably be about special situations after installation is complete, or unusual configurations that don't apply to you (how to use a UPS power unit, how to share a CD-ROM drive, and so on). But anything that might change the way you should install the LANtastic software is your current concern.

The information in README.DOC takes precedence over anything in the LANtastic manuals or this book. The only sources of information to override README.DOC are a loose piece of paper inserted with the manuals to show a late change, or information from Artisoft's Technical Support group after you ask them a question.

If you have a favorite utility for browsing text files, use it. You can also load README.DOC into your word processor and read it that way. If you

LANtastic/AI Installation

The *adapter independent* version of LANtastic, called *LANtastic/AI,* is installed slightly differently. Remember that you have to buy a separate copy of LANtastic/AI for every independent (non-Artisoft) LAN card you install. This is true for three reasons:

- The LANtastic/AI version contains LAN card driver software for these independent cards, but the regular LANtastic software supports only LANtastic cards.
- Each copy of LANtastic/AI has a unique serial number, and two different computers that use copies with the same serial number will not run at the same time.
- That's the way Artisoft wants to sell it, and they have the right to set up whatever pricing structure they like. (You can choose not to buy it.)

The result of all this is that you cannot use the same LANtastic/AI floppy disk to install the software on all your servers and workstations. You have to use a separate original (or copies of each original) for each computer.

More details about LANtastic/AI and how to configure it for various LAN cards are on the LANtastic/AI floppy disks. Unfortunately, the files are compressed and not visible until after you run INSTALL. So, run INSTALL, browse through the files installed on the hard disk (especially filenames that end with .DOC), and then reinstall LANtastic/AI if you need to make changes. This LANtastic/AI information is also available from the sources listed in Appendix B.

want to print the file, and you have a printer attached to parallel port LPT1, type this command:

```
copy a:readme.doc lpt1:
```

Another way to browse through the file is with the DOS TYPE command and the DOS MORE filter, which prevents the output from scrolling off your screen before you can read it. Type this command:

type a:readme.doc|more

That character just before "more" is the vertical bar, which on most keyboards looks like two stacked vertical lines due to the space in the middle. Most keyboards have it on the same key as the backslash (not the regular forward slash that is on the same key as the question mark). The vertical bar tells DOS to route the output of the TYPE command through the DOS MORE program, which pauses until you press a key each time the screen fills up.

Start INSTALL

To start the INSTALL program, type

a:install

If the characters are difficult to read (common on a laptop computer or a black-and-white monitor), press ESC to end INSTALL. Start it again using the mono switch by typing this:

a:install /mono

Select INSTALL Options

INSTALL displays an opening screen of information, as shown in Figure 5-1. Read the information and then press ENTER to continue.

As you go through the INSTALL process, you will be shown options, most of which have default selections. Accept a provided default value if it applies, and use the cursor keys to move down to the next choice. If a default is not appropriate, press ENTER. In some cases ENTER causes INSTALL to "toggle" (switch back and forth) between alternate selections. In other cases, ENTER prompts you to type in your own entry, or presents a small window with a list of choices. Hints appear at the top of the screen for each option.

Machine Name

The first thing INSTALL asks is for you to type a unique machine name (see Figure 5-2). The maximum length is 15 characters. Type in a name and

Figure 5-1. The INSTALL program's opening screen

```
LANtastic (R) INSTALL - V4.10                (C) Copyright 1991 Artisoft Inc.

LANtastic INSTALL Utility

                          Welcome to  LANtastic
Before installing the software on any machine, choose a unique name (1-15
characters) for each computer on the network and decide which machines will
share their printers and disk drives with the rest of the network. Computers
that share their resources are called servers. Machines that use these
resources are called workstations. With LANtastic, a server is also a
workstation, so a server can use the resources of other servers.

INSTALL will place several default resources on a server (A-DRIVE, B-DRIVE,
C-DRIVE, @PRINTER, @MAIL), and a group account name (*). If you do not want
these resources installed, you can instruct INSTALL not to create them. You
may add or change resources with the NET_MGR program after installation is
complete. If you are upgrading from a previous version of LANtastic, all
accounts & resources already set up will be preserved.

If you have any questions about the LANtastic INSTALL program, please refer
to "Chapter 3: Software Installation" in the LANtastic Network Operating
System User's Manual.

Enter-Continue,  Esc-Exit
```


Figure 5-2. INSTALL asks for a machine name

```
LANtastic (R) INSTALL - V4.10                (C) Copyright 1991 Artisoft Inc.

 Install Hints...

Enter a machine name.  Each machine must have a unique name in order to
communicate with other machines on the network.  For further help on machine
name press the F1 key or press Enter to continue...
```

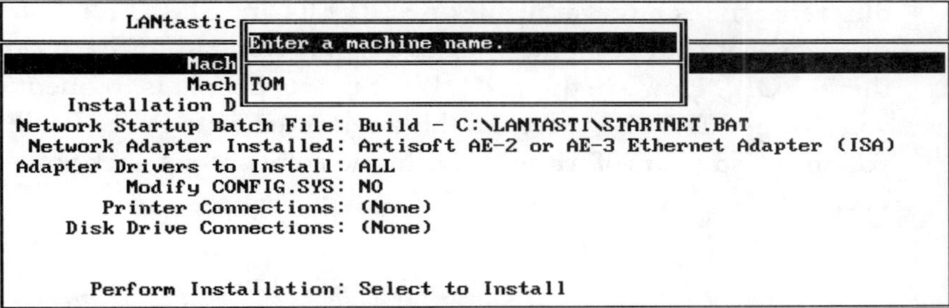


```
Input the requested data then press Enter, Esc-Exit, F1-Help
```

press (ENTER). Don't use embedded blank spaces or punctuation characters. This is the name that LANtastic uses to identify this computer to the people who access it from other computers. Because other LAN users will so frequently refer to these names, pick simple, short, memorable names. The most common types of names to pick for computers, especially in a small office, are the first names of PC users. The names are short and everyone knows them. As long as all names are different, this approach is fine. If you have two Bobs in the office, add last initials or use nicknames—whatever makes each name unique (BOBR, BOBJ, ED, EDDIE, LEFTY). Names are displayed in capital letters, even if you type lowercase letters.

If you don't want to use first names (maybe the office has six Bobs), use some other naming scheme that people will find easy. You can just assign sequential names to each server (SERVER1, SERVER2, SERVER3), or use organizational names (SALES, ACCOUNTING, SHIPPING). If the characteristics of each computer or its peripherals are important, use descriptive names (486SERVER, SRV300MB, CDROM1). The danger of this approach is that the names become obsolete if you change the computer configurations. You can use functional names, based on the use for each server (FILESERVER, PRINTSERVER, DB1). Finally, you can use whimsical names and let your creativity run wild (JAWS, PRATFALL, FROG, WATERCOOLER).

Of course, you can combine these naming schemes. If you plan to have servers dedicated to serving only (not doubling as workstations), you might want to give functional names to servers (GROUPDISK, PRINTERS) and people's names to workstations (JIM, TOM, SHIRLEY, BOB).

People will use these names constantly, so pick names that you can keep even after you later add more computers to the LAN. People are amazingly good at adapting to whatever names you pick. Everyone will quickly learn the difference in resources available on SERVER1 and SERVER2. You might even discover that your computer names become standard office nicknames ("Hi there, BOBJ. How are things?"). What upsets people is frequent changes. If you change SERVER1 to SALES this week and then to DATABASE next week, you may find yourself without lunchtime companions. Pick your names and keep them.

Machine Type

The default value for the Machine Type field is Workstation. Press (ENTER) to change this to Server (see Figure 5-3). Making this choice brings up two more options at the bottom of the screen, which will be covered in sequence.

Installation Directory

The default directory name into which INSTALL will put all LANtastic software is C:\LANTASTI. (Undoubtedly Artisoft would have preferred C:\LANTASTIC, but a file or directory name can be only up to eight characters without an extension. Too bad.) Unless you have a good reason to change the name, accept this default by moving the cursor down to the next option. One reason you might prefer a different name is if your DOS PATH is becoming too long. You might want a short name like LAN or LT instead. To change the name, press (ENTER) and type the name you want.

Figure 5-3. Pressing (ENTER) selects Server instead of Workstation

Network Startup Batch File

INSTALL will create a batch file that you can use to start the LANtastic software whenever you like. The default name is STARTNET.BAT in the C:\LANTASTI directory. Again, unless you have a good reason not to, accept the default name. If you changed the installation directory name in the previous step, be sure to change the directory name in this step to match.

Network Adapter Installed

The default Network Adapter Installed is Artisoft AE-2 or AE-3 Ethernet Adapter (ISA), as shown in Figure 5-4. Earlier versions of LANtastic had different defaults. If this is the LAN card you installed on this computer, accept this choice.

If you installed another type of LAN card (such as the Micro Channel version of the AE-2), press ENTER to bring up a window with other choices. Move the cursor key to highlight your LAN card type, and then press ENTER to select it, as shown in Figure 5-5.

Figure 5-4. The default value for the Network Adapter Installed option

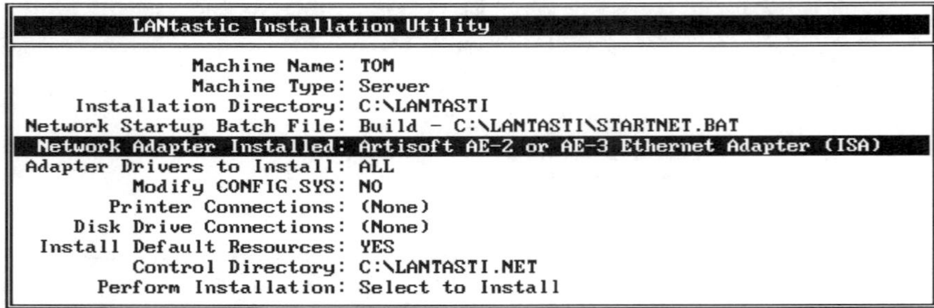

```
LANtastic (R) INSTALL - V4.10            (C) Copyright 1991 Artisoft Inc.

Install Hints...

Network adapter card model installed in this machine.  To change the default
selection press Enter.  A driver associated with the selected model will be
run in the startup batch file.  Press F1 for help or ↓ to continue...

              LANtastic Installation Utility

                Machine Name: TOM
                Machine Type: Server
      Installation Directory: C:\LANTASTI
  Network Startup Batch File: Build - C:\LANTASTI\STARTNET.BAT
   Network Adapter Installed: Artisoft AE-2 or AE-3 Ethernet Adapter (ISA)
  Adapter Drivers to Install: ALL
             Modify CONFIG.SYS: NO
         Printer Connections: (None)
      Disk Drive Connections: (None)
   Install Default Resources: YES
           Control Directory: C:\LANTASTI.NET
        Perform Installation: Select to Install

Enter-Select Option, Del-Clear Option, Esc-Exit, F1-Help
```

Figure 5-5. Selecting a different entry for the Network Adapter Installed option

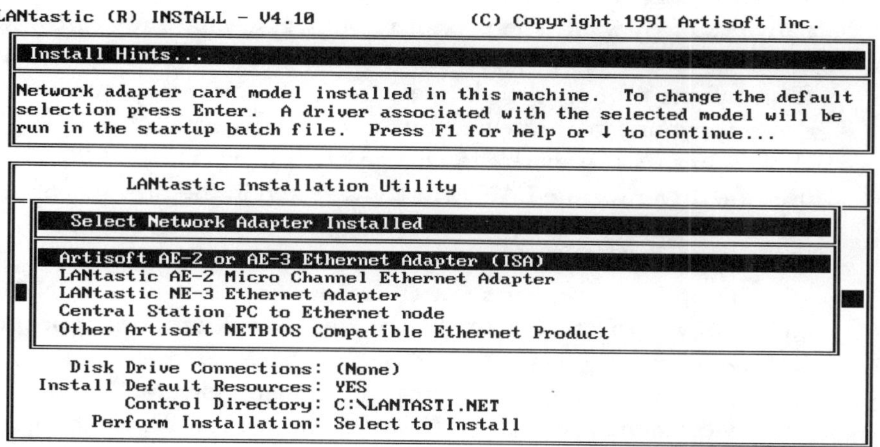
```
LANtastic (R) INSTALL - V4.10                 (C) Copyright 1991 Artisoft Inc.

 Install Hints...

Network adapter card model installed in this machine.  To change the default
selection press Enter.  A driver associated with the selected model will be
run in the startup batch file.  Press F1 for help or ↓ to continue...

          LANtastic Installation Utility

   Select Network Adapter Installed

   Artisoft AE-2 or AE-3 Ethernet Adapter (ISA)
   LANtastic AE-2 Micro Channel Ethernet Adapter
   LANtastic NE-3 Ethernet Adapter
   Central Station PC to Ethernet node
   Other Artisoft NETBIOS Compatible Ethernet Product

      Disk Drive Connections: (None)
   Install Default Resources: YES
           Control Directory: C:\LANTASTI.NET
        Perform Installation: Select to Install
Enter-Select Option, Esc-Exit, F1-Help
```

5

The LANtastic/AI Network Adapter

You have to buy the special LANtastic/AI software for each computer in which you use an independent (not LANtastic) LAN card. This is the first point in which the difference is apparent. The INSTALL program that comes with LANtastic/AI displays all the supported independent LAN cards. If you did not buy LANtastic/AI for this computer, you can't choose the LAN card you installed and the driver software you need, and therefore you can't run LANtastic. In addition, each copy of LANtastic/AI has a unique serial number. If you install the same copy of LANtastic/AI software on two different computers, you cannot run both at once because the software detects the duplicate serial numbers and refuses to run.

Adapter Drivers to Install

This seems redundant after the previous option, but gives you an alternative you may want. The previous option asks what LAN card you installed in the computer. This option asks what LAN card software drivers you want to install on your hard disk (see Figure 5-6). Normally, you want only the driver for your card; however, you can choose to install all drivers (the default choice) in case you expect to change cards later. The STARTNET.BAT file uses the driver for the LAN card you selected in the previous option.

Modify CONFIG.SYS

This option shows you some critical parameters in your CONFIG.SYS file, and gives you the chance to change them to values more appropriate for a LANtastic server. Press ENTER to display these parameters, shown in Figure 5-7. (If you like, you can highlight and change individual parameters.) After you review them, press ESC. Unless you have a specific reason not to accept the suggested changes, type **yes**. INSTALL will update CONFIG.SYS and save your old file as CONFIG.BAK. If you prefer, you can make a note of the

Figure 5-6. Selecting the Adapter Drivers to Install option

```
LANtastic (R) INSTALL - V4.10               (C) Copyright 1991 Artisoft Inc.

 Install Hints...

Adapter drivers control the network adapter cards.  You may install all
available drivers, only the driver associated with the adapter card you have
installed or none.  Press Enter to change selection or press ↓ to continue.

                  LANtastic Installation Utility

             Machine Name: TOM
             Machine Type: Server
   Installation Directory: C:\LANTASTI
Network Startup Batch File: Build - C:\LANTASTI\STARTNET.BAT
 Network Adapter Installed: Artisoft AE-2 or AE-3 Ethernet Adapter (ISA)
 Adapter Drivers to Install: Artisoft AE-2 or AE-3 Ethernet Adapter (ISA)
         Modify CONFIG.SYS: NO
       Printer Connections: (None)
     Disk Drive Connections: (None)
   Install Default Resources: YES
         Control Directory: C:\LANTASTI.NET
      Perform Installation: Select to Install

Enter-Select Option, Del-Clear Option, Esc-Exit, F1-Help
```

Figure 5-7. *Current and suggested CONFIG.SYS parameters*

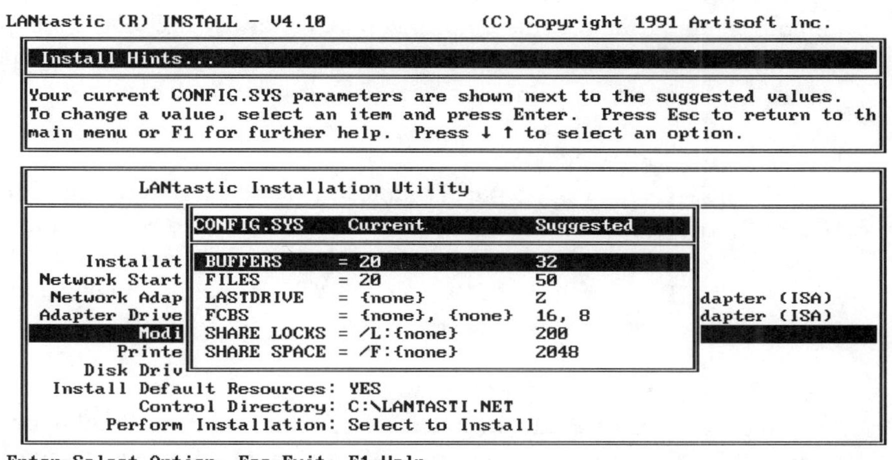

parameter changes and then make the changes yourself. However, it's best to let INSTALL do it to save time and avoid mistakes.

Caution

If you do not have acceptable parameters in CONFIG.SYS, LANtastic may not run correctly. Most importantly, the LASTDRIVE parameter must specify a letter higher (or later in the alphabet) than the server's highest lettered hard disk (usually C) if you want this server to access another server's shared hard disk, and FILES and FCBS must be large enough for your LAN workload. After you run INSTALL, you have to reboot your computer to activate the changes to CONFIG.SYS before you start LANtastic.

Printer Connections

Your simplest choice is to accept the default (None) for Printer Connections. You can instead enter a printer port number (such as **LPT1**), a server name, and resource name. If you do, INSTALL will put commands in the STARTNET.BAT file to automatically give this server, when started, access to the shared printer you specify. If this server has an attached printer that you want to use as a shared LAN printer, entering this information enables this server to access its own printer over the LAN. (Otherwise a conflict would arise between this computer's access and other nodes' access to the printer.) If you accept None for this option, you can later use NET or insert your own commands in STARTNET.BAT to get access to a printer from this server. More explanation on printer connections is given in Chapter 6.

Disk Drive Connections

For a server you will typically want to accept the default (None) for Disk Drive Connections. This means the server when started will not automatically have shared access to *another* server's hard disk. Like printer connections, you can use NET or update STARTNET.BAT yourself to make a disk drive connection later. This topic is covered in Chapter 6.

Install Default Resources

Set the Install Default Resources option to the default value of YES and INSTALL will cause this server to offer several resources to workstations automatically when started. If you don't offer resources this way, you need to either manually insert a series of commands into the STARTNET.BAT file or else select the resources using the NET_MGR program. (See Chapters 6 and 10.) If you don't use one of these methods to offer server resources, other computers are not able to access this server's hard disk and printer.

If you select YES, INSTALL makes these resources available to other computers: The server's A floppy disk drive, B floppy disk drive (if present), C hard disk drive, the printer attached to LPT1, electronic mail access, and a group user account called * (asterisk). This group user account permits anyone to have access to any of these server resources without entering a password or any other restriction. Chapters 6 and 10 have details about how to limit access to these resources if you prefer not to offer wide-open access to everything, and also explain how to offer additional shared resources.

Control Directory

LANtastic sets up a special directory on each server's hard disk called the *control directory*. This directory stores user account and resource sharing information. The default name is C:\LANTASTI.NET. It's best to leave this as is unless you have a reason to change it. Note that this is a separate directory name, not a filename within the C:\LANTASTI directory. Some people are surprised to learn that a directory name is allowed to have an extension (the

".NET" portion). That's perfectly legal under DOS rules, although by convention most people use directory names that have no extensions.

Perform Installation

The bottom line option INSTALL presents is not an option like the others. Instead, when you highlight Perform Installation (see Figure 5-8) and press ENTER, INSTALL begins to actually perform the installation of LANtastic software using the options you selected.

INSTALL asks you to press ENTER again to verify that you want to perform the installation, and then begins reading files from the installation disk and setting everything up on your hard disk. Depending on which options you choose, INSTALL creates disk directories, copies files to the hard disk, modifies CONFIG.SYS, and creates a STARTNET.BAT file. INSTALL displays messages so you can watch its progress, and finally displays a completion message when finished, as shown in Figure 5-9.

Press ESC to end INSTALL. Now you can go on to the next server or workstation computer to install the LANtastic software there. When you have

5

Figure 5-8. The Perform Installation option actually begins installation

```
LANtastic (R) INSTALL - V4.10              (C) Copyright 1991 Artisoft Inc.

 Install Hints...

If you are sure the parameters viewed on this menu are correct, press
the Enter key to perform the installation.  The procedure will create the
resources selected and copy the necessary files from the INSTALL disk.

             LANtastic Installation Utility

                 Machine Name: TOM
                 Machine Type: Server
       Installation Directory: C:\LANTASTI
 Network Startup Batch File: Build - C:\LANTASTI\STARTNET.BAT
  Network Adapter Installed: Artisoft AE-2 or AE-3 Ethernet Adapter (ISA)
 Adapter Drivers to Install: Artisoft AE-2 or AE-3 Ethernet Adapter (ISA)
            Modify CONFIG.SYS: YES
          Printer Connections: (None)
       Disk Drive Connections: (None)
   Install Default Resources: YES
            Control Directory: C:\LANTASTI.NET
       Perform Installation: Select to Install

Enter-Select Option, Del-Clear Option, Esc-Exit, F1-Help
```

Figure 5-9. *INSTALL's completion message*

```
LANtastic (R) INSTALL - V4.10                (C) Copyright 1991 Artisoft Inc.
Summary...

        LANtastic software installation is now complete.

    If you chose to have INSTALL create a startup batch file (the
    default name is STARTNET.BAT), you may view it with the DOS
    TYPE command or edit it with any ASCII text editor such as EDLIN.
    If your network is already started you will need to reboot your
    machine to start this version of the network.

    For further information on INSTALL or using your LANtastic network,
    please refer to the LANtastic Network Operating System User's Manual.

                    Press Esc to exit.
```

installed LANtastic on all computers connected to the LAN, go on to the section of this chapter called "Starting and Testing LANtastic."

Detailed Software Installation for a Workstation

The same installation disk you created to install server software installs the workstation software, too. A server also can act as a workstation, but a workstation is only a workstation–it cannot offer its shared hard disk or printers to other workstations.

Most of the INSTALL options for a workstation are the same as for a server. The instructions here are therefore shorter, focusing on differences where they occur.

Insert your copy of the installation disk (the one you made before installing the server software) into the A floppy disk drive on a PC you will use as a workstation. As before, you can use the B drive if you prefer, but examples here will assume you use the A drive. (Again, if you use independent LAN cards, you need a separate copy of LANtastic/AI for each computer.) You have already reviewed the README.DOC file for any late changes in the installation process, so proceed directly to starting INSTALL.

Start INSTALL

To start the INSTALL program, type either

a:install

or, if the computer has a black-and-white monitor, you may need to type this:

a:install /mono

Machine Name

After the opening screen INSTALL asks for a unique machine name. The maximum length is 15 characters. Don't use embedded blank spaces or punctuation characters. Follow the guidelines explained for a server's machine name in the "Machine Name" section earlier in this chapter.

Machine Type

The default value for the Machine Type field is Workstation. This is what you want, so move the cursor down to the next option.

Installation Directory

The default directory name into which INSTALL will put all LANtastic software is C:\LANTASTI. Accept this unless you have a reason to change it.

Network Startup Batch File

Accept STARTNET.BAT as the default batch filename to start LANtastic unless you have a reason to change it.

Network Adapter Installed

Press ENTER to bring up a window with LAN card choices. (Remember, if you installed an independent company's LAN card, you need to install a fresh version of LANtastic/AI on each node.) Move the cursor key to highlight your LAN card type, and then press ENTER to select it.

Adapter Drivers to Install

You probably need only the driver that was designed for your specific LAN card. If you wish, you can instead choose to install all drivers, in case you expect to change cards later. If you select ALL with LANtastic/AI, after INSTALL is done you can browse all the driver DOC files to see if another driver is more appropriate for your card. The STARTNET.BAT file uses the driver for the LAN card you selected in the previous option.

Modify CONFIG.SYS

As was true when you installed server software, this option provides your simplest method to update critical parameters in your CONFIG.SYS file. Press ENTER to display these parameters, and then press ESC after you review them. Unless you have a specific reason not to make the suggested changes, type **yes** to accept them. INSTALL will update CONFIG.SYS and save your old file as CONFIG.BAK. If you prefer, you can make the updates yourself later, but INSTALL can do it quickly and painlessly.

Caution

If you do not have acceptable parameters in CONFIG.SYS, LANtastic may not run correctly. Most importantly, the LASTDRIVE parameter must specify a letter higher (or later in the alphabet) than the workstation's highest lettered hard disk (usually C). Otherwise, the workstation will not be able to access a server's shared drive at the same time as its own hard disk. After you run INSTALL, you have to reboot your computer to activate the changes to CONFIG.SYS before you start LANtastic.

Printer Connections

Just as for a server installation, your simplest choice is to accept the default (None) for Printer Connections. If you wish, you can instead enter a printer port number (probably **LPT2** if this workstation already has a printer attached to LPT1), a server name, and resource name. If you do, INSTALL will put commands in the STARTNET.BAT file to automatically give this workstation, when started, access to the shared printer you specify. By specifying None for this option, you can later use NET or insert your own commands in STARTNET.BAT to get access to a printer from this node. Chapter 6 fully covers printer connections and sharing.

Disk Drive Connections

Accept the default (None) for Disk Drive Connections. This means the workstation will not automatically have shared access to a server's hard disk when started. Chapter 6 explains how to use NET or update STARTNET.BAT yourself to make a disk drive connection later.

Perform Installation

Highlight the bottom line option, Perform Installation, and press ENTER to tell INSTALL to do its installation job. INSTALL displays messages while it copies files to the hard disk and finally displays a completion message when finished.

Press ESC to end INSTALL, remove the installation disk, and go on to the next server or workstation until all installations are done.

Starting and Testing LANtastic

You have spent a lot of time installing the LAN hardware and software. Now comes the moment of truth. You will try to start LANtastic and see if it works. Let's rephrase that in a more positive way: You will start LANtastic and verify that it works!

Starting LANtastic

You need to start the LANtastic software on all servers and workstations that will use the LAN before they can do any LAN-related work. The STARTNET.BAT file that INSTALL created is the easiest way to start LANtastic, whether on a server or a workstation.

Starting a LANtastic Server

Try starting a server first. Power up the computer as you normally would. Be sure you rebooted the computer after you ran INSTALL in order to activate CONFIG.SYS changes. Switch to the LANtastic disk directory. If you installed LANtastic on your C hard disk and didn't change the default directory name during INSTALL, these two commands make the C drive the current disk drive (if it wasn't already) and make the LANTASTI directory the current directory:

```
c:
cd \lantasti
```

Be sure that you use the backslash (\) and not the forward slash (/) in the second command. Don't insert extra blank spaces unless you know where DOS allows them; you can accidentally change a command's meaning.

Now that the current directory is the one containing the STARTNET.BAT file, you can execute the commands INSTALL put there simply by typing

```
startnet
```

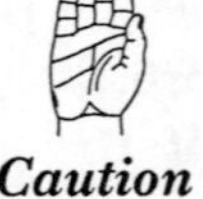

Caution

If you changed jumper settings for IRQ or IOBASE, or if you use LANtastic/AI and an independent LAN card, first look at STARTNET.BAT to verify the software and hardware settings match. Use the DOS TYPE command, your favorite line editor, or the DOS EDLIN command (or, for DOS 5, the EDIT command). Look for the line in STARTNET.BAT that contains AEX (or the driver software name for your independent card) and parameters for IRQ and IOBASE. Change IRQ and/or IOBASE if necessary (using an editor, not TYPE) to match your card's jumper settings and save the file. Then execute the STARTNET command.

If you used a LANtastic LAN card and took the default settings during INSTALL, you should see messages displayed on the screen that look like Figure 5-10. Be patient. Some of the messages may take several seconds to appear.

If your messages look the same (except for the LAN card's unique IEEE 802.3 node address and perhaps version numbers), congratulations! You just started a LANtastic server.

If you received any error messages or never received one of the four "installed" messages, something went wrong. Don't panic. A solution is probably not difficult. Write down exactly what all the messages say, and stand by for a short explanation of how the LANtastic software works.

Figure 5-10. The messages after successfully starting a LANtastic server

```
C:\>cd lantasti

C:\LANTASTI>startnet
SHARE installed
AEX AI-LANBIOS(R) driver V3.01 - (C) Copyright 1992 ARTISOFT Inc.

Command line               IRQ=15 IOBASE=300 VERBOSE
IEEE 802.3 node address   00006E230D97    Network packet size      1500
MPX interface number      C7              IO base address          0300
Interrupt request (IRQ)   15              Network buffer size      16384
Packet type               IEEE 802.3      Transmit buffers         20
Bytes of memory used      3648

                      ---- AEX driver installed ----
Adapter Independent AI-LANBIOS(R) V3.01 - (C) Copyright 1992 ARTISOFT Inc.
AEX AI-LANBIOS(R) driver V3.01 - (C) Copyright 1992 ARTISOFT Inc.
                    ---- AI-LANBIOS(R) Installed ----
LANtastic (R) Redirector V4.10 - (C) Copyright 1992 ARTISOFT Inc.
U.S.A. version only - NOT FOR EXPORT.
          ---- LANtastic (R) Redirector Installed ----
LANtastic (R) Server V4.10 - (C) Copyright 1992 ARTISOFT Inc.
U.S.A. version only - NOT FOR EXPORT.
          ---- LANtastic (R) Server Installed ----
C:\LANTASTI>
```

5

How LANtastic Software Works

Whether your first attempt to start a LANtastic server worked or not, you need a little more background in order to understand what your computer has just done. Here is a short explanation of the software components that make LANtastic work.

All LAN operating systems and related software, including LANtastic, are designed in multiple layers. LANtastic is not just one big computer program. It's several small programs that logically sit on top of each other, each performing its designated functions and then passing control to the next layer. Rather than get bogged down in technical details, let's just look at the practical implications of these multiple layers.

When you execute STARTNET.BAT for a server that contains a LANtastic AE-2 or AE-3 card, four different pieces of software are loaded into your computer, in this sequence.

- *AEX* AEX is the Artisoft low-level LAN card driver software.
- *AILANBIO* AILANBIO is Artisoft's "adapter independent" version of NetBIOS (Network Basic Input/Output System), a LAN

software standard for exchanging data between nodes and for application programs to communicate with other programs over the LAN. Even though this software is called "adapter independent," the same software runs on Artisoft LAN cards and independent manufacturer's cards.

- *REDIR* REDIR, the redirector program, works with DOS to redirect a workstation's disk and printer requests to a shared device on the LAN instead of to the workstation's own disk and printer.
- *SERVER* SERVER, the server program, processes requests from workstations and sends the results back over the LAN.

You don't have to understand much about these programs. The main point is that they must be loaded in the sequence shown: AEX, AILANBIO, REDIR, and then SERVER. Think of them as four layers of a child's pyramid toy; if you don't stack them in the right sequence, they are unstable and your LAN doesn't work (see Figure 5-11). Fortunately, the four pieces are in

Figure 5-11. *The four layers of LANtastic software in a server*

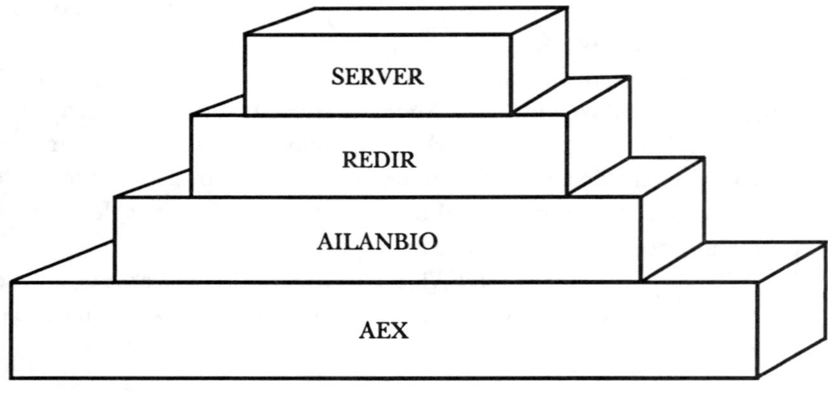

alphabetical order, which makes the sequence easy to remember. A workstation runs only the first three programs and a server runs all four. If you use an independent LAN card, the card driver software is named something other than AEX, depending on which LAN card you use. Sample names are WD8003 and 3C503MM. Look for the IRQ and IOBASE parameters on the same line.

The most likely cause of a problem with these programs is a mismatch between the AEX software (or other LAN card driver) and the jumper settings on the LAN card. If INSTALL set up STARTNET.BAT to specify IRQ number 15, but you set the jumper on the card to use IRQ 10, AEX can't talk to the card. The card and the software are, in effect, on different wavelengths. Similarly, if you install, say, a Western Digital 8003 LAN card and set it to use IRQ 5, but INSTALL defaulted to IRQ 3, the driver can't interact with the card. The same kind of mismatch can occur for IOBASE.

To fix this problem, you need to either change the card's jumper settings or change the IRQ or IOBASE parameter in the STARTNET.BAT file. Assuming you set the card jumpers to the values you want, follow these steps to change STARTNET.BAT:

1. Use your line editor or the DOS EDLIN command (or, for DOS 5, the EDIT command).
2. Look for the line in STARTNET.BAT that contains AEX and parameters for IRQ and IOBASE.
3. Change IRQ and/or IOBASE to match your card's jumper settings, save the file, and try again to start the server using STARTNET.
4. If some of the four LANtastic programs successfully installed but others did not, you can reboot the computer first to be sure you start fresh.

If you are still unable to get successful "installed" messages from each software component when you run STARTNET, you may have a more basic problem. Perhaps the card is not the model you think, and therefore the driver software you chose is incompatible. Maybe the card is not properly inserted in the PC expansion slot. For that matter, maybe you didn't run INSTALL all the way to completion, and the LANtastic software wasn't installed on the hard disk. Possible cable problems are not yet significant; the cable isn't part of what is tested so far. Any problems at this stage are between the software and the LAN card.

Go back and review the entire installation process. Make sure you followed all the steps properly. Reread the appropriate sections of the manuals, plus the README.DOC file. Look for a step you overlooked, misinterpreted, or followed incorrectly. Fix your mistake and try again. If all else fails, call for help (see Appendix B).

Starting a LANtastic Workstation

Once you have a server successfully started, pick a workstation PC to start. (If you configured your LAN to contain all servers and no workstations, start another server. Follow the directions in the previous section, "Starting a LANtastic Server.")

To start a workstation, follow the same steps as to start a server. The only difference is the messages displayed. First, make the C drive the current disk drive and LANTASTI the current disk directory, then enter the STARTNET command to run STARTNET.BAT, as done in these steps:

1. Type **c:** and press (ENTER).
2. Type **cd\lantasti** and press (ENTER).
3. Type **startnet** and press (ENTER).

The messages displayed should look like Figure 5-12.

If you fail to get completion messages from each of the three levels of software (remember, a workstation doesn't use the SERVER component), follow the same procedure described for server startup problems.

Testing LANtastic

You now have at least one server and one workstation (or two servers) successfully running the LANtastic software. That's good–it shows that some parts of the LANtastic software interact properly with the LAN card. You need to work up to the big test: Can each PC communicate with the others?

Figure 5-12. The messages after successfully starting a LANtastic workstation

```
C:\>cd lantasti

C:\LANTASTI>startnet
AEX AI-LANBIOS(R) driver V3.01 - (C) Copyright 1992 ARTISOFT Inc.

Command line              IRQ=15 IOBASE=300 VERBOSE
IEEE 802.3 node address   00006E244C6D  Network packet size     1500
MPX interface number      C7            IO base address         0300
Interrupt request (IRQ)   15            Network buffer size     16384
Packet type               IEEE 802.3    Transmit buffers        20
Bytes of memory used      3648

                    ---- AEX driver installed ----
Adapter Independent AI-LANBIOS(R) V3.01 - (C) Copyright 1992 ARTISOFT Inc.
AEX AI-LANBIOS(R) driver V3.01 - (C) Copyright 1992 ARTISOFT Inc.
                    ---- AI-LANBIOS(R) Installed ----
LANtastic (R) Redirector V4.10 - (C) Copyright 1992 ARTISOFT Inc.
U.S.A. version only - NOT FOR EXPORT.
              ---- LANtastic (R) Redirector Installed ----
C:\LANTASTI>
```


The LANCHECK Program

In addition to the LANtastic programs already mentioned (AEX, AILANBIO, REDIR, and SERVER), LANtastic includes a number of utility programs. A *utility program* is a program that performs some limited but useful function, such as maintenance or analysis. One of these programs is called LANCHECK. As the name implies, LANCHECK checks the status of your LANtastic LAN. You can use it to verify that your LAN stations can communicate. This is a way to verify that the LAN cables and connectors are not faulty and that all LAN cards are working.

To run LANCHECK, go to any node (server or workstation) and type the command

lancheck

or, if the computer has a black-and-white monitor, type

lancheck /mono

(Note that the slash is a regular forward slash, not a backslash.)

Then go to all the other computers on the LAN (on which you have successfully started the LAN software) and do the same thing. The LANCHECK program on each computer tries to communicate with all others that also run LANCHECK. A line on the screen shows each computer that is successfully contacted. Figure 5-13 shows the LANCHECK screen for a two-computer LAN, one called CMS and one called TOM. If any computer is not listed, it is not communicating with the others. Most likely problems are disconnected cables, bad cables, bad connectors, or a faulty LAN card. If a computer "freezes up" (doesn't display anything new and won't respond to keyboard entries) when you run LANCHECK, you may have an IRQ or IOBASE conflict on that computer.

The *LANtastic Network Operating System Reference Manual* explains more about LANCHECK and what the information on the screen means. Briefly, the *NAME* is the name assigned to the computer (or a name you assign temporarily when you start LANCHECK). The *NODE NUMBER* is a unique serial number assigned to each LAN card at the factory. *MINUTES RUNNING*

Figure 5-13. *The LANCHECK display for a two-computer LAN*

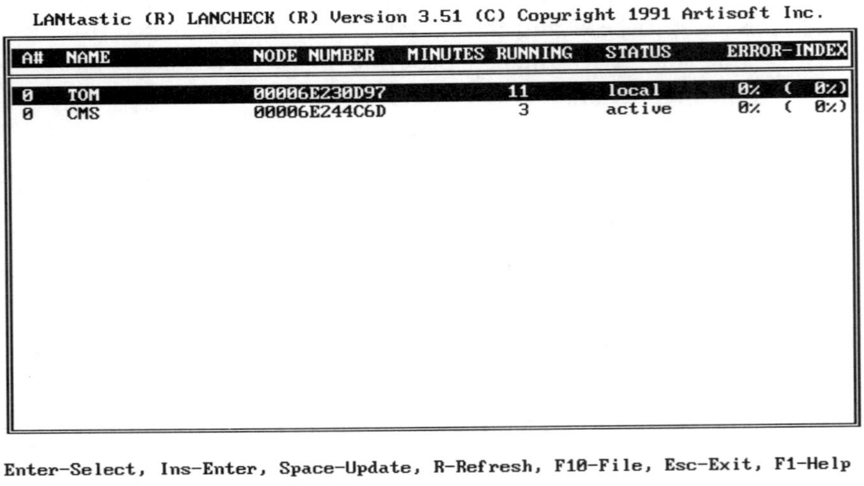

```
LANtastic (R) LANCHECK (R) Version 3.51 (C) Copyright 1991 Artisoft Inc.

A# NAME         NODE NUMBER    MINUTES RUNNING   STATUS     ERROR-INDEX

0  TOM          00006E230D97          11         local      0%  (  0%)
0  CMS          00006E244C6D           3         active     0%  (  0%)

Enter-Select, Ins-Enter, Space-Update, R-Refresh, F10-File, Esc-Exit, F1-Help
```

shows how long since you started NetBIOS (AILANBIO). *STATUS* shows *(local)* for the LAN card in the same computer, *active* for another PC's LAN card with which LANCHECK can communicate, and **inactive** for a LAN card with which LANCHECK no longer can communicate (either the LAN card or cable is working erratically, or someone stopped running LANCHECK on that computer). *ERROR-INDEX* shows a measure of error transmissions over the LAN. A computer that consistently has an error-index number much higher or lower than other computers on the LAN may be experiencing hardware problems.

You can see even more statistics about a single LAN card by highlighting that card's name and pressing ENTER. Check the manual for explanations of each entry. To end LANCHECK, press ESC.

The NET SHOW Command

Another quick test for connectivity is possible with the NET SHOW command. NET is an important part of LANtastic that will be covered fully in Chapters 6 and 7. Simply type **net show** from a workstation and you should see output like this:

```
Machine CMS is being used as a Redirector
File and record locking is currently ENABLED
Unsolicited messages will BEEP and POP-UP
LPT timeout in seconds: 10
Server \\TOM                is available on adapter 0
```

This shows a variety of information. For the moment, the important sections are the first and last line. The first line shows that this computer (named CMS) is being used as a redirector only (a workstation, but not a server). The last line shows that a server named TOM is available on the LAN. This demonstrates that this workstation recognizes a remote server, so the connection, both LAN cards, workstation software, and server software are all functioning.

LANCHECK and NET SHOW are quick and easy ways to check the status of your LANtastic LAN. Use them any time you want to verify that the LAN hardware and software are working properly. If problems persist, read Chapter 9.

Installing LANtastic Z

LANtastic Z is a special version of LANtastic that does not use a LAN card. Instead, the hardware consists of a supplied serial cable (called a null modem cable) to connect the serial ports of two computers, plus a special parallel cable in case you prefer to connect the parallel ports of two computers. You can also use LANtastic Z to connect two remote computers using modems and a telephone link.

Installing LANtastic Z Hardware

To install the hardware for LANtastic Z, you choose either the serial or the parallel cable and connect the appropriate ports. Often your decision about which to use is based entirely on the ports available on the two computers to be connected. Most computers have a spare serial port (often called a COM port or an RS232 port), so a serial connection is often easier than disconnecting printers to use parallel ports. Once you connect the ports on the two computers, your hardware installation is complete. You don't even need to remove the computer cover. If you connect two remote computers, the hardware installation consists of installing a modem, either internal (inside the computer) or external (outside the computer, connected using a serial port), and connecting the modem to a telephone line.

Installing LANtastic Z Software

The software installation for LANtastic Z is nearly identical to the process when you use a LAN card. The LANtastic Z package includes an installation disk with the same INSTALL program. You follow the same steps explained earlier in this chapter–select a computer name, specify if each computer will be a server or workstation, and so on. The difference comes when you reach the Network Adapter Installed option. The choices for LANtastic Z are a serial cable, a parallel cable, and a modem. Choose the one you plan to use the most. Then, for Adapter Drivers to Install, choose All and you will have the ability to use any of the three.

Starting LANtastic Z

You start the LANtastic software for LANtastic Z the same way, with the STARTNET command. The one difference is that you must specify which type of connection you want to use–serial (S), parallel (P), or modem (M). Choose the appropriate letter and enter it right after the STARTNET command (following a blank space). For example, to start the LANtastic software for a serial connection, type

```
startnet s
```

The four software components are almost the same for LANtastic Z. The difference is the low-level driver. Instead of AEX, LANtastic Z uses either SPORT (serial), PPORT (parallel), or MPORT (modem), depending on the letter you enter after STARTNET. The other components (AILANBIO, REDIR, and SERVER) are the same.

Testing LANtastic Z

Test your LANtastic Z hardware and software installation the same way as for a conventional LANtastic LAN, using LANCHECK and NET SHOW.

Everything you as a user see on the screen is the same for LANtastic Z as it is for the regular LANtastic. You also have the same capabilities to share files and printers, send electronic mail, and implement security measures to protect your data. The only difference you will notice is that data transfer takes longer due to the slower speeds of these three ports. The parallel port is faster than the serial or modem connection, but all are much slower than an Ethernet or 2Mbps LAN card.

6

Sharing Primary Resources: Disks, Printers, and E-Mail

In Chapter 5 you learned how to install LANtastic hardware and software, start the software, and verify that servers and workstations could communicate. This chapter and Chapter 7 take the next step: actually sharing resources over the LAN. This chapter covers the most commonly shared resources: a hard disk, one or more printers, and electronic mail (e-mail). The next chapter covers other shared resources: CD-ROM disks, tape backup units, and modems, plus attachment of portable computers.

In both Chapters 6 and 7, the LANtastic program that makes all this sharing possible is NET. From a workstation, your vehicle to get access to server resources is the NET program.

Shared Hard Disks

To start, let's look at how you use a workstation to access a server's shared hard disk if you installed the server and workstation using the INSTALL choices suggested in Chapter 5. This means the server has a C drive hard disk that any workstation can access immediately after the server runs STARTNET.BAT without any security obstacles. (Sharing a floppy disk works the same way.) Chapter 10 shows how to limit the resources a server offers.

The NET Menu

The easiest way to gain access to a server's hard disk from a workstation or another server is to use LANtastic's NET menu. Once you start LANtastic using STARTNET, as explained in Chapter 5, you can use NET.

Tip

*If you add the command **C:\LANTASTI\STARTNET** as the last line in your AUTOEXEC.BAT file, the LANtastic software starts automatically whenever you turn on your computer. This tip works for either a workstation or a server. If your workgroup's PCs need access to shared resources every day, this is the easiest way to start the LAN software automatically.*

Redirection from the NET Menu

Enter the command **net** without any parameters and you see a menu screen as shown in Figure 6-1. If your computer display is unclear, enter **net /mono** instead to get a monochrome (black-and-white) display.

NET's menu works like most menus. You use the ↑ and ↓ keys to select options from the Main Functions list. When you highlight the choice you want, press ENTER. The screen's bottom line shows other choices, and you can press F1 any time to get more help. Starting with LANtastic version 4.1 you can press a highlighted letter to select a menu entry, rather than using the arrow keys.

To access a server's hard disk, select Network Disk Drives and Printers, the top choice. After you make this selection, a menu box called Drive and Printer Connections appears, as Figure 6-2 shows.

This menu box lists all your device connections whether the connections are physical or redirected. Drives A, B, and C are physical—the workstation

Figure 6-1. The opening menu from the NET command

```
LANtastic (R) Connection Manager V4.10        (C) Copyright 1991 Artisoft Inc.

Main Functions

Network Disk Drives and Printers
Printer Queue Management
Mail Services
Chat With Another User
Login or Logout
User Account Management
Monitor & Manage Server Activity



Enter-Select Option, Esc-Exit, F1-Help
```


Figure 6-2. The result of selecting Network Disk Drives and Printers

```
LANtastic (R) Connection Manager V4.10        (C) Copyright 1991 Artisoft Inc.

Drive and Printer Connections

PRN
LPT1
LPT2
LPT3
COM1
COM2
A:      (Physical)
B:      (Physical)
C:      (Physical)
D:
E:
F:
G:
H:
I:
J:
K:
L:

Enter-Redirect Drive or Printer, Del-Cancel Redirection, Esc-Exit, F1-Help
```

actually has physical devices connected to it called A, B, and C. The other device names (D and above) are not assigned to anything, so you can use them for redirection to a server's hard disk. Follow these steps to see how:

1. Pick a disk drive name you want to use to refer to the server's hard disk.

In this example, you can use any name from D up through the LASTDRIVE parameter you specified for CONFIG.SYS during the INSTALL process. To minimize mistakes you might want to pick the same drive name every time. You also might want to standardize your workgroup by having everyone use the same name to simplify procedures and training. That way everyone will know that the G drive, for example, is the shared drive. Some workgroups like to use L as in LAN, or else N as in network. Don't set up procedures using D as the shared drive; someone in the group may have (or soon get) a second hard disk called D and then the name would conflict with the shared disk's name. Of course you don't *have* to be consistent–you can use G now and N another time if you like. However, being consistent helps avoid errors.

Anyway, step 2 is when you assign the name you will use for the server's disk.

2. Let's say you pick G this time. Select G either by typing **G** or by repeatedly pressing the (↓) key until you highlight the G: line. Then press (ENTER). After you do, the screen looks like Figure 6-3.

The Server Connections menu box on the right side of the screen appears and displays the available servers. Our example shows a server named TOM. (The name is in parentheses to indicate this workstation is not logged in to the server. More on this in a moment.) If several servers are running on the LAN, you need to move the cursor to select the one whose disk you want to access. Since only TOM is available and its name is already highlighted, press (ENTER) to select it. Figure 6-4 shows the result for LANtastic version 4.0. Starting with version 4.1 an automatic log-in feature bypasses the following username-password dialog and skips to the screen shown in Figure 6-5. However, even if you use version 4.1 your LAN administrator may implement security for your workstation and force you to go through this username-password dialog.

NET now asks for your username if this is the first time you have tried to access this server since starting LANtastic. This process is called *logging in* to

Figure 6-3. Selecting G: to redirect to a server's disk

```
LANtastic (R) Connection Manager V4.10        (C) Copyright 1991 Artisoft Inc.

Drive and Printer Connections                   Server Connections

PRN                                             (TOM)
LPT1
LPT2
LPT3
COM1
COM2
A:      (Physical)
B:      (Physical)
C:      (Physical)
D:
E:
F:
G:
H:
I:
J:
K:
L:

Enter-Select, Ins-Login, Del-Logout, Esc-Exit, F2-Set Defaults, F1-Help
```


Figure 6-4. Selecting the server causes a USERNAME prompt

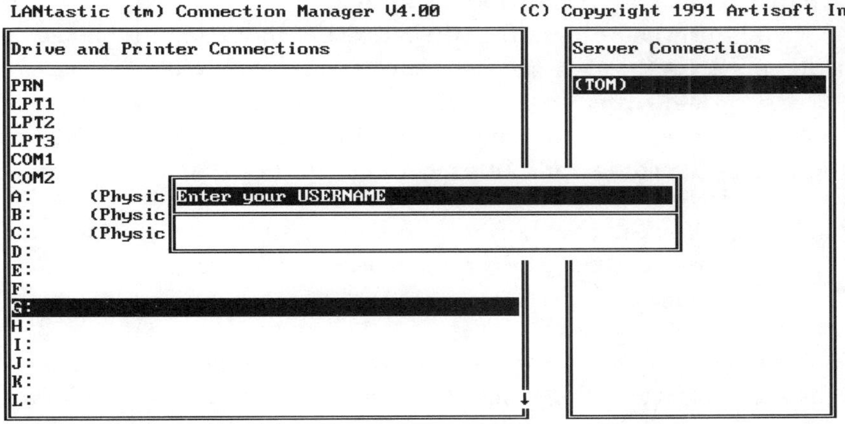

Figure 6-5. *NET asks if you want to synchronize clocks*

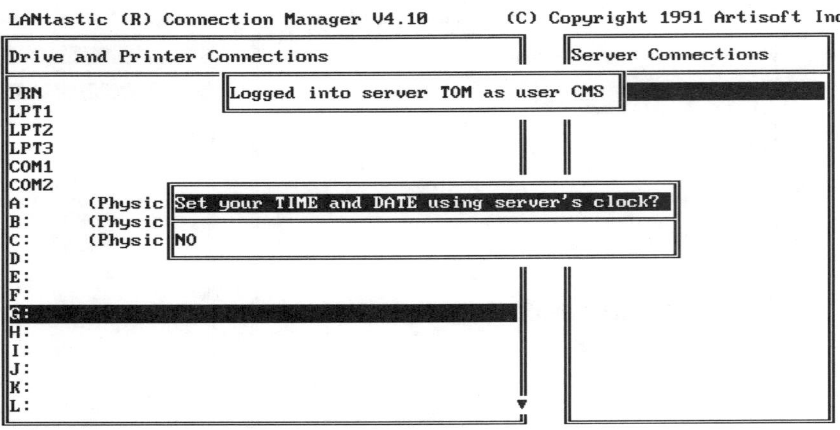

the server, or a *server LOGIN*. (You may have noticed that Login or Logout is another option in NET's Main Functions menu box. If you prefer, you can choose to log in that way instead. If you don't log in before you ask to redirect a disk drive, NET makes you log in first.)

The username identifies you in case LANtastic was installed using security features. LANtastic's security can require each user to use a name and password in order to limit who can access which resources. Chapter 10 explains user accounts and security. If you installed LANtastic the way Chapter 5 recommends, this security is not implemented.

3. You can enter any username, but you *do* have to enter one. Let's just enter **CMS** (the brand name of the computer in this case) and continue.

Tip

Enter the same agreed-upon, unique username every time you log in to a server, even if you aren't required to by your LAN administrator. Unless you use the same name each time you log in, you will lose track of printer output you send to shared printers and you will miss electronic mail sent to you. Note that this username may or may not be the same as the machine name you (or your LAN administrator) chose for your computer during the INSTALL process. If two or more people share the same computer, each should use a unique username. If you have your own computer, your best username is probably the same name as the machine name.

4. NET now asks for your password. No password is necessary because security is not in force, so you can just press ENTER.

Next, NET asks if you want to "Set your TIME and DATE using server's clock," as shown in Figure 6-5. (Figure 6-5 shows the screen from version 4.1 after automatically logging in with the machine name, which is CMS.) The default choice is No, which means you do not want to change the workstation's clock to match the server's. If you choose Yes instead, NET synchronizes clocks. Keeping the clocks in sync is not critical in most environments, but some software packages produce meaningful results only if every PC in the workgroup has an accurate date and time. A simple example is electronic mail. Inaccurate clocks produce meaningless time stamps on messages between users. Enter **yes** or **no** as you prefer. If the workstation computer has no automatic clock, or the battery is running low and causes the clock to be set slow when you boot the computer, Yes is a convenient way to set the clock to match the server's.

6

5. Enter **Yes** for "Set your TIME and DATE using server's clock."

Now NET displays a menu box that shows the resources available on the server. Remember that you previously chose G as the name you would redirect to the server. In this step you pick the server's C drive to make the link between your G name and the server's C hard disk.

6. Move the cursor down to the line that says C-DRIVE (see Figure 6-6) and press ENTER.

The connection is now complete. The Drive and Printer Connections menu box now shows that the G disk drive is redirected to the C-DRIVE resource on server TOM. Figure 6-7 shows how NET displays this.

NET has done its job. Press ESC once to return to NET's Main Functions menu box, and press ESC again to quit NET and return to the DOS C:> prompt.

Figure 6-6. *Selecting the server's C disk drive to be called drive G on the workstation*

```
Shared Directories/Devices on Server \\TOM        C) Copyright 1991 Artisoft Inc.

Drive and Printer Connections

PRN
LPT Directory      Access Rights  Description
LPT
LPT .              R---L---E---   Server's network directory
COM A-DRIVE        RWCMLDKNEA--   Drive A on Server
COM B-DRIVE        RWCMLDKNEA--   Drive B on Server
A:  C-DRIVE        RWCMLDKNEA--   Drive C on Server
B:
C:
D:
E:
F:
G:
H:
I:
J:
K:
L:

Enter-Select a Directory or Device on the Server, Esc-Exit, F1-Help
```

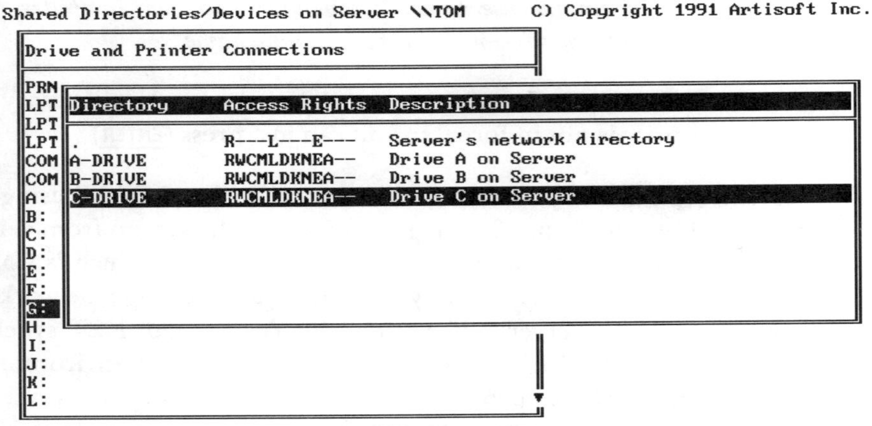

Figure 6-7. *NET shows that G is redirected to C on server TOM*

```
LANtastic (R) Connection Manager V4.10       (C) Copyright 1991 Artisoft Inc.

Drive and Printer Connections

PRN
LPT1
LPT2
LPT3
COM1
COM2
A:     (Physical)
B:     (Physical)
C:     (Physical)
D:
E:
F:
G:      \\TOM\C-DRIVE
H:
I:
J:
K:
L:

Enter-Redirect Drive or Printer, Del-Cancel Redirection, Esc-Exit, F1-Help
```

What has this accomplished? The workstation now can use drive G as if it is a hard disk on the workstation. Any usage of drive G really refers to drive C on server TOM. For a simple test, change to the G drive on the workstation by entering

```
g:
```

The computer responds by displaying a G:> prompt (or G:\> if you have the **prompt pg** command in your AUTOEXEC.BAT file, which is a good idea). Enter the **dir** command and the output displayed is the directory of the server's C drive. Change the current directory using the command **cd\dos** (if DOS is a server directory name), and the current directory becomes the DOS directory on the server. Use the DOS TYPE command to display a file from the server's disk. You will quickly demonstrate to yourself that your workstation's G drive is the same as the server's C drive.

Caution

Don't get confused between physical and redirected device names. When you choose G as your local name for the server's C hard disk, that name applies only to you. Someone from another workstation might use H or T to refer to the same disk. Someone working at the server's keyboard continues to call that disk the C disk drive, instead of H or T.

Caution

Don't redirect one of your physical device names to a server device. If you have a C hard disk, don't assign C to the server's disk. If you do, from that point on C refers to the server's disk and not your own. The results are confusion and the inability to access your own hard disk.

Caution

By default from the INSTALL process, a workstation can log in to at most two servers at a time. If you need to use resources from three or more different servers at once, edit the REDIR line in STARTNET.BAT to change LOGINS=2 to LOGINS=5 (or whatever number you need). Chapter 14 explains the LOGINS parameter for REDIR along with the parameters for other LANtastic programs.

Canceling Redirection from the NET Menu

After you gain access to a shared disk drive, you may want to end that access. Another way to say this is that you want to *cancel redirection* to the disk drive, or break the virtual connection.

To cancel redirection, type **net** and press (ENTER). From the Main Functions menu, select Network Disk Drives and Printers. Select the drive letter you want to cancel. Then press (DEL). Figure 6-8 shows the result of following these steps to cancel redirection of the G drive.

NET prompts you to press (ENTER) to verify you want to delete the resource (cancel redirection). Press (ENTER) and the G connection to the server's hard disk disappears.

Why would you want to, for our example, eliminate your access to the G drive? Several reasons are possible.

- *To prepare to stop running LANtastic so you can free up the RAM it occupies* See the "Stopping LANtastic" section that follows.
- *To reassign that same drive letter to another server's hard disk* In most cases you instead simply assign a different drive letter to a different server's disk so you can access both. However, if you install software, such as a word processor, on your own disk and specify that data files are on the G drive, you may need to use G to access both servers in turn. Also you may have BAT files or other procedures that expect to find programs or data files on a certain drive name, such as G.
- *To "clean up" and make sure you don't accidentally manipulate data on the server's disk* As long as you continue to redirect G to the server's disk, you are capable of absentmindedly copying or deleting files from the wrong disk. Suppose you want to clean up your own C disk by deleting some files and copying others to floppy disks. For safety you should first cancel your access to a server's disk. Of course, if your cleanup process involves the server's disk too, you need to retain your access to it. Just be careful, as usual, that you point to the right disk drive with each command.

Caution

If you try to delete redirection to a disk drive while that drive is your current disk drive, you can do so. However, when you end NET and return to the DOS prompt, DOS displays a message saying the "Current drive is no longer valid." You have to enter C: after the message to make C the current drive again.

Stopping LANtastic

Deleting your redirection of a disk drive is one thing, but it's another to actually stop the LANtastic software. The four software components (three

Figure 6-8. The result of pressing DEL *to cancel redirection*

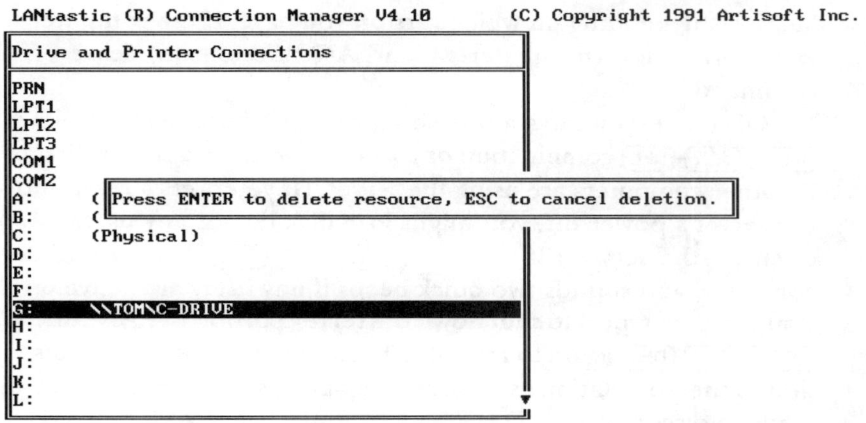

for a workstation) discussed in Chapter 5 all reside in RAM and take up space. You can eliminate them from memory to recover that space—about 30K for a workstation and usually 60K for a server. The actual RAM LANtastic uses on your system depends on what options you select, as discussed in Chapter 13.

You have to remove the software components in the *opposite* sequence in which you installed them. The last one installed has to be the first removed. Each software component has a /remove parameter (sometimes called a *switch*) that you must specify. For a server with a LANtastic AE-*x* LAN card, the removal command sequence is as follows:

```
server /remove
redir /remove
ailanbio /remove
aex /remove
```

You can create a simple batch file to do this if you like. Use EDLIN or another line editor and call the file STOPNET.BAT or any other available name that you will easily remember. If you use an independent LAN card, replace aex with the name of your card's driver software. If you use the LANtastic 2Mbps card, delete aex and replace ailanbio with lanbios2 or lanbios3, depending on which version you have. If the computer was started as a workstation (no matter which LAN card it uses), leave off the server command.

Of course, you can simply reboot your computer instead, either using the CTRL-ALT-DEL combination or a reset button. On a server, first be sure that no other computers are using the server. (If you press a reset button or turn the server's power off, you might lose disk data if any users have disk files open on the server.) If you use CTRL-ALT-DEL, LANtastic intercepts the command and sounds two quick beeps if any users are active on the server. You can then type **S** to shut down the server portion of LANtastic. Then press CTRL-ALT-DEL again to reboot the computer. LANtastic breaks the connection to the workstation as soon as you type **S**, so be sure first that all users are ready to disconnect.

Commands at the DOS Prompt

Even though using the NET menu is easy, sometimes you may want to accomplish the same results without going through the menu interaction. If so, you can enter commands at the DOS prompt and specify the complete action you want taken. These commands are most useful for insertion into batch file commands. You can either insert the commands into the STARTNET.BAT file to customize it to your preference, or make your own specialized batch files.

Server Log In from the DOS Prompt

Before you redirect a workstation drive to a server's shared disk, you have to log in to the server. The following command accomplishes the same login you saw earlier in the chapter:

```
net login \\tom cms
```

The name of the command is NET; LOGIN is the subcommand or action you request NET to take. The third parameter is the name of the server you want to log in to, preceded by two backslashes. The fourth parameter is the username. (Chapter 14 explains these commands in detail.)

NET does not display any output after you enter this command. You can't be sure anything happened unless you look. Enter the **net show** command to see. It displays several lines of output, the last one of which says

```
Logged into \\TOM as CMS on adapter 0
```

The NET LOGIN command has other options besides the ones this example uses. Here is the complete command in general form:

net login[/wait] \\servername username password adapternum

In most cases you don't need any of these other parameters, but here's a quick explanation of them. The /wait parameter means to keep trying to log in to the server until it is available. (Your computer is tied up until you succeed or decide to give up.) You can abbreviate the /wait option as /w if you like; the square brackets around it indicate that it is optional. Don't type the square brackets when you enter the command.

The password is the assigned password for the username and is required if security is implemented (see Chapter 10). The number of the LAN adapter (LAN card) is represented by adapternum. If you install only one LAN card in a computer, it is called number zero. (Welcome to the world of computers—almost all counting begins with zero, not one.) LANtastic allows you to have as many as four Ethernet LAN cards in a computer, numbered zero through three. If you omit adapternum from the command, NET assumes you mean adapter zero.

Redirection from the DOS Prompt

Once a workstation is logged in to a server, you can enter the command to redirect a disk drive name to the server's shared disk. This NET USE command duplicates the example done previously using NET's menu.

net use g: \\tom\c-drive

The first parameter after NET USE is the disk drive name you want to redirect. The next parameter provides the server name and the resource name, using two backslashes before the server name, one before the resource name, and no spaces. Notice that you have to use the exact resource name c-drive (except for capitalization, which is irrelevant in virtually all commands) because that is the way LANtastic defined the name during the INSTALL process on the server.

Like the NET LOGIN command, net use displays no output or reassuring message to confirm it did what you want. Again, you can enter **net show** to see verification. A new last line of output says

```
Disk G: is redirected to \\TOM\C-DRIVE
```

Redirection Cancellation from the DOS Prompt

If NET USE is the command to redirect a disk drive, what would be the command to cancel redirection? Why, NET UNUSE, of course.

net unuse g:

Notice that there is no need to provide the name of the server or resource name to cancel redirection. That's because after you redirect g: LANtastic knows what server and disk resource g: refers to.

You can also cancel redirection by logging out from a server. Whenever you log out from a server you cancel all redirection active to that server. This command logs a workstation out from a server named TOM.

net logout \\tom

Shared Printers

The process to access a shared printer is virtually the same as the process to access a shared disk. Once again the NET program is the vehicle to establish the access and you can either use NET's menu or DOS commands.

Printer Redirection from the NET Menu

A typical LANtastic LAN has one or more shared printers on a server, plus individual printers on some workstations. First, in the next section, consider how to use the NET menu to access a server's shared printer from a workstation. The way to use NET's menu to access a server's printer from the server itself follows that, in the "Printer Access from a Server" section.

Printer Access from a Workstation

A workstation might have an individual printer physically attached. If so, the printer is most often attached to the LPT1 parallel printer port. From this workstation you might want to preserve access to your LPT1 printer, in which case you should choose LPT2 to redirect to a server's shared printer. If your software expects to send output to LPT1, or if you simply don't need access to your personal printer right now, you can assign LPT1 to the shared printer. The example here assigns LPT2 to the shared printer.

Type the command **net** without any parameters and press ENTER to bring up the NET menu screen. Select the top choice in the Main Functions menu box, Network Disk Drives and Printers. This choice displays the familiar Drive and Printer Connections menu box. Press ↓ until you highlight the LPT2 line and press ENTER. The result is shown in Figure 6-9.

6

The Server Connections menu box on the right side of the screen appears with the names of available servers. The server named TOM has the shared printer, so select it by pressing ENTER. If you haven't logged into the server, you may be prompted as before for a username and password. Once logged in, NET displays the available printer devices on the server, as shown in Figure 6-10.

The device name on the server is @PRINTER, described as being the "Server's parallel printer LPT1." Press ENTER to select this shared printer. Then press ESC twice to end the NET menu program.

The workstation's LPT2 device name is now redirected to TOM's printer connected to port LPT1. Any commands on the workstation that send output to LPT2 cause the data to be sent over the LAN to the server's LPT1 printer. To test this connection, be sure the printer is turned on and enter this command at the workstation.

```
copy c:\config.sys lpt2
```

Figure 6-9. *Selecting LPT2 from the Drive and Printer Connections menu box*

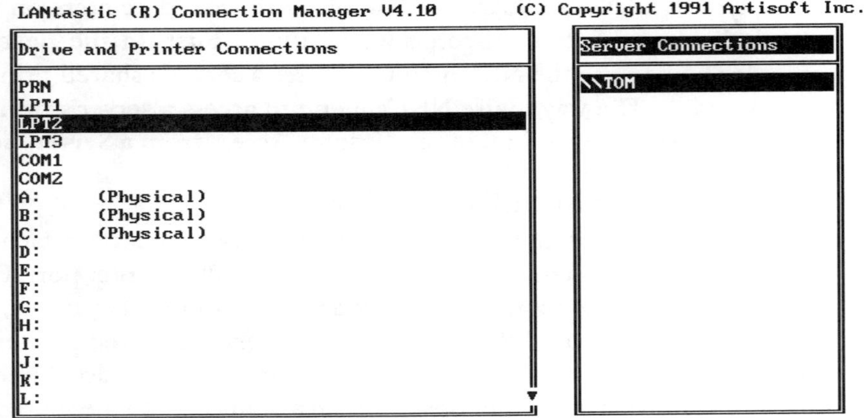

LANtastic (R) Connection Manager V4.10 (C) Copyright 1991 Artisoft Inc.

Drive and Printer Connections

PRN
LPT1
LPT2
LPT3
COM1
COM2
A: (Physical)
B: (Physical)
C: (Physical)
D:
E:
F:
G:
H:
I:
J:
K:
L:

Server Connections

\\TOM

Enter-Select, Ins-Login, Del-Logout, Esc-Exit, F2-Set Defaults, F1-Help

Figure 6-10. *The available printer devices on server TOM*

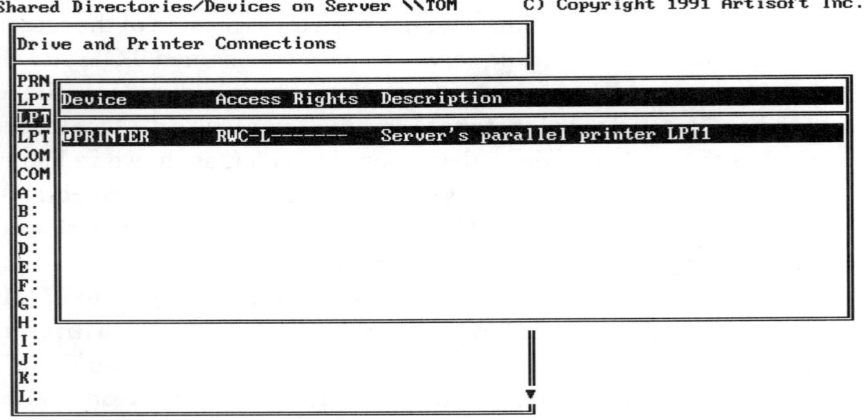

Shared Directories/Devices on Server \\TOM C) Copyright 1991 Artisoft Inc.

Drive and Printer Connections

Device	Access Rights	Description
@PRINTER	RWC-L-------	Server's parallel printer LPT1

Enter-Select a Directory or Device on the Server, Esc-Exit, F1-Help

This command prints the contents of your CONFIG.SYS file on the server's printer. Note that if the printer is a laser printer, you may need to manually take the printer off-line and press the form feed button to eject the partial page you printed.

Printer Access from a Server

If you are working from a server's keyboard and want to access a printer attached to another server, you follow the same procedure. You act as a workstation when you access another server's resources, so the steps are the same.

However, accessing a printer's server from that same server is a little tricky. You might think there's no need to do anything special. After all, this computer has a printer attached to LPT1 (for example), so why not just use it the same way as if the computer were not on the LAN?

The problem is that other computers share the use of this server's printer over the LAN. Because some computers will use the printer over the LAN, all must do so including the server itself. You must use NET to tell the server to access its own shared printer through redirection. That way the server software can coordinate every computer's printer use.

So, if this server has a printer connected to LPT1, and the printer will be shared over the LAN, type **net** and press (ENTER) at the server's keyboard to start the NET menu. Select the Network Disk Drives and Printers option under Main Functions. Move the highlight line down to LPT1 and press (ENTER). Select this server's own name (TOM) and its own printer (LPT1), and then end NET. From that point on, you can use the server's shared printer from that server without conflicting with other workstations that also use the printer.

Canceling Printer Redirection from the NET Menu

To cancel printer redirection, follow the same steps that you followed to cancel disk redirection. Type **net** to start the NET menu. From the Main Functions menu, select Network Disk Drives and Printers. Move the cursor down to the LPT2 line or whichever redirected printer you need to cancel. Press (DEL). Then press (ENTER) to confirm the cancellation. Finally, press (ESC) twice to end NET.

Printer Redirection from the DOS Prompt

As was true for disk redirection, you can use DOS commands to control printer redirection instead of the NET menu.

Printer Access from a Workstation or Server

This command performs the same function as the example that used the NET menu to redirect the workstation's LPT2 to a server's shared printer.

```
net use lpt2 \\tom\@printer
```

You can probably guess the command that redirects the server's own LPT1 port to its own printer. Here it is.

```
net use lpt1 \\tom\@printer
```

In place of lpt1 and lpt2 in these commands, you can instead use lpt3, com1, or com2. A server can have up to five shared printers attached, and a workstation can redirect up to five device names to shared printers (not necessarily all on the same server): LPT1, LPT2, LPT3, COM1, and COM2. You can add these commands to your STARTNET.BAT file to automatically redirect printers whenever you start LANtastic.

Printer Redirection Cancellation

To cancel printer redirection, use the NET UNUSE command and specify the printer device name you want to cancel. This example cancels redirection of LPT2:

```
net unuse lpt2
```

Printer Queue Control

When you redirect your workstation's printer port to a server's shared printer, you cause something to occur that may not be obvious. Consider for a moment what must happen if two workstations both redirect printer output to the same shared printer. They both can send output to the printer at the same time. How can this possibly work? Won't the printer print a garble of both sets of output mixed together? Or maybe it will print one page from one workstation, then one from the other, then another page from the first workstation, and so on?

The correct answer is neither. Instead of sending your printer output directly to the shared printer, LANtastic temporarily stores your printer output on the server's hard disk. Each workstation's output is printed in its entirety when it is completely ready. (Because of this need for temporary disk storage, be sure your server has plenty of extra disk space if a shared printer is attached.)

LANtastic keeps track of separate printer output by the use of a *printer queue*. A queue (pronounced like the letter Q) is simply a waiting line—the computer equivalent of what you stand in while waiting for a bank teller. LANtastic copies each workstation's printer output to a separate disk file and keeps track of which files are associated with each user. If several users send printed reports to the same shared printer when the printer is already busy printing, LANtastic organizes a waiting line (a queue) for those print files; each file waits in its place until the printer is available. The area on the server's disk where all this printer information is stored is called the *printer spool area,* or just the *print spool.* (The disk area is located in the LANTASTI.NET directory unless you chose a different name during INSTALL.) When your workstation sends printer output to the server's hard disk, the process is called *spooling.* Afterwards, when the server sends the data from its hard disk to the printer, the process is called *despooling.* Each printer file the server stores on disk is called a *print file* or a *print job.*

Because the printer queue can build up (like a bank on Friday afternoon), and also because printers sometimes jam or run out of paper, LANtastic has facilities under the NET menu to control the print files in a server's printer queue. Here is a brief description of how you can use the NET menu to work with a printer queue from your workstation.

Type **net**, press ENTER, and select the second option in the Main Functions menu box, Printer Queue Management. Select the server name for the printer queue you want to work on. The screen then looks like Figure 6-11.

This example shows what the screen looks like after user CMS sends three print files to printer LPT1 on server TOM. The main printer queue manipulation screen has three data areas. The top area shows all print files this user has sent to the printer and that still remain on the queue. This example shows three such jobs, and as you can see from the center column in Figure 6-11,

Figure 6-11. *The NET menu's printer queue manipulation screen*

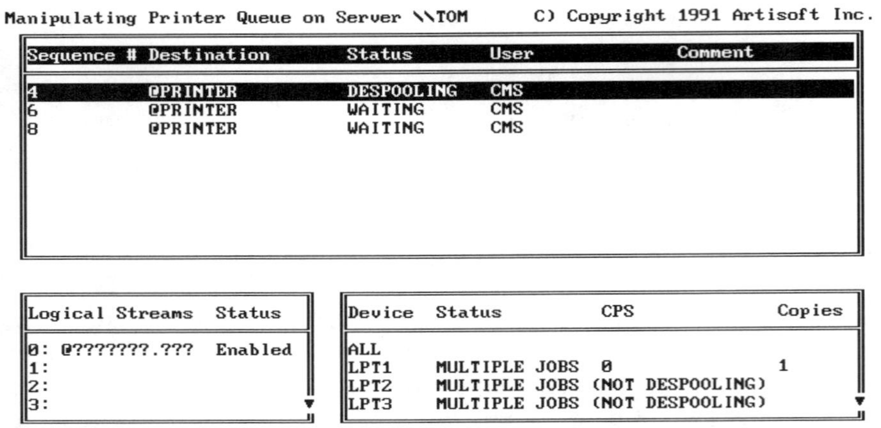

one of the files is *despooling* (being sent to the printer) while the other two are *waiting.* Other typical status indicators are *held* (because a workstation user asked to hold the job rather than print it immediately), *updating* (the print job is in the process of transferring from the workstation to the print queue), and *deleted* (the job was canceled while printing).

The lower-left area shows the logical print stream names that are enabled. A print stream is a separate category of printed output. You might want to establish a special stream name for a special preprinted form you sometimes need to print on. With a special stream that is disabled, you can use your word processor to send a print job to the shared printer and direct it to this special print stream name. The output won't start printing because you have disabled this print stream. Then, after you load the special form paper into the printer, you can enable the print stream to print your output on the forms.

The logical stream named @???????.??? refers to all print stream names, so in this example all print streams are enabled.

The lower-right area shows the status of each print device. You can use this area to control a shared printer, much like the top screen area controls a single print file.

Put yourself in the CMS workstation user's position at a workstation. You sent three print jobs to the printer, but not all are done printing. What can you do to control these jobs?

Select the first job on the list in the top window. (Use the TAB key to move the highlight from one window to another if necessary; then use the ↑ and ↓ keys.) After you press ENTER with the top job highlighted, the screen looks like Figure 6-12.

The one-line descriptions for each command explain your options. You can do any of these things:

- *Show* more information about the print file, such as the date and time created and the size in bytes.
- *Delete* the print file from the queue, as is desirable after a document starts printing and you discover it isn't formatted the way you want.
- *Hold* the print file so it won't print now.
- *Release* the print file from the hold you previously put on it.
- *View* the print file to see exactly what data you sent to the shared printer, including printer control codes.
- *Copy* the print file to another filename that you select.
- *Rush* the print file, which puts it at the top of the print queue so it will print next. This option is available to you only if you are granted the *Q privilege,* sometimes called *Super Queue.* This is a special privileged status usually reserved for the LAN administrator. (Otherwise, everyone might try to increase print file priorities.) If you use the default INSTALL settings, no one has the Q privilege. You can use the NET_MGR program, explained in Chapters 10 and 14, to assign the Q privilege.

6

Of these queue control options, the most commonly used are View, to see which print file is which when you print several in succession, and Delete, to cancel printing a document you don't want.

The NET program even includes a simple text editor so you can create a small temporary text file and send it to the printer, or send a text file that already exists. Select the upper window and press INS to insert a new print file. Then press ENTER to select the Use Screen Editor option, and ENTER again to route the output to the server's shared printer. NET then displays a

Figure 6-12. *The Queue Control options for a print file*

```
Manipulating Printer Queue on Server \\TOM      C) Copyright 1991 Artisoft Inc.

Sequence # Destination        Status       User              Comment

4          @PRINTER           DESPOOLING   CMS
6          @PRINTER           WAITING      CMS
8          @P
              Queue Control

              Show    More information about selected entry
              Delete  Remove selected entry from queue
              Hold    Suspend despooling of selected entry
              Release Allow selected entry to be despooled
              View    View contents of selected entry
              Copy    Copy selected entry to file
              Rush    Gives queue entry top priority
Logical Strea                                                   Copies

0: @???????.???  Enabled     ALL
1:                           LPT1     MULTIPLE JOBS  0               1
2:                           LPT2     MULTIPLE JOBS (NOT DESPOOLING)
3:                           LPT3     MULTIPLE JOBS (NOT DESPOOLING)

Enter-Select Option, Esc-Exit, F1-Help
```

screen on which you can type whatever printed message you like. After you enter the message, press F2 to dispatch the new print file to the print queue. For most users, this feature is not often needed—people are much more likely to send printed output to a shared printer from a word processor or spreadsheet program. However, little niceties like this editor explain why LANtastic has become so popular.

Sometimes you want to control everything that goes to a printer, not just a single print job. The lower-right area of the printer queue manipulation screen gives you this capability. Use the TAB key to highlight the lower-right area. Then use the ↓ key to select the line for LPT1 and press ENTER. Figure 6-13 shows the options NET presents when you select TOM's printer LPT1. Note that these device names, such as LPT1, refer to the physical device connection on the server and not the redirected name you use on your workstation.

As you can see, the options are similar to the options NET provides for individual print files. Note that you don't have to select these options from a server. You can control the printer queues for shared printers from a workstation.

Figure 6-13. *The Printer Control options for a server's shared printer*

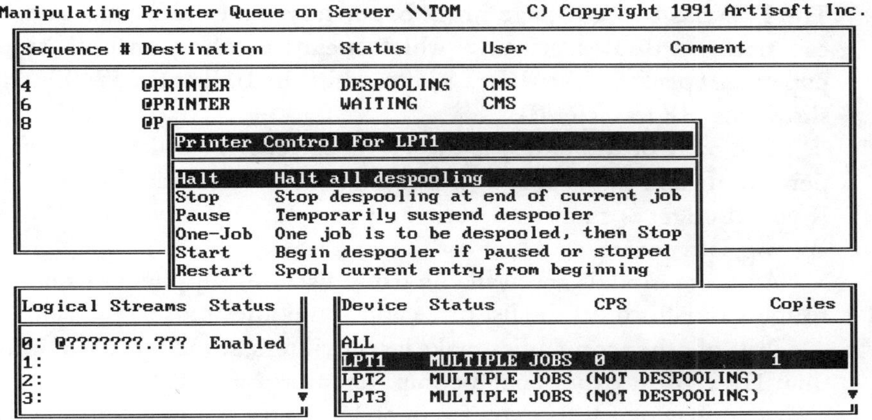

Shared Printer Products

If you have worked with several PC printers you have undoubtedly already formed opinions about what you do and don't like. A printer in a LAN environment is a slightly different situation, however. This section briefly discusses a few products that are worth considering for your LAN.

In today's PC world, the most desirable workhorse printer is a laser printer. And in today's marketplace, Hewlett-Packard makes the leading laser printers. Beginning with the original HP LaserJet printer, HP has established the standards against which other printer products are compared. The current product line is the HP LaserJet III series. The top of the line is the HP LaserJet IIISi, shown in Figure 6-14. This model prints at a rate of 17 pages per minute (ppm). It has two 500-sheet input paper trays, an optional feeder for up to 100 envelopes, and can stack up to 500 pages of output. These capacities make it ideally suited for high-volume printing on a medium to large LAN, and it has collected an impressive array of awards as a LAN printer. The list price is steep, however: $5495.

On a smaller LAN with lower volume printing needs, the regular HP LaserJet III or IIID are more appropriate. Both print eight pages per minute. The IIID has two 200-page input paper trays and the III has one. The IIID can perform duplex printing, which means printing on both sides of the paper. List price for the IIID is $3495, while the III lists for $2495. Figure 6-15 shows the HP LaserJet III.

The baby of the family is the HP LaserJet IIIP, which prints four pages per minute and holds only 70 input pages in a single tray. List price is $1695. If your budget is small and your output volume is low, the IIIP may be an appropriate choice.

All these models are available from discount suppliers or mail order for roughly one-third off the list price and sometimes more.

Lots of other companies make laser printers, some for sale at lower prices than HP's. Most experienced computer users have discovered that printers are worth paying a little extra for in order to ensure high quality and minimal problems. Unless you can save a lot of money compared to an HP printer, you are safest sticking with HP. For most HP models, the price difference

Figure 6-14. *The Hewlett-Packard LaserJet IIISi*

Figure 6-15. *The Hewlett-Packard LaserJet III*

from a discount source compared to other brands isn't very much. However, if you need the speed of an HP IIISi but can't handle the price, consider the Texas Instruments microLaser XL PS35. It prints at 16 ppm, has built-in PostScript capability (an extra-cost option for the HP models), and lists for $3149. Unfortunately it doesn't accept HP-compatible font cartridges and has only a 250-page input paper tray. A second input paper tray that handles 500 pages is $345 extra.

Laser Printer Font Cartridges If you share a laser printer on a LAN, you may want a special font cartridge. Laser printers come with only a few built-in fonts (typefaces). If you need fonts other than the built-in ones, you have to use either a font cartridge or downloadable soft fonts. Soft fonts are disk files that you copy to a laser printer to temporarily give it the capability to print other special fonts. For a printer connected to a single PC, this soft font approach is fine. However, using soft fonts on a shared printer on a LAN is generally not practical. Different users want to download different fonts, and the printer's memory has room for only so many. Each user would have to reset the printer with a special command and then download his or her own special fonts. This is a slow process. Instead, install a multi-font cartridge. Then a wide variety of fonts is always available to everyone immediately.

Font cartridges come in two varieties. One has a set of unchangeable fonts and the other is "customizable," meaning that you can put your own soft fonts in it for semi-permanent usage. Some models are for early HP printers–typically the model II family and earlier–and others are for the HP III family, which supports scalable fonts. *Scalable fonts* are fonts the printer can change to virtually any size. The HP II family cannot scale fonts; a Times Roman 10-point font and a Times Roman 12-point font are separate fonts and each takes up space in the printer. In fact, a Times Roman 10-point medium upright portrait-orientation font is different from the same font in landscape orientation. (*Portrait* means vertically oriented on the paper as a portrait in a gallery might be; *landscape* means horizontally oriented on the paper.) For the HP III family, a single Times Roman scalable font exists and can be scaled to any size you choose.

The following gives information about the two leading companies in the multi-font cartridge field:

- Pacific Data Products (9125 Rehco Road, San Diego, CA 92121, 619-552-0880). For the HP III family, Pacific Data Products sells the Complete Font Library Cartridge, which supports 51 typefaces that are all scalable by the HP III from .25 point to 999.75 point size in .25 point increments. (For your reference, 72-point type is one inch high; people seldom need fonts smaller than 6 points or larger than 36 points.) For the HP II family and earlier (and it also works on the HP III) they sell the "25 in One!" cartridge, which contains 172 combinations of typestyle, size, symbol set, and orientation. Their customizable cartridge, called the FontBank Cartridge, works for both the HP II and III printer families. It comes with either .75 or 1.5 megabytes of storage space for fonts you select. All these products have list prices of $399 except the .75 megabyte FontBank Cartridge, which is $299.
- IQ Engineering (685 N. Pastoria Ave., Sunnyvale, CA 94086, 800-765-3668 or 408-733-1161). IQ Engineering has a similar line of products. The Super Cartridge 3 Creative Collection has 66 scalable typefaces. The Super Cartridge 2 is a competitor to the Pacific Data Products "25 in One!" cartridge for portrait orientation; they also

have a landscape model. The list price is $399 for each. IQ has no customizable cartridge at this time.

Electronic Mail

LANtastic's built-in electronic mail feature is a convenient way to improve communication within a workgroup. Users can send computer messages to other users over the LAN. Recipients can read the messages and delete them without wasting paper. In practice, most small workgroups with all users in the same small office area find no advantage to using electronic mail. However, if everyone in your workgroup has a computer connected to the LAN and everyone makes frequent use of the computers, give e-mail a try to see if you find it useful. On the other hand, if some key group members often go for days without turning their computers on, they won't receive e-mail messages in a timely way and as a result e-mail isn't a good communications solution.

LANtastic's e-mail is adequate for the simple requirements of most workgroups. Other e-mail products, such as the groupware products listed in Chapter 2, have additional capabilities and conveniences.

Setting Up E-Mail

LANtastic's e-mail is extremely easy to set up. In fact, you don't really have to set up anything at all. The e-mail capability is built into the LANtastic network operating system. When you send a message, it is stored on a server's hard disk. This server is sometimes called a *mail server,* and can be the same server you use for file sharing and printer sharing.

Even though you don't really *need* to do anything to set up LANtastic's e-mail, some preparation is helpful. Before you start using e-mail in your workgroup, take a few minutes to do these things.

- *Agree upon a server* If you have more than one server on your LANtastic LAN, you need to decide which server will store the mail messages. In most workgroups this is an easy decision because either the group uses only one server or, if the group uses several servers, one server is the primary server. You can have more than one mail server if you like, but expect confusion when users forget to search all servers for mail messages. Better to have just one.

- *Have enough disk space* Even though most e-mail messages are small, they do take up disk space. Be sure the server's hard disk has plenty of room and that someone periodically cleans up the hard disk. Server disk cleanup should be one of the regular duties of a LAN administrator, discussed in Chapter 11.
- *Be sure the server is always available* LANtastic is so flexible that some workgroups constantly find reasons to reconfigure their servers and workstations. However, after users become dependent on e-mail as a fundamental means of group communication, the need for *reliable* e-mail service becomes critical. If the LAN administrator or LAN users frequently reconfigure, rename, or reboot the mail server, users can't depend on e-mail for communication. Neither snow nor rain nor heat nor gloom of night should stay your server from the swift completion of its appointed e-mail rounds.
- *Set up user accounts* If your workgroup really plans to rely on e-mail, you should set up user accounts for everyone. That way each user can see the precise name of every other user. Otherwise, you might send a message to JIM and not realize he decided to start calling himself JAMES. JAMES will never receive a message sent to JIM. If you set up user accounts, each user can display a list of all other usernames available, whether those users are currently logged on to the mail server or not. In addition, user accounts and passwords promote privacy in e-mail communications. Chapter 10 explains user accounts.

Using E-Mail

LANtastic's e-mail is most easily available through the NET menu. Type **net** and press (ENTER) to bring up the menu. Use the (↓) key to move the cursor to the third option in NET's Main Functions menu box, Mail Services. Press (ENTER) and you bring up a Server Connections menu box. Select the server name where mail messages are stored. If you haven't logged in, NET either automatically logs you in (in LANtastic version 4.1 with no security) or prompts you for your username and password. Be sure to enter the username that other group members know you by. Otherwise, LANtastic has no way to connect you to your mail. If you automatically log in, your username is your machine name as selected during the INSTALL process.

Figure 6-16 shows what the opening mail screen looks like when you first bring up NET's mail services. The top half of the screen shows incoming mail addressed to you. The bottom half is for mail you send to other people. The TAB key moves the highlight line back and forth between the top and bottom halves.

Sending E-Mail

Suppose you are a user named CMS (Charlie M. Smith, perhaps?) and you want to send a message to TOM. Press INS to tell NET you want to send mail. NET brings up a menu box called Send Mail Options. This box presents you with three choices.

6

- *Use Mail Editor* This option puts you under control of NET's simple text editor, which you can use to type your mail message.
- *Send Text File* If you have already written your message and saved it in a disk file, use this option to send the file as your message.
- *Send Voice File* This option only applies if both you and the message recipient have an Artisoft Sounding Board. Chapter 8 explains how to install and use this device as well as how to use it to send and receive voice messages.

Select the first option, Use Mail Editor. This brings up a mostly blank screen (except for key reminders on the top and bottom) in which you can type your message. Enter a message using the standard editing keys: The four cursor movement keys (↑, ↓, ←, →), BACKSPACE, DEL, HOME, END, and ENTER. Figure 6-17 shows the screen with a typed message.

Once you are satisfied with the message, press F2 to send the message. NET prompts you for the name of the user you want to receive the message. Enter **TOM**, as shown in Figure 6-18. Even though the prompting message says you can press F10 to see a list of possible recipients, you really can't unless your LAN administrator has set up user accounts for all the users. If

Figure 6-16. *The initial screen for manipulating mail*

Manipulating Mail on Server \\TOM C) Copyright 1991 Artisoft Inc.

INcoming Mail From Comment

OUTgoing Mail To Comment

Enter-Select Entry, Ins-Send Mail, Del-Delete Entry, Tab-Switch Windows, F1-Help

Figure 6-17. *A message entered using NET's text editor*

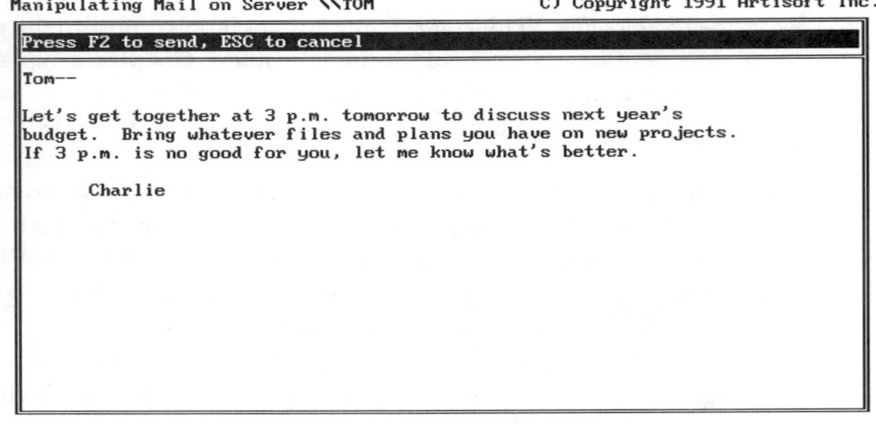

Figure 6-18. After pressing (F2)*, enter the recipient's name (in this case, TOM)*

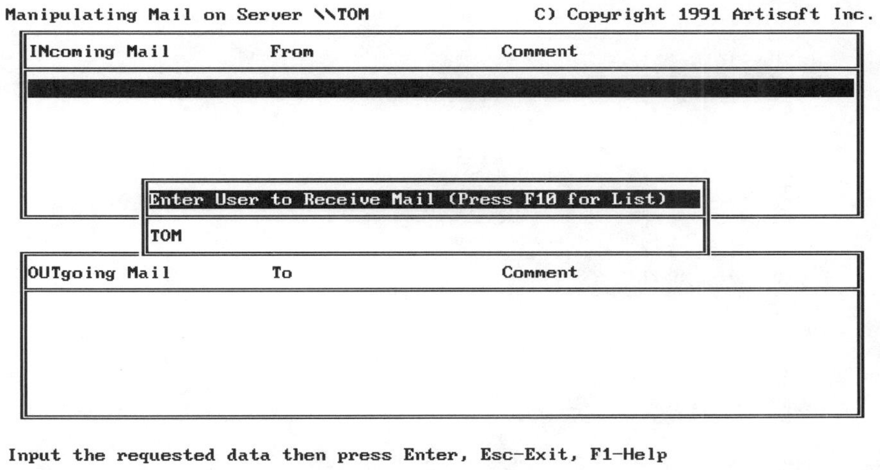

```
Manipulating Mail on Server \\TOM                C) Copyright 1991 Artisoft Inc.

INcoming Mail          From                 Comment


              Enter User to Receive Mail (Press F10 for List)
              TOM

OUTgoing Mail          To                   Comment


Input the requested data then press Enter, Esc-Exit, F1-Help
```

6

you use the default options from the INSTALL program, the only user is * (an asterisk), which is a group user account for all users. Therefore, you have to know the exact name for the user and spell it right (another reason why short, simple usernames are best).

Next NET prompts you for a comment. While a comment is optional, it's best to enter one because that way the recipient can quickly see what each message is about if there are several of them. Figure 6-19 shows the screen after CMS enters a comment for this message.

Finally, CMS presses (ENTER) and NET sends the message. After a brief delay, CMS sees the message in the incoming (no, not his outgoing) mail area. This means that CMS can look at the message to review its contents if he likes.

Receiving E-Mail

If TOM is logged in to server TOM when CMS sends the mail message, he immediately receives a pop-up message on his screen and hears three beeps. If TOM currently has his screen in graphics mode (as he would if running a graphics program or some word processors in graphics mode), the beeps sound but no message is displayed. The message stays on the screen

Figure 6-19. *CMS enters a comment to identify the message*

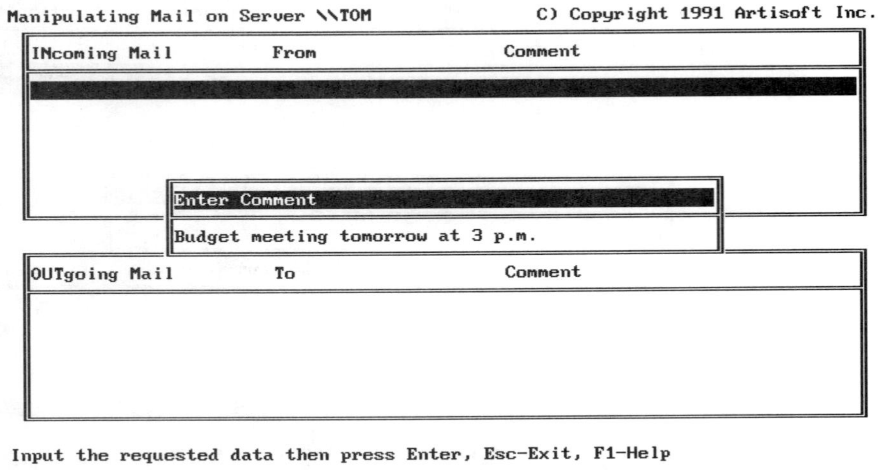

```
Manipulating Mail on Server \\TOM            C) Copyright 1991 Artisoft Inc.

INcoming Mail          From                  Comment

            Enter Comment
            Budget meeting tomorrow at 3 p.m.

OUTgoing Mail          To                    Comment

Input the requested data then press Enter, Esc-Exit, F1-Help
```

for 15 seconds or until the recipient presses (ESC). This pop-up message does not show the actual mail message that CMS sent. It's just a message to tell him mail just arrived.

If TOM is not logged in, he won't receive a pop-up message. Instead, he has to check for mail using NET in order to see that he has a message. He can either use the NET menu and select the Mail Services function, or he can enter the command **net postbox** to get a summary of mail waiting for him on all servers.

To view the contents of the mail message, TOM can use the NET menu, choose Mail Services, and select the mail server name. He then sees a screen like Figure 6-20 that shows his incoming mail.

The incoming mail list shows the date and time the mail was sent, who it came from, and the short comment or title of the mail message. When TOM highlights the message and presses (ENTER), NET displays his options for handling the incoming message, plus a description of the message, as shown in Figure 6-21.

Now TOM has four choices, listed in the Mail Options menu box.

- *Read Mail* This displays the mail message on a screen like the one in which CMS composed the message.
- *Forward Copy of Mail* TOM can send the mail to another user. All he has to do is enter the name of the new user. He can forward the same comment/title that the sender (CMS) used or enter his own. The sender can also use this option to send the mail to multiple users, if he likes. All he has to do is enter each user's name in turn and accept the existing comment for each.
- *Copy Mail to File* To save the mail, TOM can put it in a file with a name he chooses. TOM can also simply leave the mail on the mail queue for future reference, but if he wants to save it he should save it in his own file instead. This prevents the mail queue from growing endlessly due to everyone leaving old mail there. Also, saving the message in his own file allows TOM to use filenames of his choosing. Unfortunately NET does not save the mail's comment or to/from names, so everyone should get into the habit of showing such information in the message body. Also, NET has no capability to append a mail message to the end of a file that already contains other saved mail messages. Each mail message is saved in its own file and if you save a new message in a filename that already exists, the old file is replaced (after you give permission), not extended. This makes accumulation of a sequence of messages awkward.
- *Delete Mail* Use Delete Mail to delete the mail from the mail queue on the server. After you read a mail message you should delete it, as just explained. Save the message in a file first if you want to, or print it by selecting Copy Mail To File and entering LPT1 (or whatever port has a printer connected or redirected). The sender can also delete a message, and if he does so before the recipient reads the message then the recipient will never see it. The sender in this way can correct an erroneous message. Normally, however, the recipient deletes a message after reading it.

Mail Security

Under normal circumstances only the sender and recipient can view or delete a mail message. However, if you do not establish user accounts and passwords (discussed in Chapter 10), then anyone can log in to any server

Figure 6-20. *TOM sees his incoming mail from CMS*

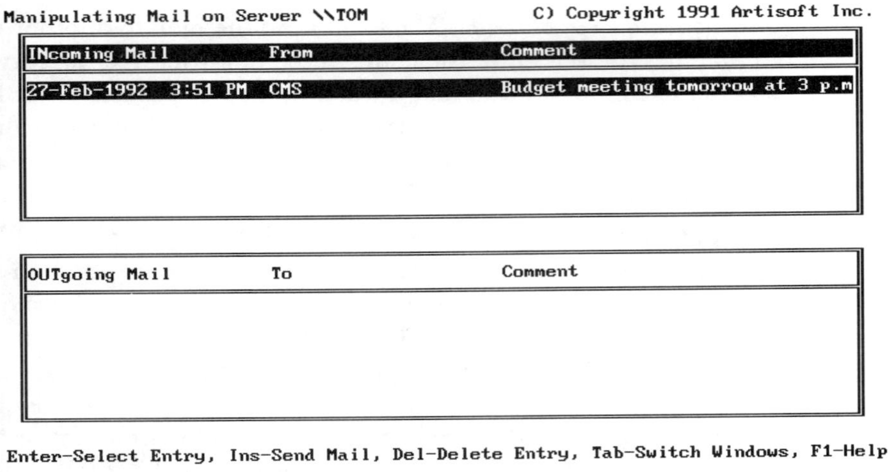

Manipulating Mail on Server \\TOM
C) Copyright 1991 Artisoft Inc.
INcoming Mail
From
Comment
27-Feb-1992 3:51 PM CMS Budget meeting tomorrow at 3 p.m
OUTgoing Mail
To
Comment
Enter-Select Entry, Ins-Send Mail, Del-Delete Entry, Tab-Switch Windows, F1-Help

Figure 6-21. *TOM selects the incoming mail message from CMS*

Manipulating Mail on Server \\TOM
C) Copyright 1991 Artisoft Inc.
INcoming Mail
From
Comment
27-Feb-1992 3:51 PM CMS Budget meeting tomorrow at 3 p.m
Mail Options
Read Mail
Forward Copy of Mail
Copy Mail to File
Delete Mail
Description of Mail
OUTgoi
To: TOM
From: CMS
Date: 27-Feb-1992 3:51 PM
Size: 213
Comment: Budget meeting tomorrow at 3 p.m.
Enter-Select Option, Esc-Exit, F1-Help

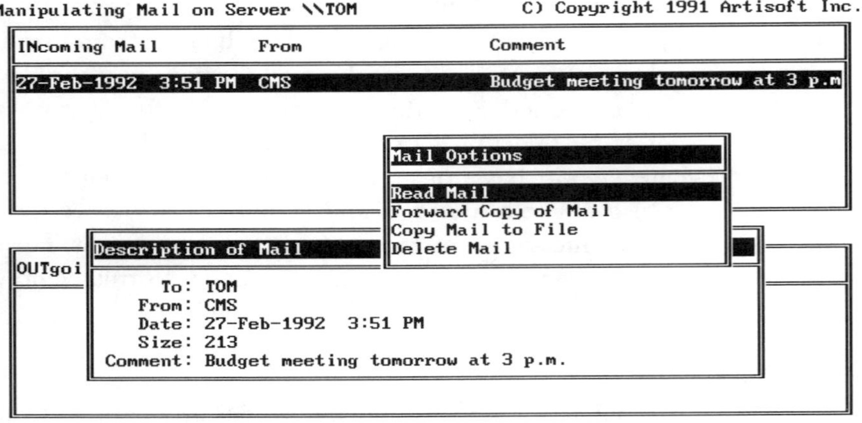

using any username. (With LANtastic version 4.1, the automatic login causes you to use the computer's machine name; however, someone could easily reinstall LANtastic and provide a different machine name or simply use the **net login** command.) Even if you are not TOM, you can say you are TOM and retrieve TOM's mail. You can also send mail to someone else as if it came from TOM. You might find this entertaining, but TOM might be considerably less amused. Many people think of their mail as personal, whether it's e-mail, office mail, or U.S. Mail. Before your workgroup starts using e-mail, be sure everyone understands the security, or lack of security, that is in effect. If everyone can read and delete everyone's mail, be sure everyone understands and accepts this lack of privacy. If this lack of privacy is not acceptable, take advantage of user accounts and passwords to provide security.

If you implement security, some lack of privacy still exists. The LAN administrator needs to have the *M privilege* (sometimes called the *Super Mail privilege,* and assigned using the NET_MGR program explained in Chapter 10) to perform maintenance on the server's hard disk. This means the LAN administrator can choose to read everyone's mail. That's better than allowing everyone to read all the mail, but it's still less than total privacy. Be sure users understand the limitations of their privacy. Also be sure the LAN administrator is a trusted individual who does not abuse this capability.

7

Sharing Other Resources: CD-ROMs, Modems, and Other Devices

The first six chapters covered the basics of LANs and LANtastic. Many people successfully use LANtastic every day without knowing anything more than what those six chapters cover. You might decide to join them. If so, that's fine. However, LANtastic has some additional capabilities that can make you and your workgroup more productive. This chapter begins the discussion of some additional topics that are less commonly implemented by LANtastic users, but nevertheless can be worthwhile, interesting, and even fun. (Don't tell the boss.)

This chapter discusses attachment and use of the following devices:

- CD-ROM disk drives
- Shared modems and two-way plotters
- Tape backup systems
- Portable PCs

Two Artisoft products, ArtiCom and Central Station, are explained as part of this discussion. ArtiCom is designed to share two-way serial devices, such as modems and certain plotters that require two-way communication. Central Station allows you to connect a portable PC to a LANtastic LAN.

Sharing CD-ROM Disk Drives

The CD-ROM (compact disk, read-only memory) is a relatively recent data storage and retrieval development with rapidly growing popularity. Think of a CD-ROM as an incredibly high-capacity floppy disk drive with which you can read but not write data—that is, you can copy data *from* the CD-ROM, but not *to* it. As a result, the CD-ROM disk is called a read-only device. The similarity to a floppy disk drive is that a CD-ROM consists of a removable *CD-ROM disk* plus a *CD-ROM disk drive* that reads it. Using LANtastic, you can install a CD-ROM disk drive on a server computer to let everyone on the LAN access the CD-ROM disk in it. Because a CD-ROM works a bit differently from a regular hard disk or floppy disk, you need to take a few extra steps to make it available to workstations. These steps are explained in this section.

The familiar audio CD, which has virtually replaced vinyl record albums, can hold over 60 minutes of music. The computer CD-ROM disk is based on the same technology and looks identical, but instead of music can hold over 600 megabytes of data. (In fact, most CD-ROM drives can also play audio CDs.) In both cases, the CD-ROM disk is a silvery platter about 4.7 inches in diameter and 1/16 of an inch thick.

Just how much is 600 megabytes? Well, this book contains about 600,000 characters of text. Each character occupies one byte, so this book is 0.6 megabytes of text data. (Assume a megabyte is one million bytes, not 1,048,576, which is 1024 × 1024, and is sometimes what people mean by a megabyte.) Divide 600 by 0.6 and the result is that the text of one thousand books the size of this one could all fit on one single CD-ROM disk. Using some simple data compression techniques, even more data would fit. Either way, that's an awful lot of data in such a small package.

Not all of the 600 megabytes is available for data storage. Because so much data is stored on each disk, CD-ROMs are designed to quickly find data in a number of ways. In order to speed up the access time to any data on the

CD-ROM disk, elaborate indexing schemes are employed. These indexes work like the card catalog in a library—you can look in the card catalog to find which books the library has about a subject. Then you can go straight to the proper shelf based on the Dewey Decimal System number (or, in some libraries, the Library of Congress number). You don't have to search through every book on the shelves until you find the one you want.

CD-ROM indexes work much the same way. For example, the *Los Angeles Times* database (available from Dialog Information Services) contains on one CD-ROM disk all that newspaper's articles published in a six-month period. You can search for all articles that contain a single word that you provide. For example, if you enter the word **lawsuit** the software quickly searches an index file and tells you within a second or two (timings vary depending on the CD-ROM disk drive model) that 1636 articles from January through June of 1991 contain that word. If you ask how many of those articles also contain the word "copyright," within another second you learn that 31 do. Then you can read each article, and it takes about one or two seconds to retrieve each one. Instead of searching for words, you can search by title, author, subject, and many other criteria or combinations. Without extensive indexes to speed up the search process, the software would have to sequentially read through all the data until it finds what you request. You wouldn't sit still long enough to wait for that. Even though these indexes sometimes occupy 100 megabytes or more of CD-ROM space, that still leaves lots of space for data.

An important aspect of CD-ROM disks is that they are relatively inexpensive to manufacture. Once the manufacturer creates an original master disk, which can cost several thousand dollars, each disk copy can be produced for about $2. Costs vary depending on manufacturing techniques used and the size of the production run, but this gives you a rough idea. Do a little arithmetic and you'll see that a manufacturer who produces a few thousand CD-ROMs can make them for $4 to $10 each.

Of course, that's just the manufacturing cost. The data that goes on the CD-ROM disk doesn't come free. Someone has to research, acquire, and prepare the data and indexes. An encyclopedia, atlas, newspaper, or other CD-ROM database doesn't write itself. Also there are the typical business costs for advertising, distribution, sales commissions, profit, and so on. All of these costs greatly dwarf the manufacturing cost. As a result, a CD-ROM disk can cost anywhere from $10 to over $1000. Specialized databases for businesses or professionals generally cost the most. Mass market databases, promotional materials, and data from the public domain (such as old literary works that no longer have copyright protection) cost the least.

These are all costs for the CD-ROM disk and what is recorded on it. (People who produce and sell CD-ROM disks use the terms *CD-ROM title* or *CD-ROM software* for the disk and the data recorded on it. Sometimes CD-ROM software refers only to the computer software you run to access the CD-ROM data. This software is also called the *search engine* or *search software.*) What about the cost for a CD-ROM disk drive? You can't read the data on a CD-ROM disk unless you insert it into a CD-ROM disk drive.

As popularity has increased, prices for CD-ROM disk drives have dropped. A few years ago you had to spend $1000 or more to buy a CD-ROM disk drive. Today the most popular models are priced in the $400 to $600 range. The lower-cost models usually access data slower than more expensive models. Many models are available in "package" deals that include several CD-ROM titles, either in the base price or perhaps for $100 to $200 more. Some packages include two, three, or even six or more CD-ROM disks that might cost $500, $1000, or more if you bought them separately from the disk drive. If you shop for a CD-ROM drive, look carefully at the different package deals available.

So, for about $500 (less if you shop rigorously) you can buy a CD-ROM disk drive with a lot of reference materials included. This price is steep enough that most buyers pay it only if they have a strong need or desire for CD-ROM. Suppose you could buy one for $100. Would that make it more attractive?

In a way, that's just what you can do if you have a LANtastic LAN. Connect the CD-ROM disk drive to a server and make a few changes to software commands. Then, if you have five PCs on the LAN, all five can access the CD-ROM disk. In effect, each one pays 20 percent of the cost. If you have 10 PCs, the cost is only $50 each.

Some warnings before you run off and spend that $500:

- Some CD-ROM disk titles are sold only for a single user's use. Others permit multiple users to access the data over a LAN but charge a higher price.
- Some CD-ROM search software doesn't work over LANtastic (or any LAN). Most popular software does.

- The CD-ROM disk drive reads only one CD-ROM disk at a time. If one person needs to search an encyclopedia while another searches a newspaper database, one has to wait. Every time you want to change to a different CD-ROM disk, you have to go to the server, manually remove one disk, and insert another. Some special multi-disk CD-ROM players are available to automatically switch between different CD-ROMs, but they are much more expensive. One model takes seven seconds to switch CD-ROM disks. That may seem quick, but computer users who are accustomed to instantaneous responses find the delay interminable. See the section on "CD-ROM Disk Drive Products" later in this chapter for more information. Another alternative, of course, is to install more than one CD-ROM drive on your LAN so you can always leave a different database on each one.
- A CD-ROM disk is much slower than a hard disk. If more than three or four users search the disk at once, everyone's response can become extremely slow. Instead of waiting one or two seconds to find a dictionary entry or a magazine article, you might wait 10 or 20 seconds. Many users become impatient after five seconds or so.

Installing a CD-ROM Disk Drive

Not all CD-ROM disk drives are the same, but most are pretty similar. Here's a short description of how to install two different models, the Toshiba TXM3300 (shown on the right in Figure 7-1) and the Chinon CDC-431, each in a different computer. Both of these models are external CD-ROM drives, meaning that they are separate boxes that sit outside your computer's system unit. Internal CD-ROM drives are also available, which install like a floppy disk drive inside your computer. Toshiba's internal model that is equivalent to the TXM3300 is called the XM-3300 and is shown at the left in Figure 7-1.

An external CD-ROM drive kit typically consists of the drive itself, an interface card you install in the server, a connecting cable, a power cable, and a floppy disk with CD-ROM driver software. Be sure the interface card is included unless you don't need one. If your computer's hard disk uses a SCSI (small computer system interface) controller card, you may be able to connect the CD-ROM drive to the same interface.

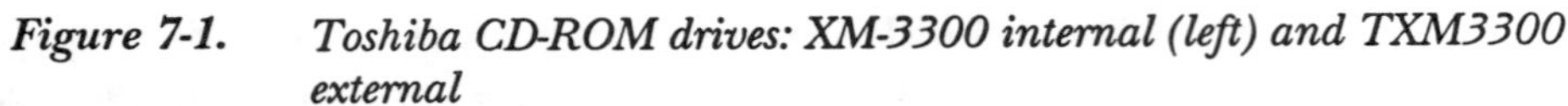

Figure 7-1. *Toshiba CD-ROM drives: XM-3300 internal (left) and TXM3300 external*

CD-ROM Hardware Installation

Step one of the hardware installation is to install the interface card, if you need one, on the server computer. Both the Toshiba and the Chinon products come with SCSI interface cards that install much like any other add-on card, such as the LAN cards described in Chapter 5. The only difficulty might arise if the CD-ROM card's settings for IRQ, a RAM memory area, or I/O ports conflict with the LAN card or some other card in your computer. The Toshiba's interface card comes with default settings of 5 for the IRQ (which can instead be set to 3), and an 8K memory area starting at hex address CA00:0000, switchable instead to C800:0000, CE00:0000, or DE00:0000. The Toshiba card does not use I/O port addresses, so there's no chance to conflict with the IOBASE setting of a LANtastic AE-2 LAN card, for example.

The Chinon interface card needs a range of 16 I/O port addresses and by default uses ones starting at hex address 300. This is the same range used by default for IOBASE on a LANtastic AE-2 or AE-3 card, so you have to change one or the other if you want both to run in the same computer. Removing a jumper on the Chinon board changes the address to 320 and solves the problem. (On an XT computer, the 320 address range would conflict with the hard disk controller, so leaving the CD-ROM controller at 300 and switching the LAN card to 340 would solve the conflict.) The Chinon interface card doesn't use IRQ or RAM memory settings.

Once the card is installed, the next step is to install the cable between the interface card and the CD-ROM drive. For both brands, the cable connects easily and is secured by screws or clips.

Then, because these are both SCSI devices, you have to set the SCSI device number on the drive. Because you can daisy-chain several SCSI devices on the same SCSI interface card, each needs a unique number. The Chinon drive has a default setting of 0 (zero) and the Toshiba is set to 4. Both can be left to these settings unless they conflict with another SCSI device on the same interface card. If there's a conflict, it's a simple matter to flip a few switches or change jumpers to select a new number.

The end of each SCSI daisy chain requires a terminator. The Toshiba drive requires attachment of a plug device. The Chinon uses switches, which by default are set to the terminator position.

Finally, you connect a power cable between the drive and a wall outlet or other power source to complete hardware installation.

CD-ROM Software Installation

Like the LAN NOS software, CD-ROM software is designed in layers. A low-level CD-ROM driver controls the CD-ROM disk drive itself. A high-level CD-ROM driver, called Microsoft CD Extensions, or MSCDEX, interfaces between the low-level driver and DOS. On top of that layer is the application program for the particular CD-ROM database product you use. The application program contains the search software. Figure 7-2 shows these layers.

As a result, the software installation process requires several steps. Each step is simple, but follow them carefully in order to fit all the pieces together properly.

1. Install the CD-ROM driver software on your hard disk. The CD-ROM driver disk that comes with the CD-ROM drive typically comes with a SETUP or INSTALL program that performs this step. Instead you may have to, or choose to, copy the files to your hard disk yourself. At least two files are necessary—the low-level driver and the high-level driver. For the Toshiba drive, the SETUP procedure

creates a directory called DEV on the hard disk in which it puts the low-level driver program, called MDSCD_FD.SYS. SETUP creates another directory called BIN for the high-level driver, MSCDEX.EXE. The Chinon drive also includes a SETUP program, but it's just as easy to copy the two files into the root directory of the hard disk. The low-level driver is called CHINON02.SYS and the high-level driver is again called MSCDEX.EXE.

Figure 7-2. Layers of software between you and a CD-ROM drive

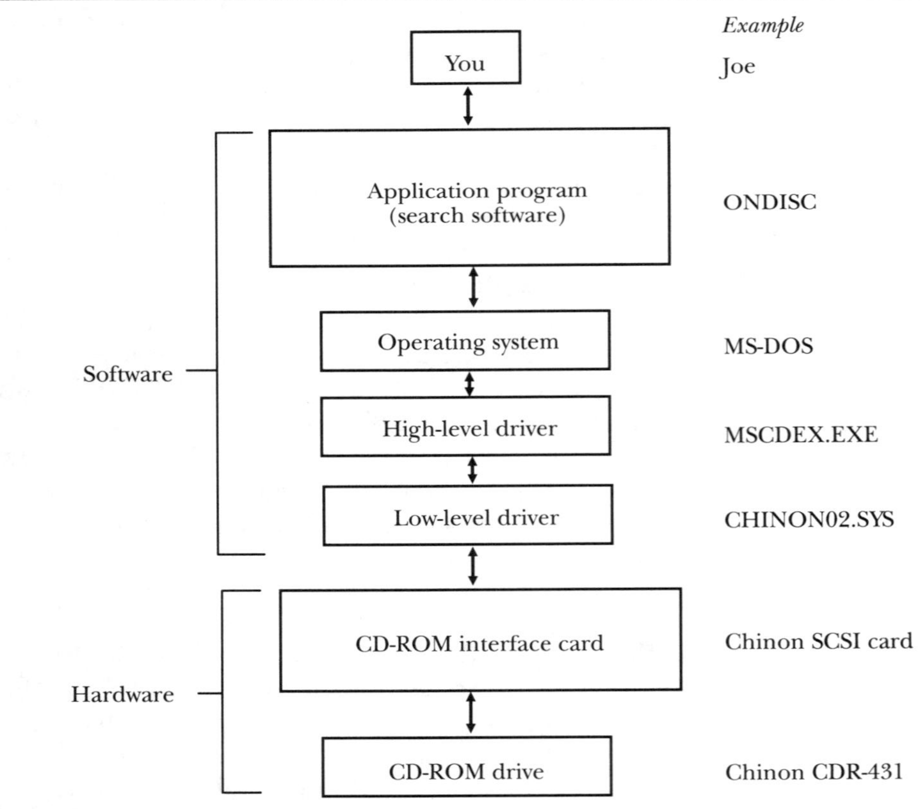

2. Change your CONFIG.SYS file to include the low-level driver software. Use EDLIN or another line editor to update CONFIG.SYS and include a line to install the low-level driver when you boot your computer. For example, this is the command for the Toshiba drive:

   ```
   device=\dev\mdscd_fd.sys /d:mscd000 /n:1
   ```

   And this is the command for the Chinon drive:

   ```
   device=chinon02.sys /d:mscd000 /a:320
   ```

   The command for the Toshiba drive specifies the location of the driver file, including the DEV subdirectory name. The parameter /d:mscd000 provides an internal name for the CD-ROM drive. The name was chosen by the SETUP program, but could be any DOS-type name up to eight characters. The last parameter, /n:1, specifies the number of CD-ROM drives installed in this computer.

   The command for the Chinon drive has a few differences. First, because the driver program is in the C drive's root directory, no subdirectory names or backslashes are needed. Second, the /a:320 parameter gives the I/O base address to which the interface card is set. The default value on this driver is 300, but you'll recall we had to change to 320 to avoid a conflict with the LANtastic AE-2 LAN card. The /d parameter provides the same device name, although there is no reason to make them the same. If these two CD-ROM drives were both installed in the same computer, different names would have to be chosen.

3. Change the LANtastic STARTNET.BAT file to run the high-level driver software, MSCDEX. Use EDLIN or another line editor to update the STARTNET.BAT file that by default LANtastic puts in your C:\LANTASTI directory. LANtastic requires you to run MSCDEX after REDIR, but before SERVER. To do this, insert a line just before the line in STARTNET.BAT that starts the server. In some versions of LANtastic this line says C:\LANTASTI\SERVER and in others, just SERVER. The added line should say:

   ```
   c:\mscdex /d:mscd000
   ```

If the MSCDEX program is in a subdirectory, as is the case for the Toshiba example, specify that directory:

```
c:\bin\mscdex /d:mscd000
```

The /d parameter again provides the device name and must match the name you used in CONFIG.SYS to install the low-level driver program. You can also provide a disk drive name by adding an /l parameter, such as /l:R to make the CD-ROM drive your R drive. Otherwise, MSCDEX uses the next available name, usually D unless you have extra hard disks or a RAM disk. The /l parameter is useful if you want to cause everyone in the workgroup to use the same drive letter for the CD-ROM drive, and therefore simplify batch files and other procedures you set up. MSCDEX has other parameters you might also want to use. They are /e to use expanded memory, /m:*x* to use *x* number of two-kilobyte buffer memory units, and /v to display at startup how MSCDEX uses memory. If you expect to have several people heavily access the CD-ROM drive, you might want to experiment with different /m values to see if performance improves. Try /m:8 or /m:12 or even more if you can afford the extra RAM used. Use /v to see how much buffer memory (called "dynamic DATA") MSCDEX uses by default.

Caution

If you used the CD-ROM SETUP program and permitted it to update your AUTOEXEC.BAT file, remove the MSCDEX command line that SETUP inserted there. LANtastic requires you to run MSCDEX after REDIR and before SERVER.

4. Install the application software on each workstation. Follow the application software manufacturer's instructions to install the search software on each workstation's hard disk.
5. Run LANtastic's NET_MGR program on the server with the CD-ROM drive to tell the server to make the CD-ROM resource available to workstations. You will learn more about NET_MGR in Chapter 10, but here's a simple introduction to let you share a CD-ROM drive. On the CD-ROM server, type the command **net_mgr** and press ENTER. (Note that the character between "net" and "mgr" is the underscore character, not the hyphen.) This command brings

up the LANtastic Network Manager main menu. Move the cursor down to the Shared Resources Management line, as shown in Figure 7-3, and press (ENTER).

This selection brings up the Resource Name menu box, which lists the resources offered to workstations. You need to add a new resource, so press (INS). LANtastic prompts you to enter a resource name. Type the name **CDROM** (as shown in Figure 7-4) and press (ENTER). Note that NET_MGR forces the name to be all capital letters.

After you enter the name, NET_MGR asks you to "Enter server's true path for this resource." Type **D:** or **R:** or whatever physical device name you assigned to the CD-ROM drive with MSCDEX, and press (ENTER). Let's say you force the name R: for this example. After you press (ENTER), NET_MGR displays the resource name list with the addition of the CDROM resource name having a local device name R:. That's just what you want, but there's another action you must take. Highlight the CDROM line and select it by pressing (ENTER). This produces a menu screen that reads, "Detailed Informa-

Figure 7-3. The LANtastic Network Manager (NET_MGR) main menu

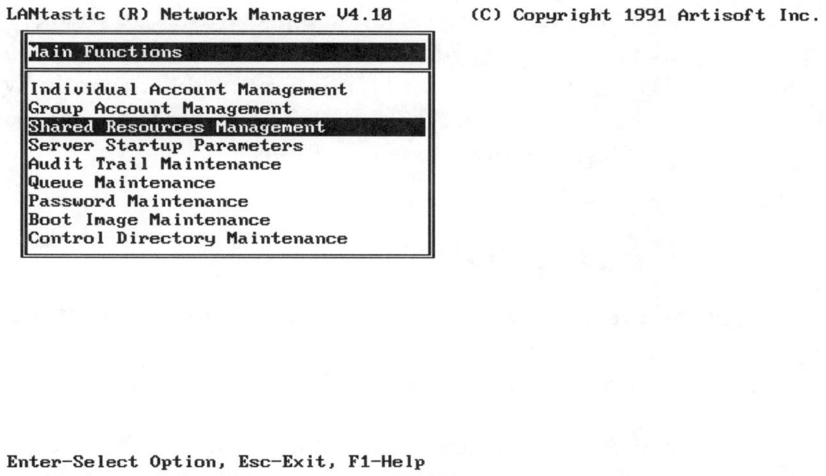

```
LANtastic (R) Network Manager V4.10        (C) Copyright 1991 Artisoft Inc.

 Main Functions

 Individual Account Management
 Group Account Management
 Shared Resources Management
 Server Startup Parameters
 Audit Trail Maintenance
 Queue Maintenance
 Password Maintenance
 Boot Image Maintenance
 Control Directory Maintenance

Enter-Select Option, Esc-Exit, F1-Help
```

Figure 7-4. *Pressing* INS *to add a resource causes NET_MGR to prompt you for a resource name*

```
NET_MGR USING: C:\LANTASTI.NET                (C) Copyright 1991 Artisoft Inc.

Resource Name => Local Path/Device

.             => C:\LANTASTI.NET
@MAIL         => MAIL
@PRINTER      => LPT1
A-DRIVE       => A:
B-DRIVE       => B:
C-DRIVE       => C:
                    Enter resource name

                    CDROM

Input the requested data then press Enter, Esc-Exit, F1-Help
```

tion for CDROM." Move the highlight down to the third line, which says " CD-ROM Drive: No," and press ENTER to change the selection to Yes, as Figure 7-5 shows. Now LANtastic knows this device is a CD-ROM disk drive and can interact with it accordingly. Press ESC three times to end NET_MGR. The server is now prepared to offer the CD-ROM drive to workstations.

Accessing a CD-ROM Drive

All the previous steps to install the hardware and software need to be done only once. Once they are done, you typically need to follow these steps each time you want to access the CD-ROM from a workstation:

1. If the CD-ROM drive is external, turn on the CD-ROM disk drive power switch. This switch is typically on the back of the drive.

Figure 7-5. *Telling NET_MGR the device is a CD-ROM drive*

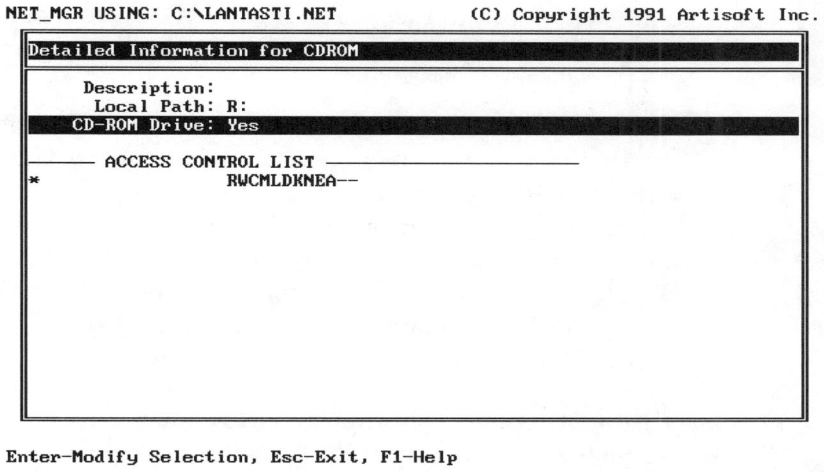

```
NET_MGR USING: C:\LANTASTI.NET            (C) Copyright 1991 Artisoft Inc.

Detailed Information for CDROM

     Description:
      Local Path: R:
    CD-ROM Drive: Yes

——— ACCESS CONTROL LIST ———
*                 RWCMLDKNEA--

Enter-Modify Selection, Esc-Exit, F1-Help
```

Internal drives get their power from the computer and don't need to be turned on separately.

2. Boot the server computer. If the CD-ROM drive is not powered on first, the low-level driver software may not install. Some will, some won't. Experiment once by leaving the CD-ROM drive powered off when you boot the server. Look for an error message that says the driver software is not installed. If you see such a message, you know the CD-ROM disk has to be turned on first.
3. Start LANtastic on the server, including the MSCDEX driver. Your start-up procedure is no different from before, except now the MSCDEX command is part of STARTNET.BAT and therefore gets loaded at the proper time.
4. Start LANtastic on the workstation if it is not already running.
5. Run NET on the workstation to redirect a disk drive name to the server's CD-ROM disk. Select Network Disk Drives and Printers from the opening menu and then select a device name for the

CD-ROM drive. The name doesn't have to match the physical name you assigned on the server. After you select the server (and log in, if necessary), you will see the added CDROM resource listed. Select it, end the NET program, and the workstation has access to the CD-ROM drive.

6. Run the application software on the workstation. You may need to specify the disk drive name you chose on the workstation, or the software may be smart enough to figure out the name. For example, Dialog Information Services provides a program called ONDISC to use with the L.A. Times and Standard & Poor's databases. To use ONDISC with a CD-ROM disk that is redirected using drive name K you type the command **ondisc k:** and press ENTER. This produces ONDISC's opening screen.

Some CD-ROM application software checks to make sure you are running MSCDEX on your computer. But MSCDEX will run only on a computer that has a CD-ROM drive attached. On the LAN, MSCDEX can run only on the server, not the workstation. As a result, these applications will refuse to run on a workstation. To solve this problem, get a program called MXSUB from Artisoft's computer bulletin board system or CompuServe (see Appendix B). This program fools the application into thinking MSCDEX is installed on the workstation.

CD-ROM Disk Drive Products

CD-ROM disk drives and CD-ROM titles are available from many sources. Popular CD-ROM disk drive brands, in addition to Toshiba and Chinon, are Sony, NEC, Hitachi, Philips, and Magnavox.

Two special hardware products are worthy of mention if you need to access more than one CD-ROM drive. Meridian Data, Inc. (5615 Scotts Valley Drive, Scotts Valley, CA 95066, 408-438-3100) makes a line of products called CD Net. The low end of the product line is the CD Net Model 100NC, which can contain from one to eight CD-ROM drives in one cabinet that is roughly a 16-inch cube. Artisoft has tested CD Net and verified its compatibility with LANtastic. This is a sophisticated device that includes its own microprocessor and has many security features and performance enhancements. The bad news is that prices start at $4995 and go as high as $11,000. Software is extra, starting at about $500.

The second hardware device of note is the Pioneer DRM-600 MiniChanger. This is a single CD-ROM disk drive with a changer that permits six CD-ROM disks to be interchanged on the drive. List price is $1200. The time to change disks is seven seconds. Other manufacturers have recently announced devices that allow access to multiple CD-ROM disks simultaneously. One is the Toshiba TXM-3301A4, which lists for $3170 and includes four CD-ROM drives stacked on top of each other, all of which run from a single controller card on the host computer. Artisoft does not yet list these devices as compatible with LANtastic, so check with Artisoft before you buy.

CD-ROM titles are available from many vendors, most of which also sell drives. Here are some of the vendors who offer large catalogs of CD-ROM titles:

- Updata Publications, Inc., 1736 Westwood Blvd., Los Angeles, CA 90024, 800-882-2844, 310-474-5900. Offers a variety of titles and hardware. Has an excellent catalog, logically grouped and indexed.
- Compact Disk Products (CDP), 272 Route 34, Aberdeen, NJ 07747, 908-290-0048. Offers a variety of titles and hardware.
- CD ROM, Inc., 1667 Cole Blvd., Suite 400, Golden, CO 80401, 303-231-9373. Offers a variety of titles and hardware. Excellent catalog.
- PhoneDisc U.S.A. Corp., 8 Doaks Lane, Marblehead, MA 01945, 800-284-8353, 617-639-2900. Specializes in phone directories on CD-ROM.

Sharing Modems and Other Two-Way Serial Devices

LANtastic in its standard configuration does not allow you to share modems over a LAN. Artisoft requires you to buy its ArtiCom product to share modems and other vendors sell similar products.

Let's first look at modem sharing from a financial perspective. Modems have become so inexpensive that most workgroups don't find the economics of modem sharing attractive. If you can install a $50 internal 2400 bps modem in every PC, why spend the money to buy modem-sharing software? Two answers might fit:

- The 2400 bps modems may not be fast enough. If various group members each need occasional use of 9600 bps modems, the cost is much higher and modem sharing may be a good answer.
- Telephone line costs may overshadow other costs. If the cost to install and use, say, eight individual phone lines for your eight-person workgroup is too high, and three shared lines would be enough, modem sharing makes sense.

Determine your modem and phone line needs, both for shared and individual usage. Do all eight individuals really need modems? Do all need 9600 bps? If the eight users share modems, are three enough, or do four people sometimes all need to use modems at once? Check current prices for the types of modems you need and also your local telephone costs, both for installation and monthly usage. Then compare the costs, benefits, and drawbacks for shared and unshared configurations and make your decision. This section shows how to use ArtiCom so you can understand how modem sharing works in case it is the best choice for your circumstances.

What ArtiCom Does

ArtiCom sets up a special communication process between your LANtastic nodes in order to support serial devices that require two-way communications–usually a modem but also certain plotter models or other devices. ArtiCom routes messages back and forth between a PC with a modem and another PC that needs to use the modem. It uses up only about 6K of RAM on each PC.

Without special hardware you can have up to four serial devices on a PC, attached to ports COM1 through COM4. However, you can also buy special devices called *multiport serial adapters,* which allow you to connect up to eight serial devices on one COM port. As a result, you can have up to 32 serial devices on one computer. ArtiCom supports multiport serial adapters made by four companies: Stargate, Arnet, Quatech, and DigiBoard.

This means you can install from one to 32 modems on one PC and let all LAN users access these modems. This gives everyone access to outside computer facilities without the need to install a modem in every computer. And you can put these modems on any computers, not just a LANtastic server. If you like, you can install modems on one or two workstations for everyone to use, which avoids bogging down a server that has a heavy database workload.

Once you use ArtiCom to make the connection between a modem PC and another user's PC, the user can use ArtiCom software to dial a remote computer, upload and download files, and capture the dialog in a disk file. If you prefer you can use your own favorite communications program, as long as the program adheres to a standard called the *INT 14h standard* (interrupt 14 hexadecimal). This standard specifies how the PC communicates with the modem. Many newer versions of communications products follow this standard, or at least have an option to let you configure the product to follow the standard. Some of these products are Procomm Plus Network, CrossTalk Mark IV, Mirror III, SmarTerm, Softerm, and BLAST PC.

Installing ArtiCom

ArtiCom is a software product. You have all the hardware you need if you have a LANtastic LAN (or any other LAN that conforms to NetBIOS standards) and at least one modem or other bidirectional serial device. Because your most likely use of ArtiCom is to share a modem over your LANtastic LAN, that is the usage covered here. For simplicity, this discussion is based on a LAN with one modem on one computer that all other computers want to share. The computer with the modem for others to use is called the *modem server,* even if it is not a LANtastic server.

Note

Any LANtastic workstation or server can be set up as a modem server. A computer that makes use of the shared modem is called a modem workstation.

The ArtiCom software is installed much like the LANtastic NOS software discussed in Chapter 5. The software comes on both 5.25-inch and 3.5-inch floppy disks, so you can use either one and put it in either your A or B drive. The example here assumes you use the A drive.

Modem Server Installation

Put the ArtiCom floppy disk in the A drive of the computer that has the modem. Type **a:ainstall** and press ENTER. This displays the screen shown in Figure 7-6.

Like the main LANtastic INSTALL program, AINSTALL expects you to press the cursor-movement keys to highlight different options and then press ENTER to change them. The first option is Type of Software Installation, which has a default value of Workstation AND Server. This setting would allow this computer to offer its modem to other computers that need access, and also to connect to other modem servers to use their modems. Because this computer has the only modem on our example LAN, press ENTER to change the setting to Server ONLY.

The default settings for the next three options are fine and you can leave them unchanged. As a result, AINSTALL will load the ArtiCom software from the A drive into a disk directory named ARTICOM on the C drive, and this modem server will be named MODEM-SERVER to identify it when users want to access its modem.

Figure 7-6. *The opening screen from ArtiCom's AINSTALL program*

```
ArtiCom Install V1.00 - (C) Copyright 1991 ARTISOFT Inc.

Software Installation

          Type of Software Installation: Workstation AND Server
          Software will be copied FROM: A:\
            Software will be copied TO: C:\ARTICOM
            Asynchronous server name: MODEM-SERVER
 Number of automatically selected ports: 2
     Maximum NETBIOS adapters to be used: 6

Enter-Modify, F2-Start Install, ESC-Exit, F1-Help
```

Move the cursor to the option called Number of automatically selected ports, set by default to 2. Press (ENTER) to see the screen shown in Figure 7-7.

This screen shows the devices that this modem server will make available to modem workstations. Rather than make all these devices available, delete the ones that are not modems. (Otherwise users may try to share your mouse.) On this computer, the modem is configured by jumpers on the modem card to use the COM2 port. The COM1 port is connected to a mouse. Delete the COM1 port from being offered. (Do so by highlighting it and pressing (DEL), and then pressing (ENTER) when prompted to confirm the deletion. If a computer has only one COM port and it is connected to the shared device, this step isn't necessary.) Finally, press (ESC) to return to the main menu box.

The last option is Maximum NetBIOS adapters to be used, with a default value of 6. This option refers to the number of LAN cards (which run NetBIOS software) in the computer. ArtiCom needs to make allowances to communicate with all the cards. Most likely you have only one LAN card in each computer and can set this option to 1. Be sure the number you select is at least as large as the number of LAN cards that run NetBIOS in this computer.

Figure 7-7. *Press (DEL) to delete any COM device you don't want to offer for sharing*

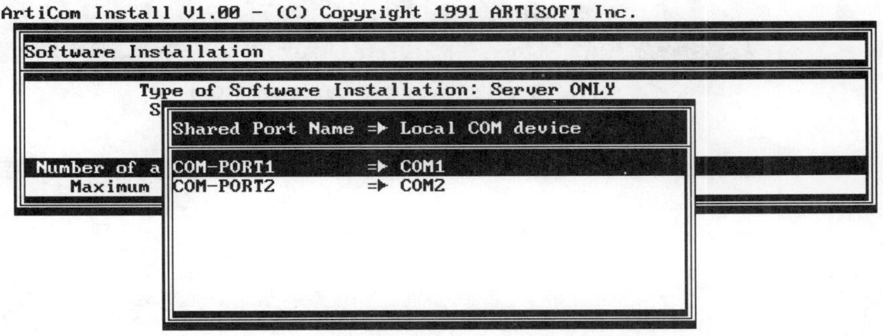

Finally, press the (F2) key to tell AINSTALL to copy the files from the floppy disk to the hard disk and use the settings you chose. The program displays progress messages to show you what files are copied and then displays a screen to say that the installation is complete.

That's all it takes for a modem server's installation. The files are on the modem server's hard disk and ready to be used. The ArtiCom software is not yet started.

Workstation Software Installation

The process to install a modem workstation's software starts off the same as for a modem server. Type **a:ainstall** and press (ENTER) to start the AINSTALL program. Then press (ENTER) twice to change Type of Software Installation to Workstation ONLY. This selection causes the screen to look like Figure 7-8.

Only the first three options remain. The default values should be appropriate. If not, change them. Then press (F2) to install the workstation software.

Figure 7-8. The AINSTALL screen for installation of workstation software only

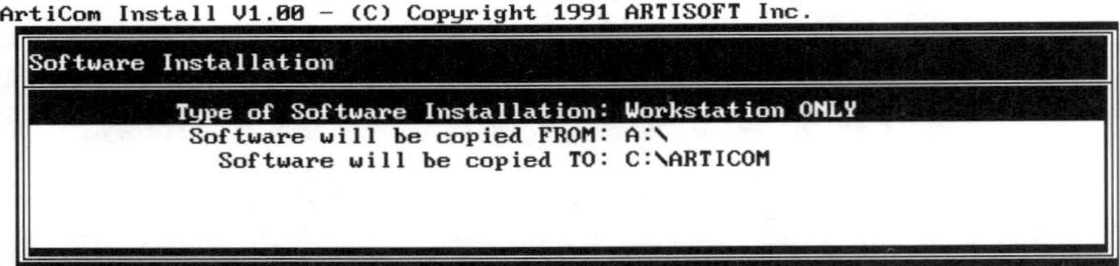

The AINSTALL program displays the filenames it installs and then a completion message. The workstation software installation is complete.

Running ArtiCom

To run ArtiCom, whether on a LANtastic server or workstation, you first need to start the regular LANtastic network operating system software if you have not already done so. Type **cd c:\lantasti** and press ENTER to switch to the LANtastic disk directory and then type **startnet** and press ENTER to start the software.

Once the LANtastic software is running, type the command **cd \articom** to make ArtiCom's directory the current directory and then type either **a-server** on the modem server computer or **a-redir** on a modem workstation. Then press ENTER. The modem server displays output like this:

```
Asynchronous Server (A-SERVER) V1.00 - (C) Copyright 1991 ARTISOFT Inc.
                 ---- A-SERVER installed ----
```

The modem workstation displays this output:

```
Asynchronous Redirector (A-REDIR) V1.00 - (C) Copyright 1991 ARTISOFT Inc.
                 ---- A-REDIR installed ----
```

If you like, of course, you can add the ArtiCom startup commands to the end of your STARTNET.BAT file on each computer to start the ArtiCom software automatically whenever you start LANtastic.

These two programs communicate with each other across the LAN: A-REDIR on a modem workstation and A-SERVER on the modem server.

Now you are ready to actually make contact between the workstation and the modem on the modem server. On the workstation be sure ARTICOM is still the current directory and type the command **acom** (or, on a black-and-white display, type **acom /mono**) and press ENTER. The ACOM program displays the screen shown in Figure 7-9.

Highlight the first choice in the Main Functions menu box, Terminal Emulator, and press ENTER. This brings up a menu box called Select COM Port for Terminal Emulation. This workstation computer has two serial ports

Figure 7-9. *The ACOM program's opening menu*

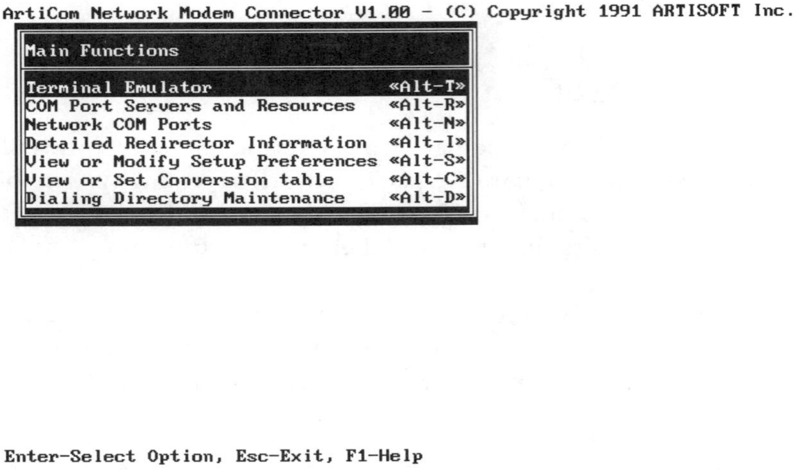

```
ArtiCom Network Modem Connector V1.00 - (C) Copyright 1991 ARTISOFT Inc.

 Main Functions

 Terminal Emulator                   «Alt-T»
 COM Port Servers and Resources      «Alt-R»
 Network COM Ports                   «Alt-N»
 Detailed Redirector Information     «Alt-I»
 View or Modify Setup Preferences    «Alt-S»
 View or Set Conversion table        «Alt-C»
 Dialing Directory Maintenance       «Alt-D»

Enter-Select Option, Esc-Exit, F1-Help
```

on it, neither with a device attached. Therefore this box says (as you'll see in a moment in Figure 7-10) that COM1 and COM2 are local and available, which means they are actual ports on the computer. The third choice, COM3, is shown as available. COM3 is a nonexistent port that is available for assignment to the server's modem, just like a workstation can assign a nonexistent disk drive name to a server's disk drive.

Move the highlight line down to COM3 and press ENTER. This brings up a menu box on the right that lists modem servers available on the LAN. There is only one, called MODEM-SERVER, so press ENTER to select it. The result is the screen shown in Figure 7-10, which lists the available resources on the modem server.

ArtiCom shows the workstation the resource named COM-PORT2, which is the modem on the server's COM2 port. The "In use by" column shows the modem is "Not in use," which means that no other modem workstation has already taken control of the modem. The modem is available to use. Press ENTER and the screen then shows COM3 assigned to COM-PORT2 on MODEM-SERVER (as shown in Figure 7-11).

Figure 7-10. The ACOM program shows the server's available serial devices

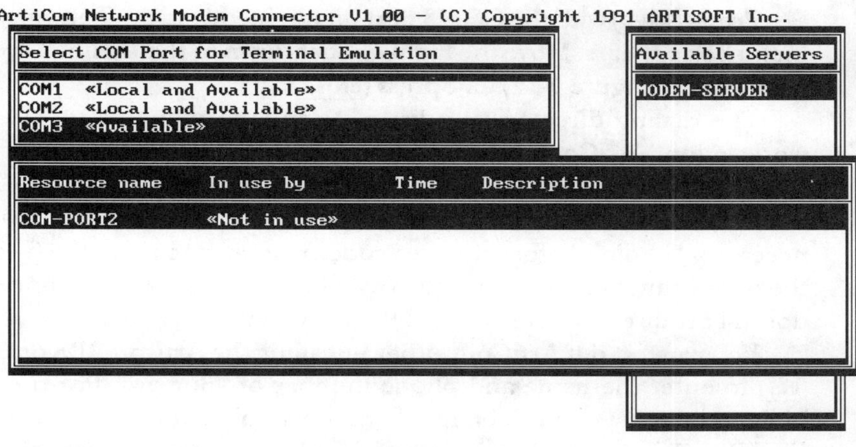

Figure 7-11. The workstation's COM3 is now assigned to MODEM-SERVER's COM-PORT2

Enter-Select Option, Del-Cancel, Space-Update, F10-Attach *, Esc-Exit, F1-Help

7

The modem workstation now has access to the modem server's shared modem. How does the workstation place a call?

Press (ENTER) with the COM3 port highlighted, and the Terminal Emulator menu box appears. Move the highlight bar down to the Dialing Directory line (as shown in Figure 7-12) and press (ENTER).

The dialing directory is a list of telephone numbers to call from this workstation. ArtiCom arrives with one phone number already in the directory—the phone number for the Artisoft Technical Support BBS. Unfortunately, the initial release of ArtiCom provides a phone number without the necessary "1" digit before the area code. You need to press the (E) key to edit the phone number and correct this oversight, unless your telephone company doesn't require 1 before you dial the area code.

You can test out ArtiCom either by calling the Artisoft BBS or by pressing (INS) to enter the name and phone number of your own favorite computer bulletin board system. Then highlight the number you want to call and press (ENTER) to dial the number. You might find the experience strange to hear the

Figure 7-12. *Use the Dialing Directory option of the Terminal Emulator menu to place a call*

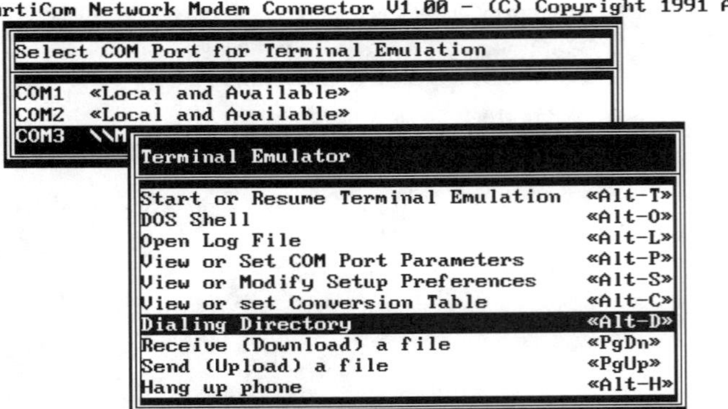

modem server computer making the phone call (if the modem has a speaker) while your modem workstation computer does the dialing.

When the remote computer answers your call, press ALT-T to switch to the terminal mode and start your dialog. When you are done with your call to the remote computer, press ALT-T again to end the terminal emulator and return to the Terminal Emulator menu box. Press ESC to see the menu box labeled Select COM Port for Terminal Emulation (as shown in Figure 7-11). Then press DEL to cancel COM3's redirection to the server's modem. This frees up the modem for someone else to use.

The Terminal Emulator menu box has options to customize the terminal program to your needs. The View or Set COM Port Parameters option lets you select the baud rate (speed of the modem in bits per second), parity, word length, and number of stop bits to match the remote computer's requirements. Another option, View or Modify Setup Preferences, provides options to select the type of terminal emulation you want, to choose a download protocol (XMODEM, YMODEM, or YMODEM batch), and to select other preferences. If you have no experience calling remote computers, the first part of this paragraph probably looks like Greek. You will need to do some self-education to understand the language of data communications and the resources you can tap into. For a wealth of information, see *Dvorak's Guide to PC Telecommunications,* second edition, by John Dvorak and Nick Anis, (Berkeley, CA: Osborne/McGraw-Hill, 1992).

ACOM_MGR

An important program that comes with ArtiCom is called ACOM_MGR. This program is similar to the NET_MGR program that comes with LANtastic in that it performs management functions for all users that share the modem servers. When you install ArtiCom, the ACOM_MGR program is installed only on modem server computers, not modem workstations.

Use ACOM_MGR to change what resources the modem server offers to workstations. For example, if you add a second modem to the modem server, you use ACOM_MGR to tell ArtiCom to make it available to workstations. You also use it to provide the technical specifications the modem will use by default (baud rate and so on). You can also change the parameters you provided when you first installed ArtiCom, such as the server name. After you make any of these changes, you must start the A-SERVER program again.

If A-SERVER is already running, you must stop it (with the command **a-server /remove**) and restart it in order for your changes to take effect.

This book won't go into the details of ACOM_MGR options. The choices are straightforward from the menus, much like for ACOM. If you need further explanation, refer to the *ArtiCom Modem Sharing Software User's Manual* that comes with ArtiCom.

Other Modem-Sharing Products

Besides ArtiCom, other modem-sharing software products are also on the market. These products have a wide variety of features and pricing options. Contact the manufacturer for latest specifications, features, and prices. Here are some with which users report success, or for which the manufacturers claim LANtastic compatibility:

- LAN+Modem NetBIOS, from Cross Communications Company, 1881 9th Street, Suite 302, Boulder, CO 80302, 303-444-7799. For dialing out only. Cross also has a product called Cross+Touch, which allows outside users to dial in and control a computer on the LANtastic LAN. Another product, Cross+Connect, performs both dial-out and dial-in.
- Modem Protocall NetBIOS, from Protocall Communications, 526 Queen Street East, Toronto, ON, Canada M5A 1V2, 416-866-8833. Modem Protocall NetBIOS performs both dial-out and dial-in.
- Norton pcANYWHERE/LAN, from Symantec Corporation, 10201 Torre Ave, Cupertino, CA 95014, 800-441-7234, 408-253-9600. In addition to other capabilities, pcANYWHERE/LAN performs dial-in to control a computer on the LAN.
- Carbon Copy Plus, from Microcom, Inc., 500 River Ridge Drive, Norwood, MA 02062, 617-551-1000. Along with other capabilities, Carbon Copy Plus allows remote computers to dial in and control LAN computers.

Using a Tape Backup System

Almost everyone who has ever put important data on disk over an extended period of time has learned the value of making backup copies of files. An amazing number of things can go wrong when you depend on computers. If any one of them does, you need a spare copy of your data. Otherwise those documents you took so long to write and those spreadsheets you so meticulously created are gone forever.

The following gives just a few of the reasons why you might need a backup copy of your data:

- *Hard disk failure* After about three years of use, your chances increase that a disk will fail due to wear and aging.
- *Theft* Burglars have discovered that computers are valuable and relatively easy to sell. When your computer disappears, the data on its hard disk does too.
- *Viruses* Computer viruses continue to increase in number and sophistication. If you ever use a computer program you get from someone else (even from a reputable manufacturer), you run the risk of losing data from a virus.
- *Software failures* A computer program may malfunction and create corrupt disk files without notice. After you discover the problem, you need to go back to backup copies created prior to the problem.
- *Disasters* Fire, flood, lightning, spilled coffee, or any natural or human-made disaster can destroy your hard disk and/or floppy disks.
- *Sabotage* A disgruntled co-worker or sneaky competitor might destroy or modify your critical data.
- *Your own mistakes* You might accidentally save a new file using the same name as an old one and wipe out the old one, or you might delete a group of supposedly obsolete files and later discover you need one of them. Human errors like these undoubtedly cause more lost data than any other kind.

The list goes on and on. They all lead to the same conclusion: your best protection against data loss is to have a backup copy. You can use the backup copy to restore the lost data to its previous form and then continue as if the problem never happened. To be useful, the backup copy has to be current and complete. A year-old copy of your current inventory won't do you much good. Neither will a floppy disk that contains only a quarter of your client history information.

Everything said so far about backup also applies to a stand-alone computer, not just a LAN-connected computer. However, once you put your entire workgroup's critical data on a server computer so everyone can use it, any data loss affects the whole group instead of just one user.

Of course, if your workgroup consists of only two or three people who create only a small amount of word processing documents and spreadsheets (or whatever) each week, backup methods can be easy. All you need to do is convince everyone to copy any new or changed file to a floppy disk regularly. "Regularly" can mean immediately after saving a file or at the end of each day. If people develop this habit, backing up data is painless. However, human nature tends to keep even the smallest group from achieving 100 percent consistency in backing up all updated files.

In addition, the more data your group collects and the more you all use it, the more critical it is for you to make regular, frequent, complete backup copies of your data.

There are several ways you can make backup copies:

- *Use floppy disks* This is the time-honored way to make backup copies. The process is awkward if each floppy disk can hold only 1.4 megabytes of data or less while your server stores 40 megabytes of data or more.
- *Use other computers* If two computers are connected on a LAN, one can copy its data to the other and vice versa. Then if either computer loses data, the other has a copy ready for immediate use. This is better than nothing, but each disk drive has to be twice the size a single user needs in order to hold both computers' data. And what if you have five or ten computers? The disks need to be even bigger and, of course, more expensive. And what if the copy you make is already corrupt? You need to go back to a previous version of a backup copy but all you will have is the copy you just made.

- *Use a tape backup system* A tape backup system can avoid the problems inherent in the previous two methods. Most tape backup systems consist of an interface card you install in a PC (although some models use your floppy disk controller card instead and some even connect through a parallel port), a tape drive (either internally or externally installed), a connecting cable, tape cartridges, and software. The tape drive looks much like a floppy disk drive, except you insert a tape cartridge where the floppy disk would go. A single cartridge can hold as much data as even a large server disk. Most cartridges are about midway in size between an audio cassette and a video cassette. Low-cost tape systems typically store from 40 to 525 megabytes on a cartridge and cost from $300 to $1500. The interface card is sometimes priced separately. More expensive tape systems store even more data on a cartridge.

Tape Backup Strategies

Before you start making backup copies of your data, you need to decide on a methodology or strategy to make backups as efficient and painless as possible. This section gives some ideas.

To determine which backup strategy makes the most sense for your workgroup, first ask yourself these questions:

- How long will it take us, and at what cost, to re-create our data if we lose it?
- If we can't re-create it somehow, how much does it hurt my workgroup if we never have access to it again?

Be aware that the answers to these questions change over time. When you first install your LAN you may not immediately put much valuable data on a server. But several months later the server might hold large amounts of irreplaceable data. If your data is costly to replace and your organization would suffer without it, backup copies are critical to you. Backup is a form of insurance. A few hundred dollars for equipment plus a few minutes work each day or two can save many companies from a disastrous loss.

The Rotation Method

You need several tape cartridges (which typically cost $20 to $50 each) so you can rotate your backups and have more than the most recent copy available. Never make a backup copy on a tape cartridge that already contains your most recent backup—if something goes wrong, you lose your best backup copy. One way to avoid this is to make a complete backup copy of your server's hard disk every day using one of three tape cartridges. On Monday use #1, on Tuesday use #2, and on Wednesday use #3. Then on Thursday use #1 again. If on Friday you need to restore a file from the backup tape, you can use Thursday's tape. If it is damaged or missing, you can use either Wednesday's or Tuesday's backup. In olden sexist days this method of rotating backup tapes was called the grandfather-father-son method. Now it's the grandparent-parent-child method, or just the rotation method.

A variation on the rotation method is to designate a tape cartridge for each day of the week. Every Monday you make a backup copy on the tape labeled "Monday" and in doing so replace last Monday's copy. On Tuesday you use the "Tuesday" tape, and so on.

Other Backup Concepts

Another important backup technique to protect yourself is to be sure you have an *off-site backup,* which means to keep a copy of your critical data somewhere other than right near your computer. Ideally the location should be in another building. An off-site backup copy reduces your risk in case of fire, flood, theft, or sabotage. In a small office, the easiest way to guarantee you have an off-site backup might be to take the next-most-recent backup copy home with you each night. Then if the most recent backup is damaged, you can go home and get the previous backup. In a larger company, you can arrange to ship backup copies back and forth between your office and a different building with storage facilities.

Many backup software products give you the capability to make an *incremental backup* as well as a complete backup copy. An incremental backup is a copy of only those files which have changed since the last time you made a backup copy. Suppose you have a 300-megabyte hard disk that is nearly filled with data files. To copy the entire disk to tape might take an hour or more, depending on your tape drive and LAN. If each day users typically change only about five megabytes of this data, why not just copy the changed portion?

That would take only a couple of minutes. You might want to make a full backup copy every Friday, but only incremental backups on other days. The tape backup software keeps track of which files are on each tape cartridge so you can retrieve the most current backup copy of any particular file.

The best place to install a tape backup system usually is on a workstation. From the workstation the tape backup software can access all servers if you have more than one. Some people like to define all PCs on their LANtastic LANs to be servers so the tape system can back up everyone's hard disk, not just a single shared server's hard disk.

Ideally you should back up a server when no one is using it. If anyone is using a file on the server, the backup software can't copy it because the data might be in the middle of being updated. Most workgroups handle this by making backups at the end of the day just before going home or else scheduling the backup process during the night when no one is around. Many backup software products provide the facility to perform a tape backup automatically at a pre-set time. As long as you leave the computers turned on overnight, this approach is fine. Be sure you monitor the first few automatic backups to verify they work correctly. Later you can simply review the report generated by the backup software to be sure all is well.

The manual that accompanies a backup software product usually provides tips and recommendations for making backups based on the features of the product. Read the manual, evaluate your situation, and decide on a backup strategy.

Using Tape Systems with LANtastic

DOS doesn't communicate with most tape systems the same way it does with disk drives. However, special backup programs know how to write to and read from tape systems. Most tape systems come with backup programs customized to work with those tape systems. Most of these programs have a menu from which you choose the actions you want to take. The simplest way to back up a server's disk is to tell the program to copy all the files from the L drive (or whatever you designate as the network drive name on the workstation) to the tape cartridge. Figure 7-13 shows the menu screen from the SY-TOS software that comes with a Tapemaster 250 tape backup system from CMS Enhancements. In this example the tape system and SY-TOS software are installed on a workstation. The workstation user used the LANtastic NET program before running SY-TOS and directed the name L: to the server's hard disk. Then, for the purpose of a short example, the user chose SY-TOS options to make a *selective backup* (certain files only) to copy to the tape cartridge all the ".DOC" (document) files from the L disk's WORD55 directory. The sample screen shows the result after making the backup copy.

SY-TOS, like other backup programs, has many features such as incremental backups, automatic timed backups, batch file control (so you can automate the steps you want SY-TOS to take), and tape verification (so you can verify the files you just copied to tape are readable).

LANtastic's server control directory (which has a default name of LANTASTI.NET) always contains open files when the server is active. You need to back this directory up, but you can do so using the LANtastic NET_MGR program. Then you can tell the backup software (such as SY-TOS) that it should not try to back up this directory. Otherwise SY-TOS displays a message to indicate the files in the directory could not be backed up.

Figure 7-13. *A menu screen from the SY-TOS backup program after completing a backup to a tape cartridge*

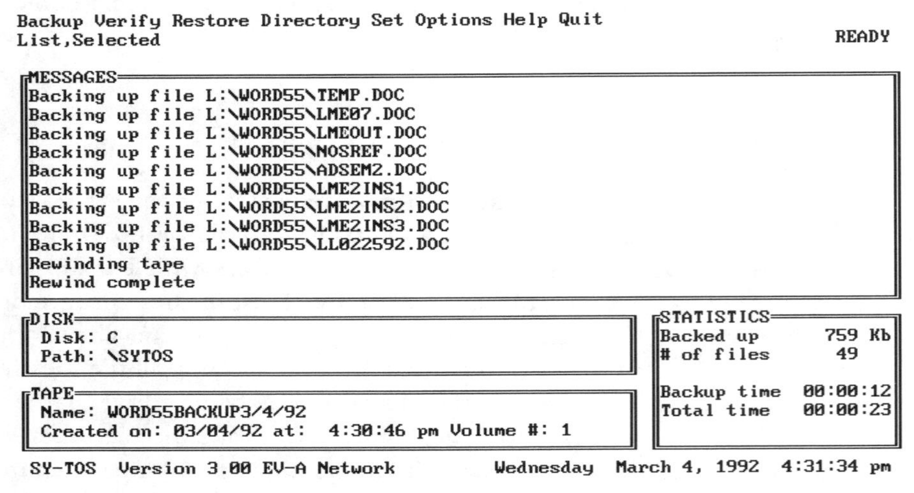

Tape Backup Suppliers

Most popular models of tape backup systems are compatible with LANtastic. Some of the leading names on tape backup hardware in the low to medium price range are Cipher, CMS Enhancements, Colorado Memory Systems, Everex Systems, Mountain Computer, Tallgrass Technologies, and Tecmar. Nearly all models seem to be compatible with LANtastic (provided you avoid conflicts with IRQs and I/O port base addresses). To make sure, check with Artisoft or the tape drive manufacturer for verification.

Software products to perform backup copies with these tape systems are either included with the tape system or are available from independent companies. The following lists some of the independent software products:

Product	**Company**
Back-It 4 LAN	Gazelle Systems
CPBACKUP (part of PC Tools)	Central Point Software
SY-TOS	Sytos Plus, Sytron Corporation

Before Choosing a Tape Backup System

You have two main concerns when you buy a tape drive system, in addition to your obvious concern of whether you can afford the price. First, make sure you can copy all the data you need to back up onto one cartridge, both now and in the foreseeable future. One of the big advantages of a tape system compared with floppy disks is that a tape system permits unattended backups. You can automate the entire process by using batch files or script files, depending on the software product. Then the backup is done automatically. All you have to do is insert a tape cartridge before the process starts and then check the results afterward to be sure everything ran properly. Floppy disks, on the other hand, require manual intervention to change disks. So, when you shop for a tape system, be sure a single cartridge's storage capacity is larger than the total amount of data you need to back up. Or, if that's not possible, make sure the tape can at least hold the largest incremental backup you expect to make.

Your second concern is that you must be sure the backup process will occur fast enough to complete in the time you have available. This is generally not a problem if you make automated backups overnight because in most workgroups you have about 14 hours to complete the job (6 P.M. until 8 A.M. the next morning). However, some workgroups have people who work the swing shift, which reduces the window of opportunity. Other workgroups work around the clock. You need to find a time slot when no one needs the servers that must be backed up. The time slot might be 2:00 to 2:30 A.M. Is the tape system fast enough to do the job in 30 minutes? Another time constraint might be that your boss decides, for security and safety reasons, not to leave any computers in your workgroup powered on all night. You must make the backup copies at the end of the day after everyone else leaves. How late you stay depends on how fast the tape drive can copy data. Most tape drives copy data at a rate between two and eight megabytes per minute. Some low cost models are slower.

Attaching Portable Computers

Chapter 4 mentioned four ways to connect a portable computer to a LANtastic LAN. Two of those ways, LANtastic Z and laptop file transfer products, connect the portable computer to a single computer on the LAN. The other two ways, Artisoft Central Station and a portable LAN adapter, connect the portable computer to a LANtastic Ethernet LAN to provide full access to all LAN resources. This section covers these last two ways.

Artisoft Central Station

Chapter 3 briefly introduced the Artisoft Central Station Connectivity Processor and showed a photo in Figure 3-7. Central Station is a convenient way to attach a portable computer to a LANtastic Ethernet LAN, either thin Ethernet or 10BASE-T. Other devices such as printers can also be connected using Central Station, but the focus here is on portable computers.

To connect a portable computer to a LANtastic LAN by means of a Central Station, you need:

- A portable computer that has a standard parallel printer port

- A connecting cable for the LAN, either thin coaxial for thin Ethernet or twisted pair for 10BASE-T, with appropriate connectors
- Central Station, which includes a special five-foot cable to connect the portable computer's parallel port to Central Station, a BNC T connector to connect to thin Ethernet, floppy disks (both 5.25-inch and 3.5-inch sizes) containing special Central Station software, a power cord, and the *Central Station Connectivity Processor User's Manual*

Central Station also has an RJ45 socket for connection to a 10BASE-T hub, plus connectors for a PC attachment, a parallel printer, two serial devices, and an auxiliary device. Software called the LANtastic Printer Server is available from Artisoft to support a printer you attach to Central Station. Other products that support devices attached to the other connectors may be available by the time you read this.

Hardware Connection

The hardware setup to connect a portable computer to Central Station is not at all difficult. Follow these steps:

1. With both Central Station and the portable computer powered off, attach one end of the included connecting cable to the LPT1 or LPT2 port of the portable computer and the other end to the PC port on Central Station. Either end of the cable works on either port.
2. Attach the appropriate LAN cable between Central Station and your LANtastic LAN. For thin Ethernet, attach the BNC T connector to the "THIN ETHERNET" connector on the rear of Central Station. Then attach a thin Ethernet cable between one side of the T connector and another node on your LAN. On the other side of the T connector, either attach another cable or a terminator, depending on if you make Central Station an end point on your daisy chain. For 10BASE-T, attach a twisted-pair cable between the "UTP ETHERNET" port on Central Station and a port on your 10BASE-T hub.
3. Make sure Central Station's power switch is in the "OFF" position. Attach one end of the power/transformer cable to the "POWER"

jack on Central Station and the other end to an electrical outlet. Be sure the power connection uses a surge protector.

Software Installation and Startup

Starting with version 4.1 of LANtastic, the necessary software for Central Station is included with the regular LANtastic NOS. For version 4.0 you need a combination of the LANtastic NOS and software that comes with Central Station. This section explains the LANtastic 4.1 method and then notes differences for 4.0. Follow these steps:

1. Run the INSTALL program on the portable computer the way the software installation process is described in Chapter 5. It usually makes the most sense to configure the portable computer as a workstation, but you can make it a server if you like. Because of the limiting speed of the parallel port, the portable computer will be a slooooow server. If the portable computer has a hard disk, the only difference in the software installation process is that for Select Network Adapter Installed you should choose Central Station PC to Ethernet node, as shown in Figure 7-14.

   If the portable computer has no hard disk, install the software on a floppy disk. To do this put the installation disk in the A drive and put a previously formatted floppy disk in the B drive. You'll probably want to format this floppy disk using the /s parameter of FORMAT so you can boot the computer from this disk. Then for INSTALL's Installation Directory option, change the entry to b:\lantasti to cause INSTALL to install the files on the floppy disk. If your portable has only one floppy disk drive and no hard disk, you can't run INSTALL on that computer. Instead, run the INSTALL program on a desktop computer to create the floppy disk. You can either put the LANtastic software directly on the floppy disk or else install the software first in a hard disk directory and then copy the files from the desktop's hard disk to a floppy disk. In the latter case, you must configure the portable PC as a workstation and you need to change STARTNET.BAT's statements to point to the floppy disk drive instead of the C drive.

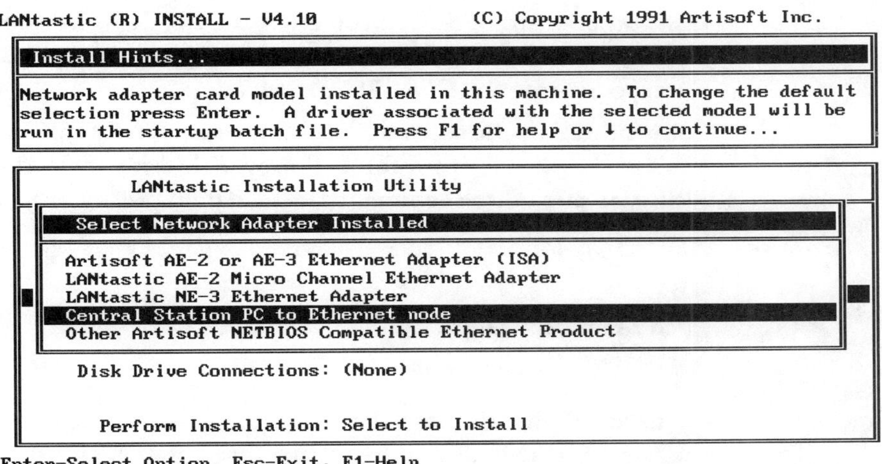

Figure 7-14. *Using INSTALL to configure Central Station software*

2. If you connect the LPT1 port on your portable to Central Station, you need no changes to the STARTNET.BAT file that INSTALL creates. If you connect LPT2 you need to change the "PORT=LPT1" parameter in STARTNET.BAT to "PORT=LPT2" using EDLIN or another line editor program.
3. Check the instructions that came with Central Station. You may need to use the version of AILANBIO.EXE that comes with Central Station instead of the version that comes with LANtastic 4.1. If so, use the DOS COPY command to copy the file from the Central Station floppy disk to the LANTASTI directory on your hard disk (or to the floppy disk if you installed LANtastic there). In case you need it later, save the original AILANBIO.EXE somewhere (or rename it) before you copy the replacement file.
4. Be sure you modify the CONFIG.SYS file the way INSTALL recommends if you did not allow INSTALL to make the changes for you.

If you installed LANtastic on a floppy disk and you boot from another floppy disk, you need to make the changes on the floppy disk you boot from. Before you enter the STARTNET command to start the LANtastic software, be sure to reboot your portable computer to activate the CONFIG.SYS changes.

5. Start the LANtastic software the same way you did in Chapter 5. If you run LANtastic from the B floppy disk drive instead of a hard disk, type these three commands instead (and press ENTER after each one):

```
b:
cd \lantasti
startnet
```

These commands make the B floppy disk drive the current drive, then make LANTASTI the current directory on the B drive, and finally run the STARTNET batch file that INSTALL created. Watch for the usual messages that indicate each software component installs correctly. Instead of AEX for a low-level driver, Central Station uses a driver called CSPPORT. Once the software is started, use the portable computer connected to Central Station the same way you would any other workstation (or server, if you installed it that way). The only difference you should notice is that data moves between the portable computer and the LAN slower than it does between a desktop computer and the LAN because the parallel port cannot transfer data nearly as fast as an Ethernet LAN card.

Differences for LANtastic 4.0 Version 4.0 of LANtastic does not provide Central Station as an alternative under INSTALL's option called Select Network Adapter Installed. Instead you have to select another adapter, such as the AE-2 ISA adapter, and continue with INSTALL as before. After INSTALL is complete, you need to edit the STARTNET.BAT file and make a change, and copy two files from the Central Station Configuration Software disk to your LANTASTI directory. Assuming you installed LANtastic on the portable computer's C disk, here are the steps to follow after you run INSTALL but before you run STARTNET.BAT:

1. Using EDLIN or another line editor, change the STARTNET.BAT line that executes the AEX driver program so the line executes Central Station's CSPPORT program instead. Before the change, the line looks like this:

```
C:\LANTASTI\AEX IRQ=15 IOBASE=300 VERBOSE
```

   Change the line so it reads instead like this:

```
C:\LANTASTI\CSPPORT ACK_TIMEOUT=20 RETRY_PERIOD=20 PORT=LPT1 VERBOSE
```

2. Use the DOS COPY command to copy the files CSSPORT.EXE and AILANBIO.EXE from the Central Station Configuration Software disk to the LANTASTI directory on your C drive. If you put the floppy disk in your A drive, type these two commands and press (ENTER) after each:

```
copy a:cssport.exe c:\lantasti
copy a:ailanbio.exe c:\lantasti
```

Portable LAN Adapters

Another approach to connecting a portable computer to a LANtastic Ethernet LAN is to use a portable LAN adapter. The leading vendor is Xircom (26025 Mureau Road, Calabasas, CA 91302, 818-878-7600).

At the present time, Xircom makes two models of interest to LANtastic users. The Pocket Ethernet Adapter model PE10B2 works with a thin Ethernet LAN and the Pocket Ethernet Adapter model PE10BT works with 10BASE-T. Each has a list price of $495. Xircom also has two similar models of a new line called the Pocket Ethernet Adapter II, but as of this writing no software drivers for LANtastic are available.

A Pocket Ethernet Adapter actually can fit in a shirt pocket. It weighs five ounces and is about 5 inches by 2.5 inches by 7/8 inch—roughly the size of an audio cassette box or a medium-size hand calculator. Its compact size makes this adapter a better choice than Central Station if you carry a laptop around to different LANtastic LANs (or other Ethernet LANs, with which these adapters are also compatible).

On one end of a Pocket Ethernet Adapter is a connector for the portable computer's parallel port. On the other end is a connector for the LAN—a BNC connector on the thin Ethernet model and an RJ45 socket on the 10BASE-T model. On the same end is a connector for the supplied power cord.

Hardware installation is simple. Follow these steps:

1. Attach the Pocket Ethernet Adapter to a parallel port of the portable computer. LPT1 is the default choice the software assumes, but you can override it and use LPT2 or LPT3 if you prefer.
2. Connect the appropriate type of LAN cable (not supplied) to the other end of the adapter. A BNC T connector is supplied with the thin Ethernet model.
3. Attach the power cord and plug it into a power source. The adapter has no power on/off switch; when the power cord is connected, the unit is powered on.

The software installation is also straightforward. You need to buy the adapter independent version of LANtastic, LANtastic/AI. When you run INSTALL, select the option for the Xircom PE10B2 Pocket Ethernet Adapter. The driver software works for the PE10BT model, too. Even though LANtastic driver software comes with the Xircom adapter, you must use the driver that comes with LANtastic/AI, which is a newer version. After INSTALL is done copying the software to the portable computer's hard disk or a floppy disk, you need to change the STARTNET.BAT file if you connected the pocket adapter to LPT2 or LPT3. Change the line that starts PE (the adapter's driver software for the Pocket Ethernet Adapter) to include the parameter /LPT=2 or /LPT=3 along with any other parameters. You can enter either capital letters or lowercase; INSTALL uses all capital letters. For the LPT2 port, the line would look like this:

```
PE /LPT=2 /VERBOSE
```

Artisoft recommends that you also include a parameter for AILANBIO in STARTNET.BAT. The current recommendation is to make the line look like this:

```
AILANBIO /ACK_TIMEOUT=4
```

Artisoft also suggests that if you have problems transferring data between the portable computer and servers that you make the same change for all servers on the LANtastic LAN. If you have problems, check with Artisoft (see Appendix B) or Xircom to see if recent studies cause them to recommend another value or other changes.

Be sure you run DOS 3.1, 3.3, or higher on the portable computer, and that the printer port is configured for use as a standard printer. Some portables have switches you can set or SETUP commands you can enter to configure printer ports in various ways. As a test, attach a printer to the port and verify that the computer can send data to the printer. If you can set the printer port to a bidirectional or high-speed mode, you might get faster throughput between the Pocket Ethernet Adapter and the computer. Check your portable computer's documentation to see if you can change the printer port's configuration.

Once you run STARTNET to start the LAN software on the portable computer, it should work like any other computer attached to the LAN. Like Central Station, throughput will be much slower than for a computer with a LAN card because of the limitations of the parallel port.

8

The Artisoft Sounding Board

The one capability of LANtastic that makes it perhaps unique among other network operating systems is its support for voice messages. All you have to do is add a relatively low-cost voice system called the Artisoft Sounding Board Adapter (called the Sounding Board or voice card for short) to each computer and you can send and receive voice messages in addition to typed electronic mail. For people who don't like to type, this capability is an attractive alternative to conventional e-mail.

The Sounding Board was introduced in Chapter 3 and is pictured in Figure 3-10. Originally called the LANtastic Voice Adapter, the Sounding Board has a list price of $99 for the ISA bus and $199 for the Micro Channel. You need to install one on each computer to which you want to add the capability to send or receive voice messages. If you aren't sure how useful the Sounding Board would be in your workgroup, consider buying just two of them to start. Use the two to experiment and understand the possibilities. Later you can buy additional Sounding Boards for the other workgroup members who would benefit.

Included with the Sounding Board are the following:

- An 8-bit expansion card that you install in an available slot in your PC
- A telephone handset
- A coiled cord that stretches to a length of about seven feet and connects the card to the handset using standard RJ-11 modular telephone plugs
- Two stick-on Velcro pads to enable you to "hang up" the handset in a position near your computer
- A floppy disk containing software drivers and utility programs
- An instruction book that explains hardware and software installation

The expansion card has RCA-type phono jacks on the back for audio input and output in case you want to connect a tape recorder, small speaker, amplifier, or stereo system.

The sound quality of the messages you create using the Sounding Board is extremely good. The Sounding Board *digitizes* your spoken sounds, which means that it converts the sounds into digital form so they can be saved in a regular disk file. The shortcoming of this method is that the disk files can become large quickly. Each ten seconds of sound takes about 80K in a disk file. When you use LANtastic's e-mail to send voice messages, these disk files are stored on a server in the spool area. Unless you have a huge amount of available server disk space, you need to be sure that everyone in the group listens to messages promptly and deletes voice messages afterward. Otherwise you will soon run out of disk space. The Sounding Board software also supports a compressed form of digitizing, which cuts the file size requirement in half but makes sound quality slightly worse. However, even this compressed mode has sound quality better than the average long-distance phone call.

The Sounding Board's main competition does not come from other similar LAN add-on products, but instead from telephone voice mail systems. If you have telephone voice mail in your workgroup, you might decide the Sounding Board is redundant.

One other point is that Artisoft has just announced a Windows-compatible version of the Sounding Board. At the time of this writing, however, no other information was available. Check with Artisoft for details.

Installation

The installation process for the Sounding Board takes two steps. First you install the hardware and then the software. After installation you can run some supplied test programs to verify that the Sounding Board is working correctly. Then you can begin using the Sounding Board to "chat" directly with another user or to exchange voice messages over your LANtastic LAN.

Hardware Installation

The only jumper settings on the ISA version of the Sounding Board expansion card are for enabling or disabling DMA (direct memory access) channels. DMA channels are hardware mechanisms in the PC by which the Sounding Board can move data to and from the computer's memory without going through the microprocessor. The Sounding Board uses DMA channels 1 and 3. If you don't have one of these DMA channels available because of usage by some other device, you need to disable one of the two channels using jumpers J1 and J2 in the upper-left corner of the card. (Using jumpers is described in more detail in Chapter 5.) J1 controls DMA channel 1 and J2 controls DMA channel 3. By default both channels are enabled. To disable either one, remove the jumper from its default location in which it connects the two pins on the right of the jumper area and instead connect the two pins on the left. If you disable either channel you can't use the Sounding Board to record and play sounds, or send and receive sounds, simultaneously. You *can* both record and play, just not at the same time. Unless you have an unusual expansion card installed in your PC you should encounter no conflicts and be able to use both DMA channels.

Now install the Sounding Board expansion card in an available slot in your PC. The card works in either an 8-bit or a 16-bit slot. Follow the instructions in Chapter 5 if you need reminders about how to open the computer's system unit and install an expansion card. Be sure to observe the standard precautions: turn off the computer, disconnect the computer's power cable, avoid damaging components from your body's static electricity by first touching an electrical ground, and handle the expansion card carefully by the edges.

Once the card is installed, put the computer's cover back on and connect the handset to the card using the supplied cord. That's all it takes to install the Sounding Board hardware.

Software Installation

Software for the Sounding Board comes on a 5.25-inch floppy disk. No INSTALL program is provided, so you can use the DOS COPY command. Follow these steps:

1. Review the README.DOC file on the Sounding Board floppy disk to be sure there are no late changes to the installation procedure. Use your favorite text editor or, with the disk in your A drive, type the command **type a:readme.doc|more** and press ENTER. (Be sure your DOS PATH includes the DOS directory so you can use the MORE filter as this command shows.)
2. Make the LANtastic directory the current directory. First type **c:** and press ENTER to make the C drive the current drive. Then type **cd \lantasti** and press ENTER.
3. Rename the README.DOC file that is already in your LANTASTI directory to avoid it being overlaid by the same-named file that comes with the Sounding Board. To rename the file, type **rename readme.doc readmeln.doc** and press ENTER.
4. Copy all the files from the Sounding Board disk into your LANTASTI directory. To do this, type **copy a:*.* c:\lantasti** and press ENTER. Be careful to type only the two blank spaces shown in this command! One blank is after the word "copy" and the other is after the second asterisk. After you enter the command, DOS shows the names of the files copied to your hard disk.

This completes the installation of the software. However, you have not *started* the software yet. You only copied the software onto your hard disk.

Starting the Software

The ISA version of the Sounding Board uses a software driver program called LANVOICE.EXE. The Micro Channel version uses MC-LANV.EXE. The appropriate driver accompanies the type of card you bought. Examples here use LANVOICE.

You can start LANVOICE even if you are not running the LANtastic network operating system. Of course, without running LANtastic you can't send voice mail messages to other LAN users. You can, however, test the Sounding Board and also record and play digitized voice files on disk. But because most people use the Sounding Board with LANtastic, the following explains how to use them together.

First, start your LANtastic software as you always do with the STARTNET command from the LANTASTI disk directory. The examples here work on either a nondedicated server or workstation, so use whichever you like. Once LANtastic is successfully started, type **lanvoice** and press ENTER. (For the Micro Channel version, type **mc-lanv** instead.) The result should be two lines of output that look like this:

```
LANtastic Voice PC-bus Driver V1.17 - (C) Copyright 1990 ARTISOFT Inc.
                         ---- VOICE driver installed ----
```

If during installation of the Sounding Board card you changed a jumper to disable a DMA channel, when you start LANVOICE you have to specify which DMA channel you *will* use. For example if you disabled channel 1 then you can use only DMA channel 3, so type **lanvoice /dma=3** and press ENTER.

If you find that you use the Sounding Board regularly, you can edit your STARTNET.BAT file to add a line with LANVOICE to start the Sounding Board's software whenever you start LANtastic. LANVOICE uses less than 6K of RAM and therefore doesn't take up much space. As a result, you might want to always run LANVOICE even if you don't always use it. LANVOICE seems to work fine whether you run it before the other LANtastic programs or after. By convention, most people start it after the other programs in

STARTNET.BAT. So for a server, add the LANVOICE line after the SERVER line. For a workstation, add it after the REDIR line.

Testing the Sounding Board

Now that you have run LANVOICE, you're ready to test the Sounding Board. Artisoft provides several ways to test the hardware and software, all explained in a file called VCTEST.DOC. The tests use programs included on the Sounding Board floppy disk (that you copied to your hard disk). The programs–HTEST, LTEST, SAY, and RECORD–are explained individually next.

HTEST: The Handset Test

The first test program is called HTEST, which tests the handset with the Sounding Board. To run this test you must use both DMA channels, which is called full-duplex mode. If you use only one DMA channel, skip this test. Put the handset facing downward on a smooth, hard surface. This connects the earpiece and the mouthpiece of the handset in what is called an *acoustical coupling*, which simply means that sounds can easily travel between the two by bouncing off the hard surface. Then type **htest** and press ENTER. If all is well, you will hear a beep and see HTEST display the message "Handset passed" on the screen. If a problem exists, you might see one of several messages. The most likely is "ERROR: Handset not functioning." If you see this error message, try HTEST several more times using different hard, flat surfaces. If insufficient sound bounces between the earpiece and mouthpiece, your surface may not be adequate for this test.

LTEST: The Line-In and Line-Out Test

Even if you have a problem with HTEST, move on to the next test. This test also requires full-duplex connection (both DMA channels). Get a connecting cord that has RCA-type male phono plugs on both ends. These cords are sometimes supplied with stereo systems or videocassette recorders. Use the cord to connect together the two phono jacks on the back of the Sounding Board card. These jacks are called the line-in and line-out connections. Remove the handset cord from the jack on the Sounding Board. Then type **ltest** and press (ENTER). This test program should display the message "Line-In and Line-Out passed" on the screen. If not, check that the connecting cord is securely inserted in both jacks. However, don't try to force the cord. You may be using a cord with the wrong plugs on each end.

SAY: Play a Prerecorded Message

The remaining tests work in either full-duplex mode or half-duplex mode (one DMA channel only). If the previous tests don't work, the reason may be simply an inadequate hard surface for HTEST or a faulty cord for LTEST. Try this next test even if one or both of the previous tests fail.

Plug the handset back into the card and remove the connecting cord from the last test. Artisoft provides a test file called ARTIBLAB.SPK, which has about eight seconds of speech on it. Type **say artiblab.spk** and then hold the handset to your ear and press (ENTER). The SAY program converts the digitized test file into sounds. You should hear a message through the handset's earpiece thanking you for buying the Sounding Board.

RECORD: Create and Play Your Own Message

Finally, you can record your own test message and play it back. Type **record tt** and press (ENTER). The RECORD program displays two messages on the screen. You'll see this:


```
Recording...
Hit any key to exit
```

You should immediately begin speaking into the handset. Talk for a few seconds and then press any key. You have just recorded a speech message in a file called TT. (You can pick any filename you like, of course; the name TT simply puts a minimal strain on your typing skills.) Next, play the message back. Type **say tt** and then hold the handset to your ear and press ENTER. The SAY program displays this message:

```
Hit any key to exit
```

Immediately afterward, the SAY program begins to play your test message into the handset. You should hear the message you just spoke. If you don't, go back and review the installation process. Verify that you installed the hardware and software correctly. If you can't find your problem, see Appendix B for information about getting help.

Compressed Files

The RECORD and SAY tests you ran used standard, uncompressed messages. Try another test using a compressed message. Type the command **record/c squash.msg** and press ENTER to record a brief test message as before. To play the message, type **say/c squash.msg** and press ENTER. (As before, the filename SQUASH.MSG is arbitrary; you can use any filename you like.) The /c parameter says to use the compressed message format. Be sure to use /c with SAY if you used /c with RECORD to create the message. Otherwise, SAY plays an indecipherable static message for your listening displeasure. Unfortunately, there seems to be no way to look at a file to see if it is in compressed form or not. You might want to establish a filenaming convention to keep each kind identifiable, such as an extension of .CMP or .VC for compressed files and .UNC or .VU for uncompressed files.

Using Voice Chat

All the previous tests work fine without connecting your computer to a LAN or running STARTNET to start your LANtastic software. All you really need to use the Sounding Board are the hardware, the LANVOICE driver software, and the RECORD and SAY programs. In fact, you can use RECORD and SAY to send messages to someone who is not connected to your LANtastic LAN. Just use RECORD to record a message file, and then copy the file to a floppy disk and give it to a friend. If the friend also has a Sounding Board, he or she can listen to your message using SAY. Sure, it would be simpler and cheaper to record an ordinary audio cassette tape with a $30 cassette recorder instead, but that just doesn't seem as technically exciting.

Now let's actually send messages across your LANtastic LAN. LANtastic's network operating system provides two ways to communicate using Sounding Boards. One is with the voice chat feature of the NET program. The other is with voice mail, also part of the NET program.

Voice chat is simply a LAN software connection between two LANtastic users who have Sounding Boards. The two users can use the handsets to carry on a conversation just as if they were using a telephone. To start voice chat, type **net chat** and press ENTER to display NET's chat menu. Or, if you prefer, you can type **net** and press ENTER, and then move the cursor down to select the Main Functions option that says "Chat With Another User." In either case, NET displays a screen that looks like Figure 8-1.

This screen shows that the local machine is called CMS. This is the machine name on the computer that entered the NET command. The bottom part of the screen shows that this computer is "Unconnected" right now, which means CMS wants to chat but no one is yet listening. To make a connection, press INS to make a call to the other computer. NET prompts you to enter the name of the machine you want to call. In this example the

Figure 8-1. *NET's chat screen before making a connection*

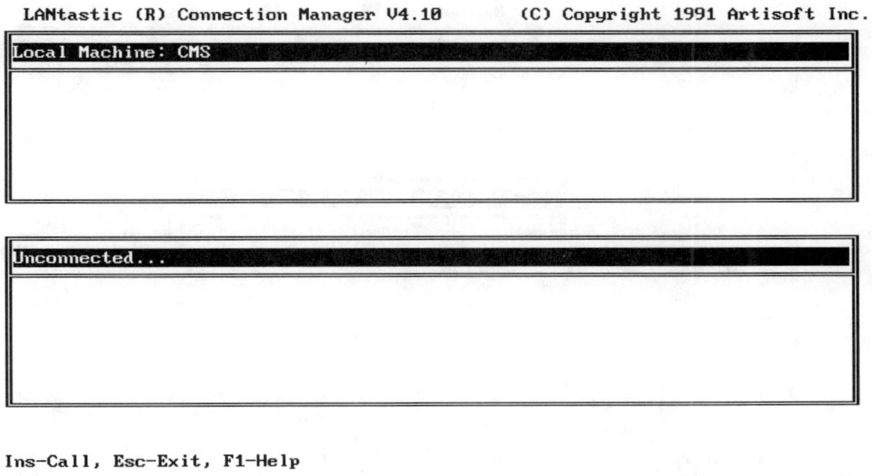

```
LANtastic (R) Connection Manager V4.10      (C) Copyright 1991 Artisoft Inc.

Local Machine: CMS



Unconnected...



Ins-Call, Esc-Exit, F1-Help
```

8

other computer is named TOM, so type that name (as shown in Figure 8-2) and press ENTER.

The bottom part of the screen then displays a message that says "Calling Machine TOM" while the system waits for TOM to answer. A message is displayed on TOM's screen (unless his screen is in graphics mode) that tells him to run NET CHAT and a triple beep sounds every 15 seconds until TOM answers or CMS presses ESC to give up. If TOM is not currently on the LAN (meaning that he did not run STARTNET to start his LANtastic software), CMS receives an error message that says "Name not found on network."

For our purposes, Tom is on the LAN. He answers the call by typing **net chat** and pressing ENTER. Once he does this, CMS sees that a connection is made because a message saying "<< Connect >>" appears in the bottom part of the screen. Either CMS or TOM can then press F2 to enable voice chat, which will result in the screen shown in Figure 8-3, and the voice conversation begins. (Pressing F2 works only if both chatting parties have Sounding Boards and are running the LANVOICE software.) When either person talks, a brief delay of about one-half to one second occurs while the message is digitized and transmitted over the LAN.

Figure 8-2. CMS enters the name of the computer to call

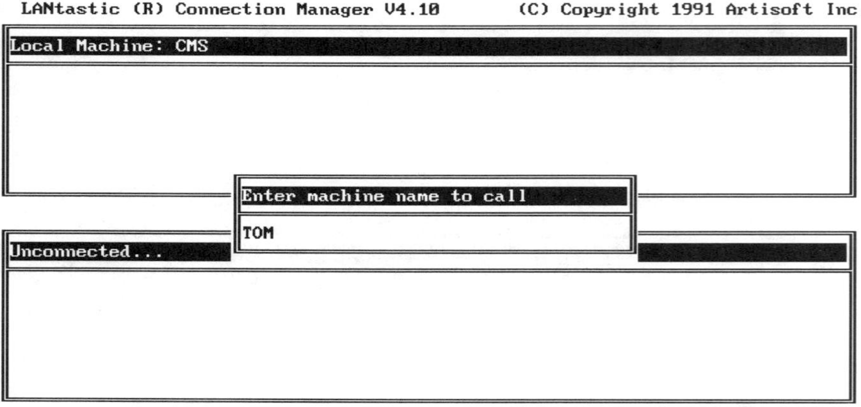

Figure 8-3. Once the connection is made, CMS presses F2 *to enable voice chat*

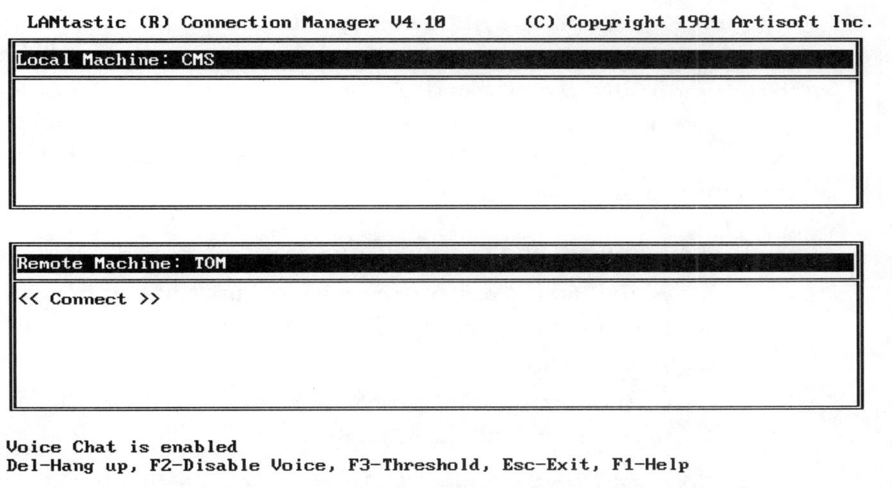

To end the conversation, either person can press DEL to end the voice call only, or press ESC to end the entire chat session. When voice is disabled, you can still chat in writing by using the keyboard. (This is the standard written chat feature built into LANtastic.) In fact, when voice is enabled you can type messages to each other while you talk if you like.

While chatting, you can press F3 to set a voice-activated threshold level. In a noisy room you might need to increase the default value of 32 to avoid constantly transmitting background noise, which would put an extra load on the LAN. You might need to decrease the threshold value to avoid missing occasional words if you talk from a quiet room and speak softly.

Using LANtastic Voice E-Mail

Voice chat is a fun feature, but unless one computer is in a location without a phone you might as well use a normal telephone. However, voice mail is more practical. If regular written electronic mail is useful in your workgroup, voice mail is an extra method of communication that can be worthwhile when you want the recipient to hear the excitement or urgency in your voice. Sometimes written communications don't have the spark that an actual voice does. Also, of course, if you don't like to type you'll find verbal messages more attractive to send.

You saw in Chapter 6 how to send written mail messages between LANtastic users. Voice mail works the same way until the last steps. Follow these steps to send voice mail:

1. First type **net** and press (ENTER).
2. Move the cursor down to the Main Functions option called Mail Services and press (ENTER). NET displays available servers where mail might be stored.
3. Move the cursor to the proper server and press (ENTER). NET's "Manipulating Mail" screen appears.
4. Press (INS) to send a message. This brings up a menu box called Send Mail Options.

All the previous steps are the same as explained in Chapter 6. Here's where your steps begin to differ from how you sent written mail messages.

5. Select the option that says Record Voice Mail (see Figure 8-4). NET then continues, at least for the moment, the same way it operates for written mail. First it prompts you to enter the name of the user who will be the recipient of the voice mail message.
6. Type the name, such as TOM. NET prompts you for a comment to associate with the message. After you type the comment, NET displays the Voice Message Recorder menu box shown in Figure 8-5. This box shows you what takes place while you record your voice message. As the bottom line shows, you press the (SPACEBAR) to begin recording or to pause during the recording.
7. When you finish recording, press (ENTER) to save the message for transmission. If you want to record the message in compressed mode to save disk space, press (F2) before you begin recording. While you record the message, the Message Length field and timer clock increase to show you how much disk space the message uses

Figure 8-4. *Voice mail is the same as regular e-mail until you press* (INS) *to send a message and then select Record Voice Mail*

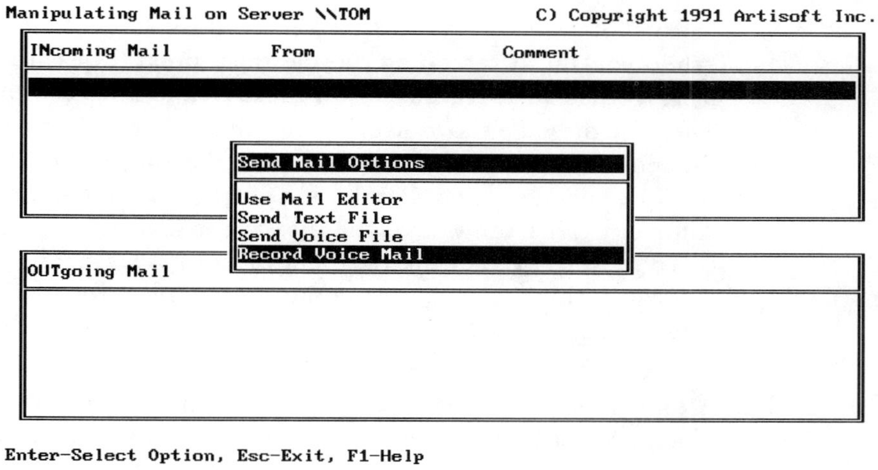

```
Manipulating Mail on Server \\TOM                    C) Copyright 1991 Artisoft Inc.

INcoming Mail          From                  Comment

                   Send Mail Options

                   Use Mail Editor
                   Send Text File
                   Send Voice File
                   Record Voice Mail
OUTgoing Mail

Enter-Select Option, Esc-Exit, F1-Help
```

Figure 8-5. *The bottom line of the screen with the Voice Message Recorder menu box shows you how to begin recording and save your message*

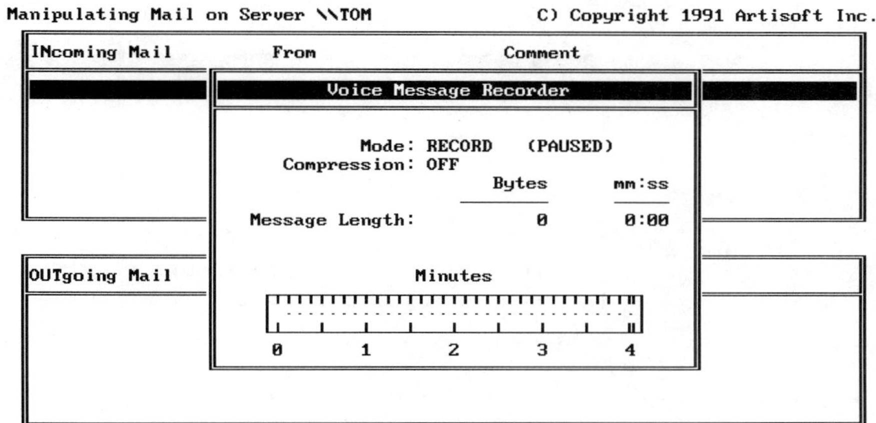

and how much time the message takes. These are good reminders of how quickly your spoken messages can fill up your server's hard disk. Figure 8-6 shows the box while message recording is in progress.

8. When you finish recording the message, press ENTER to save the message. The message is sent over the LAN and stored on the server. Then the message shows itself in the "INcoming Mail" box on both the sender's and recipient's Mail menu. The only visible difference from a typed message is the addition of "(V)" in front of the message comment. That shows that the message is a voice message, not a typed message. Either the recipient or the sender can listen to the message by highlighting the message in the Incoming Mail box and pressing ENTER. This brings up a Mail Options box that has as its first option Listen to Mail. An example is shown in Figure 8-7.
9. After the recipient presses ENTER to select the Listen to Mail option, a Voice Message Recorder box appears. This box is almost identical

Figure 8-6. *The box shows the size of the message in bytes and time during recording*

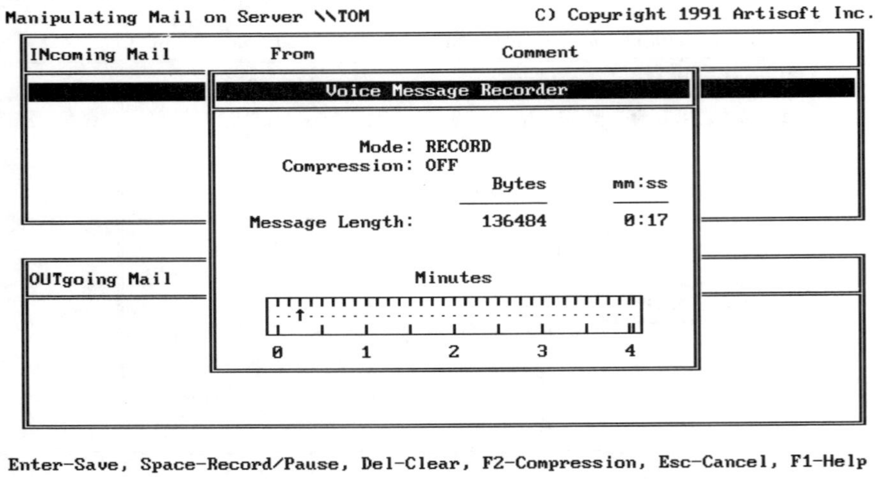

```
Manipulating Mail on Server \\TOM                    C) Copyright 1991 Artisoft Inc.

INcoming Mail          From                Comment

                    Voice Message Recorder

                          Mode: RECORD
                   Compression: OFF
                                           Bytes        mm:ss

              Message Length:             136484         0:17

OUTgoing Mail                    Minutes

                   0        1        2        3        4

Enter-Save, Space-Record/Pause, Del-Clear, F2-Compression, Esc-Cancel, F1-Help
```

Figure 8-7. *The recipient selects the voice message and gets to choose from several options*

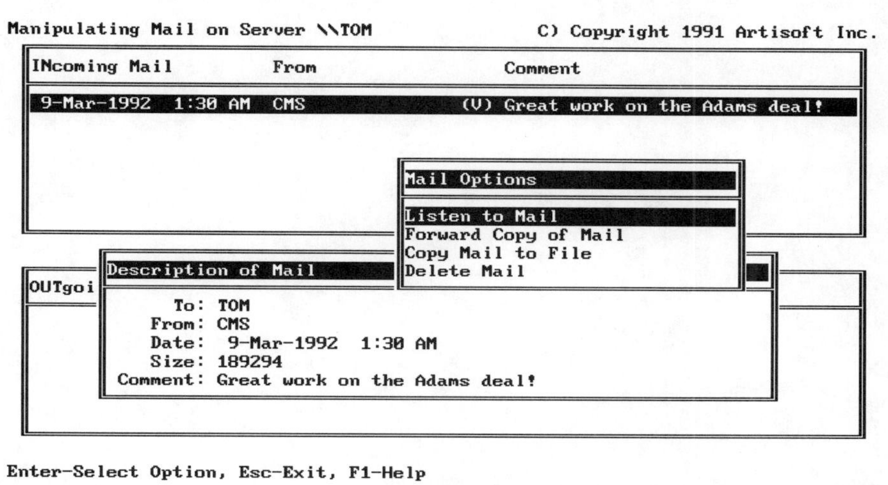

to the one shown previously in Figure 8-5, except that the recipient presses the (SPACEBAR) to play the message, not to record it.

Remember that these voice messages are large and you should delete each one after you hear it to avoid filling up your server's disk. You can reduce the disk space usage by always pressing (F2) to create compressed files. When a recipient plays back a compressed message, NET automatically recognizes the fact that the file is compressed and plays it correctly.

9

Troubleshooting

Life would be nice if everything you tried to do or build worked perfectly the first time and every time thereafter. A little dull, maybe, but nice.

But life isn't like that. Many things don't work when you first attempt them or set them up. The ones that do work the first time have a tendency to fail after a while. "Nothing works forever" is an undeniable fact of life.

This weak attempt at philosophy leads us to the subject of this chapter: troubleshooting. You may never need the discussion in this chapter, but here it is in case you do.

When you read all the things in this chapter that might go wrong with your LANtastic LAN, you might react negatively. You might think, "With all of these things that can cause problems, one of them is *sure* to hit me!" Don't. These things seldom happen. Especially if you keep your LANtastic set-up simple and you don't play football in your office area, you should have few if any problems. In fact, interviews with several Artisoft dealers yielded surprisingly few "common problems." Once your LAN is installed and working, it tends to stay working unless something obvious causes a problem–like accidentally ripping a cable off a LAN card, or a user mistakenly deleting some LANtastic files. So, yes, it's true that anything in this chapter *might* happen to you. However, if you are just moderately careful these things are all either unlikely or easily diagnosed and fixed.

General Troubleshooting

Before getting into specific types of problems, consider some general guidelines that apply to many types of problems you might encounter.

Start with the Obvious

Some people fall into the trap of assuming any problem has a tricky, hidden cause. They can't believe something obvious would be the cause. After all, if the cause is obvious they'll see it immediately, right? Wrong. Failing to see the forest because of all the trees is part of human nature. Check these simple, seemingly obvious things before you start tearing your computers and cables apart to look for obscure gremlins. Some of these ideas apply more to some types of errors than others, but most apply to all problems.

Assume You Made the Mistake

In this context "you" might refer to anyone in your workgroup, but the point is not to blame the LANtastic hardware or software for problems until you absolutely rule out any mistake you might have made. Yes, there are always bugs in software and yes, hardware can fail, but the overwhelming percentage of problems you might encounter will be caused by human error. It's easy to press a wrong key or misinterpret an instruction. Don't assume LANtastic is no good until you rule out any mistakes that a user may have made–such as forgetting to reboot the computer after running INSTALL or misspelling a parameter that was changed in STARTNET.BAT.

First Look for the Most Obvious

A tired cliche on television situation comedies is the joke about a do-it-yourselfer who works for hours to fix an appliance–when the problem is that it's unplugged from the wall socket. Many LAN problems have equally obvious causes. Some incredibly obvious questions to ask are as follows:

- Is the computer plugged in? Is the monitor? The keyboard?
- Are all LAN cables still firmly connected to all LAN cards?
- Does the LAN use only cables that meet specifications? Is the cable length maximum exceeded?
- Is every computer running MS-DOS version 3.1, 3.3, or higher? Enter the DOS VER command to see. Type **ver** and press ENTER.
- Are all the DOS and LANtastic files still on the hard disk?
- Does everything else work on the computer? Is it just when you start LANtastic that something goes wrong? Maybe the problem has nothing to do with LANtastic. Maybe someone accidentally reformatted the hard disk.
- Are you entering the right commands in the right sequence? Are you spelling all of them correctly?
- Did the computer display an error message you overlooked when you powered it on?
- For thin Ethernet, do you have terminators at the ends of the daisy chain of cables?
- For 10BASE-T, is the hub powered on?

Examine Recent Changes

If your LAN worked yesterday but doesn't work today, did any change or unusual event occur between then and now? If so, something done during the change or event is the most likely cause of things working differently or not working at all. Do some detective work to see what anyone in the workgroup might have done. Some questions to consider:

- Did someone move a PC from one location to another? This could damage the LAN cable or connection to the LAN card.
- Did someone change CONFIG.SYS or delete it? Both on a server and a workstation, CONFIG.SYS must contain the right settings for LANtastic to work correctly.
- Did someone install new application software on a server or workstation? During the installation process, critical files may have been changed, replaced, or deleted. Also, the application software may

not be compatible with LANtastic, or it may have been installed for a stand-alone computer instead of a network environment.

- Did someone update the STARTNET.BAT file to "improve" it or eliminate some "unnecessary" portions? Verify that it still runs the right LANtastic programs in the right sequence and using the right parameters.
- Did someone install some special software such as a disk cache program or a TSR (terminate-and-stay-resident) utility program? Some of these products are either incompatible with LANtastic or need to be installed in a certain way to coexist with LANtastic.
- Did someone reconnect a cable that "fell off?" It may have fallen off because it was kicked and damaged.
- Did someone run a "harmless" game or utility program borrowed from a friend or downloaded from a computer bulletin board? This program may have introduced a computer virus to the LAN, which could destroy critical files or cause any number of other problems. See Chapter 11 for more information on computer viruses.
- Did someone install a new expansion card in the computer that has a problem? The card may use conflicting IRQs, I/O port base addresses, or memory addresses. Also the LAN card or cable may have been damaged during the new card's installation.

These and a thousand other things could cause a problem on your LAN. Find out what change has been made lately and try to figure out how the change or new activity might cause a problem. People often can't recognize that a change could cause a seemingly unrelated LAN problem. Encourage your workgroup members to tell you of *any* kind of change since the last successful use of the LAN (or the PC, printer, or whatever), even if in their minds the change *could not possibly* cause a problem. You may see a cause-and-effect relationship that others don't. Yes, sometimes a failure occurs when nothing has changed—hard disks fail, memory chips go bad, and so on. Even so, a huge percentage of problems result from seemingly innocent and unrelated actions and changes.

Look Up Error Messages

LANtastic's numerous software components are carefully designed to display specific error messages when certain problems are detected. These error messages are all listed in alphabetical order with explanations in Appendix E of the *LANtastic Network Operating System Reference Manual.* (Also listed are informative messages that don't indicate error situations.) Carefully read the message on the screen, write it down, and look in the manual for an explanation. The messages themselves are very brief so as not to take up much space in the LANtastic programs (and to not take up extra RAM). However, the explanations in Appendix E have much more information, usually pointing you precisely to the cause of the problem.

Look at the first error message if several are displayed. For example, if you run STARTNET and the first program (AEX or another low-level LAN card driver) detects an error, it displays a message and then ends. Depending on the structure of STARTNET, the second program (AILANBIO) may also try to run, even though the first program did not run successfully. The second program will undoubtedly display an error message, too. However, the second error message is not your concern; it only occurs because the first program failed. Pay attention to just the first error message.

Run LANCHECK

If you want to verify that everything is properly connected, LANCHECK is your best friend. Chapter 5 tells you how to run LANCHECK and perform other fundamental tests. If LANCHECK shows an inability of all computers to connect to each other, look for a bad cable or terminator (for thin Ethernet) or a bad hub (for 10BASE-T), or a problem with the software setup for all the computers. If LANCHECK shows just one computer that can't communicate when all the others are fine, look for a problem with that one computer's hardware or software.

Isolate the Problem

A fundamental fact about a LAN makes it harder to troubleshoot than a stand-alone computer: A LAN consists of many different computers and software components connected together. Because of these multiple components and connections, a problem can exist anywhere on the hardware chain or software chain that connects them. If a workstation can't communicate with a server, a hardware problem might be in the workstation itself, the workstation's LAN card, the server itself, the server's LAN card, or the cable connecting them. A software problem might be in any of the software components on either computer: drivers, system software, application software, or parameters you specify for any of them. If any one piece of the hardware or software chain has a problem, communication doesn't work. How do you find that piece?

The basic answer is to take steps to isolate the problem. Divide and conquer. A number of simple techniques are helpful to track down hardware and software problems. Unfortunately, you can't always tell up front if the problem is caused by hardware or software. Sometimes you have to try both types of problem isolation. Following are some general techniques to isolate hardware and software problems.

Hardware Problem Isolation

Two isolation approaches work best to pin down hardware problems: part swapping and conflict elimination.

Part Swapping If one computer can't communicate with the others, swap (exchange) a cable that connects that computer with another cable. The other cable can be a spare cable you have on hand or can be a cable you already use in another part of the LAN. After the swap, has the problem moved with the cable? If so, the cable is bad. If not, the cable isn't the problem. With thin Ethernet, one bad cable can prevent *all* computers from communicating. You need a spare cable to test for this bad cable. Swap the spare cable with one of your cables and then test your LAN with LANCHECK. If the problem persists, swap another cable and test again. If you replace every cable and the problem remains, the cable is not your problem (or else you have two bad cables).

If one computer can't communicate, you can swap LAN cards between two computers to see if the problem follows the LAN card. If you have a spare terminator, replace each terminator in turn to see if the problem goes away. A bad or missing terminator, like a bad thin Ethernet cable, can prevent the *entire* LAN from communicating. Notice the value of having available at least one spare cable and, for thin Ethernet, one spare terminator and one spare BNC T connector. These components are not expensive and can help you isolate problems quickly.

Conflict Elimination If one computer won't work on the LAN, the problem may be a hardware conflict inside that computer. Remove all possible conflicting cards, such as a CD-ROM controller, a backup tape controller, a bus mouse, and any other I/O card except the hard disk controller and the LAN card. Test the computer without these cards. If the computer then works with the LAN, the problem is a conflict between the LAN card and one of the removed cards. Add them back one at a time, testing after each addition. When the problem comes back, the conflict's cause is the card you just added. Then you can try (either on the conflicting card or the LAN card) a different IRQ, I/O port base address, or other setting, or get a replacement card if the one you have is faulty.

Software Problem Isolation

A LAN that runs application programs has many more software components than hardware components. If a single computer won't work on the LAN, the best basic approach to isolate a software problem is to start with a simple software configuration and build it up until something fails. Make a backup copy of your CONFIG.SYS, AUTOEXEC.BAT, and STARTNET.BAT files. Then change these files to their simplest possible configuration to test the LAN, as shown in the following sections (*xxxx* indicates to use whatever is appropriate on your computer).

AUTOEXEC.BAT Use only PATH=*xxxx* and PROMPT PG.

CONFIG.SYS Use only the statements that the LANtastic INSTALL program created. These are FILES, BUFFERS, LASTDRIVE, and FCBS. Don't use the "/X" parameter on any statement. You can also use the STACKS statement. On a server with DOS 4 or 5, or a workstation with DOS 4 and a large hard disk, include the INSTALL=C:*xxxx*\SHARE*xxxx* statement that the INSTALL program or DOS created. On a server with DOS 3.1 or 3.3, start SHARE from AUTOEXEC.BAT or STARTNET.BAT.

STARTNET.BAT Use only the statements INSTALL created.

Examples of all three files are shown in Appendix A. If your LAN works with this minimal configuration, then start adding to these files the other statements you previously had, one by one. Test the computer on the LAN after each change. Depending on your problem, the test might be to run LANCHECK or to run a software application that causes your problem, or both. When you run a test that won't work, you know that the cause of your problem is the statement you just added to one of these three files. After a test fails, try the test again to be sure the problem is repeatable.

In general, if you want to run TSR utilities such as SideKick or ProKey you should start them *after* you start the LANtastic software, not before. Usually the best way to ensure the correct startup sequence is to copy the contents from your STARTNET.BAT file into the end of AUTOEXEC.BAT, and then add the statements that start the TSR programs after those statements at the end of AUTOEXEC.BAT.

If you run Windows, see Chapter 12. If you run optimization utilities such as a disk cache (including LANtastic's LANcache) or a memory manager such as QEMM or 386MAX, see Chapter 13. Any of these products can cause problems if you don't use them correctly.

Specific Problems

If you read the first part of this chapter carefully and try the methods suggested, you should find the cause of most problems. However, some specific problems might occur for which there are specific solutions. This section discusses the most common ones.

Single Computer Lockup

A *computer lockup* is an unresponsive computer. You can press keys until doomsday but you never get a response except maybe a beep. A lockup indicates an internal error of some kind that causes DOS to be unable to accept your keyboard entries. The only solution is to reboot the computer, by using the three-key combination CTRL-ALT-DEL (which sometimes gets no response either), or by pressing the hardware reset button (if your computer has one), or by powering off the computer, waiting a few seconds, and powering it back on again. In any event, you lose any work you have done since you last saved your word processing files or other data. A lockup has an assortment of other colorful names, some of them not acceptable in polite company. Some of the acceptable ones are a hung computer, a dead computer, a keyboard lockout, a system loop, and a system crash. Whatever you call it, it's a pain and you want to avoid it.

Many types of internal conflicts can cause a lockup. Some lockups occur when you first run a LANtastic program, such as AEX, AILANBIO, REDIR, or LANCHECK. Others occur when you run an application program. Here are some things to check if you have a lockup problem:

IRQ or IOBASE Conflicts

The conflict can either be between the LAN card and the LAN software, or between the LAN card and another add-on card. Be sure the LAN card's hardware jumper settings match the low-level driver software's parameters. Use the /verbose parameter on AEX (or whatever driver your LAN card uses) to verify what the software specifies, and then check that your LAN card jumpers are set to the same settings. For conflicts with other cards, check your hardware manuals to see what the other cards require. Be sure you don't use an XT-type hard disk controller in an AT-type computer. The XT controller uses IRQ 5, but a disk controller on an AT is supposed to use IRQ 14. Some independent LAN cards use IRQ 5, which is usually available in an AT.

RAMBASE Conflicts

Some LAN cards use a block of memory in the area from 640K to 1024K (often referred to by hexadecimal segment addresses A000 to FFFF). The LANtastic 2Mbps card and some independent Ethernet cards (but not the LANtastic AE-x cards) require part of this memory and use a parameter called RAMBASE to specify it. Other hardware and software can conflict with the memory block. Possible problems come from expanded memory (EMS) hardware, memory management programs such as EMM386, QEMM, and 386MAX, and VGA video cards in 16-bit mode when using certain graphics modes. Be sure these products don't conflict with your LAN card. Specify to the memory manager program that the LAN card's RAMBASE address range is to be excluded from the program's control. Put your VGA card in an 8-bit slot (and/or set a switch on the card to specify 8-bit mode) to be sure it is not the cause.

TSR Program Conflicts

A TSR (terminate-and-stay-resident) program occupies memory and in most cases waits for you to press a certain keyboard combination before it "pops up" and becomes active. (Other TSRs are activated by internal computer events.) Some of these programs are not compatible with LANtastic. Start TSR programs after you start LANtastic. If you have lockup (or other) problems, don't run the TSR program and see if the problem goes away. If it does, the TSR program is the cause. Contact the program's manufacturer or Artisoft to see if a way exists to run the TSR and LANtastic together. Sometimes a lockup occurs only because of a rare combination of events—several programs all happen to do a certain unusual thing at once. You might be able to reboot your computer and never see the problem again. However, if the problem is frequent you need a solution.

Computer Viruses

If a computer virus wiped out critical DOS files you may not be able to even boot your computer. Try to boot from a virus-free write-protected floppy disk and then run a virus-checking program. See Chapter 11 for more information about computer viruses.

Inability to Communicate

Another type of problem is a computer that doesn't lock up, but can't communicate with other LAN computers. In some cases none of the computers can communicate with the others. Sometimes this problem is consistent, other times it's intermittent. As discussed earlier, your best tool to diagnose connection problems is LANCHECK. Use it to pin down the scope and consistency of the problem. If your LAN computers aren't communicating, see if any of these problems are the cause:

- *Computer lockup problems* The same things that can cause a computer lockup can cause an intermittent inability to communicate by one system (or all systems if you set them all up the same way). See the section, "Single Computer Lockup," earlier in this chapter.

- *Bad cable* On a thin Ethernet LAN, one bad cable can prevent all computers from communicating. Substitute a good spare cable for each LAN cable in turn, as explained in the "Hardware Problem Isolation" section earlier in this chapter. If any cables are exposed to view, the exposed area is the most likely location for damage. If you are handy with electronics, use an ohm meter to test each cable for continuity and shorts.
- *Bad connector* This is a variation on a bad cable. Sometimes a cable itself is fine, but the connector on the end of a cable is damaged. If the connector itself isn't damaged, the cable may have been pulled hard, which may have caused contact between the cable and connector to be broken. Either install a new connector or replace the entire cable-connector combination. Another possibility is a bad BNC T connector. Especially if you frequently pull hard on cables or disconnect and reconnect cables, the T connector can become cracked or otherwise damaged. Try replacing each T connector in turn with a spare to see if the problem goes away.
- *Nonstandard cable type or length* The need to use the right cable was stressed in chapters 4 and 5. For thin Ethernet, be sure you use RG58 a/u (the most readily available type that meets specifications) or RG58 c/u. Do not use plain RG58 or RG58/U. These other cables have slightly different electrical characteristics and may cause erratic problems or even damage to your LAN cards. Sometimes these nonstandard cables will work in small configurations but fail when you either expand the LAN or begin using it heavily. Don't take a chance. Replace nonstandard cable with the proper type and use the same kind of cable throughout the LAN. Be sure the total length of the cables does not exceed the 185-meter (607-foot) specification for thin Ethernet. For 10BASE-T, be sure each cable meets specifications and does not exceed the 100-meter (328-foot) length limit.
- *Environmental hazards* Especially for 10BASE-T cable, be sure to avoid electrical interference from motors, power supplies, electromagnets, and light fixtures. Thin Ethernet is less susceptible to such hazards, but some installers claim that even a fluorescent light fixture can cause problems with thin Ethernet if you put them together just right (or wrong).

- *Missing or faulty terminator* A missing or faulty terminator can prevent all or part of a thin Ethernet LAN from being able to communicate. Have spares on hand and check the terminators at both ends.
- *Bad LAN card* If one computer can't communicate but all others can, you might have a bad LAN card. Swap the card with another computer's LAN card and see if the problem moves to the other computer. If so, either the LAN card is bad or its jumper settings are wrong for both computers. If the problem stays with the computer, the problem is probably either a conflict on that computer (IRQ or other) or a bad card slot in that computer. Try moving the LAN card to another slot.
- *Bad hub* For 10BASE-T, the hub/concentrator may be powered off, faulty, or configured incorrectly.

Corrupt Disk Files

A disturbing type of problem is if everything seems to work properly with your LAN but sometimes disk files you save or copy are corrupt. The data seems to be successfully saved on disk but when you later look at it, the data is all or partially wrong. These are some possible causes:

- *User error* You may have simply made a mistake and not saved what you thought. If the problem happens only once or extremely rarely, user error is the most likely cause. Try to reconstruct the exact steps you followed to see if you entered a wrong command at some point.
- *Disk cache conflicts* A disk cache program is designed to speed up disk access by storing certain disk data in RAM storage instead of on disk. A computer can process data in RAM much faster than on disk. LANtastic comes with its own special disk cache program called LANcache, which does not run unless you make changes to STARTNET.BAT to make it run. Some other disk cache programs are either incompatible with LANtastic, or require careful setup to work properly. See Chapter 13 for more information.

- *Incompatible application software* If an application program is incompatible with LANtastic or any other network, there is a chance that using the program in a LAN environment can permit two users to corrupt files. Be sure your program is LAN compatible if two users may try to use the same file at once.
- *Failure to use SHARE on a server* The SHARE program is the DOS mechanism that prevents two users from simultaneously updating the same file on a server. You must run SHARE on a server to avoid file corruption problems. (You don't need to run SHARE on a workstation, except that DOS 4 requires SHARE to support a hard disk over 32 megabytes.) In DOS 4 or 5, SHARE is best installed using CONFIG.SYS. In DOS 3.1 or 3.3, start SHARE in AUTOEXEC.BAT. Some people stop running SHARE on a server after encountering a "Share violation" error message when two people try to use a file at once. DON'T DO THIS! On a server, *always* run SHARE. The "Share violation" problem is solved safely only by using software that is designed properly to share files on a LAN or by setting the shared files' attributes to read-only.
- *Using FASTOPEN* Some users report problems caused by the DOS FASTOPEN statement in CONFIG.SYS when using DOS 5.0, whether running LANtastic or not. To be safe, remove FASTOPEN. See your DOS manual for details.
- *Failure to bring down the server gracefully* Don't simply turn a server's power off. The server may be in the middle of writing output data on a disk file. By powering it off (or pressing a hardware reset button) you may prevent the server from leaving data files in good condition. Instead, be sure no workstations are actively using the server and then either type the command **server /remove** and press ENTER, or else press CTRL-ALT-DEL and then type **s** to shut down the server.
- *Power problems* If your server or workstation loses power occasionally, two bad things can happen. First, you can corrupt disk files for the same reasons just mentioned—because a power failure does not bring down the server gracefully. Second, power failures are often accompanied by power surges and spikes that can damage your LAN

card or other computer components. Use a surge protector as minimum protection. If you have frequent power failures, consider using a UPS system (see the box on UPS Systems).

- *Computer lockup problems* The same things that can cause a computer lockup can cause corrupt disk files. See the "Single Computer Lockup" section earlier in this chapter.

UPS Systems

Chapter 4 briefly mentioned the advantages of using a UPS (uninterruptible power supply) system if your office is susceptible to power failures or your applications are especially critical. This section tells how LANtastic works with UPS and where you can get more information.

Several types of UPS systems are on the market. The most useful type to protect your LANtastic server is often called a standby UPS system. You connect your computer's power cord to the UPS system, and the UPS system to the commercial power source. The commercial power passes through the UPS, which under normal circumstances simply uses a little power to recharge its own internal batteries and passes the power on through to the computer. If the UPS system detects a power loss or brownout, it continues providing power from its batteries so the computer is unaffected by the power problem. Different UPS models continue to provide the server's power from batteries for different time periods, but 5 to 30 minutes is common for inexpensive models.

When the commercial power fails, the UPS system communicates to the LANtastic server by sending a signal over a cable connected to a serial port on the server. The server then takes whatever action you have planned for it. Depending on your needs, the actions may vary. At the least, you want the server to perform an orderly shutdown so you avoid corrupt disk files. You may also want to make backup copies of files or take other protective action. Of course, if the power failure is only momentary, you don't want to take these actions at all. You just want the UPS system to continue providing power for a few seconds until the commercial power returns.

LANtastic comes with a program called UPS that you must run on a server to process the signal the UPS system sends to the serial port. You run UPS after the SERVER program, so you can simply add it to the end of your STARTNET.BAT file. When you start the UPS program you can specify numerous parameters (listed in Chapter 14) to determine what the server will do. The most important parameter that you'll set is for a brownout minimum, which says how long the power failure must last before LANtastic schedules a shutdown. The other important parameter to set is for minutes until shutdown, which specifies the number of minutes before the shutdown actually occurs. You might want to ignore a power failure of less than 60 seconds, but then schedule the shutdown for 10 minutes later. If the power returns during that 10 minutes, you want to cancel the server's scheduled shutdown. When LANtastic schedules a shutdown, it sends a message to users logged in to the server to tell them when the shutdown will occur. That way users who still have their own power (or a UPS system) can take whatever actions they need to save files or make backup copies before the server shutdown occurs.

Prices for low-capacity UPS systems (one to five computers) typically range from $200 to $1000. UPS systems that are compatible with LANtastic are available from several manufacturers, including these:

- American Power Conversion, 132 Fairgrounds Road, West Kingston, RI 02892, 800-541-8896, 401-789-5735
- PARA Systems, 1455 LeMay Drive, Carrollton, TX 75007, 800-238-7272, 214-446-7363
- SOLA Electric, 1717 Buss Road, Elk Grove, IL 60007, 800-BUY-SOLA, 708-439-2800
- Tripp Lite, 500 N. Orleans, Chicago, IL 60610, 312-329-1777

Other Problems

Other problems with LANtastic are usually more localized than the ones already covered. These problems may involve the inability of a user to access a certain server from a certain workstation, or problems printing output under certain circumstances, or many other specific things. If the problem is accompanied by an error message from LANtastic, your best bet by far is to read the message explanation in the *LANtastic Network Operating System Reference Manual.*

Here are some common problems and solutions:

- *One application program doesn't work* Review the program's installation instructions for a LAN environment. Follow the directions for a "NetBIOS LAN" or a "PC LAN", *not* a NetWare LAN. If the documentation has no such instructions, maybe it won't work on a LAN. Call the manufacturer and find out. You may have to buy a special LAN version of the product.
- *The AEX driver program won't work with your LAN card* The AEX program works only with Artisoft (LANtastic) Ethernet cards. If you have the LANtastic 2Mbps card, use LANBIOS for the old cards, LANBIOS2 for the newer "enhanced" cards (called E2MBPS), and LANBIOS3 for the newest 2Mbps cards (called A2MBPS). For independent (non-Artisoft) Ethernet cards, you must buy LANtastic/AI, the adapter independent version of LANtastic for each node. This version has different drivers for many independent cards. AEX will not work with them.
- *Only five users can log in to a server at once* Five is the default maximum. If you need more users at once on a server, change the SERVER statement in STARTNET.BAT to include the /logins= parameter. If you prefer, you can run NET_MGR on the server and select the Server Startup Parameters function to increase the "Maximum Users" number. Increasing the number uses more RAM on the server, as discussed in Chapter 13.
- *Only ten users can log in to a server at once* Ten is the default maximum number of users for the * group account that everyone uses if you don't set up your own individual or group accounts. Use NET_MGR's Group Account Management function to increase the "Number Concurrent Logins" from ten to whatever you need. See Chapter 10 for more information about group accounts.

- *A workstation can't log in to a server* Be sure the computer you think is a server is running the SERVER program.
- *A workstation can log in to only two servers at once* This limit is set by the /logins= parameter on the workstation's REDIR statement in STARTNET.BAT. Usually two is enough, but you may want more. Increasing this number uses more RAM.
- *A workstation can access the server's hard disk but not its own C drive* Don't redirect the workstation's C drive to the server. If you do, you are telling LANtastic to use C to refer to the server's hard disk, not to your own disk. Pick another letter such as L—a letter that doesn't correspond with one of the workstation's own hard disks.
- *A sharing violation when trying to run a program on a server* Use the DOS ATTRIB command to set all the server's shared executable files to "read-only" status. Executable files are ones that have a filename extension of EXE, COM, BAT, and OVL.
- *Unacceptably slow server response* See Chapter 13.
- *Unacceptably slow printing* See Chapter 13.
- *Erratic printing speed* Increase the NET LPT TIMEOUT value in STARTNET.BAT.

10

LANtastic Security

LANtastic security is simply another phrase that means LAN protection. You have valuable assets on your LANtastic LAN and you don't want them damaged or lost. In effect, LANtastic security is no more than a restriction on your LAN users' freedom. Although restricting freedom may seem in opposition to worldwide political trends, it's really no different from installing a lock on your front door and giving keys only to those you trust. You don't want everyone who passes by to have the freedom to enter your home unless you give permission. Similarly, you may decide you don't want everyone who can enter your building to have the freedom to read, change, or delete the files on your LANtastic servers. (This chapter focuses on LANtastic's built-in security features; Chapter 11 gives details on protecting against another type of threat to your system–viruses.)

The LANtastic software provides four methods for imposing security on your LAN:

- *Controlling logins to servers* LANtastic lets you set up user accounts to control who can log in to a server and when.

- *Controlling the type of access allowed to a server's shared resources* LANtastic uses access control lists (ACLs) to decide what kind of access is allowable for each shared resource.
- *Limiting the resources a server offers* LANtastic lets you give users access only to specified server disk directories if you don't want them to have access to the entire hard disk.
- *Maintaining audit trails* LANtastic can keep track in a disk file who did what to each server, so you can review server usage after the fact.

These are all software security measures. It's up to you to provide whatever physical security you believe appropriate, such as limiting physical access to your servers and workstations. None of these software security measures prevent anyone from walking up to your server, rebooting it from a floppy disk, and reading or deleting any files on the server's hard disk. The best way to prevent this type of security breach is to put your server in a locked room.

Also note that all of LANtastic's security is centered around servers. The philosophy is that your servers contain your valuable shared data and access to other resources such as printers. LANtastic's goal is to protect these valuable shared resources from unauthorized or erroneous access or data destruction.

This chapter goes through each of these four LANtastic security mechanisms in turn.

Controlled Logins

When you set up LANtastic's software using the INSTALL program, you establish virtually no security restrictions. Anyone can access any resource available on any server. Actually, what INSTALL creates for each server is a group user account called * (asterisk). The asterisk acts like a wildcard, much like it does for DOS filenames, and allows anyone to log in to a server using any username and no password. Everyone who uses a server accesses it through this group account.

The mechanism by which LANtastic controls access to a server is called a user account. A *user account* is a set of information that describes who a user is and what that user can do on a LANtastic server. When user accounts are activated, nobody can access a server unless a user account is previously set up for that user. You can set up user accounts for individuals or for groups, or both.

An unscientific survey of a few LANtastic dealers and sites leads to the conclusion that in 90 to 95 percent of all LANtastic installations, user accounts are not implemented. No security restrictions are placed on anyone. If you see no need to restrict access to your LAN servers in any way, fine. It's your choice. However, you might find this chapter worthwhile reading so you can decide if security will help you control your LAN and protect your data.

Here's a brief summary of the kinds of restrictions you can place on your LANtastic users if you implement LANtastic's security features to control server logins. You don't have to establish all these restrictions. You can use as many or as few as you like.

- Require anyone who wants access to a server to first enter a valid username and password.
- Prevent certain or all users from using a server on some days of the week or certain hours of the day, such as outside of normal office hours.
- Require users to change passwords periodically to reduce the damage if an outsider discovers someone's password.
- Make a user account expire on a pre-set date so the user (such as a temporary employee) can no longer access a server after that date.
- Give some users special privileges to manipulate jobs on the printer queue or access all server resources, while restricting other users.
- Decide if each user should be allowed to access a server from more than one workstation simultaneously.
- Set up a group account so that everyone in a group has the same rights, so you don't have to set up an individual user account for each member one at a time.

When you use LANtastic's security features, you need someone to take the role of the LAN administrator. This is a person who controls usernames, passwords, resources offered, expiration dates, and other security-related constraints. Sometimes the LAN administrator goes by other names: LAN manager, system manager, network administrator, and network manager are a few examples. Chapter 11 discusses other duties a LAN administrator should also perform. For a small LAN, this person only spends a small percentage of each week handling administrative duties. On a large LAN with stringent security, the LAN administrator might perform these functions nearly full time.

For the purposes of this chapter, assume that you are the LAN administrator for your LANtastic LAN. If your LAN uses security or might in the future, you need to understand the material in this chapter. Other users also might want to know this information so they will understand just what they can and can't do with LANtastic when security is in force.

The program the LAN administrator uses to control security (and a few other things) is NET_MGR. You were introduced briefly to NET_MGR in Chapter 7. In this chapter you learn much more about it. In addition, individual users have limited control over their accounts through use of the NET program.

Establishing User Accounts

This section takes you through the process of setting up user accounts, both for individuals and groups. The process is straightforward; before long you will find you can add a new user quickly and effortlessly.

Individual Accounts

To start, create a user account for an individual. These accounts are regulated on each server, not for the whole LANtastic LAN at once. From the keyboard on the server you first want to control, type **net_mgr** and press ENTER. NET-MGR displays its opening screen of Main Functions, as shown in Figure 10-1.

The first function, Individual Account Management, is highlighted. That's the one you need to create an individual user account, so press ENTER to select it. NET_MGR displays a menu box titled Current Users. You haven't created any user accounts so far, so the box is empty. Press INS to add a new user. This brings up a box that prompts you to enter the username. You can make the username as long as 16 characters, but you probably want a short name. Unless several people share each PC, use the same name as the machine name

Figure 10-1. *The Main Functions screen of NET_MGR*

```
LANtastic (R) Network Manager V4.10        (C) Copyright 1991 Artisoft Inc.

 Main Functions

 Individual Account Management
 Group Account Management
 Shared Resources Management
 Server Startup Parameters
 Audit Trail Maintenance
 Queue Maintenance
 Password Maintenance
 Boot Image Maintenance
 Control Directory Maintenance

Enter-Select Option, Esc-Exit, F1-Help
```

you assigned to the user's computer when you ran INSTALL. The name cannot contain any blank spaces, colons, commas, or semicolons. (You can press F1 to get help with these rules and other tips at any time.) Type the name **BOB** in this example (see Figure 10-2) and then press ENTER.

NET_MGR then prompts you for the user's password, which must follow the same rules as the username. For best security, a password should not be too short. However, for convenience the name shouldn't be too long either. Usually five to eight characters is a good compromise. The name should *not* be something that anyone else could easily associate with BOB. Examples of bad choices are BOB, ROBERT, TREBOR (Robert backwards), Bob's middle or last name, his spouse's name, his children's names, his hobbies, his anniversary, or any other personal information. These passwords are too easily guessed by others. The best choice might simply be a random word of the right length you pick out of a dictionary. Avoid one that Bob might take as an insult or a compliment (NASTY, PIMPLE, HANDSOME, JACKASS). He might find any of these so amusing or outrageous that he would talk about it to others, and the whole point of a password is to keep it secret.

Figure 10-2. *After you press* INS *to add a name, type the username*

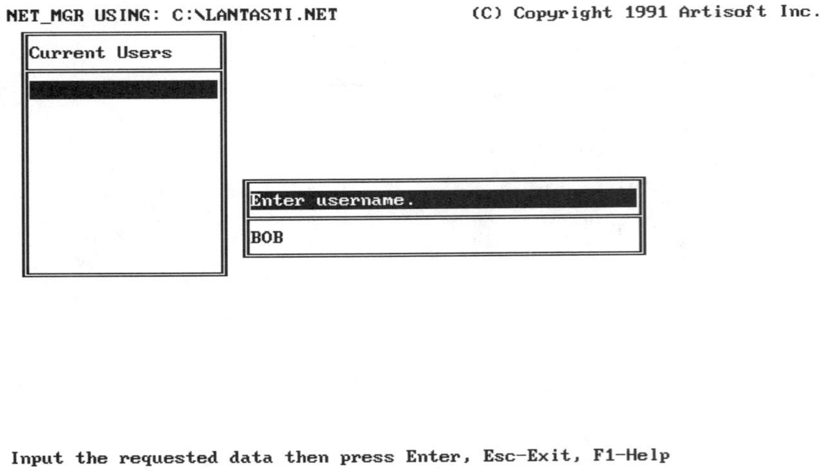

```
NET_MGR USING: C:\LANTASTI.NET              (C) Copyright 1991 Artisoft Inc.

Current Users

                                   Enter username.
                                   BOB

Input the requested data then press Enter, Esc-Exit, F1-Help
```

Each user on the LAN should understand these basics of password construction. Users have the option to change their own passwords whenever they like. They simply have to run the NET program and select the User Account Management function from the opening menu. You waste your time picking an unguessable random password for BOB if he immediately changes his password to ROBERT the next day.

Let's say you randomly pick the word "GROUND" for BOB's password. You can type it either in capital letters or lowercase letters, but NET_MGR shows it in all caps and treats caps and lowercase letters the same. Type **GROUND** (as shown in Figure 10-3) and press ENTER.

Next NET_MGR asks you for the user's description. You can type any description you like here, up to 64 characters, although only the first 20 or 25 are shown in some output displays. If you have a lot of users on your LAN, this helps keep track of which username goes with which person. In a small office you may not need to enter anything here. In this example type Bob's full name and department, as shown in Figure 10-4, and press ENTER.

The next entry is the number of concurrent logins for this user (see Figure 10-5). If Bob might need to log in from two or more workstations at once to

Figure 10-3. *Type a password, which NET_MGR automatically converts to all caps onscreen*

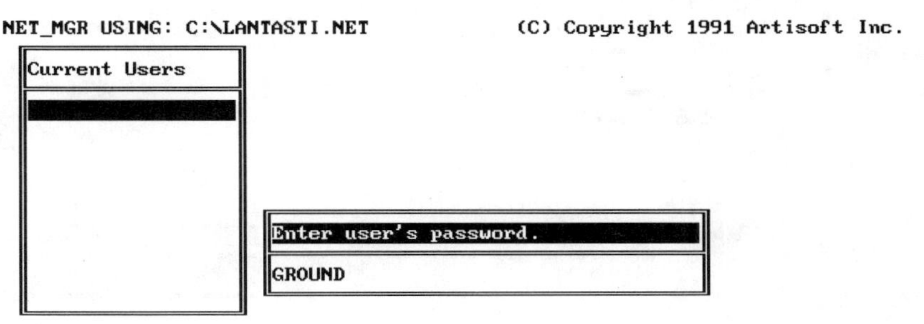

Figure 10-4. *Optionally, enter the user's description*

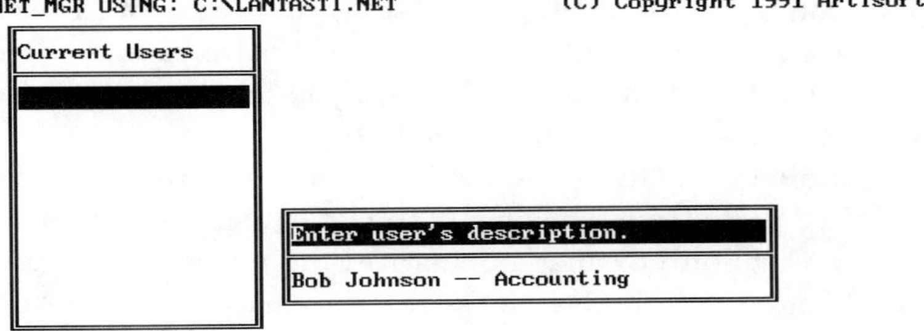

Figure 10-5. *Unless Bob needs to access the server from two workstations at once, leave the number of concurrent logins as 1*

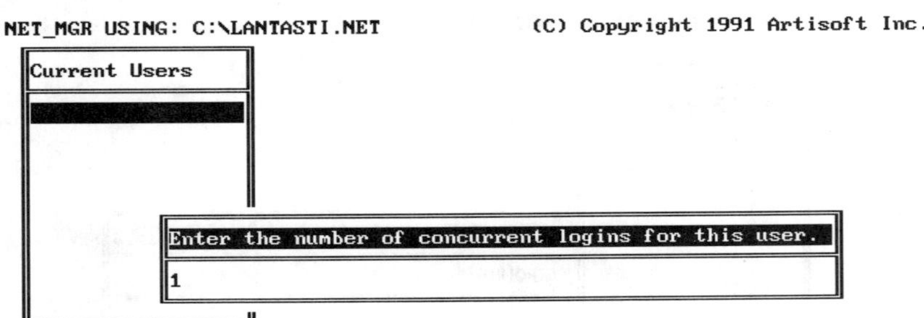

access this server, change the default value of one to a larger number. Most users use only one workstation at a time, so you can just press ENTER to accept the default number.

That completes the creation of a user account for Bob. The changes you made don't take effect until you press ESC twice to end the NET_MGR program; don't do that yet, but be sure you jot down the username and password you assigned so you can tell Bob.

The username BOB now shows itself in the Current Users menu box. Press ENTER again (with the name BOB highlighted) and the screen displays a User Information box that summarizes the entries you made for BOB. Figure 10-6 shows this display. Notice that the password is not displayed. Once you assign the password, you don't see it again. You can't even find it on disk because LANtastic encrypts (encodes) the password. As the LAN administrator you can delete the username BOB and start over again, or you can assign BOB a new password, but you can't see his current password.

Figure 10-6. *BOB is now set up as a username with the information shown*

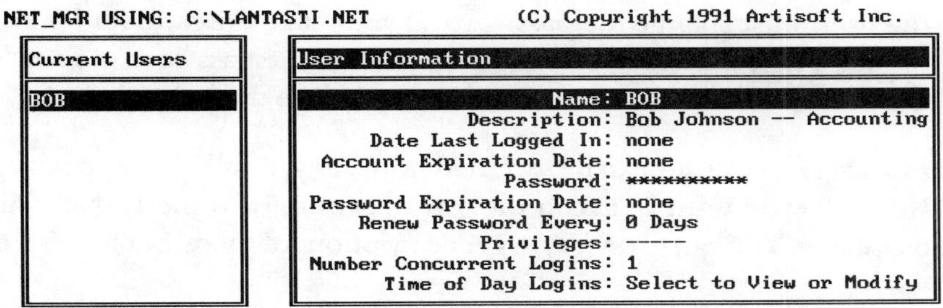

From this User Information menu box you can use the cursor keys to highlight the entries and change them, except for the Date Last Logged In. LANtastic maintains that based on when Bob last logged in to the server.

Four of these entries you entered yourself when you set up BOB's account: Name, Description, Password, and Number Concurrent Logins. You can use the cursor to select these entries and change them whenever you like. Following are brief explanations of the other entries you can change.

Account Expiration Date To limit the lifetime of this user account, highlight the Account Expiration Date entry and press ENTER. NET_MGR displays a dialog box into which you enter a date. After that date, the user can no longer log in to the server.

Password Expiration Date Select the Password Expiration Date entry and a dialog box lets you set a date after which the user will have to come to you to get a new password. The user account will still exist, but you will have to assign a new password. An easier way to force users to periodically pick a new password is the next option.

Renew Password Every Press ENTER with the Renew Password Every entry highlighted and NET_MGR prompts you to enter the number of days before the user must change the password. If you make the number 30, the user has to pick a new password every 30 days. When the password is about to expire, the user gets a warning that it's time to change the password.

Privileges A user can be assigned none, any, or all of five special privileges. Normally you want to assign these privileges only to the LAN administrator's username. You can press F1 to get descriptions of them, but here's a quick look:

- A *Super ACL Privilege* Lets the user access all shared resources on the server, even if access control lists (ACLs) limit the resources that other users can access. ACLs are discussed in a separate section later in this chapter.
- Q *Super Queue Privilege* Lets the user see and manipulate all jobs on the print queue, not just his or her own.
- M *Super Mail Privilege* Lets the user see and manipulate all e-mail, not just his or her own.
- U *User Auditing Privilege* Lets the user enter NET AUDIT commands to place entries in the server audit log.
- S *System Manager's Privilege* Lets the user do system management functions such as logging off users and remotely shutting down the server.

Time of Day Logins This is the method by which you limit the user's access to the server to certain days of the week and certain times of each day. By default the user can access the server any time on any day. Press ENTER with this entry highlighted and NET_MGR displays a weekly calendar that you can change to limit the user's access. Figure 10-7 shows this calendar display without any limitations on the user. Each diamond symbol is a half-hour time block.

Group Accounts

If your LAN has no more than a dozen users, individual user accounts are probably all you need to control LAN usage. If you have more users, you might want to use group accounts.

Figure 10-7. *The Time of Day Logins entry displays a calendar for limiting the user's access time*

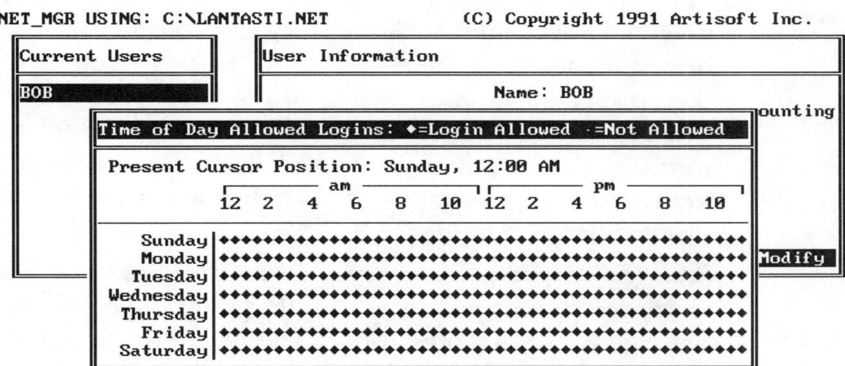

As the name suggests, a *group account* is a single account for an entire group of users. With a group account, you don't have to create individual user accounts for each group member.

A group account works the same way that an individual account does with a few exceptions:

- The first few characters of everyone's username are the same.
- Everyone in the group uses the same password, unless you specify that no password is needed.
- The "number of concurrent logins" you enter sets the limit of how many group members can log in at once.

An example will clarify this. Suppose you have seven users in the shipping department and all need access to a LANtastic server. You decide to set up a group account for them. All will use any usernames they like that start with "SHIP-" such as SHIP-JOE, SHIP-DORIS, and SHIP-AL. The following are the steps to take:

1. Type **net_mgr** and press ENTER. Select the Group Account Management function from the opening menu.
2. This brings up the Group Users menu box, which may still have the universal * account that allows everyone to log in with no password or restrictions. If so, press DEL to delete this account. The screen then displays a message telling you to press ENTER to verify the deletion (see Figure 10-8). Press ENTER to finish the deletion. From now on, or at least after you end NET_MGR, everyone will need to log in to this server using either an individual or group user account that you have established.
3. Press INS to add a new group account. This brings up a menu box asking you to enter a username for the group. Type the name **SHIP-*** (see Figure 10-9) and press ENTER. The asterisk at the end of the name indicates that any text can follow the previous characters to form a legal name. The maximum length for the entire name is 15 characters.
4. When prompted for a password, type a password that everyone in the group will use and press ENTER. Continue by typing the user's description, such as "Shipping Department," and pressing ENTER.

Figure 10-8. *Delete the unrestricted * account before adding a new group account*

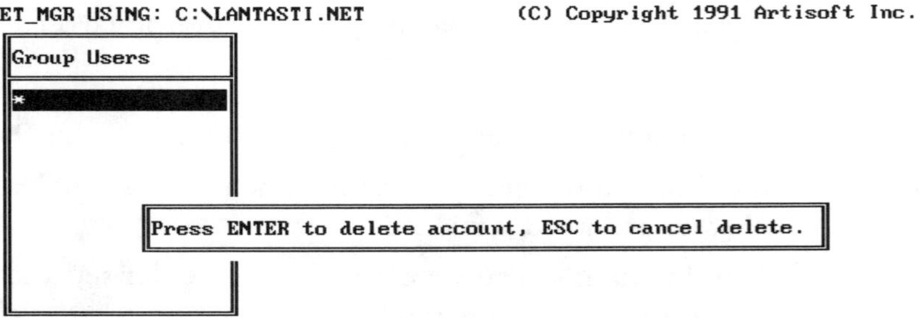

Figure 10-9. *Type the group name prefix plus an asterisk*

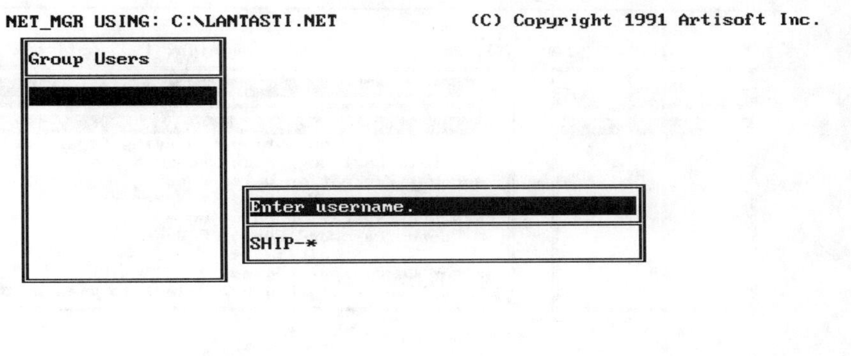

5. When prompted for the "number of concurrent logins for this user" type **7** and press (ENTER). This overrides the default value of 10 that NET_MGR provides for a group account.
6. The NET_MGR program now displays the name SHIP-* in the Group Users menu box. Press (ENTER) to see the User Information for this group account, as shown in Figure 10-10. As was true for an individual user account, you can change these entries if appropriate.
7. Press (ESC) repeatedly until the NET-MGR program ends. The group account is now ready for use.

Access Control Lists

You may recall from Chapter 6 that when you use NET to redirect a disk drive name to a server's hard disk, NET displays a column of alphabet soup under the heading "Access Rights." Figure 10-11 shows this screen from NET.

Figure 10-10. *The User Information box summarizes information about this group account*

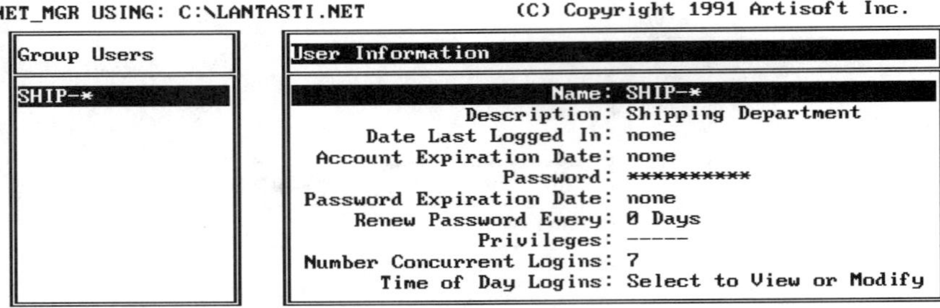

Access Rights

These jumbles of letters refer to 12 different *access rights* that each user may or may not have when using server resources. Users who lack certain access rights cannot perform corresponding operations on the server resource. For example, if you want to be sure that a certain user can read files from the server's hard disk but cannot update or delete those files, you can grant the user the R (read) access right but no other rights.

On each server, LANtastic maintains an *access control list,* which is simply a list of all the access rights granted to each username for each resource the server makes available. Here are brief descriptions of what a user can do if granted each of the 12 access rights.

- R *Read access* Can open files to read
- W *Write access* Can open files to write or update data in them
- C *Create file* Can create new files, but can write in them only if also granted the W right

Figure 10-11. *The Access Rights column that NET shows when you redirect a disk drive name to a server*

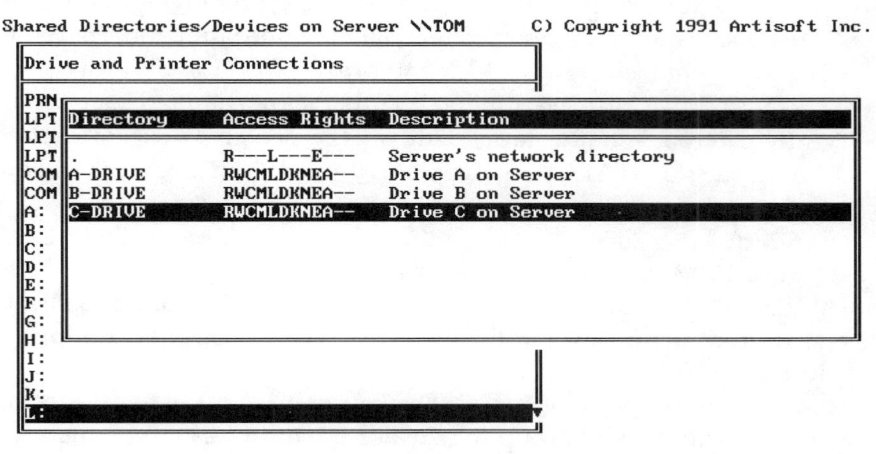

- M *Make directory* Can create disk directories
- L *File lookups* Can display or search disk directories
- D *Delete file* Can delete disk files
- K *Delete directory* Can delete disk directories
- N *Rename file* Can rename disk files
- E *Execute program* Can execute (run) programs from the server
- A *Change file attributes* Can change the DOS file attributes of disk files
- I *Indirect file* Can use indirect files to point to other files
- P *Physical access* Can connect to DOS devices directly instead of through LANtastic's normal server mechanisms (Artisoft warns you not to grant this access right because incorrect use can conflict with LANtastic functions such as the despooler)

By default under LANtastic 4.1, users are granted the first ten access rights for disk drives and access rights R, W, C, and L for printers.

Changing Access Rights

Use the NET_MGR program on the server to change the access rights you authorize for any resource on that server. Type **net_mgr** and press ENTER. Then move the cursor down to highlight the third function, Shared Resources Management (see Figure 10-12) and press ENTER to select it.

NET_MGR displays a menu box that shows all its resource names presently offered and the local path on the server to access each resource. LANtastic's INSTALL program set up these default resources and their access rights.

Move the cursor down to the bottom resource, called "C-DRIVE" as Figure 10-13 shows. Then press ENTER.

Now NET_MGR shows a screen titled Detailed Information for C-DRIVE. Move the cursor down to highlight the access control list options, as shown in Figure 10-14.

Now press INS, not ENTER. This causes NET_MGR to prompt you for the name of the user or group for the access control list. Type the username of the individual or group name for which you want to change access rights. Figure 10-15 shows entry of the username BOB.

Figure 10-12. *Selecting the Shared Resources Management function from NET_MGR*

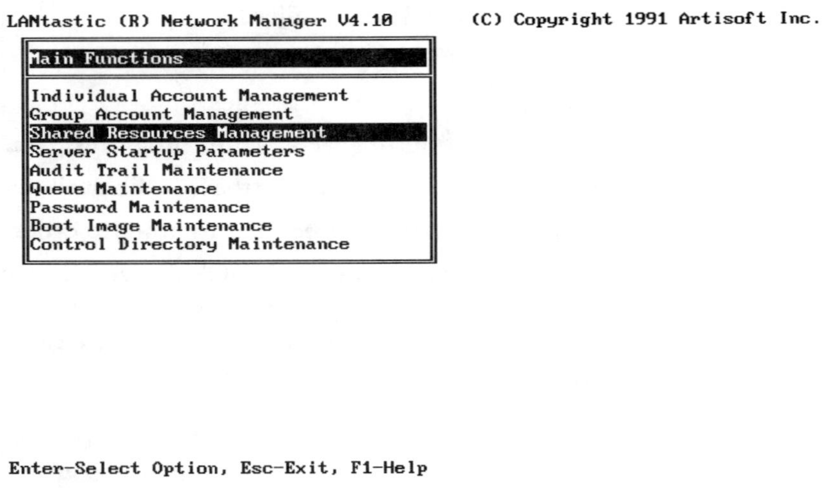

```
LANtastic (R) Network Manager V4.10        (C) Copyright 1991 Artisoft Inc.

 Main Functions

 Individual Account Management
 Group Account Management
 Shared Resources Management
 Server Startup Parameters
 Audit Trail Maintenance
 Queue Maintenance
 Password Maintenance
 Boot Image Maintenance
 Control Directory Maintenance


Enter-Select Option, Esc-Exit, F1-Help
```

Press (ENTER) after you type the username and the screen displays a new set of access rights for the username you entered. To change the access rights for BOB, type the keys of the letters that correspond with the rights you want to change. When a letter is displayed, the user has that access right. When a hyphen is displayed in the letter's place, the user does not have the access right. Each time you type a letter on the keyboard, the access right switches to the opposite state. For example, type **W** once and the W access right disappears. Type **W** again and the W right reappears.

Suppose BOB is a low-level clerk who needs only to read information from a shared file on the server. All he needs are the R (read access) and L (file lookups) access rights. Type all the other keys to turn the other access rights off: **W, C, M, D, K, N, E,** and **A**. (Rights I and P are already off by default in LANtastic 4.1.) If you prefer, you can press (F4) to clear (turn off) all access rights, and then type **R** and **L** to turn those two back on. Figure 10-16 shows the screen with BOB's new access rights.

Finally, press (ESC) repeatedly (three times) to end NET_MGR. BOB's new access rights are now in effect.

Figure 10-13. *Selecting the C-DRIVE resource*

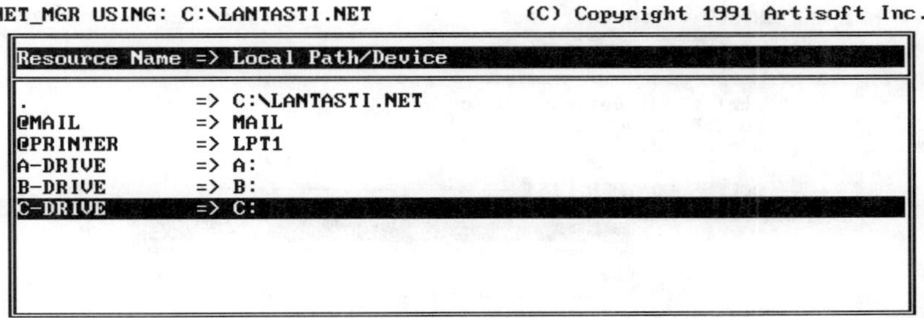

Figure 10-14. *Selecting the access control list for the server's C-DRIVE*

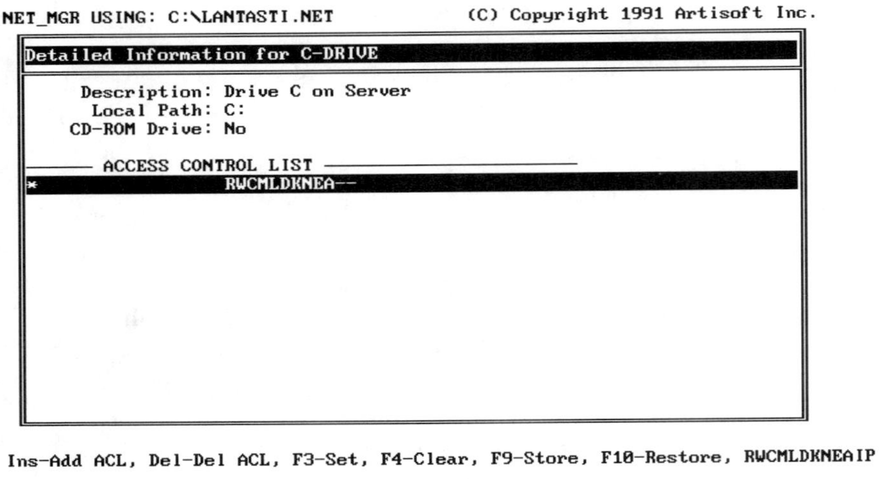

NET_MGR USING: C:\LANTASTI.NET
(C) Copyright 1991 Artisoft Inc.
Detailed Information for C-DRIVE
Description: Drive C on Server
Local Path: C:
CD-ROM Drive: No
ACCESS CONTROL LIST
* RWCMLDKNEA--
Ins-Add ACL, Del-Del ACL, F3-Set, F4-Clear, F9-Store, F10-Restore, RWCMLDKNEAIP

Figure 10-15. *Enter the username for the individual or group whose rights you want to change*

NET_MGR USING: C:\LANTASTI.NET
(C) Copyright 1991 Artisoft Inc.
Detailed Information for C-DRIVE
Description: Drive C on Server
Local Path: C:
CD-ROM Drive: No
ACCESS CONTROL LIST
*
Enter the user or group for this ACL.
BOB
Input the requested data then press Enter, Esc-Exit, F1-Help

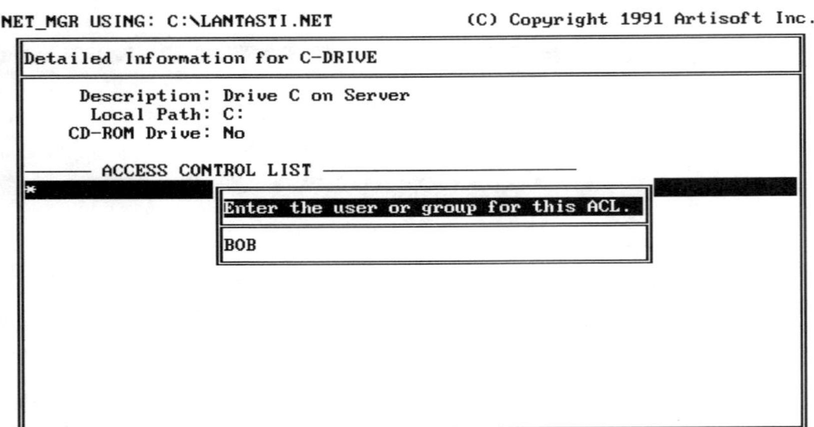

Figure 10-16. *Turn off all of BOB's access rights except for R and L*

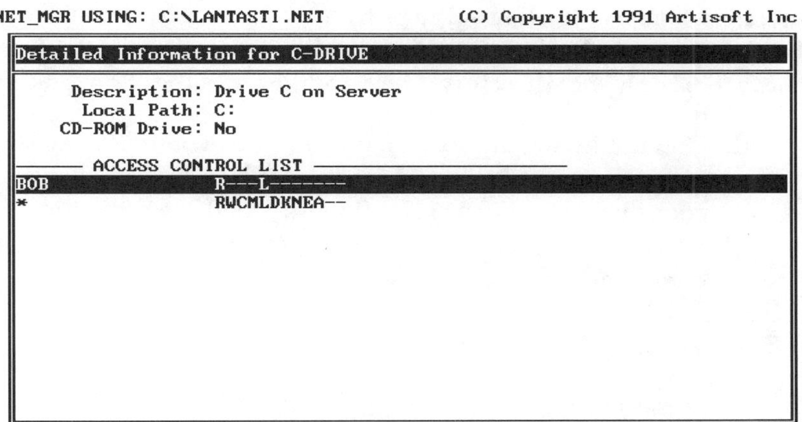
```
NET_MGR USING: C:\LANTASTI.NET              (C) Copyright 1991 Artisoft Inc.

Detailed Information for C-DRIVE

     Description: Drive C on Server
      Local Path: C:
    CD-ROM Drive: No

────── ACCESS CONTROL LIST ──────────────────────
BOB                R---L-------
*                  RWCMLDKNEA--

Ins-Add ACL, Del-Del ACL, F3-Set, F4-Clear, F9-Store, F10-Restore, RWCMLDKNEAIP
```

Similarly, you can alter the access rights for any specific username of an individual or group. If you decide not to assign usernames, but instead just use the global asterisk account for everyone, you can change access rights for the account. That way, everyone in that group account has only the access rights you grant.

Limited Server Resource Offerings

Another type of security restriction is to limit the resources a server offers to other computers on the LAN. Consider an example of a small office that has three computers connected to a LAN. The three computers are named LES, ED, and KATE (the names of the three workers). The computer named LES is configured to be a server and the other two are workstations. The three people in the office therefore use LES's hard disk to share files that they all need access to.

But suppose Les (the person) doesn't want the other two people to have full access to the entire hard disk. The server computer may contain confidential information that shouldn't be available to the other users or other files that the less-experienced Ed and Kate might accidentally delete.

The solution is to offer only a portion of the hard disk to the other users. Make a separate disk directory that you will use for shared data. Let the other users access only that directory. Here are the steps to follow on the server:

1. Create the directory you want to share. The following sequence of commands makes the C drive the current drive, makes the C drive's root directory the current directory, and creates a directory called GROUP (you can use another name if you like, of course). Type each command and press ENTER after each:

   ```
   c:
   cd\
   md group
   ```

2. Type **net_mgr** and press ENTER to start the NET_MGR program.
3. Move the cursor down to the Shared Resources Management function and press ENTER.
4. NET_MGR displays the same box of resource names and local paths that was shown in Figure 10-13. Press INS to add a new resource. When NET_MGR prompts you to enter the resource name, type **group** (converted automatically to all caps even if you type in lowercase) as shown in Figure 10-17 and press ENTER. You can give the resource any name you like as long as the name is no more than eight characters and does not duplicate another resource name on the server.
5. NET_MGR prompts you for the "server's true path for this resource." Type **c:\group** (automatically converted to all caps again) as Figure 10-18 shows, and press ENTER. This entry must provide the exact path to get to the resource and doesn't necessarily have to match the resource name you assigned in step 4. To avoid confusion, however, it's a good idea to keep the names the same.
6. NET_MGR now displays the list of assigned resource names again, this time with GROUP, your new resource, added to the list and highlighted. Press ENTER again to modify this resource.

Figure 10-17. *After pressing INS, type a resource name for the directory*

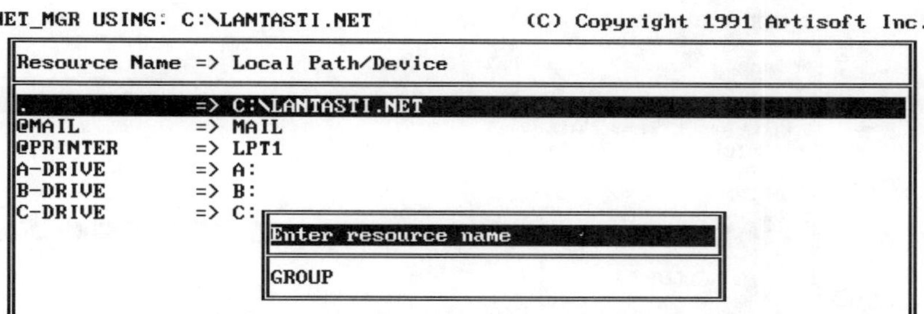

7. NET_MGR displays the Detailed Information screen for this resource, as you previously saw in Figure 10-14. Highlight the Description line and press ENTER. NET_MGR now prompts you to enter a description for this resource. Type a description, such as the one shown in Figure 10-19, and press ENTER. The description becomes part of the detailed information for this resource. At this point, you can also change the access control list information for this resource if you like.
8. Press ESC to return to the NET_MGR screen that displays the list of resource names. Move the cursor to the line that shows the C-DRIVE resource and press DEL. NET_MGR prompts you to press ENTER to verify that you really want to delete the resource, as shown in Figure 10-20. Press ENTER to confirm the deletion. Then you can also delete the A-DRIVE and B-DRIVE floppy disk resources if you like. Deleting the floppy disk resources prevents workstations from accessing the server's floppy disks, which may be desirable for security reasons and to prevent workstations from erroneously selecting them instead of the shared GROUP directory.

Figure 10-18. *Enter the path on the server to reach the resource*

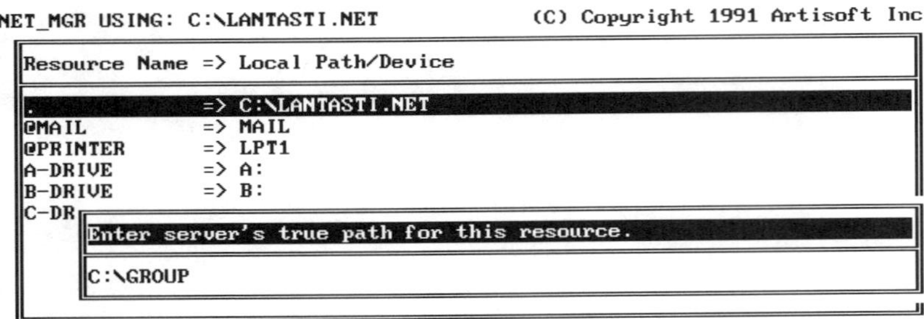

Figure 10-19. *Enter a description for the newly added resource*

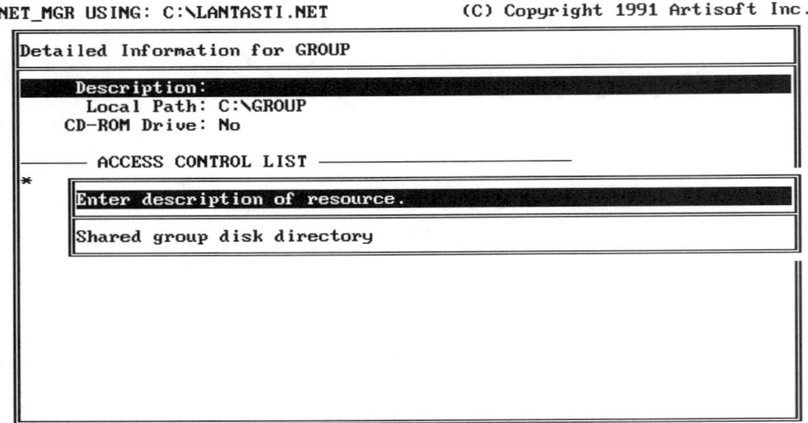

Figure 10-20. *Highlight the C-DRIVE resource and press* DEL *to delete it*

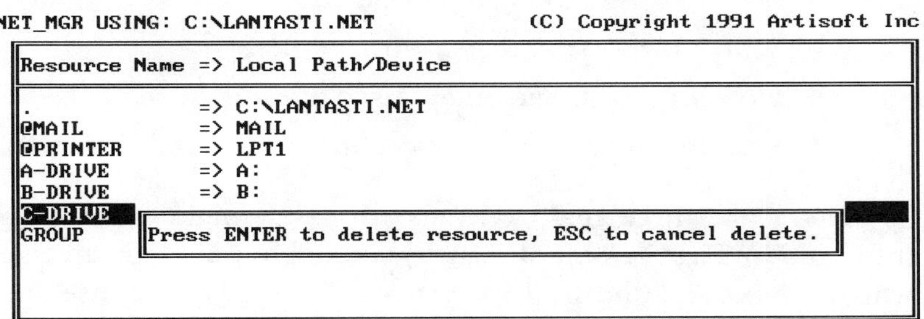

9. Press ESC twice to end the NET_MGR program. From now on, the other users can access only the disk directory called GROUP on LES's C drive. (They can also access any subdirectories created under the GROUP directory.) The other users no longer have access to LES's entire hard disk. LES can continue to access the entire C hard disk on the server, but can use NET to redirect another drive letter to the GROUP directory only.

Audit Trails

The fourth method to implement LANtastic security is to use audit trails. An *audit trail* is a log of evidence that shows what users have done on a server. You can keep track of virtually everything anyone does on the server or customize your audit trail to track only certain activities. The following list shows some of the things you can track:

- Who has logged in to the server
- Who has tried to log in but failed
- Who has tried to access restricted files
- How long each person has used a resource
- How much data each person printed on a LAN printer

There are three main reasons why you might want to record such information. First, as part of security you might want to keep an eye on users who try to get unauthorized access to confidential files or use the server after normal office hours. That's why audit trails are discussed in this chapter. Second, in some work environments you might need to bill users for their use of server resources. Third, on a large LAN you can review audit data to see how busy each server is and what kind of work people are doing on it. You might want to take steps to balance the workload between multiple servers, or to change server parameters to improve performance.

The audit trail capability of LANtastic carries with it two costs that you might not want to pay: disk space and performance degradation. All the audit data obviously has to be recorded somewhere, and the place is on the server's hard disk. Depending on how active the server is, the amount of disk space used up can be substantial. A megabyte or more per day is possible on a busy server. To record all this data also puts an additional workload on the server. Some users report a noticeable slowdown in server performance when the Audit Trail feature is enabled. If you decide to use an audit trail, test carefully to determine if you can tolerate the server disk space usage and performance loss that come along with it. However, if you track nothing more than when each user logs in and out, the overhead and disk space usage are not large. Tracking every time a user opens a file can be another story.

To enable an audit trail, run the NET_MGR program and select the Server Startup Parameters function from the Main Functions menu. Eight different audit trails are available and you can enable any or all of them. By default, none of them is enabled. Once you enable them, you use the Audit Trail Maintenance function from NET_MGR's Main Functions menu to look at the data recorded, to copy the data to a regular DOS file, or to clear the data out of the audit file. The *LANtastic Network Operating System Reference Manual* has details about how each of the audit trails work and the information recorded in the audit file. You can also press F1 to see brief explanations.

Here are the eight audit trails:

- *Server Up* Makes an audit entry when the SERVER program starts
- *Logins* Makes an entry when a user logs in
- *Logouts* Makes an entry when a user logs out
- *Queuing* Makes an entry when a mail message or print job is added to the spool queue
- *Printing* Makes an entry when a print job completes printing
- *User Entry* Allows users to use the NET AUDIT command to make audit entries (see Chapter 14)
- *Access Allowed* Makes entries when the server allows any of the types of access you specify in an access rights list; for example, if you specify R, an audit entry is made when anyone reads a server file
- *Access Denied* Makes entries when the server disallows any of the types of access you specify in the access rights list

Protecting NET_MGR

One more capability of NET_MGR is important to mention. All the security options covered in this chapter sound like good ways to control access to your LAN servers, but what stops all the LAN users from running the NET_MGR program to get access to anything they want?

One approach is the physical security method mentioned at the beginning of the chapter. You can put your servers in locked rooms to keep people from fooling around with them.

But in most office environments, locked-up servers aren't practical. After all, one of LANtastic's biggest benefits is that you don't have to buy extra computers to use as servers. As a peer-to-peer LAN it allows you to use anyone's PC as a server while the person continues using the PC for individual work. You can't lock that person in a closet. Not with the number of attorneys advertising on television these days.

A second approach is practical. You can password-protect the NET_MGR program itself. Select the Password Maintenance function from NET_MGR's

Main Functions menu. Then you can force anyone who starts the NET_MGR program to enter the secret password before using NET_MGR. If only you, the LAN administrator, know the password, then no one else can cause mischief with NET_MGR. If you set up multiple servers, assign a password to the copy of NET_MGR on each one. Then only the person or persons who know the password can use NET_MGR on each server.

11

LAN Administration

Earlier chapters mentioned the need for a LAN administrator to perform some management functions. For a small LAN, these efforts can be simple and not at all time-consuming. On a large or very active LAN, administrative work is a bigger job. In either case, the critical point is that *someone* has to take the role of the LAN administrator and be responsible for a few regular maintenance and management duties. If not, the result is the same as if you choose not to perform regular automobile maintenance: you later pay a big price to fix problems that maintenance could have avoided.

If you have a small LAN, you may think it ridiculous to appoint a full-fledged LAN administrator. Fine. Don't make it a big deal. Maybe you'll find it more palatable to call someone the network manager, the LAN coordinator, or even "our LAN guy" or "Ms. LAN." The name doesn't matter. Just be sure that someone thinks of himself or herself as the one responsible for keeping the LAN running right. If not, everyone will assume that someone else will do it. They'll say, "Hey, it's not *my* LAN! Why should I go looking for more work to do?" Instead, make sure someone says, "Well, let's see how my LAN is looking today."

In many workgroups, selecting the LAN administrator is simple. The best candidate is the person who has already displayed the most interest in the workgroup's computers. If that person is also a meticulous, reliable person who likes to keep things organized, you've got your LAN administrator. All that remains is to announce it officially and tell him or her not to spend more than a half an hour a day "playing with" the LAN once it is installed and running.

If the office computer guru isn't well organized or reliable, or can't spare the time to perform extra duties, the decision is harder. Computer knowledge, or at least a willingness to learn, is important but other personal traits are even more important: trustworthiness, organizational skills, and reliability (including a good attendance record) are perhaps the most significant ones. You may want to take the second or third best computer person if that person ranks way ahead of the computer guru in these personal traits.

In addition, you should either officially or unofficially name a secondary LAN administrator. Even in a small office where the LAN connects only two or three computers, the primary LAN administrator will occasionally be sick, on vacation, traveling, or busy with a high-priority project. Also, of course, the primary LAN administrator may get hit by a truck on the way to work or decide to quit. At least one other person should be in a position to fill in temporarily and take over permanently if necessary. Don't put all your eggs in one LAN administrator.

Why is a LAN administrator so important? What does one do? The duties can be grouped into four categories:

- *LAN Security* Coordinate the security discussed in Chapter 10, ensure the integrity of shared resources, back up disk files, monitor server disk space, check for computer viruses, and coordinate physical security measures
- *User support* Perform troubleshooting, answer user questions, develop new procedures for users, and train new users
- *Configuration management* Set up the LAN initially, set up new users' hardware and software, upgrade LANtastic software, install new applications, and implement new procedures
- *LAN optimization* Improve server response time, reduce RAM usage on servers and workstations, reduce disk space usage, make

parameter changes to improve performance, monitor LAN usage, and determine the need for upgrades and new products

For the rest of this chapter, assume you are the LAN administrator for your LANtastic LAN. Each of these four categories of duties is explained so you can see what kind of a job you have.

LAN Security

The LAN administrator coordinates use of LANtastic's built-in security features, which are covered in depth in Chapter 10, but the LAN administrator's security duties go much farther. Think of LAN security as broadly including everything that might relate to the integrity of data available on the LAN. If for some reason a shared file on a server becomes corrupt or unavailable, LAN security is at fault. If you think the computers are the most valuable resources on a LAN, you're wrong. In most workgroups the most valuable resource is the data. You can always replace a computer, but unprotected data can be lost forever. Your first priority as LAN administrator is to protect the data and your group's ability to access the data. The basic techniques to do so involve making regular backup copies, verifying that the servers have plenty of available disk space, protecting against computer viruses, and implementing physical security measures.

Data Backup

Because of the value of your data, your most important duty as LAN administrator is to make sure current backup copies of all critical disk files are available at all times. No matter what else may go wrong, you can recover if you have a backup copy of all your important data files and system files. Backup copies are just a form of insurance for your workgroup. As LAN administrator you are in effect the person who makes sure the insurance premiums are paid and that the policy has sufficient coverage.

Most computer users don't appreciate the value of backups until after their first loss. By then it's too late. If there is anything that a LAN administrator must be fanatic about, it is making and protecting backup copies.

Chapter 7's discussion of tape backup systems covered the causes of data loss and methods of making backup copies. Read that section carefully, even if you have no intention of buying a tape backup system. You don't have to use a tape backup system to make backup copies, but a tape system is usually the most convenient way to make backups. If your workgroup creates such a small amount of updated data that backups on floppy disks are practical, you may not need a tape backup system. However, you still need backups. You, as LAN administrator, must evaluate your workgroup's backup needs and set up procedures to make regular backups of all important files. Ask your users, "What files would you need to recover if you came to work tomorrow morning and discovered that all our computers were stolen or burned?" Because of the possibility that the entire office area could be destroyed, make sure your backup plans include off-site backup copies as discussed in Chapter 7.

Server Disk Space

Because a LAN server's disk space is shared by everyone in the group, it shares some traits of an office lunchroom. If no one is assigned the job of keeping it well stocked and clean, it soon runs out of the items you need and becomes an unusable mess.

Like the lunchroom, the server's disk must be kept well stocked and clean. The resource that a server's disk must keep stocked is disk space. Disk space is like home closet space: no matter how much you have, an occasional cleanup effort is necessary to make space available for new things. A shared disk can quickly become a repository for everyone's junk. You, the LAN administrator, have to ask why a server disk that had 40 megabytes of space available yesterday has only 2 megabytes today. Then you have to figure out who put the new data there and what to do about it. You can't allow your server's hard disk to become full. You need plenty of available space at all times to have room for printer spool jobs and new data files. Sometimes your only choice is to back up an unidentifiable big new file onto a tape cartridge (or a stack of floppy disks) and then delete it from the server's disk. The owner will come screaming about the missing file, at which time you can ask if the owner has any idea how large it was. If you then decide the file should stay on the server you can restore it there from your backup copy.

You (the LAN administrator) may already have one or more favorite software tools to help you manage your hard disk. Very likely the same products work on server disks. However, some products do not. Some disk management products that do work with LANtastic are Q-DOS LAN, XTree Pro Gold, PC Tools, and Norton Utilities.

Computer Viruses

Destructive computer viruses have become big news items in recent years. It seems that hardly a month goes by without dire warnings of a new virus that may destroy some or all of your computer's data. Is this a bunch of news hype, or are viruses a real threat?

The computer virus threat is real. Computer vandals release new strains upon an unsuspecting public almost daily, and most experts agree that computer virus problems will continue to increase in the foreseeable future. Every computer user should understand some fundamentals about computer viruses. LAN administrators need to be especially educated and alert to computer viruses.

What Is a Computer Virus?

A *computer virus* is a piece of software that does two things: it spreads from one computer to another and it causes damage or mischief to your computer's data and software. The damage typically is destruction of the data on your hard disk. Note that the disk itself is not damaged physically; the data on it is altered or erased. Some viruses don't really cause much damage. Mischief or annoyance is a better description. The virus might simply display a message on your screen periodically, or otherwise make itself known by altering your screen display in some way.

A computer virus is not a by-product of nature the way a biological virus is. Someone took the time to design the software to make each computer virus work. It takes a fair amount of computer programming knowledge to write an effective virus program. Speculation varies, but many observers think that most virus authors are stereotypical computer nerds between the ages of 15 and 25 who create viruses for the challenge and to inflate their egos. To these authors, creating a virus program is the equivalent of writing clever high-tech graffiti on walls. Some other people believe that viruses (at least some of them) are created by terrorist groups bent on destruction of establishment institutions. And some cynics believe viruses are created by the companies that sell anti-virus software products. Which one is closest to the truth is irrelevant. The point is that any time you execute a computer program you receive from an outside source, you run the risk of contracting a computer virus that can destroy your data. Because on a LAN everyone shares the same hard disk, if one user unknowingly runs a virus-infested program everyone is exposed. That's why the LAN administrator has to be on guard.

How a Virus Works

A virus works in two stages, which you might call the contagious stage and the destructive stage. During the contagious stage, the virus attaches itself to programs on your computer's hard disk or floppy disks. The most common targets are the three basic MS-DOS boot programs: COMMAND.COM, IO.SYS, and MSDOS.SYS. (If you run IBM's version of DOS, these last two programs are called IBMBIO.COM and IBMDOS.COM.) These last two programs are "hidden" files that you can't see when you use a DIR command. They reside in your root disk directory and cause your system to boot when you turn on the power. The other program, COMMAND.COM, is the DOS program that processes the commands you type from the keyboard. Some viruses attack other programs, but virus authors know that these three programs are on every DOS computer and that they are executed every day.

The virus program attaches itself to one of these DOS programs, which means the program modifies the DOS program and makes its own programming instructions part of the DOS program. From that point on, the DOS program works slightly differently. Instead of performing only its normal work, it also follows the virus program's instructions. These instructions might say to attach the virus program to additional programs, such as any program you copy onto a floppy disk. Then when you give the floppy disk to another user, that user runs the program you supplied and another computer becomes infected. Like a biological virus epidemic, a computer virus epidemic can spread very fast. If you give floppy disks to three people and then they each give floppy disks to three others, before long thousands are infected.

Please notice that you have to run an infected computer program in order to infect your computer with the virus. You cannot become infected just by being near an infected computer or floppy disk. You must actually run an infected program, usually one you obtain on a floppy disk. Other possible sources are programs you download from a computer bulletin board system or programs you obtain or run from a LAN server's hard disk. If you just copy an infected program from a floppy disk, BBS, or server to your own hard disk, you do not infect your system. The infection takes place only when you run the program and the virus attaches itself to a host DOS program.

Now you see how the contagious phase of a virus causes it to spread. How does it do damage or mischief? A virus is programmed with some sort of "trigger" logic to cause it to enter its destructive phase. The trigger might be based on the computer's internal date. The virus can sit benignly for months and then do major damage when your computer registers the specific date that triggers the virus. This kind of trigger means that a virus might spread to other computers for as long as 364 days before it suddenly does any damage. Other viruses keep count of how many floppy disks they infect. After they spread to a certain number of disks, they destroy the hard disk data of the computer they infect. Either of these trigger mechanisms is effective because both assure that the virus spreads to other computers before it makes itself known by destroying data or displaying messages. If instead the virus destroyed hard disk data immediately upon infecting a computer, the virus wouldn't have time to spread to other computers. That's why a delayed trigger mechanism is necessary for a computer virus to spread. Some other destructive programs, usually called bombs or Trojans, do damage immediately upon being run without going through a contagious phase.

Virus Treatment

Now that you understand the basics of computer viruses, what can you do about them? Your three courses of action are identical to the actions you can take for contagious diseases.

Prevention The best way to avoid virus damage is to never become infected. Never run a new program on any of your computers until you verify that the program is free of viruses. Use a *virus-checker program* (sometimes called a *virus-detection program*), which is a program that scans a new program before you run it to verify that no known virus infects the new program. If the virus-checker shows that the new program is infected, don't run the program. Other products, called *anti-virus programs,* are designed to monitor your PC and intercept any of the actions that viruses are known to take in order to spread infection or do damage. As long as these products monitor all the right actions, they can prevent virus damage even when you do unknowingly run an infected program. However, if a virus finds a new way to spread or cause damage, the anti-virus program won't know how to prevent it.

Frequent Checkups Suppose one of your LAN users runs an infected program without first checking it for virus infection. Because most viruses stay in their contagious state for some time before they cause destruction, you can usually detect a virus on your hard disks or in your computers' memory by running a virus checker. Then you can take steps to eliminate the virus before it causes you harm. Many LAN administrators run virus-checker programs every day to verify that server hard disks are free of viruses. For a group with active users, especially if they frequently bring in programs from outside the workgroup, daily virus checking is a good idea. In a small group where new programs are seldom used, less frequent checking may be adequate.

Treatment Once you discover you have contracted a virus, you need to take action to eliminate the virus before it does damage. Use a *virus-cleanup program*, which is a program that in most cases can remove the viral portions of infected programs. For some viruses, cleanup programs can't fix the infected programs; you have to delete the infected programs and reinstall them from your original floppy disks or backup copies. If you don't detect the virus before it destroys data, your treatment may consist of restoring all your programs and data from backup copies. If you don't have current backup copies, you learn the valuable and painful lesson of why you should have paid attention to backups.

Virus-Protection Products

A staggering array of virus-protection products has appeared on the market in recent months. Some are anti-virus programs, some are virus-checking programs, and some are virus-cleanup programs. Most leading products now perform all three functions, or can if you tell them to.

When you buy a virus-protection product, you put your trust in the company that created it. How thoroughly did they test it? Does it really catch all current viruses? How much of an effort do they make to update the product so it protects you from new viruses? What is their policy for providing you with upgrades to new versions of the product? You must use a recent version of any virus-protection product to have any confidence that it will prevent, detect, or clean up new viruses. Virus authors constantly develop new viruses from which old protection products fail to protect you.

Investigate the products available and find out which suits you best. Be sure to follow the manufacturer's directions carefully. Here are some of the leading products:

- *VIRUSCAN Series (VIRUSCAN, VSHIELD, CLEAN-UP)* From McAfee Associates, 4423 Cheeney Street, Santa Clara, CA 95054, 408-988-3832 (voice), 408-970-9727 (fax), 408-988-4004 (BBS). If you use CompuServe, type **go virusforum** to gain access to McAfee-led discussions about viruses. McAfee distributes these products as shareware for home use, but you must license them for business use. Either way, they are the best bargain in virus protection. Home users can get the products free from McAfee's bulletin board system (BBS) and use them for five days free. Then you are expected to register the products. VIRUSCAN (also called SCAN) is a virus checker and costs $25 to register. CLEAN-UP does virus cleanup for $35. VSHIELD is an anti-virus program for $25. Registration gives you free updates for one year and hot-line assistance. Business users have to call McAfee to arrange a site license. With VIRUSCAN, McAfee provides a list of agents around the world whom you can contact for assistance with virus problems. Revised versions of VIRUSCAN usually are developed every two or three months.
- *ViruSafe/LAN* From XTree Company, 4330 Santa Fe Road, San Luis Obispo, CA 93401, 800-395-8733, 805-541-0604. This product has a list price of $595 for ten users and is available in a NetBIOS version that works with LANtastic. A single-computer version costs $99. ViruSafe/LAN performs anti-virus, virus-checker, and virus-cleanup functions.
- *Virex-PC* From Microcom, Inc., P.O. Box 51489, Durham, NC 27717, 919-490-1277. List price is $99.95 for the single-computer version. Virex-PC performs anti-virus, virus-checker, and virus-cleanup functions.

- *Central Point Anti-Virus* From Central Point Software, 15520 N.W. Greenbrier Parkway, Beaverton, OR 97006, 503-690-8088. List price is $129. Central Point Anti-Virus performs anti-virus, virus-checker, and virus-cleanup functions. Another Central Point software product, PC Tools, includes a virus-checker capability among its utility programs.
- *Norton AntiVirus* From Symantec, 10201 Torre Avenue, Cupertino, CA 95014, 408-253-9600. List price is $129. Norton AntiVirus performs anti-virus, virus-checker, and virus-cleanup functions.

Physical Security Measures

Chapters 4 and 10 mention the need for physical security measures in addition to software security. As LAN administrator, you might be the only person who keeps an eye on overall office security, so take the initiative and verify that physical security is adequate. You are in the best position to remind management of the value of the group's computer data, so make an argument to improve physical security. If you don't succeed in improving door locks, fire prevention, and other measures, be extra sure you arrange for regular rotation of off-site tape backup copies. Your chance of needing one someday increases if other physical security factors are weak and improvements are turned down.

User Support

Even though LANtastic is easy to learn and use, your workgroup's LAN users will need occasional support. A new user needs training, even if it is no more than ten minutes of your time to demonstrate how to use NET to redirect a disk drive and printer. Even longtime LANtastic users may become confused occasionally and need questions answered or error messages explained. If someone accidentally deletes an important disk file on the server, you may be called on to help restore the file from your most recent backup copy.

Even if you don't feel comfortable as the office LANtastic expert, you are the closest thing the workgroup has available. If you can't figure out answers to questions yourself, you are the best choice to call Artisoft Technical Support (as explained in Appendix B) to explain the problem's symptoms and your LAN configuration.

In addition, you are the person who will develop new or simplified procedures for users. Your workgroup might benefit from having customized STARTNET.BAT files, or by including the LANtastic start-up commands in each user's AUTOEXEC.BAT file. For example, you may want all users, upon booting their computers, to redirect disk drive L to a server's shared disk and LPT2 to a shared laser printer. You can also customize everyone's word processing program to use these shared resources. Evaluate your workgroup's needs and LANtastic's capabilities. Then design and test batch files or written procedures that simplify everyone's LAN usage.

Configuration Management

If you were named the LAN administrator from the beginning, you probably were the one who coordinated the original installation of the LAN hardware and software. Even if you became LAN administrator later, you are the logical choice to install hardware and software for new users. An inexperienced computer user is likely to make mistakes either installing the LAN card or the LANtastic software. You have installed them before and can do it again quickly and accurately. Also, you can coordinate the LAN downtime necessary to cable a new user's computer to the LAN, if you use thin Ethernet.

New LANtastic software is released by Artisoft periodically. You should be aware of these new versions and decide if your workgroup should upgrade. If so, you make the plans and perform the new software installation. In general, you should avoid falling too far behind the current versions. The new versions generally fix bugs in past versions and also include new features and performance improvements. However, it's usually a good idea to wait a month or two after a new version is released before you install it. That gives you (and Artisoft) a chance to see if any major problems exist with the new version. Check the Artisoft technical support bulletin board (see Appendix B) to find out if users are complaining about unresolved problems. (Most such problems are caused by user mistakes, such as using nonstandard cables or trying to use independent LAN cards without using LANtastic/AI.) No matter how thoroughly a software company like Artisoft tests new software, sometimes bugs show up only after real-world users begin running a new version. If you have a pioneering spirit, however, you can upgrade immediately. Just be aware of the hardships pioneers often face. After you let the pioneers run the new version for a couple of months, you can more safely upgrade.

When your workgroup's management wants to implement new functions using the LAN, you should get involved as soon as possible to evaluate alternative software products, plan the installation, and install the software.

Once your workgroup becomes dependent on the LAN, your role as LAN administrator becomes more important. The LAN is a shared resource. As a result, it needs a central control point to be sure configuration changes don't cause problems. You are that control point. You have to be sure that the LAN is available whenever group members need it, and that configuration changes (hardware or software) don't cause problems for group members who are trying to get work done.

LAN Optimization

Chapter 13 discusses LANtastic optimization in depth. *Optimization* is sometimes called performance improvement or tuning and refers to any efforts that result in the more efficient use of resources. On a LAN, optimization falls into three areas: improved speed, reductions in RAM usage, and disk space savings. You can take many steps to accomplish these results. As part of the effort you may run *benchmark tests*, which are timed tests of controlled workloads. By comparing the timings before and after you make changes you can determine if your changes are beneficial.

Also as part of optimization, you should perform *capacity planning*, which consists of tracking the workgroup's LAN usage in order to anticipate the need for hardware upgrades because of an increasing workload. You need to decide if upgrades (such as larger disk drives or faster servers) are really necessary to increase capacity or if optimization efforts can handle the increasing workload. See Chapter 13 for details about these optimization activities.

12

LANtastic and Windows

Microsoft Windows has been on the market for many years, but became popular in 1990 only after the release of version 3.0. An estimated 5 million people bought Windows 3.0 during 1991. At the time of this writing, Windows 3.1 is about to be released.

There are four main reasons for Windows' popularity:

- A consistent, graphical user interface that most people find easier to use than typing commands at the DOS C:> prompt
- More automatic installation and execution of many applications
- The ability to share data between applications
- The ability to run more than one application at a time

These are attractive advantages. However, some observers claim that the majority of users who bought and installed Windows have since removed it or seldom use it because of shortcomings. The following are shortcomings of Windows 3.0 (which might be improved in subsequent versions):

- High RAM requirements compared to using DOS without Windows
- High disk space usage (about 8 megabytes)
- Slow performance
- Reliability problems
- The high cost of buying Windows versions of software when DOS versions are already paid for

If you have Microsoft Windows version 3.0 or later and LANtastic version 4.0 or later, you can run LANtastic and Windows together in three different ways (each will be explained individually in the remainder of this chapter):

- *Single-user Windows configuration* For a single-user configuration, you install a separate copy of Windows on each computer connected to your LAN. Each computer runs its own copy of Windows from its own hard disk and can access shared resources over the LAN.
- *Multiuser Windows configuration* For a multiuser configuration install Windows once on a server instead of installing a copy of Windows on each workstation. Then each computer accesses Windows on the server. This approach saves disk space on each workstation but usually results in slower performance, plus greater setup complexity and bigger workloads on both the server and LAN.
- *LANtastic for Windows* Optionally, you can use Artisoft's LANtastic for Windows product in combination with either of the previous two configurations. LANtastic and Windows work fine together without this product. However, LANtastic for Windows adds a Windows interface and more flexibility in using the LAN while Windows is running.

This book makes no attempt to teach you about Windows itself. That's a big job better addressed either by books devoted to the subject or by the *Microsoft Windows User's Guide* that comes with the product. The focus of this chapter is how to install LANtastic and Windows so they work together.

Single-User Windows Configuration

The most common way to run LANtastic and Windows together is to install a separate copy of Windows on each LAN node, whether a workstation or server. Each computer runs its own copy rather than everyone sharing a common copy from a server. In fact, when you run separate single-user Windows copies on each workstation, you probably do not want to run Windows on a server unless the server is used by someone who needs Windows. A server runs LANtastic faster if Windows isn't causing additional overhead.

This section shows you how to install and run a single-user setup for Windows on a workstation or server.

Installation of Single-User Configuration

To install LANtastic and Windows together on either a workstation or server, follow these steps. (When you see this long list of steps, you may question if Windows really makes things easier for users. Don't panic. The steps here have been made elementary; the entire process really isn't bad.) These instructions are based on a system using Windows 3.0 or 3.1, LANtastic 4.0 or 4.1, and any acceptable version of DOS (3.1, 3.3, 4.0, or 5.0). If you still use an earlier version of LANtastic, either upgrade to the current version first or else get document WIN300.TXT from Artisoft to see if your version is compatible. If you use later versions of any of these products, the process might change.

1. Install LANtastic hardware and software normally, as explained in Chapter 5. Run the tests shown in Chapter 5 to verify that everything is working correctly. Then follow the instructions in Chapter 6 to share a disk drive and a printer, to verify that you understand how to do so and to further confirm that everything works properly without Windows. If you already have Windows installed on one or more of these computers, run these LANtastic tests from the normal DOS prompt, not from a virtual DOS machine through Windows.

2. Before you install Windows, use STARTNET to start the LANtastic software as explained in Chapter 5. (You should have already done this in step 1, but if you install Windows at a separate time be sure to start LANtastic first.) If you previously installed Windows before installing LANtastic, skip to step 4 to reconfigure Windows.
3. Install Windows on a workstation's hard disk. Follow the instructions in Chapter 1 of the *Microsoft Windows User's Guide.* For version 3.0 of Windows, the SETUP program detects that LANtastic is running and selects "Microsoft Network (or 100% compatible)" for the Network option. Accept this choice and continue the Windows installation.
4. After you complete the installation of Windows 3.0, you must run SETUP again to configure Windows for LANtastic. (These steps should not be necessary for Windows 3.1 because it will make the configuration automatically. You can skip to step 8.) Assuming you installed Windows on your C drive and used the default disk directory name, type **c:** and press (ENTER), then type **cd \windows** and press (ENTER). Finally, type **setup** and press (ENTER). SETUP displays a screen that looks like Figure 12-1.
5. Move the cursor up to highlight the Network option line that shows "Microsoft Network (or 100% compatible)" and press (ENTER). SETUP displays a new screen with a selection box in the middle. Move the cursor down until you highlight "Other (Requires disk provided by a network manufacturer)" as Figure 12-2 shows. Then press (ENTER).
6. SETUP displays a screen that asks you to insert a floppy disk. Press (BACKSPACE) three times and type **c:\lantasti** instead, as shown in Figure 12-3, then press (ENTER). This entry causes SETUP to use a file called OEMSETUP.INF that LANtastic's INSTALL program has put in your LANTASTI directory. This file provides the Windows SETUP program with information about LANtastic.
7. SETUP displays a screen showing the network name LANtastic provides, as shown in Figure 12-4. For LANtastic 4.1 the name is "LANtastic Network Operating System 4.1." Press (ENTER) to accept this network driver. SETUP then displays the screen shown pre-

12

Figure 12-1. *The SETUP screen when run after installing Windows 3.0*

```
Windows Setup

     If your computer or network appears on the Hardware Compatibility List
     with an asterisk next to it, press F1 before continuing.

     System Information
        Computer:            MS-DOS or PC-DOS System
        Display:             VGA
        Mouse:               No mouse or other pointing device
        Keyboard:            Enhanced 101 or 102 key US and Non US keyboards
        Keyboard Layout:     US
        Language:            English (American)
        Network:             Microsoft Network (or 100% compatible)

        Complete Changes:    Accept the configuration shown above.

     To change a system setting, press the UP or DOWN ARROW key to
     move the highlight to the setting you want to change. Then press
     ENTER to see alternatives for that item. When you have finished
     changing your settings, select the "Complete Changes" option
     to exit Setup.

 ENTER=Continue  F1=Help  F3=Exit
```

Figure 12-2. *Select Other to change the type of network installed*

```
Windows Setup

     You have asked to change the type of network to be installed. This
     list includes all the types of networks that have an asterisk on the
     Hardware Compatibility List because they are not 100% compatible
     with Windows 3.0 and therefore require special handling. If your
     network does not appear in this list, accept Setup's original choice.

      Microsoft Network (or 100% compatible)
      No Network Installed
      Novell Netware 2.10 or above, or Novell Netware 386
      IBM PC LAN Program
      Other (Requires disk provided by a network manufacturer)

     (To see more of the list, press the (↓) arrow key)

     To select a network from the list, press the UP or DOWN ARROW key to
     move the highlight to the item you want to select. Then press ENTER.

     If you want to return to the System Information screen without
     changing your network type, press ESC.

 ENTER=Continue  F1=Help  F3=Exit  ESC=Cancel
```

Figure 12-3. *Point SETUP to the LANTASTI directory to get information about LANtastic*

```
Windows Setup

    Please insert your network driver disk provided by the hardware
    manufacturer. If the files on this disk can be found at a different
    location, enter a new path to the files in the prompt below.

                c:\lantasti

ENTER=Continue  F1=Help  F3=Exit  ESC=Cancel
```

Figure 12-4. *SETUP gets network driver information from LANtastic's OEMSETUP.INF file*

```
Windows Setup

    You have chosen to install a network driver provided by a hardware
    manufacturer. Select a network driver from the following list:

      LANtastic Network Operating System 4.1

    Press the UP or DOWN ARROW key to move the highlight to the item you
    want to select. Then press ENTER.

    If you want to return to the System Information screen without
    changing your network driver type, press ESC.

ENTER=Continue  F1=Help  F3=Exit  ESC=Cancel
```

viously in Figure 12-1, except the Network option now shows "LANtastic Version 4.1." Press ENTER to accept these choices. SETUP updates your Windows configuration and returns you to a DOS prompt.

8. Use EDLIN or another line editor to edit the file SYSTEM.INI in the WINDOWS directory. First make a backup copy of the original on a floppy disk in case you make a mistake during editing and want to start over again. Find the line that says "device=*vpd" near the end of the file and delete it. If you plan to redirect port COM1 or COM2 to a shared printer, then also find the line that says "device=*vcd" and delete it. Other lines are similar! Be sure to delete the right ones.
9. If the computer uses the LANtastic 2Mbps LAN card or an independent Ethernet card that maps a RAM address range onto the card's RAM, you need to tell Windows to exclude that address range in 386 enhanced mode. This means that any LAN card that uses the RAMBASE parameter in STARTNET.BAT must have one or more lines inserted into the SYSTEM.INI file. The LANtastic AE-x cards do not require this insertion. For the 2Mbps card with default settings, two lines are required—one for the RAM address and another for the onboard ROM, like this:

   ```
   EMMExclude=D800-D9FF
   EMMExclude=F800-FFFF
   ```

10. The next few steps are to avoid conflicts in how Windows and LANtastic use printers. When you run Windows and LANtastic together, you should always process any shared printer output using a redirected LPT2 or LPT3, not LPT1. Use LPT1 only for a printer physically connected to the workstation. To make LPT2 available on the workstation, add a line like this one to the end of the STARTNET.BAT file, using your server's name instead of *servername*:

    net use lpt2 *servername*\\@printer

    If you use version 4.0 of LANtastic, you need to add a NET LOGIN statement immediately before the one just shown in order to log in to the server before trying to use its printer. Version 4.1's Autologin feature, unless you have disabled it, makes this extra statement unnecessary.

11. Next you need to run Windows on each workstation to make some changes. Type **win** and press ENTER. (If you need help understanding how to take any of the actions about to be covered, refer to your Windows manual.) From the Main program group choose Control Panel, and then choose Printers.
12. The Installed Printers list shows the printers you chose during the Windows SETUP process. Pick the one that describes the shared printer you plan to use on a server and select Configure.
13. Select the printer port you directed to the server's shared printer (LPT2 in step 10). Do *not* choose LPT2.OS2. You want the plain LPT2 selection.
14. Set the Device Not Selected time-out value to 900 and the Transmission Retry time-out value to 950. Then select the OK action.
15. Finally, highlight the check box for Use Print Manager and turn it off (remove the X mark). You should never use the Windows Print Manager for printed output—always use the network spooler instead. Highlight OK and accept the changes.
16. The remaining steps apply only to a server that will run Windows and has one or more shared printers attached. End Windows and then type **cd \lantasti** and press ENTER to make LANTASTI the current directory. Then type **net_mgr** and press ENTER.
17. Move the cursor down to select the Shared Resources Management function and press ENTER.
18. Select the printer this server will share (usually named @PRINTER) and press ENTER.
19. Select the option named Chars/Second and press ENTER. Then type **9600** and press ENTER.
20. Press ESC to return to the list of server resource names. If the server has any other shared printers, select each one in turn and repeat step 19. When done with all shared printers, press ESC again to return to the Main Functions menu.

21. Move the cursor down to the Server Startup Parameters function and press ENTER.
22. Verify that the Printer Tasks parameter is set to 1, even if this server shares more than one printer. If not, change it to 1.
23. Press ESC repeatedly until you end the NET_MGR program and return to a DOS prompt.
24. If the SERVER program is already running on this server, you need to restart it to activate the changes NET_MGR just made. Be sure that no other users are actively using the server. Then type **server /remove** and press ENTER to stop the program, and type **server** and press ENTER to restart it.

You have now completed the installation process for Windows and LANtastic together. Follow the process on each workstation and server on which you want to run Windows.

Using the Single-User Configuration

Once you complete installation, LANtastic and Windows are easy to use together as long as you run things in the right sequence.

Always start LANtastic and redirect disk drives and printers *before* you start Windows. This means to run STARTNET.BAT and NET before you run WIN. The simplest way to be sure you do everything in the right sequence is to put all your commands into one batch file. Either AUTOEXEC.BAT or STARTNET.BAT will do, or make your own new batch file. If you don't always want to run the LAN software, put your NET USE commands and WIN command at the end of STARTNET.BAT and then run it only when you like. If you always use LANtastic and Windows, put all the commands at the end of AUTOEXEC.BAT.

As long as you have all your disk drives and printers redirected before you start Windows, your Windows applications can use them just like locally attached devices. To have complete control of resources from *within* Windows, see the section on "LANtastic for Windows" at the end of this chapter.

Caution

Be sure you never redirect a workstation's local hard disk drive name to a server's hard disk. For example, don't use NET to redirect your C drive to the server's C drive. If you do, your computer can no longer access your own C drive (because the C drive name points to the server) and Windows no longer has access to necessary files on your hard disk. The result is a lockup, forcing you to reboot your workstation.

Multiuser Windows Configuration

Installation of the multiuser Windows configuration is similar to, but a little more complicated than, the single-user configuration. The LANtastic 4.1 manual explains all the details, which are also available in document WIN300.TXT from Artisoft. (Presumably a new document called WIN310.TXT will appear soon for Windows 3.1.) In addition, Chapter 14 of the *Microsoft Windows User's Guide* for version 3.0 is titled "Networks and Windows" and explains many of the concepts and techniques.

To remain out of jail, you still need to buy a separate copy of Windows for each workstation, even if everyone runs it from the server. You can buy the regular Windows version and install it on the server, but on workstations (or other servers) you have a choice: either buy a regular copy of Windows, or buy the "license pack" version. The license pack version costs a few dollars less and does not include manuals; it's meant for LAN installations where everyone uses Windows in the same office and all computers are set up by one person.

LANtastic for Windows

LANtastic for Windows gives you the same graphical user interface for LANtastic's NET and NET_MGR commands that you have for other Windows applications. You can use these programs without leaving Windows. The result is that you don't have to perform all your LANtastic activities outside of Windows. You can redirect disk drives, log in to servers, read e-mail, change server parameters (if you are the LAN administrator), and monitor server activity all from Windows.

Like previously covered combinations of LANtastic and Windows, LANtastic for Windows requires LANtastic version 4.0 or higher and Windows 3.0 or higher. As this is written, the current version of LANtastic for Windows is 4.0. LANtastic for Windows requires that you run Windows in either enhanced or standard mode. Real mode is not supported.

Installation of LANtastic for Windows

You can install LANtastic for Windows three different ways: from the DOS prompt, using the Windows Program Manager, and using the Windows File Manager. From the DOS prompt is easiest. You have to use the accompanying WINSTALL program, which as part of the process converts the specially compressed files that come on the LANtastic for Windows floppy disk into normal file formats.

To install LANtastic for Windows, first be sure you have installed both LANtastic as explained in Chapter 5 and Windows as explained in this chapter. Then put the LANtastic for Windows distribution floppy disk in your A drive, type **win a:winstall** and press ENTER. This command starts Windows and runs the WINSTALL program. Select the Install option to copy the necessary files into your LANTASTI directory, or another directory if you choose, and into the WINDOWS directory. Be patient. For the first one or two minutes the floppy disk spins but nothing else appears to happen. Eventually the "0-100%" meter shows some action and installation completes soon after.

Exit from Windows and then restart Windows, as WINSTALL instructs you, to activate the changes made by the WINSTALL program.

Using LANtastic for Windows

After the LANtastic for Windows installation is accomplished, you can access LANtastic for Windows by selecting it from the Program Manager window, as shown in Figure 12-5. Be sure you run STARTNET.BAT or its equivalent to start the LANtastic software *before* you start Windows. Don't try to run AEX, AILANBIO, REDIR, or SERVER from a DOS virtual machine in Windows.

Figure 12-5. *Selecting LANtastic from the Program Manager window*

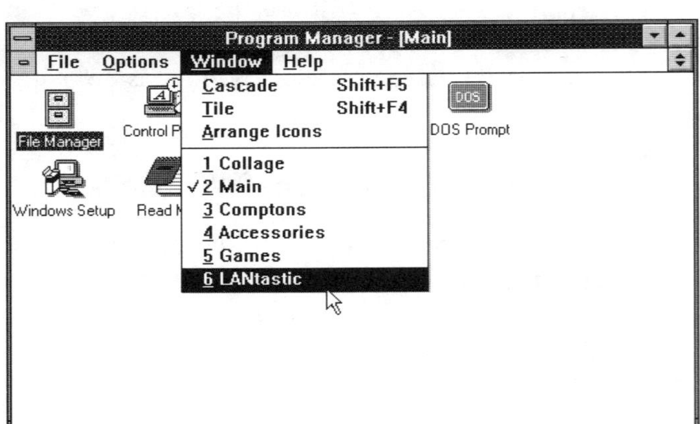

After you select LANtastic, Windows displays the LANtastic Net icon, a symbol that shows four PCs networked together. If you are running on a server, you also see the Network Manager icon. The LANtastic Net icon selects the equivalent of the NET program and the Network Manager icon selects the equivalent of the NET_MGR program. Figure 12-6 shows the icons.

Select the LANtastic Net icon to run the NET program. Windows displays eight icons that correspond with the Main Functions on the regular NET menu from a DOS prompt. (NET has only seven main functions, but the LANtastic for Windows version separates the selection of disk drives and printers into two different icon options.) Figure 12-7 shows the LANtastic Net icon choices.

Press (TAB) or use the mouse to select whichever choice you want. For example, select the Drives box to redirect a disk drive name to a server's shared hard disk. Windows displays a Drive Connections window that gives you the same options as NET's Drive and Printer Connections menu box.

Use the mouse to click on the server's C-DRIVE resource in the left half of the screen and then on the drive name E in the right half. Then move the mouse up to the Connect action at the top of the screen to make the

Figure 12-6. *The LANtastic Net and Network Manager icons await your selection*

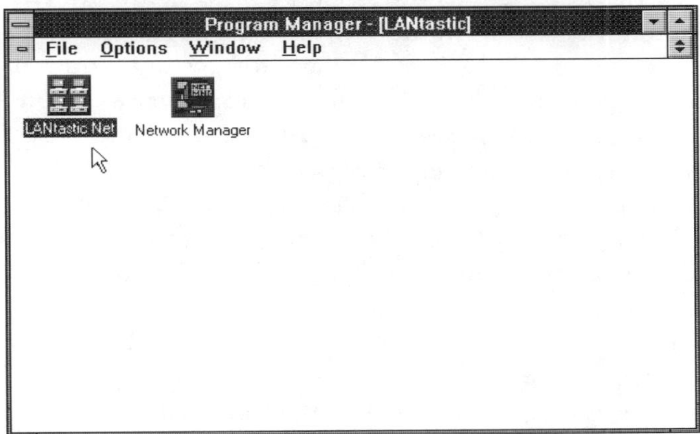

Figure 12-7. *Selecting LANtastic Net displays eight icons that correspond with the DOS NET program's Main Functions menu*

connection. The result is that the E drive is redirected to the server's shared C drive, as shown in Figure 12-8.

The other options work similarly. All use the standard Windows interface to perform the functions you already learned about for NET and NET_MGR. The difference is only in the way you select your options.

One new capability is particularly interesting. You can use LANtastic for Windows to monitor a server's activity level over a period of time. Select the lower-right icon, Server Mgt, from the eight LANtastic Net choices shown in Figure 12-7. From the Server Management screen that appears, select View and then Graph. After a few seconds, LANtastic begins to display a three-dimensional graph that shows how busy the server is. The front line of blocks shows the number of input/output kilobytes per second that users are causing the server to perform. The back line shows the number of user requests per second. By default a new pair of blocks is added every six seconds, but you can select Options and change the time period if you like. This display provides a way to examine the effect on your server when users perform certain activities. You might be surprised how much server activity a user

Figure 12-8. *The user redirects drive E to the server's C drive*

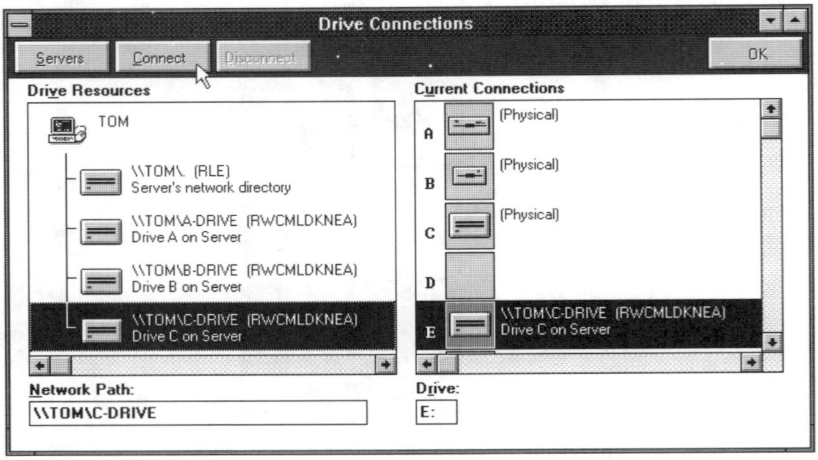

Figure 12-9. *A graphical display of server activity from the Server Mgt function of LANtastic Net*

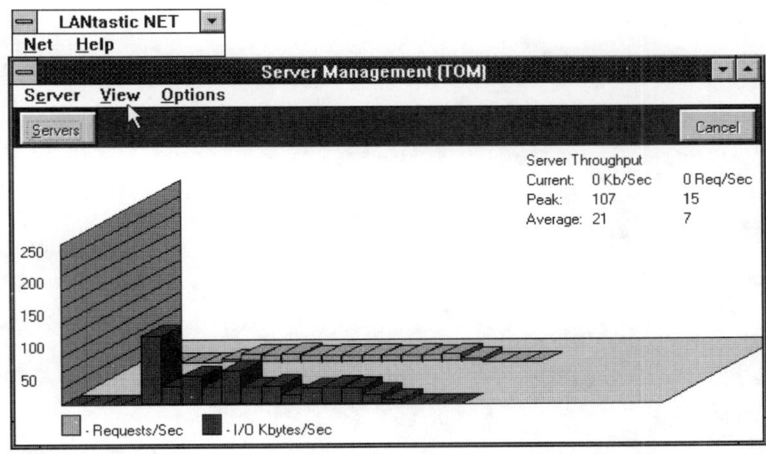

generates by starting an application program or by entering a simple database search command. Figure 12-9 shows a sample graphical display of server activity.

All the other options of LANtastic Net and Network Manager work the same way, using the normal Windows interface. These options and the selections you can make from them will all look familiar from your use of the NET and NET_MGR programs under plain non-Windows DOS.

13

LANtastic Optimization

It's one thing to make LANtastic run. It's another to make it run well. *Optimization* in a LAN environment refers to making a LAN or its components run better. Other names are often used, including system tuning, network tuning, performance analysis, performance tuning, resource optimization, and response time improvement. Some people just call it tweaking the LAN.

But "better" is such a vague, subjective word. How do you decide if one LAN configuration runs better than another? The answer is not absolute. Different observers could look at the same two LANs and draw different conclusions about which one runs better. In general, however, optimization efforts try to make improvements in these areas:

- Faster response when a workstation interacts with a server
- Increased overall throughput on the LAN, meaning that more work is processed by the entire group in a given time period, even if any one individual's response time is slower

- Increased RAM availability for applications that run on servers or workstations (in other words, reduce the RAM that operating system components use)
- Increased disk space availability on servers or workstations

Most people think of only the first item, faster response, when they consider optimizing a LAN or improving a server's performance. However, an effort that results in better usage of *any* resource is a form of optimization. Because time is the most valuable resource in the minds of many people, speed usually is the focus of optimization efforts. In some environments, however, an improvement that avoids the need to add another big, expensive hard disk to a server might be even more important. For reasons like these, opinions can differ about which LAN runs best.

This chapter looks at a number of optimization topics and provides recommendations about how you can make your LAN run better. But you must be the judge about which types of improvements matter most in your environment. Often an improvement in one area comes only at a cost in another. In particular, you can often gain more speed if you use up more RAM on a server. Is such a trade-off worthwhile? You must judge for yourself based on your own needs and resources.

Optimization Methodology

If you are an amateur (or even professional) scientist at heart, optimization will appeal to you. Optimization consists of a series of experiments. You measure how well your LAN runs, make a change, and then measure again. If the second set of measurements show improvements from the change, the change stays. If not, step back and try again.

So, to run these optimization experiments you need some way or ways to measure how well your LAN runs. To measure speed, the classic method is to run benchmark tests. A *benchmark test* is a controlled, repeatable chunk of work that you can measure to compare results. Most benchmarks are measured either in terms of time (how long did the benchmark take?) or work per time unit (the number of bytes transferred per second or the number of responses per minute).

To know if your optimization efforts are working, you have to have some sort of a benchmark. Having several benchmarks is even better, to see if your changes improve response for some kinds of work but not others.

Benchmarks are available from many sources. Utility software products, such as the Norton Utilities and PC Tools, include benchmark programs. Popular computer magazines, such as PC Magazine and Byte, construct benchmark work loads for their comparative tests. You can obtain these benchmarks from the magazines' bulletin board systems and use them if you like. A set of benchmark tests is sometimes called a *benchmark suite.*

However, the best benchmark for you is one that reflects your particular work load. If your workgroup uses Paradox databases heavily but you test with a dBASE IV benchmark, the results may not apply to your situation–that is, you might make an optimization change that, according to the benchmark results, improves response time by 15 percent. For your Paradox programs, however, you may end up with a slower response time than you had before.

Even if you find a Paradox benchmark, the benchmark may not use Paradox the same way you do. Maybe the benchmark includes equal amounts of database reads and database writes, while your workgroup reads the database 98 percent of the time.

While no benchmark is a perfect representation of your real work load, you should try to figure out a relatively simple set of tests that at least is a rough approximation of the work your group does most. If the main way people use your server's shared disk is to use the DOS COPY command between their hard disks and the shared disk, a benchmark with a lot of COPY commands similar to yours is a good benchmark. If your group doesn't use many COPY commands, than a benchmark with a lot of them doesn't make sense for you.

A fundamental problem with running a benchmark test on a LAN is that a real-world LAN has lots of things going on at once. Your LAN might have eight computers connected, and sometimes all eight are active and doing different things. How do you set up a test and run all eight things at the same time? And even if you manage to test, how do you measure the results and interpret the measurements?

No simple answer exists. A few possible benchmarks are suggested here, but you may find them too complex, too simple, or too artificial for your needs. In most cases, well-selected benchmarks are valuable in optimization efforts, but be aware of their limitations.

Possible Benchmarks

Both benchmark programs and the real work people do on a LAN fall into two broad categories:

- *Transfers of large data blocks* Programs that read or write entire files of data at once transfer large blocks of data across the LAN. Examples are the DOS COPY and XCOPY commands for medium or large files, file management programs that copy files, and starting up programs that reside on a shared hard disk.
- *Transfers of small data blocks* Some programs and DOS commands send only small chunks of data across the LAN at a time. Examples are most random reads and writes by database programs, the DOS DIR command on a server's disk, and the DOS COPY command for very small files.

Any single benchmark test you choose will most likely perform either large or small data block transfers almost exclusively. Many optimization changes you make will improve performance for one type of processing but not the other. If your real work load consists of both types of work, use both types of benchmarks. If your work load is primarily one of the two types, use benchmarks of the same type.

Large Block Benchmarks

Here are a few suggestions for benchmark tests you can set up and run to test the speed of large data block transfers:

- A series of DOS COPY or XCOPY commands of large files from a workstation to a server and vice versa
- Starting up a large application program that resides on a server's hard disk, such as WordPerfect, Microsoft Word, Lotus 1-2-3, or dBASE
- Running artificial benchmark programs such as the Norton Utilities SYSINFO or one you write yourself that reads and writes data and times the results

Small Block Benchmarks

Benchmarks that test transfers of small data blocks are more difficult to construct and measure. Here are some possibilities:

- A database program that searches and updates a known database file (that you restore before each test) using a fixed script of commands
- A word processing spell-check in which the dictionary file is on the server's shared disk
- A batch file that executes a series of DOS DIR commands and/or COPY commands of very small files (no more than 2000 bytes each; most smaller) to and from a server
- An artificial benchmark program that performs small block data transfers

Benchmark Tips

Here are some general tips and guidelines to follow whenever you run benchmarks. If you overlook these methods, your results may be false or misleading.

Be Sure Results Are Repeatable Run your tests only on a LAN that no one else is using at the time. Otherwise your results will vary depending on what other users happen to be doing during your test. Don't use tests that rely on humans at each keyboard to "enter commands as usual" to simulate a real work load. People won't do the same thing each time (and will judge the LAN's responsiveness inconsistently) and your results will be worthless. Run each test at least twice to be sure the results are consistent. If the results vary, either your benchmark has a problem or some variable factor is at work. If the benchmark consists of copying or querying files, be sure the files are identical before each test. Be aware of the varying results you can get due to disk fragmentation (discussed later in this chapter).

Run Tests That Last Long Enough to Overcome Measurement Errors Don't use a stopwatch to time a DOS COPY command that takes less than three seconds. Your reaction time can vary so much that you won't know if a test with a 1.6-second run time is really better than one that supposedly ran 1.8 seconds. Be sure any timed test runs at least five seconds, and preferably over ten seconds. If you use the computer's internal clock, be aware that its resolution is .0549255 seconds (about 18.2 timer clicks per second); this means you should assume only one decimal place of accuracy even if two are displayed.

Don't Use Tests That Become Boring If you run a database inquiry test that takes 15 minutes, you will get bored after you run it a few times (or once, even). As a result, you won't monitor the test as carefully as you would a shorter test (which can result in unnoticed errors) and you will be less likely to run a large number of tests to investigate various optimization changes. Keep each test run under five minutes, and two minutes is even better, depending on your attention span. Of course, after you make optimization changes a two-minute test may take only one minute.

Carefully Record All Results Don't rely on your memory. Write down the timing or other results of each test along with the optimization changes you made. Record specifically which values you used for each parameter you are testing. These results are useful not only to see which changes worked best today, but also to compare with future tests you perform.

Optimizing for Speed

Speed is what computers are all about. The primary reason computers are useful is that people can do certain things faster with them than without them. The classic speed improvement needed is on a server that many users access at once. The fundamental type of change that does the most good is to put some data in RAM instead of on disk. A computer can access data in RAM much faster than on even the fastest disk.

You have a dizzying array of things you can do to try to improve the speed with which your server responds. These are just a few of the ways to optimize (the best of these methods are covered fully in this chapter):

- Use a disk cache such as LANtastic's LANcache

- Alter the number and size of buffers your LANtastic servers use to hold data in RAM
- Use the ALONE program to run your servers as dedicated servers
- Optimize your hard disks to make them respond faster
- Upgrade your hardware with faster LAN cards, faster processors, faster disk drives, or more RAM

If your LAN isn't running fast enough to suit you, don't despair. This section lists lots of things you can try to improve performance. Just keep in mind that no single change or set of changes works best for everyone. Every LAN is different—the hardware, the software, and the work loads all vary. Therefore, you have to test changes in your environment to see what works best for you.

LANcache

In most LANtastic configurations, the best way to improve server performance is clear-cut: use a disk cache. A *disk cache* (pronounced like "cash") is a piece of software that logically sits between DOS and your hard disk. The cache software sets up and manages an area of your RAM in which it stores disk data, whether the data is being read from disk or being written to disk. This improves your computer's speed in accessing disk data for two main reasons. First, your computer can transfer a large chunk of data to or from the disk instead of many more transfers of small chunks. A lot of overhead time is associated with each transfer and reducing the number of them improves performance. Second, when your program accesses data, the next data you need is most likely right near the last data you accessed. By putting a large amount of adjacent disk data in RAM, your computer can often avoid the need to go out to the disk drive for data. The data is quickly accessible in RAM instead.

Disk cache programs are complicated to create, especially when used in conjunction with LAN software. LANcache was developed by Artisoft specifically for use with LANtastic. It comes with LANtastic at no extra charge, but the INSTALL procedure does *not* add the statements to STARTNET.BAT that would activate LANcache for you. You have to add a statement to

STARTNET.BAT yourself. You can also run LANcache on a workstation, but the critical benefit comes from running it on a server.

Because a disk cache program uses your computer's RAM to store disk data, you need to be clear on the different types of RAM in a computer. If you aren't clear on the differences among conventional, expanded, extended, and XMS memory, the next section should help.

Different Memory Types

In order to know how to run LANcache (and implement other optimization techniques), you need to know how much and what kind of memory your computer has. An explanation of different memory types can get confusing, but here's an attempt to keep it simple.

To begin with, the type of memory discussed here is usually called RAM, or random access memory. RAM is inside the system unit of your PC and is made up of a series of integrated circuit chips. The information in RAM stays there only as long as the computer's power is on. When you turn off the computer you lose what is in RAM, so first you have to save on disk anything you will need later.

The original PC had only one kind of RAM, what is now called *conventional memory.* This is the first 640 kilobytes (640K) of RAM. All PCs have conventional memory—usually at least 512K and most often 640K. Most application programs are designed to use conventional memory only.

Later, people discovered the need for more than 640K of RAM, so manufacturers invented *expanded memory.* Expanded memory requires a special expanded memory card in your computer, with RAM chips installed on it, plus some software called an expanded memory manager. Expanded memory uses a tricky scheme to flip-flop 16K chunks of memory (called pages) back and forth between the expanded memory card and a 64K section of a special memory area called the upper memory area. The upper memory area is between the 640K and 1024K marks and is normally reserved for use by hardware devices such as video cards. Not all computers have expanded memory, but it was the first type of extra memory available so it is still used on many computers and by many software products. Expanded memory is often abbreviated EMS (expanded memory specification) or LIM (Lotus-Intel-Microsoft) EMS. Figure 13-1 shows the layout of the different memory areas.

A newer type of extra RAM is called *extended memory.* Extended memory exists only on computers that use the 80286, 386, or 486 processors, and it is

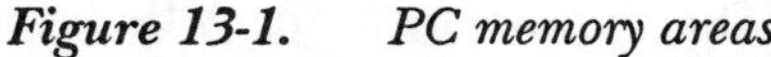
Figure 13-1. *PC memory areas*

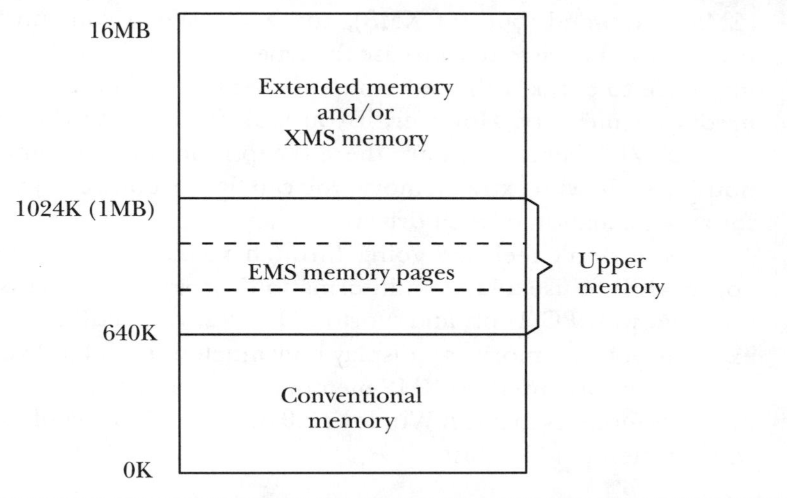

mapped into the area above the 1024K mark. Many of these computers come with one megabyte (1024K) of memory, which is configured as 640K of conventional memory and 384K of extended memory. Some software requires a special memory program called an extended memory manager program to use extended memory (and some other software isn't designed to use it at all). A standard way that such extended memory manager programs can be designed to work is to follow the XMS (extended memory specification) standard. Extended memory that is accessed using XMS standard software is called *XMS memory.* MS-DOS includes a program called HIMEM.SYS, which conforms to the XMS standard.

To use one of the memory manager software products, you have to include a DEVICE statement in your CONFIG.SYS file to run the software when you power on your computer. The software uses a small amount of your computer's conventional memory and makes the extra memory (XMS or expanded) available. Here is an example of a DEVICE statement that loads the HIMEM.SYS driver program:

```
device=c:\dos\himem.sys
```

Did you survive that explanation? The important point is that your PC might have five different kinds of memory: conventional, upper, expanded (EMS), extended (but not XMS), and XMS. When you run the LANcache program you have to tell it to use the type of memory you have available. You may have to check with your computer vendor to find out how they configured your memory. However, if you look in your CONFIG.SYS file to see what DEVICE statements are there (keep in mind that some of them have nothing to do with extra memory) you can figure it out. See your DOS manual for an explanation of each driver.

If you don't feel like going through your CONFIG.SYS file, another approach is to use a "system information" program such as SI or SYSINFO available with PC Tools and Norton Utilities, respectively. These programs examine your memory and display how much of each kind you have.

If your computer has XMS memory (this is most common on newer 386 or 486 computers that run Windows 3.0 or DOS 5), you would start LANcache with a statement like this:

```
lancache /type=xms
```

You might also want other parameters, which you will learn about shortly, but the point is that the /type parameter tells LANcache what type of memory to use. Find out what you have. If you can configure your memory any way you like (because none of your other software requires a specific type), XMS is probably the best way to go.

Using LANcache

LANcache works only with the LANtastic software, and it must be started in the proper sequence among the other programs. Start LANcache after REDIR but before SERVER. So, for a server on an AE-x Ethernet LAN, the program sequence in STARTNET.BAT must be AEX, AILANBIO, REDIR, LANCACHE, and then SERVER. Use EDLIN or another editor to insert the LANCACHE line.

The four options for the /type parameter are xms, extended, ems, and conventional. By default, LANcache uses all your available memory for xms, extended, or ems. For conventional, LANcache uses 384K by default. To limit the amount LANcache uses, add the /cache_size parameter, as shown in the following statement:

lancache /type=xms /cache_size=256

Experiment with different cache sizes to see which one gives the best performance in your environment. Give LANcache all the RAM you can spare. At least half a megabyte (512) is a good size, and one or two megabytes (1024 or 2048) is even better. For most computers, you can buy RAM chips for less than $50 per megabyte—a good investment to improve performance when you use the memory for a disk cache.

Chapter 14 lists the parameters you can specify for LANcache (as well as for other LANtastic software). Two other LANcache parameters in particular are worth mentioning:

- *The after_io_delay parameter* This parameter says how long in seconds LANcache should wait after no disk writing activity before writing output data to the disk. The default value is three. This means that after your program writes data to a hard disk, if no more write requests occur on the server for three seconds, LANcache will copy the data from its cache area to the hard disk. The three second delay gives LANcache the opportunity to wait for a lull in activity before writing the data to disk, which smooths out the work load and gives you better overall disk response time. However, if a power failure occurs on the server during those three seconds, your data never gets written to the hard disk.
- *The long_write_delay parameter* This LANcache parameter tells LANcache to write data to disk after the specified number of seconds even if after_io_delay has never lapsed. A busy disk may never wait three seconds without writing output, which would cause data in the cache never to be written to the hard disk. The long_write_delay parameter forces data to be written to disk at least occasionally. The default value is 12 seconds.

If you set either or both of these parameters to zero, you force LANcache to write output data to the disk immediately—in other words, you disable write caching. A few software or hardware products misbehave when write caching is enabled, so disable it using one or both of these parameters if you see corrupted disk files and suspect an incompatibility. If the disk corruption problem persists, stop using LANcache completely to see if that solves the problem. If the problem still persists, see Chapter 9 for tips on troubleshooting. Also, if your office is plagued by power failures and you have no UPS system, turn off write caching to minimize the risk of disk updates failing to be written to the disk drive when a power failure hits.

If you have write caching enabled, you have another reason to power down a server or workstation gracefully. If you simply turn off your computer's power, the data in the cache may not yet have been written out to disk and will be lost. Either wait until the data is written to your hard disk, or enter any one of the following commands to tell LANcache to write its data to disk:

```
lancache /disable
lancache /flush
lancache /release
lancache /remove
lancache /reset
```

(These and other LANcache parameters are explained in Chapter 14.) On a server, you can instead press CTRL-ALT-DEL and then type **s** to perform a server shutdown.

One more LANcache parameter of note: While LANcache is running, type **lancache /stat=info** and press ENTER to check periodically to see how well LANcache is performing for you. The /stat=info parameter displays how much disk I/O LANcache has performed and what part of the I/O has taken place from the cache area.

Other disk cache products are also available. As a rule, you should use LANcache because of its tight integration with LANtastic. However, you might prefer to use another disk cache product if you need to perform disk caching on more than one physical disk (LANcache supports only one) or if you occasionally run without LANtastic and want to keep a disk cache active on your computer at all times. Most other disk cache products that support write caching will work only if you disable write caching. Find out what parameter disables write caching before you use another disk cache. If you try write caching, test it very carefully. Sometimes failures occur only under a heavy I/O load.

Of the independent disk cache products on the market, the one that seems to have the most vocal satisfied LANtastic users is Super PC-Kwik from Multisoft Corporation (15100 SW Koll Parkway, Beaverton, OR 97006, 800-274-KWIK, 503-644-5644). Artisoft reports that you must use the /H- and /D- switches with Super PC-Kwik, but check with Artisoft or Multisoft to see if that is still true for the latest version. If you use Super PC-Kwik you can have a disk cache for more than one physical hard disk. The list price for Super PC-Kwik is $79.95.

A disk cache program called SMARTDRV.SYS comes with recent versions of MS-DOS, but users report its performance improvement generally does not match LANcache or Super PC-Kwik. (However, if you run Windows on the server, Artisoft recommends using SMARTDRV instead of LANcache.) Utility products such as Norton Utilities and PC Tools include disk cache programs, too. Be sure not to use write caching with any of these products unless you verify in advance that write caching is compatible with LANtastic.

Some hard disks have a built-in disk cache in the hardware, either in the disk drive circuitry or the disk controller card. These disk drives and controllers provide some of the benefits of a software disk cache without the complexity of installation or parameters. Typically, however, these hardware disk caches are much smaller than the RAM you would make available to a software disk cache. Because less data can reside in the cache at once, you have less performance improvement.

When you use LANcache (or most other disk cache programs), you should lower the BUFFERS statement in CONFIG.SYS. The DOS buffers area is the RAM into which DOS puts disk data that you read or write. The LANtastic INSTALL program sets the number of buffers to 32 on a server. That's usually a good number if you don't run LANcache. However, if you run LANcache, both the DOS buffers area and LANcache serve somewhat the same function. Too large a value for BUFFERS can slow down disk I/O because DOS will waste time searching through its buffers area instead of its cache area for data that LANcache will find. Artisoft recommends a value of eight for BUFFERS if you run LANcache. Other disk cache products have similar recommendations, typically from 3 to 12. This reduction in BUFFERS will reduce RAM usage on the computer, too. Every 20 buffers you eliminate saves about 11K of conventional memory.

Tip

The first speed optimization change you should try is to use a disk cache program. If the server has one physical hard disk (even if partitioned into more than one logical disk), use LANcache. If the server has more than one physical hard disk and both (or more) need speed improvements, consider another disk cache product such as Super PC-Kwik.

Tip

If the server doesn't have enough RAM to use at least 256K for the disk cache program, add more RAM to the computer. On a heavily used server, give at least two megabytes (2048K) to the disk cache. At some point, giving more RAM to a disk cache does little or no good. Unfortunately, you have to install the RAM and run tests to find out where that point is.

Caution

A disk cache is not the same as a processor cache. Some 386 and 486 computers are advertised as including a "64K cache" or a "256K cache" as part of the system. The cache referred to is a processor cache, which allows the processor to execute instructions faster by accessing instructions and data from this processor cache area instead of conventional RAM. The processor cache does not serve the same function as a disk cache.

Benchmark Results

To give you an idea of how optimization changes affect performance, here are some benchmark results. The test results in this chapter use a program called BENCH, created by the author and available to you (see Appendix B).

The BENCH program writes a disk file to the disk drive you select, whether the disk is a workstation's local disk or a redirected disk on a server, and then reads the file back afterward while keeping track of how long each step takes. BENCH displays the elapsed time of each step and calculates the data transfer rate (thousands of bytes per second). The write-read cycle is repeated as often as you like, but the tests in this chapter run five cycles unless otherwise stated. By specifying parameters, you can change the I/O blocksize, which is the size of each chunk of data written at a time. By default, BENCH writes and reads 10,000 bytes at a time in a 1 million byte file to simulate large block transfers. For comparison, tests are shown with 1000 byte (small block) transfers, too. The tests were run on a Teltron 386/33 server computer with a 120-megabyte IDE hard disk and the default parameters in CONFIG.SYS from DOS 5's and LANtastic 4.1's installation programs. When a cache was used, it ran in XMS memory using the DOS 5 HIMEM.SYS driver. The workstation is a CMS 386/33 running DOS 4.01 with default installation parameters. Both computers use LANtastic AE-2 Ethernet cards with thin Ethernet cable and LANtastic 4.1. You can also run BENCH from more than one workstation at once, but the results here are all for the simple case of a single workstation.

Table 13-1 shows a comparison of running BENCH with no cache, with a 1024K (one-megabyte) cache, and a 2048K (two-megabyte) cache. The numbers show the average data transfer rate in kilobytes per second (KB/second), where a kilobyte means 1000 bytes, not 1024. The speed improvements are large using a two-megabyte cache—usually more than twice as fast as when not using a cache.

The only anomaly in the results is that 10K reads actually slowed down from 192 to 159 KB/second when using a one-megabyte cache. This happened because the server had to perform delayed writes to the hard disk after the write test, and these physical disk writes took place during the subsequent read tests. These delayed writes made the cache perform somewhat worse than it would under most real-world circumstances, because the BENCH program constantly writes, reads, writes, and reads again (five total write-read cycles). However, most real LANs have users that perform work more erratically, which allows LANcache to sneak in its delayed writes during slack periods. With BENCH, delayed writes had to occur during a subsequent read test, which elongated the read time. The two-megabyte cache has more room and doesn't need to flush the cache by performing disk writes as often, and therefore gets better performance than the one-megabyte cache. Benchmark

Table 13-1. *Transfer rates (KB/second) of BENCH tests without and with LANcache*

Work Load Type	Without LANcache	With 1024K LANcache	With 2048K LANcache
10K writes	80	210	209
10K reads	192	159	373
1K writes	28	100	131
1K reads	114	122	166

results normally can vary from one run to another by 5 or 10 percent, but this LANcache flushing action can make results vary even more. Be sure to make several benchmark runs before you draw conclusions.

ALONE

Another method that Artisoft provides to improve server performance is the ALONE program. ALONE turns a nondedicated server into a dedicated server. Remember, a dedicated server is one that cannot be used as a workstation at the same time as a server. Because the computer can devote all its resources to being a server, it can handle a bigger work load. The improvement is often only a small speed increase, but in some environments it can be significant.

You can turn ALONE on or off depending on what you need to do. If you don't need to use the server as a workstation for awhile, you can fire up ALONE. When you need to use the server as a workstation, stop ALONE and do your work.

To run ALONE on a computer already functioning as a server, simply type **alone** and press ENTER. If you want a server to always run as a dedicated server, add ALONE to the STARTNET.BAT file as the last statement. When ALONE starts, it displays a screen like the one shown in Figure 13-2.

ALONE's display is similar to the display from NET's Monitor & Manage Server Activity function. In fact, if you want to take a quick look at a server to see which users are suddenly causing the server's disk light to flash wildly from a heavy work load, start ALONE to see whose numbers are changing fastest. Press the F1 key and ALONE explains what all the columns and commands mean. To end ALONE and return the server to nondedicated operation, press ESC.

While ALONE is running, you can press F3 to enable password protection. This way you can prevent other people with curious fingers from tinkering with your dedicated server. Another ALONE option is to press F2 to turn ALONE's filename display on or off. However, performance is slightly better without the constant filename display.

Do not try to run ALONE with Microsoft Windows. ALONE runs properly only from a normal DOS prompt, not from a Windows DOS virtual machine.

Figure 13-2. *The screen display from ALONE*

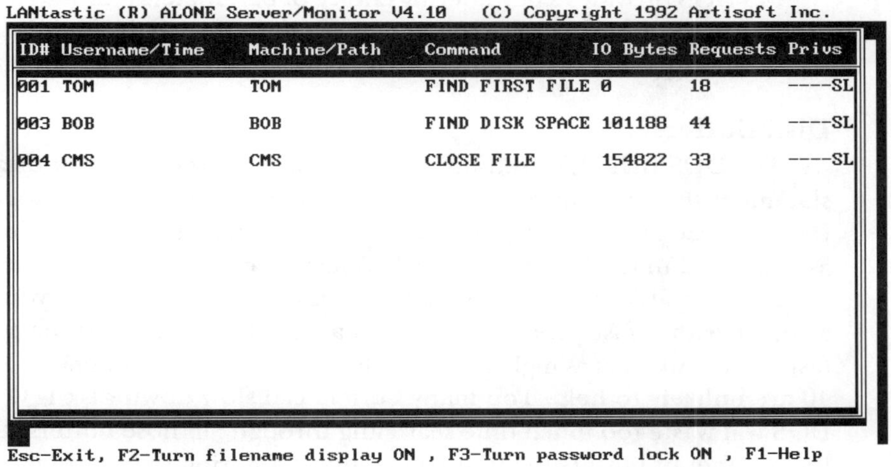

```
LANtastic (R) ALONE Server/Monitor V4.10   (C) Copyright 1992 Artisoft Inc.
ID# Username/Time     Machine/Path     Command          IO Bytes Requests Privs
001 TOM               TOM              FIND FIRST FILE 0        18       ----SL
003 BOB               BOB              FIND DISK SPACE 101188   44       ----SL
004 CMS               CMS              CLOSE FILE       154822  33       ----SL

Esc-Exit, F2-Turn filename display ON , F3-Turn password lock ON , F1-Help
```


Some users have reported problems trying to run ALONE at the same time as some memory management products, such as QEMM. The problems seem to depend on exactly what parameters are specified and the computer configuration. Test carefully if you try a combination like this. Also, you can't run any TSR programs on a computer that runs ALONE or you risk a lockup. That includes Artisoft's own The Network Eye software, although some users have reported success running them together.

If you use ALONE consistently on a server, you can change server parameters to make the server run even faster. These changes would make workstation performance unacceptable on the computer, but if you always run ALONE that's not a problem. Change the Run Burst parameter to 200. See the "Server Parameters" section later in this chapter for details.

Benchmark Results

The tests you saw in Table 13-1 were rerun using ALONE and no other parameter changes. Without LANcache, the ALONE results were virtually the same. With LANcache, the ALONE performance was typically from 4 to 15 percent faster.

DOS Parameters

MS-DOS provides a bewildering choice of parameters and statements you can use to optimize your computer's operation. This section briefly explains the most significant ones. See your DOS manuals for more information.

Disk Buffers

The DOS BUFFERS setting in CONFIG.SYS is the most important DOS statement that can improve performance on either a server or workstation. If you run a disk cache program such as LANcache, set the number of buffers as explained in the "Using LANcache" section earlier in this chapter. If you do not use a disk cache, experiment with the number of buffers you use. On a server with a fast processor (such as a 386 that runs at 20 megahertz or faster), try numbers as high as 60. On slower processors, numbers higher than 40 are unlikely to help. Too many buffers can slow down disk I/O because DOS will waste too much time searching through all those buffers. Don't set the number of buffers to 99 (the maximum), figuring that more is better.

Too few buffers will definitely hurt performance without a disk cache program. Be sure to use at least 12 or 15 buffers. LANtastic's INSTALL program's default values of 16 for a workstation and 32 for a server are good choices for most computers. However, the best number for each of your computers depends on the type of processor, the clock speed, the type of disk drive, the amount of RAM available, the type of work the computer performs, and the version of DOS. Therefore, you have to experiment to find the best value. As a rule, you are better off spending this time experimenting with a disk cache instead, unless your computer has too little RAM to support one.

Benchmark Results Increasing BUFFERS from 32 to 50 and 60 made virtually no difference in performance results shown earlier in Table 13-1, either with or without LANcache. With LANcache active, BUFFERS was reduced from 32 to 8 with no speed difference.

FASTOPEN

FASTOPEN is a DOS program that keeps track of the files and directories you open (begin to use) to speed up your access to them. Its biggest benefit comes if you run programs that repeatedly open and close files. Database programs are the best example.

Unfortunately, some users have reported problems with DOS 5.0's FASTOPEN causing corrupt disk files, independent of using LANtastic. To be safe, don't use FASTOPEN with DOS 5.0. (It seems to work fine with DOS 4.0 and 3.3.) The easiest way to start FASTOPEN is by adding a statement to your CONFIG.SYS file. For details, see the manual for your version of DOS.

Caution

If you encounter disk file corruption problems (disk files that are improperly updated), stop using FASTOPEN until you can verify that it isn't the cause of your problem.

RAM Disks

A RAM disk is another method for using RAM instead of a disk drive to improve speed. A RAM disk (sometimes called a virtual disk, to the confusion of those who call a redirected disk over a LAN a virtual disk) is software that uses a chunk of RAM to simulate a floppy disk. If, for example, your computer has two floppy disks (A and B) and a C hard disk, you can create a RAM disk called your D drive. Your software can read from and write to the RAM disk just like any other real disk, except much faster.

The disadvantages of a RAM disk are that it uses up RAM, although most versions can use expanded or extended memory as well as conventional, and that the data you put there is temporary. Unlike using a real disk, when you power off your computer the data in the RAM disk disappears. As a result, a RAM disk is best used for temporary files (ones that your program writes out to disk and then reads back in, for example), or read-only files that you can copy from a real disk to the RAM disk for temporary access. If you update any files on a RAM disk, you have to save them on a real disk before you turn off the power or else you lose the data.

DOS includes a RAM disk program called RAMDRIVE.SYS, which for DOS 5.0 can use conventional, expanded, or extended memory. The RAMDRIVE program itself uses a small amount of conventional memory, but the disk drive space can use whatever type of extra memory you have. Other companies also sell RAM disk software, which may have different features and capabilities.

Usually a RAM disk does not improve your overall computer performance as much as a disk cache. The typical situation in which a RAM disk works out better is when your software creates a large number of small files and accesses them frequently. If you think your situation might be right for a RAM disk and you have some RAM to spare, experiment and compare the results with the results you get from a disk cache.

Other DOS Tips

The following are a few more quickies about DOS parameters and their potential effect on LANtastic performance.

SHARE Be sure you use plenty of SHARE locks and filename space on the server in CONFIG.SYS. An application program uses SHARE to temporarily *lock* (get exclusive control of) an entire file or a portion of a file so no other user will access or update that data at the same time. If you run short, some applications will sit and wait until locks and space are made available. (Others will simply terminate after displaying an error message about a lock or file shortage.) INSTALL by default gives a server 200 locks (/L:200) and a filename space of 2048 bytes (/F:2048). The filename space holds for each open file the complete file and path name, plus 11 bytes of other information. For average file and path name lengths, 2048 bytes might be enough for only 50 or 60 files to be open at once. Some database products in particular make heavy use of locks, sometimes using a dozen or more locks each on many files at once. If you don't run any applications that share data files on the server, you probably don't need to increase your SHARE settings. But if your applications do share data files on the server, check each product's documentation for SHARE recommendations. If you find no recommendations but have occasional slow response from the application, try doubling both SHARE settings to see if the slowdowns decrease.

Disk Partitions If you have a giant hard disk and use it as one logical drive, consider separating it into several smaller partitions. For example, if you have a 200-megabyte hard disk that you use as your C drive (permissible under DOS 4.0 or 5.0), use FDISK to repartition the drive into several 32-megabyte logical hard disks called C, D, E, and so on. DOS uses a file allocation table (FAT) to keep track of the disk space on each logical hard disk. The FAT is a separate area on your disk that contains entries for all the used and unused disk areas. On a huge hard disk, the FAT can be very large and DOS has to spend a lot of time searching through it. A smaller disk partition has a smaller

FAT and DOS can search it faster. Of course, if your workgroup needs to share a 50-megabyte disk file then you need a disk partition at least that big, plus room for growth. Also, if you set up six or seven logical drives (C through H, let's say), you have a tougher management job to keep track of which files are on each one and what to do if a logical drive gets full. These are the trade-offs of this optimization technique.

Unfortunately, if you use FDISK to repartition a hard disk you lose all the data on the disk. So, you have to back up all your data first and then restore it after you complete the FDISK process. See your DOS manual about FDISK for details. If your 200-megabyte hard disk is already partitioned into two logical disks of 32 megabytes and 168 megabytes, try putting your most heavily accessed disk files on the 32-megabyte disk.

Server Parameters

The LANtastic SERVER program is the center of activity on a server computer. If you provide no parameters when you start the SERVER program (using the STARTNET.BAT file), you use a series of default parameters. For many servers, these parameters are adequate. However, if you want to improve performance and especially if your server has a heavier than average work load, changes to some of these parameters can make a big difference.

To change these parameters, you have three choices:

- Add the parameters to the command line for SERVER in STARTNET.BAT or whatever batch file you use to start the server
- Put the parameters in a file called a switch file, which you can name whatever you like; you then point to the switch file using an @ ("at" sign) in the batch file's SERVER statement, like this:

  ```
  server @switchfile
  ```

- Use the NET_MGR program to permanently change the Server Startup Parameters (a choice from the Main Functions menu box) to cause SERVER to always use the new parameters automatically whenever you start that server

Be aware that these recommendations point out the eternal confrontation between speed and memory. When you increase most of these server parameters, the server uses more RAM but runs its work faster (until you reach a point of diminishing returns). You have to decide from your needs and experiments how much RAM you can sacrifice to increase speed. If you use too much RAM you may not be able to use the server as a workstation to run your application programs. Of course, if you use the server as a dedicated server, the RAM usage won't be a problem.

The following sections show the key server performance parameters. For each parameter, the name shown first is the name of the parameter under NET_MGR's Server Startup Parameters menu. Immediately after that name in parenthesis is the parameter name if you use the SERVER command line or a switch file, followed by an equal sign and the default value for LANtastic 4.1. The sequence shown here is the same sequence used by NET_MGR's menu. By the way, the help text NET_MGR displays after you press F1 provides a good summary of how each parameter works and tips for which values to specify.

Network Buffer (network_buffer_size=4k)

NET_MGR specifies this parameter in bytes, not kilobytes, so 4096 in NET_MGR is the same as network_buffer_size=4k on the SERVER command line. The server's network buffer is not the same as the DOS disk buffers or the REDIR buffer or any of the many other buffers in your computer. The server sets up this area in RAM to store the data it processes for workstations. For a lightly loaded server the default value is acceptable. A server that processes a heavy volume of sequential file requests (reads, writes, copies, and program starts from the server) should use a larger value. Try 8k (8192), 12k (12288), or 16k (16384). Even larger values may be beneficial in some environments. Random reads and writes, such as are often done with database files, do not benefit so much from increasing the network buffer size.

Network Tasks (network_tasks=1)

If you have a small LAN that seldom has more than one person reading or writing on the server's disk at once, leave the Network Tasks parameter set to 1. However, if you often have two, three, or more active server users, increase this parameter to match that number of users. The key is the number of *active* users, not just users who have a disk drive redirected to the server. LANtastic sets up a network buffer area for each network task. The amount of RAM used is the product of the two, plus a little extra. For example, if you specify two network tasks and a network buffer size of 16K, the amount of RAM used by SERVER for network buffers is 32K instead of the default 4K. That makes SERVER use just over 58K of RAM instead of the 30K it uses with the default settings.

Tip

In most LANtastic environments, these first two parameters–Network Buffer and Network Tasks–are the most important server parameters you can change to speed up server performance when multiple users access a server. Try at least two tasks and 8K buffers and compare results with the default settings unless two or more workstations never access the server at the same time.

Printer Buffer (printer_buffer_size=512)

The printer buffer is a RAM storage area used by each printer task for data destined for one of the server's printers. If your shared printers run slow, consider increasing this buffer's size. Try 1024, 2048, or even more and run some timing tests. The SERVER command line parameter uses 512, 1K, 2K, 3K, and so on, but NET_MGR uses 512, 1024, 2048, 3072, and so on.

Printer Tasks (printer_tasks=1)

The Printer Tasks parameter specifies the number of simultaneous printer tasks this server can run. Consider increasing this parameter to two or three on a server that has two or three printers. Do not set the value higher than the number of printers attached to the server. If the server runs Windows, leave this parameter set at 1 even if more printers are connected.

Request Size (request_size=14)

Request size is the size in bytes of the buffer the server uses to process requests from workstations. In most environments such requests are usually small, but some are big enough to require multiple messages across the LAN if you keep the default setting. You can make this buffer as large as 2048 bytes, but over 100 probably won't help much. Be careful of excessive RAM usage. Each user in the Maximum Users parameter has one of these buffers allocated in RAM. Try using 30 or 50 bytes and see if your performance improves.

Run Burst (run_burst=2)

The Run Burst parameter sets the number of clock ticks (each measuring about .055 seconds, or roughly 1/18 of a second) that the server processes its own work before allowing interruptions to perform any local workstation work. If you set this parameter very high, anyone sitting at the server's keyboard trying to run word processing will get extremely slow response. If you want the computer to give server requests the highest priority, set this number to 5, 10, or more. If the server always runs ALONE or you don't care about how slowly it responds to its own workstation requests (it won't have any workstation requests while ALONE runs), set Run Burst to 200 or 250 (maximum is 255). If you want to give the server's own workstation good response time but don't care about great response time for other workstations, set Run Burst to 1 or 2. This feature is new in LANtastic 4.1.

Seek Cache Size (seek_cache=none)

If the server holds a database file that users often read from or write to randomly (jumping around in different parts of the database instead of going through the database sequentially from beginning to end), activate the seek cache. This causes the server to keep random access file location information in RAM.

Use the maximum size of 64K for a large database or a smaller size for smaller databases (or if you can't spare the RAM). This feature is new in LANtastic 4.1.

Other Server Parameters

Some other SERVER parameters may also help in special cases. Take a look at the descriptions in NET_MGR's help text for Cached Resources and Lock Hold Time.

Benchmark Results

Table 13-2 shows the results from running the BENCH program with differing parameters for network_buffer_size. Notice the big improvement from a large buffer when performing large block reads and writes, but virtually no change for small blocks. That's because the 1000-byte blocks used in the small block benchmark fit in the 4K buffers. However, for large block tests the 10,000-byte blocks benefit by having a larger server buffer. Also notice the huge difference in performance between the default LANtastic

Table 13-2. *Transfer rates (KB/second) of BENCH tests with differing values for SERVER's network_buffer_size parameter*

Work Load Type	4K	8K	12K	2 MB LANcache and 12K
10K writes	80	118	164	243
10K reads	192	214	224	498
1K writes	28	28	28	124
1K reads	114	115	116	170

settings (4K network_buffer_size and no LANcache) and two simple changes (12K network_buffer_size with 2-megabyte LANcache). The lesson here is to change your default settings and use LANcache if you want better performance. Also, as before, if you run ALONE on the server then most of the results that use LANcache improve by another five or ten percent.

Parameters on Other LANtastic Programs

The other LANtastic programs typically have less to do with fast performance than the SERVER parameters do, but some can be significant in some environments. The following programs are the main ones to try.

REDIR

You run REDIR on both a server and a workstation. For performance purposes, the parameters you specify for REDIR affect only how quickly a workstation accesses another server. What you specify for REDIR on a server does not affect how quickly that server responds to other workstation requests. So, to improve each workstation's performance in accessing servers, look at the Size parameter and the Buffers parameter.

Size (size=1024) The Size parameter determines the size of the buffer REDIR uses for data transfers over the LAN. If you run large file copy operations and other sequential disk reads and writes, increasing this parameter can make a difference. Try 2048, 4096, or 8192. The maximum is 16384. If you run a lot of random database queries and other small data transfer operations, a smaller value may work better. The minimum is 512.

Buffers (buffers=1) The Buffers parameter specifies the number of buffers REDIR uses. Try two buffers to see if performance is improved. The maximum is 64, but any more than two is unlikely to help and will just waste RAM.

Specify these parameters on the REDIR command line in STARTNET .BAT or whatever batch file you use to start the LANtastic software. (Like SERVER, you can instead use a switch file to provide REDIR parameters.) Here is a sample REDIR statement with the size and buffers parameters added to the parameters created by INSTALL:

```
redir whitney /logins=2 /size=2048 /buffers=2
```

AILANBIO

The AILANBIO program runs on Ethernet LAN cards (LANBIOS, LANBIOS2, or LANBIOS3 run on 2Mbps cards). One parameter change may improve performance in your environment. The jury is still out on the other parameters (given in Chapter 14).

Run Burst (run_burst=10) On a dedicated server with an Ethernet LAN card, try setting the Run Burst parameter to 254. This run_burst is different from the run_burst you can specify for SERVER.

Other Speed Tips

This section gives an assortment of other speed tips that might be effective for you. Some of these tips apply to any computer, not just a LAN server or workstation. That's because of the obvious fact that computers optimized to run their fastest are more capable of fast LAN performance than non-optimized computers are.

Check Your Interleave Factor

Check that your server's hard disk uses its optimal interleave factor. An *interleave factor* describes the number of revolutions your hard disk must perform to transfer an entire disk track of data into your computer's RAM. Most newer hard disks have an interleave factor of one, which means that only one revolution is necessary. Older hard disks often alternate their disk sectors in such a way that two, three, or more revolutions are required. Depending on the hard disk and its controller, you may be able to reduce the interleave factor and improve disk performance.

Caution

Reducing the interleave factor can also make performance much worse if the controller can't keep up with the disk revolution speed. Use a utility program to check and, if appropriate, change your disk interleave factor. Look at PC Tools, Norton Utilities, and SpinRite II. You can't run these products on a server's disk while other users access the disk. You have to stop the server and run the products directly on the server computer itself.

Fix Disk Fragmentation

As you add, delete, and update files on a disk, the space used by each file has a tendency to become fragmented, or noncontiguous. This situation, in which different portions of a file are scattered around on a disk, is called *disk fragmentation.* Special utility program are available to put these pieces together again (something all the king's horses and all the king's men can't always do). When a disk's files are fragmented, the disk takes longer to read or update each file because the disk's head has to move farther to access all the fragments. A file that is stored in one contiguous area on disk can be accessed fastest.

Unless your server's hard disk frequently becomes nearly full, disk fragmentation probably is not a severe performance problem for you. Just to be safe, you should occasionally run a "defrag" program to defragment your server's hard disk. Some people go overboard and run these programs weekly or even daily. In most environments, once a month is probably plenty. You can gauge how often you need to defragment based on the degree of fragmentation you see when you run the defragmentation software. Some products that perform defragmentation are OPTune from Gazelle Systems, PC Tools, and Norton Utilities. You can't run these products on an active server.

Have Plenty of Server Disk Space Available

As a disk fills up, performance suffers for two reasons. First, DOS has more trouble finding available space for updated disk files, which leads to more fragmentation problems. Second, each disk directory has more files in it and DOS's searches take longer. Eliminate unnecessary disk files from your server's hard disk, especially in the logical partitions that contain shared files.

Upgrade Your LANtastic Software

Each new version of the LANtastic network operating system software usually has internal performance improvements as well as new parameters you can change to improve performance. Version 4.1 in particular has improvements from version 4.0, and 4.0 had improvements from earlier versions. If you are running an old version of LANtastic, especially prior to 4.0, upgrade. Contact Artisoft for pricing.

Upgrade Your Hardware

Sometimes there's no substitute for raw power. Your best performance improvement may come only from upgrading your hardware, especially processors, disk drives, RAM, and LAN cards and cable (if you don't use Ethernet). If your server computer uses an 80286 processor or less, or a slow disk drive, an upgrade to a 386 or 486 with a faster disk drive can work wonders. If your server has only 640K of RAM, adding more RAM and running a disk cache should help greatly (as you've seen from this chapter's benchmark tests). If your LAN cards are ARCnet or Artisoft 2Mbps cards, a switch to Ethernet can make a big difference if your server has a fast processor. First try to determine which hardware component is the cause of your slowdown. Don't assume you need to upgrade to Ethernet if your bottleneck is a slow disk drive and controller on your server. On a busy server with a fast disk and processor, upgrading an AE-2 or AE-3 LAN card to 64K of on-board RAM may help performance. Upgrading an 8-bit LAN card to a 16-bit LAN card on a server is also something to try, but don't expect to double throughput.

Eliminate Cable and LAN Card Problems

If you have faulty LAN cables or a faulty LAN card, your LAN might spend a lot of time recovering from collisions or CRC errors, which degrade LAN performance for everyone. Use LANCHECK to verify that these errors are low. You should normally see an error percentage of less than one percent. Collisions might occasionally be slightly higher on an extremely active LAN with many simultaneous users. If errors are too high, follow the steps outlined in Chapter 9 to isolate and fix bad cables, connectors, or LAN cards.

Separate Your Work Load

If a server handles heavy loads of both file sharing and printer sharing, separate the two. Put the shared printers on one server and the shared files on another to reduce contention between the two work loads. Similarly, if you run two different database applications on the same server, move one to another server. This simple step of separating work loads can, in some workgroups, make a far bigger difference than any other optimization action.

Don't Use Windows

Microsoft Windows 3.0 puts a lot of overhead on a server. Remove it and see if performance improves. Also, if a particular workstation that runs Windows has performance problems, try it without Windows. Watch reports on Windows 3.1 to see if promised performance improvements prove to be a reality.

Turn Off LANtastic Audit Trails

Recording audit data can slow down a server and use up disk space. Unless you need the audit data, don't activate auditing. If you do need audit data, capture only the minimum data you need, not everything. In most cases, the overhead from capturing minimal audit data is not high.

Optimizing RAM Usage

The speed optimization techniques covered so far in this chapter often come at the expense of conventional RAM. If you make a buffer bigger then the server runs faster. However, the bigger buffer takes some of the server's RAM and leaves less RAM available for application programs that a user at the server's keyboard wants to run. Some applications require 500K, 550K, or more conventional RAM and won't run if DOS and LANtastic take up so much that this amount isn't available. In general you have two courses of action you can take to free up more RAM on your servers or workstations:

- Reduce LANtastic and DOS buffer sizes and other settings and possibly sacrifice speed

- Use upper memory and extended memory whenever possible to reduce the usage of your 640K conventional memory area (see the explanation in the "Different Memory Types" section earlier in this chapter)

To measure the results of your changes, you have three choices:

- *Use a utility program or DOS command that shows how much RAM of each type is in use at a particular time* If you have DOS 5 you can type **mem/c** and press ENTER to see a summary of memory usage. (With DOS 4 you can type **mem/program|more** and press ENTER to see similar but less concise information which, unfortunately, has numbers shown in hexadecimal.) For DOS 3.3 and earlier, you need an independent utility program such as PC Tools SI, Norton Utilities SYSINFO, or the shareware PMAP from The Cove Software Group.
- *Read the LANtastic and DOS manuals and calculate RAM usage from that information* This method helps you learn what LANtastic does, but is error prone and has to be based on only the limited (and sometimes out-of-date) information provided.
- *Use the /verbose parameter with each LANtastic program* Using the /verbose parameter lets you see how much RAM the program uses with its current settings. This is fine for the LANtastic programs but doesn't explain memory usage of different DOS parameters.

Your goal in RAM reduction is almost always to reduce usage of the precious 640K of conventional memory. That's the memory that most programs use. If you try to run an application program and it fails because of insufficient memory, the problem is nearly always a shortage of conventional memory. You need to either reduce the space LANtastic or DOS uses, or move some things to upper or extended memory if available.

LANtastic and DOS Parameters

The first way to reduce RAM usage is to be sure you don't waste RAM by specifying uselessly large parameters for LANtastic or DOS. If you do, you set up memory areas that take up RAM space but don't improve performance (or improve it by only miniscule amounts). The next two sections cover the most likely offenders.

LANtastic Parameters

RAM usage is most often a concern on a computer that acts as both a server and workstation. You need to increase some parameters to make the server perform well, but you also need to have as much conventional RAM available as possible in order to run application programs. If the server does not also act as a workstation, you can use all the RAM you like.

Minimize these server parameters to reduce RAM. (See "Server Parameters" earlier in this chapter for details.)

Network Buffer and Network Tasks The server sets up a buffer area for each network task. The default of one task with a 4K buffer is 4K (4096 bytes) for this area. If you specify five tasks and 16K buffers, you use over 80K instead. Use no more than two tasks and 8K buffers unless you need more for performance reasons.

Printer Buffer and Printer Tasks Similarly, the server uses a printer buffer area for each printer task. Multiply the number of tasks you specify times the size of the buffer to see how much RAM you cause the server to use.

Request Size and Maximum Users The server sets up a request buffer for each user in your Maximum Users parameter. If you allow 20 users at 1024 bytes each, you use 20K for this area.

Tip

The important point is that the number you specify for Maximum Users (/logins=) should reflect the number of people who simultaneously use the LAN; even if you could have up to eight people using a LAN, if in real life you never have more than four simultaneous users, reduce Maximum Users to four and save RAM.

Seek Cache Size You may need to specify a large value for the Seek Cache Size parameter to improve database response, but that means using more RAM. The amount you specify is the amount used.

Some parameters you specify for REDIR and AILANBIO also can use RAM. In particular look at any buffer size or buffer number parameter and determine if you can reduce the size or number to correspondingly reduce RAM usage. Be aware of the possible negative effect this may have on performance.

DOS Parameters

Several DOS parameters in CONFIG.SYS use RAM. The primary ones are BUFFERS and SHARE, discussed earlier in this chapter. In addition, FILES, LASTDRIVE, and FCBS each use a small amount of memory. You can reduce their settings to only the minimum you need to recover a little RAM. For example, use LASTDRIVE=L instead of LASTDRIVE=Z and save a little over 1000 bytes if you can live with having only drives A through L to redirect to servers. You can specify STACKS=0,0 in CONFIG.SYS to save another 1K of memory on most computers, especially if you don't run Windows. Finally, look at all DEVICE and INSTALL statements in CONFIG.SYS to see if you really need them. Each one uses RAM. The amount varies depending on the size of the device driver or program. See your DOS documentation for more details.

Upper Memory Usage

For an 80286, 386, or 486 computer, extended memory is your rescuer when it comes to gaining more conventional memory. With DOS 4 or 5 you can run the HIMEM.SYS extended memory manager that comes with DOS (or run an independent memory manager program such as QEMM, 386MAX, or NetRoom) to move many of your software components from conventional memory to another memory area.

The key facts are that you have to have extended memory on your computer, and the processor has to be an 80286 or higher. With a 386 or higher you can do even more because of the 386's additional memory management capabilities.

See Appendix A for sample CONFIG.SYS and STARTNET.BAT files that reduce use of conventional memory.

Optimizing Disk Space Usage

The key to optimizing disk space usage is simple human vigilance. Someone has to monitor the server's hard disk to be sure plenty of space is available. The techniques are simple: Remember to check every day and use file management utility programs to help you do the work. Use DOS commands or programs such as Q-DOS from Gazelle Systems, XTree Pro Gold from XTree Company, or PC Tools from Central Point Software. These programs help you quickly search files by date created, size, or directory to determine which files are eating up disk space.

If you have a tape backup system, you can archive programs regularly and more easily convince people that some files don't have to stay on the server's hard disk forever. Often someone's reason for keeping a file is "I might need it some day." If you save a copy on tape (or floppy disks, but that's more labor-intensive for large files) you can remove the file from the server's disk and keep your users happy.

A product exists that you must consider if you find your server's hard disk too small and your budget unable to tolerate a bigger hard disk. It's called Stacker, from Stac Electronics (5993 Avenida Encinas, Carlsbad, CA 92008, 619-431-7474). Stacker's purpose is to roughly double the amount of disk space your existing disk drive gives you. A hardware version includes a coprocessor card for the ISA bus and lists for $249. It reportedly gives you access to twice as much disk data with no perceptible speed penalty. A software-only version has a list price of $149 but doesn't run as fast. Stac has drawn rave reviews for developing data compression techniques and PC-integration methods that allow its products to work seamlessly on your computer with virtually any software products.

Highlights

This chapter has covered a lot of optimization techniques. Which are the most significant ones? Here's a quick list of the techniques that most people will find make the biggest difference:

- Use a disk cache such as LANcache. If you need more RAM in order to create a large enough cache to improve performance, get it.
- Experiment with SERVER's startup parameters, especially Network Buffer and Network Tasks, to improve performance without using up more RAM than necessary.
- Try larger or smaller REDIR buffer sizes.

- Be sure each server's hard disk uses an optimal disk interleave factor.
- Be sure each server's hard disk always has plenty of space available and doesn't suffer from severe fragmentation.
- Separate your work load between two different servers if contention is a problem.
- Change DOS and LANtastic parameters if they are so large that you waste RAM space. Use extended memory and LOADHIGH if necessary. If RAM usage is a severe problem, use a memory management product such as QEMM, 386MAX, or NetRoom.
- Sometimes there's no substitute for faster hardware or more RAM.

14

LANtastic Software Reference

This chapter is a reference list of the primary commands you can use to control your LANtastic software and hardware. This reference lists the LANtastic commands alphabetically, tells which subcommands and parameters you can enter with each command, and gives brief explanations of each. Some parameters are new to LANtastic version 4.1, but most have existed through several earlier versions.

A note on terminology: LANtastic is designed so that each command is a separate computer program. When you enter a directive from the DOS prompt telling a LANtastic program to do something, the program name is the first word of the directive and the entire line you enter is commonly called a command. Sometimes the program name itself, such as NET or REDIR, is called a command in this context. In this chapter, a command and a program mean the same thing.

Here are a few other points to remember when using this command reference:

- A timer tick is about .055 seconds (55 milliseconds) or 18.2 times per second.

- All numbers are decimal unless specifically noted as hexadecimal.
- Any parameter followed by an equal sign requires a number or other value after the equal sign.

The General Command Format

Although some commands have variations (shown throughout this chapter) most LANtastic commands follow this general format:

commandname subcommand argument /parameter1 /parameter2 ...

Some commands have one or more subcommands; some have no subcommands. Some commands require parameters immediately after the command name. Some commands have an *argument,* which is the name of something that you want to do something to, such as a server's name or a drive name. You can enter commands and parameters in capital or lowercase letters; LANtastic treats them the same. A server's name uses a double backslash (\\) before the name, although the backslashes are not always needed. A resource name is preceded by a single backslash. So, a server and its resource are connected like this:

servername *resource*

Here are some real examples of commands:

```
aex /irq=15 /iobase=300 /verbose
net login \\server1
net use n: \\server1\c-drive
net unuse n:
redir john /logins=4
server
```

For most commands, each parameter (sometimes called a switch) can be entered in several ways, as shown in the following:

parameter
parameter:value
/parameter
/parameter=value

In most cases you can use any of the four formats. Some commands don't allow all four formats. In this chapter and throughout the book, the formats preceded by the slash are usually shown because they always work and are the same format used commonly for DOS commands and by other software products.

Common Parameters

Some parameters are common to all (or nearly all) commands. Rather than explaining these common parameters under each command that uses them, these parameters are explained in this section only; when listed under the commands that use them, instead of an explanation you'll be referred back to this section. These parameters are very easy to understand, so it won't take long to commit them to memory.

The /help Parameter (/help or /?)

The /help parameter displays the command's syntax and available parameters, but does not otherwise run the program. If you are unsure if your version of LANtastic has a certain option available, use /help to see.

The /remove Parameter

The /remove parameter removes the program from memory. You can remove from memory only the last TSR program you ran. If you run the programs in the sequence 1, 2, 3, 4, you must remove them in the sequence 4, 3, 2, 1. This applies only to the TSR programs, such as AEX, AILANBIO,

REDIR, SERVER, and LANCACHE. The programs NET and NET_MGR do not stay in memory permanently and do not need to be removed. If you run DOS 5, use the mem/c command to see which programs currently occupy memory.

The /verbose Parameter

The /verbose parameter displays detailed information about the settings used when the command executes. It's valuable for debugging and optimization, especially for AEX, AILANBIO, REDIR, and SERVER.

The @filename Parameter

The @filename parameter tells the program to use the commands contained in the disk file called *filename* (substitute for *filename* any filename you choose) instead of relying only on any additional parameters on the command line. This approach is useful if you have a large number of parameters to provide, or if you maintain several different sets of parameters for use in different situations. The file can be as large as 2048 bytes for most programs, but REDIR and SERVER restrict the file size to 1000 bytes. Note that the filename is preceded by an @ ("at" sign), not a slash.

AEX

The AEX program is the low-level driver software for the LANtastic AE-x Ethernet cards. The LANtastic 2Mbps card and independent LAN cards use low-level drivers with different names.

Format

This is the format for AEX:

AEX */parameters*

Parameters

You can specify these parameters for AEX:

help or ?	See the "Common Parameters" section earlier in the chapter.
iobase=	The hexadecimal address for the beginning of a group of I/O port addresses. The address you specify must match the jumper setting on the LAN card. If you have more than one LAN card in a PC, they must use different I/O port addresses. Can be 300, 320, 340, or 360 on ISA bus computers.
irq=	The interrupt request (IRQ) number the LAN card uses. Must match the IRQ jumper setting on the LAN card. If you have more than one LAN card in a PC, each needs a different IRQ number. Can be 2, 3, 4, 5, 6, 7, 10, or 15 on ISA bus computers.
mpx=	A unique DOS multiplex number. If you run two copies of AEX they must use different MPX settings. Default is C7 (hexadecimal). Can be C0 to FF (hexadecimal).
packet_size=	The maximum size of IEEE 802.3 *packets* (data chunks) the LAN card will transmit. The default size is 1500. Can be 570 to 4300.
remove	See the "Common Parameters" section earlier.
transmit_buffers=	The number of transmission buffers AEX will use. Default is 20. Can be 2 to 80.
verbose	See the "Common Parameters" section.
xerox	Causes packets to be in a special format called the Xerox format instead of IEEE 802.3 standard.
@filename	See the "Common Parameters" section.

14

AILANBIO

The AILANBIO program is the high-level driver for most LAN cards (except the LANtastic 2Mbps card). It provides NetBIOS functionality for AE-x or other Ethernet or ARCnet cards. NetBIOS establishes communications (sessions) between LAN nodes and controls sending packets of information between them.

Format

This is the format for AILANBIO:

AILANBIO */parameters*

Parameters

You can specify these parameters for AILANBIO:

ack_timeout=	The number of timer ticks to wait for an acknowledgment signal from another node. After this time is up, this node resends data to the other node. Default is 2. Can be 0 to 254.
adapter=	The adapter number for the LAN card this copy of AILANBIO runs. Default is 0. If you install multiple LAN cards in a PC, each needs a unique adapter number. Can be 0 to 255, and each card is commonly numbered in sequence starting with 0.
buffers=	The number of buffers to use (new in LANtastic 4.1). Default is 1. More may improve performance but will use more RAM. Artisoft recommends using 0 if you use LANcache. Can be 0 to 254.

force_ack_mode	Forces frequent acknowledgments when a session is set up between this node and another. Most useful for a slow link such as over a telephone line. New in LANtastic 4.1.
help or ?	See the "Common Parameters" section.
initial_send_size=	The number of bytes in a packet of data first sent. Requires the /size= parameter to be the same size in order to work correctly. Default is 570. Can be 1 to 65535.
max_names=	The maximum number of NetBIOS names this node can handle. Can be 1 to 253.
max_ncbs=	The maximum number of NCBs (network control blocks) this node can support. NetBIOS uses NCBs to communicate between nodes. Can be 1 to 255.
max_sessions=	The maximum number of sessions this node can set up with other nodes. A NetBIOS session is a logical connection between two nodes that need to communicate. Can be 1 to 254.
mpx=	The DOS multiplex number the low-level software driver uses. Default is C7 (hexadecimal). Can be C0 to FF (hexadecimal).
ncbs=	The number of NCBs to allow when AILANBIO is started or a NetBIOS reset command is issued. Can be 1 to 255.
remove	See the "Common Parameters" section.
retry_period=	The number of timer ticks between the transmission of inquire-type messages. Can be 0 to 254.
rom_patch	Enhances AILANBIO if you have a boot ROM chip on the LAN card and run on a diskless workstation.

run_burst=	The number of timer ticks AILANBIO will run before returning control to the PC's processor to do other work. A larger value than the default 10 may improve performance on a server but will lock out the processor from running applications during the burst period. Can be 0 to 254.
sessions=	The number of sessions to allow when AILANBIO is started or a NetBIOS reset command is issued. Can be 1 to 254.
size=	The number of bytes in each buffer. Should be set to the same value as initial_send_size. Use the same value on all LAN nodes. Default is 570. Can be 1 to 4300.
timeout=	The number of half-second time units that NetBIOS waits before timing out (assuming no answer) after certain NetBIOS commands. The default 8 units means 4 seconds. Can be 1 to 254.
verbose	See the "Common Parameters" section.
@filename	See the "Common Parameters" section.

ALONE

The ALONE program turns a server temporarily into a dedicated server to improve performance.

Format

This is the format for ALONE:

ALONE */parameters*

Parameters

You can specify these three parameters for ALONE:

help or ?	See the "Common Parameters" section.
mono	Displays output for a monochrome (black-and-white) monitor.
@filename	See the "Common Parameters" section.

14

LANCACHE

The LANCACHE program improves disk performance by caching (storing) disk data in RAM to reduce the number of physical disk I/Os. See Chapter 13 for more information.

Format

This is the format for LANCACHE:

LANCACHE */parameters*

Parameters

Most LANCACHE parameters are meant to be used when starting LANCACHE, but others only apply after LANCACHE is already running.

You can specify these parameters for LANCACHE:

after_io_delay=	The number of seconds of inactivity after which output data will be written to disk. Default is 3. Can be 0 to 3600. Using 0 disables write caching.

cache_size=	Number of kilobytes of RAM to use for the cache area. Default is 384 for conventional memory, and all available RAM for other memory types. Can be 16 to 16000.
disable	Flushes (empties) the cache and stops caching. Leaves the LANCACHE program and cache area in memory.
disk=	The physical hard disk number that will be cached. Disk 0 is the first physical hard disk, which might be logically partitioned into several disk drive names. For example, a 60MB hard disk that you use as a C drive of 32MB and a D drive of 28MB is together considered hard disk 0. Default is 0. Can be 0, 1, 2, or 3.
enable	Restarts caching after it was temporarily stopped by the /disable or the /release parameter.
fast_irq=	Specifies a specially written high-speed IRQ number that you don't want LANCACHE to process. Default is "none." Can be none or 0 to 15.
flush	Flushes (empties) the cache area to disk.
help or ?	See the "Common Parameters" section.
long_write_delay=	The maximum number of seconds before the cache writes output data to disk. If zero, write caching is disabled. Default is 12. Can be 0 to 3600.
release	Flushes the cache and releases the cache RAM area for other usage. The LANCACHE program itself remains in memory.
remove	Flushes the cache, releases the cache RAM area, and removes the LANCACHE program from memory. Works only if LANCACHE is the last loaded TSR program still in RAM (on a server, you need to remove SERVER first).

reset	Flushes output data to disk, clears input data from the cache area, and resets cache statistics to zero.
shutdown_key=	The key, when combined with the CTRL and ALT keys, that starts a LANCACHE shutdown sequence. Default is the DEL key. If you run software that intercepts the CTRL-ALT-DEL key sequence, you might want to reassign to another key. Can be del or a-z.
stat=	Displays or resets cache statistics. Can be info (to display) or reset (to reset).
type=	The type of memory to use for the cache data area. Default is "extended." Can be conventional, ems, extended, or xms.
verbose	See the "Common Parameters" section.
with_windows	Makes LANCACHE compatible with Microsoft Windows in standard or enhanced mode. Requires you to disable write caching by specifying /after_io_delay=0 and /long_write_delay=0.
@filename	See the "Common Parameters" section.

14

LANCHECK

The LANCHECK program tests connectivity between LAN nodes.

Format

This is the format for LANCHECK,

LANCHECK *machinename /parameters*

where *machinename* is a unique name you can optionally assign to this computer. If omitted, the default name is the name assigned to this computer during the INSTALL process.

Parameters

You can specify these two parameters for LANCHECK:

help or ?	See the "Common Parameters" section.
mono	Displays output for a monochrome video monitor.

LANPUP

The LANPUP (LAN pop-up) program is a TSR version of NET, with which you can perform most functions of NET from within an application program. Run LANPUP after you start the LANtastic software to install it in RAM. Then, to activate LANPUP when you need it, press CTRL-ALT-L. Use the SPACEBAR or the → and ← keys to select different menu options, and the INS and DEL keys to add or cancel resource usage. The ESC key ends the program. LANPUP uses about 8K of RAM.

Format

This is the format for LANPUP:

LANPUP */parameters*

Parameters

You can specify these parameters for LANPUP:

help or ?	See the "Common Parameters" section.

line=	The screen line number on which to display the LANPUP menu. Default is 4. Can be 0 to 20.
remove	See the "Common Parameters" section.
stack	Allocates a 512-byte stack area in RAM rather than relying on the stack in use by the existing program when you activate LANPUP.
stand_alone	Runs LANPUP in stand-alone mode instead of as a TSR. Does not leave LANPUP in memory after completion.

NET

The NET program provides functionality for a workstation to interact with the LAN. NET, with its many subcommands, gives you the capability from a workstation to interact with the LAN. Most users find it easier to simply type **net** and press (ENTER) to bring up the NET menu, from which they can choose NET actions. So, the commands shown here are most often used in batch files.

Format

This is the format for NET,

NET */parameters subcommand*

where *subcommand* is one of the subcommands listed after the parameter explanations that follow. In some cases, the subcommand can be a two-word subcommand or contain additional arguments.

Parameters

You can specify the following two parameters for NET:

mono	Displays output for a monochrome (black-and-white) screen.
noerror	Says not to display error messages (typically because the command is in a batch file that checks the DOS ERRORLEVEL after the command).

The subcommands you can use with NET follow.

NET ATTACH

Function	Redirects the workstation's next available drives in sequence to all the specified server's disk resources.
Format	net attach *servername* or net attach/verbose *servername*

where *servername* is the name of the server that offers the resources. If the /verbose option is specified there must be no preceding blank space; the resources redirected are displayed. *Servername* can be specified with or without a preceding double backslash (for example, either \\server2 or just server2).

Example	net attach server2
Notes	A typical result (for a workstation with a C hard disk and a server that offers resources A-DRIVE, B-DRIVE, and C-DRIVE) is that the workstation's D drive is redirected to the server's A-DRIVE, E is redirected to B-DRIVE, and F is redirected to C-DRIVE.

NET AUDIT

Function	Writes an audit record in the server's audit file.
Format	net audit *servername reason "text"*

where *servername* is the name of the server where the audit entry is placed, *reason* is a string of as many as eight characters, and *"text"* is up to 64 characters of any information you choose between quotation marks for entry into the audit file.

Example net audit fileserver test1 "Beginning test now."

Notes The user has to have the U (user audit) privilege in order to successfully use this command.

NET CHANGEPW

Function Changes your password.

Format net changepw *servername oldpassword newpassword*

where *servername* is the name of the server where you have a user account, *oldpassword* is your current password, and *newpassword* is the new password you want.

Example net changepw server2 ground igloo

NET CHAT

Function Starts a chat session with another user.

Format net chat

Example net chat

Notes This command displays a screen that lets you specify the name of the user with whom you want to chat.

NET CLOCK

Function Sets your clock to match the server's.

Format net clock *servername*

Example net clock server2

NET COPY

Function Copies a file from and to the same server's disk.

Format net copy *sourcepath targetpath*

where *sourcepath* specifies the server, resource, and file of the source (input) file, and *targetpath* specifies the server, resource, and file of the target (output) file.

Example net copy \\srv1\c-drive\fil4 \\srv1\c-drive\copy4

Notes The source and target file must be on the same server. DOS wildcard characters (asterisk, question mark) are allowed. Using this command reduces the workload over the LAN (compared to a DOS COPY command, for example) because the data is not transmitted over the LAN, only on the server itself.

NET DETACH

Function Detaches all disk redirections at once from the workstation to a server.

Format net detach *servername*

Example net detach server2

NET DIR

Function Displays directory information for a server.

Format net dir *directorypath*
or
net dir/all *directorypath*

where *directorypath* is the server, resource, and directory you want to display. If specified, /all causes system and hidden files to be included in the display.

Example net dir \\server2\c-drive\dos

Notes To make the display pause when each screen is full, use the DOS MORE filter by adding |more after the command (assuming you have included the DOS directory in your PATH).

NET DISABLEA

Function Disables your user account by setting your number of simultaneous logins to zero (if it was previously one).

Format net disablea *servername password*

14

where *servername* is the server on which you want your account disabled and *password* is your password.

Example net disablea \\server2 swordfish

Notes This command is useful if you plan to be away from the office for an extended period of time. To reactivate your user account, the LAN administrator must use NET_MGR to reset your number of simultaneous logins to one.

NET ECHO

Function Displays a text message on the screen.

Format net echo *"text"*

where *"text"* is any text message you choose, enclosed in quotation marks.

Example net echo "Beginning benchmark test 1"

Notes You can also display LANtastic's special strings by preceding *"text"* by an exclamation mark. For example, net echo !"time" displays the current time in HH:MM:SS format. Other special strings are !"date" (the current date in DD-MMM-YYYY format), !"dir" (the current directory), and !"install" (the LANtastic programs currently installed).

NET EXPAND

Function Displays the physical or network path of a server file.

Format net expand *filename*
or
net expand*/parameter filename*

where */parameter* is either /physical (or /p) to find the physical path on the server or /recurse (or /r) to find the network path to a conventional or indirect file.

Example net expand myfile

NET FLUSH

Function Flushes all of a server's LANtastic caches (LANcache, the random access cache, and the resource cache).

Format net flush *servername*

where *servername* is the name of the server whose caches you want to flush.

Example net flush \\server3

Notes You must have the S privilege to use this command. This command is new in LANtastic 4.1.

NET HELP

Function Displays the NET subcommands or help text about any specific subcommand or certain topics.

Format net help
or
net help *subcommand*
or
net help *topic*

where *subcommand* is any of the NET subcommands, and *topic* is either errors, macros, or syntax.

14

Examples net help
net help use
net help syntax

NET INDIRECT

Function Creates an indirect file, which points to another file.

Format net indirect *indirectfilename realfilename*

where *indirectfilename* is the name of the indirect file you are creating on a redirected drive and *realfilename* is the full network name of the file being referenced.

Example net indirect ptr \c-drive\config.sys

Notes The indirect file must be on a workstation's redirected drive. Indirect files provide a way to stay in one directory and reference files that are in different directories.

NET LOGIN

Function Performs a login to a server.

Format	net login *servername username password adapter* or net login/w *servername username password adapter*

where *servername* is the server you want to log in to, *username* is your username (or default machine name), *password* is your password, if any, and *adapter* is the adapter number of the LAN card (default is zero). If you use the /w parameter (or /wait), your computer will continue attempting to log in until the server starts up and responds (or until you press ESC to stop trying).

Examples	net login server2 net login/w fileserver net login \\dbserver john magnet 2

NET LOGOUT

Function	Performs a logout from a server.
Format	net logout *servername*

where *servername* is the server you want to log out from.

Examples	net logout server2 net logout \\dbserver
Notes	A logout cancels all disk and printer redirection from this workstation to the server. Before shutting down a server, ask all users to log out from that server.

NET LPT COMBINE

Function	Combines redirected printer output to eliminate breaks between output from different programs.
Format	net lpt combine
Example	net lpt combine

Notes This command is normally used from a workstation's batch file. DOS terminates the combination when the batch file ends.

NET LPT FLUSH

Function Flushes a printer (ends a workstation's print job) after the NET LPT COMBINE command.

Format net lpt flush

Example net lpt flush

NET LPT NOTIFY

Function Sets LANtastic to notify a user when a print job completes.

Format net lpt/enable notify
or
net lpt/disable notify

Example net lpt/enable notify

Notes By default, notification is disabled. This feature is new in LANtastic 4.1.

NET LPT SEPARATE

Function Disables the NET LPT COMBINE feature for a workstation in a batch file.

Format net lpt separate

Example net lpt separate

NET LPT TIMEOUT

Function Sets the number of seconds LANtastic waits before assuming a print job is complete.

Format net lpt timeout *seconds*

where *seconds* is the number of seconds to wait.

Example net lpt timeout 10

Notes After the specified time period completes, all data is flushed from the LANtastic printer buffer. Increasing the number may cure the problem of print jobs separating where you don't intend them to. Be aware that a page-oriented printer (such as a laser printer) still may not print the last page unless the print job issues a command to eject the page or a subsequent job resets the printer.

NET MAIL

Function Sends a file as a mail message to another user.

Format net mail *filename servername recipient "comment"*
or
net mail/v *filename servername recipient "comment"*

where *filename* is the name of the file to send as mail, *servername* is the mail server, *recipient* is the username of the recipient, and *"comment"* is a comment or title (in quotation marks) for the mail. The /v option indicates the file is a voice message.

Example net mail mymsg \\server4 ralph "Staff Mtg."

NET MESSAGE

Function Enables or disables pop-up messages and beeps on your workstation.

Format net message/disable *messageform*
or
net message/enable *messageform*

where *messageform* is either beep (applying to beep tones that accompany messages) or pop (applying to pop-up messages on the screen).

Example net message/disable pop

NET PAUSE

Function Pauses the processing of a batch file.

Format net pause *"message" seconds*
or
net pause/newline *"message" seconds*

where *"message"* is a message to display on the screen and *seconds* is the number of seconds (from 0 to 999) to pause after displaying the message. If *seconds* is omitted or zero, the message is displayed until the user presses a key. The /newline option causes the cursor to advance to a new line after displaying the message.

14

Example net pause/newline "Will continue in 5 seconds" 5

NET POSTBOX

Function Displays messages showing how many mail messages (if at least one) you have waiting on each server to which you are logged in.

Format net postbox

Example net postbox

NET PRINT

Function Prints a file on a server's shared printer.

Format net print *filename printername "comment" copies*
or
net print*/parameters filename printername "comment" copies*

where *filename* is the name of the file to print (and can include DOS wildcard characters), *printername* is either a redirected printer name or a network name of a server and printer, *"comment"* is a comment to attach to the printer job (the filename is used if "comment" is omitted), and *copies* is the number of copies to print (default is 1 if omitted). If you use the second format, the following parameters are allowable:

binary	Uses binary mode to print the file.
delete	Deletes a file after printing with the /direct parameter.
direct	Prints directly to the server's printer without first spooling and despooling. Works only with files on the server.
notify	Sends a pop-up message to notify you when the job is printed.
nonotify	Turns off /notify mode.
verbose	Displays printer filenames when each is sent to the print queue.

Examples

net print myfile lpt2
net print c:\word\memo4.asc \\server2\@printer
net print/verbose graph*.* lpt1 "Transparencies" 2

Notes

The /notify and /nonotify parameters override the commands net lpt/disable notify and net lpt/enable notify respectively. The following parameters are new in LANtastic 4.1: delete, direct, notify, and nonotify.

NET QUEUE HALT

Function Halts despooling on a server or a server's shared printer.

Format net queue halt *servername printeraddress*

where *servername* is a server name and *printeraddress* is the name of the LPT or COM port of a shared printer. If *printeraddress* is omitted or "all" then all shared printer devices on the server are halted.

Examples

net queue halt \\server2
net queue halt \\server 2 lpt1

Notes You need the Q privilege to use this command. A print job in the middle of despooling (printing) when this command is issued is placed back on the print queue and restarted from the beginning after despooling is restarted.

NET QUEUE PAUSE

Function Pauses despooling on a server or a server's shared printer.

Format net queue pause *servername printeraddress*

where *servername* is a server name and *printeraddress* is the name of the LPT or COM port of a shared printer. If *printeraddress* is omitted or "all" then all shared printer devices on the server are paused.

Examples net queue pause \\server2
net queue pause \\server2 lpt1

Notes You need the Q privilege to use this command. A print job in the middle of despooling when this command is issued continues printing from the point it paused.

NET QUEUE RESTART

Function Restarts despooling of the current print job from the beginning.

Format net queue restart *servername printeraddress*

where *servername* is a server name and *printeraddress* is the name of the LPT or COM port of a shared printer. If *printeraddress* is omitted or "all" then all shared printer devices on the server are restarted.

Examples net queue restart \\server2
net queue restart \\server2 lpt1

Notes You need the Q privilege to use this command.

NET QUEUE SINGLE

Function Despools a single print job on a server or a server's shared printer.

Format net queue single *servername printeraddress*

where *servername* is a server name and *printeraddress* is the name of the LPT or COM port of a shared printer. If *printeraddress* is omitted or "all" then all shared printer devices on the server despool the print job.

Examples net queue single \\server2
net queue single \\server2 lpt1

Notes You need the Q privilege to use this command. A print job in the middle of despooling when this command is issued finishes printing and then the printer stops. If no job is printing, the next job in the queue prints and then the printer stops. The command is useful if you need to change printer forms between jobs.

NET QUEUE START

Function Starts despooling on a server or a server's shared printer.

Format net queue start *servername printeraddress*

where *servername* is a server name and *printeraddress* is the name of the LPT or COM port of a shared printer. If *printeraddress* is omitted or "all" then all shared printer devices on the server are started.

Examples net queue start \\server2
net queue start \\server2 lpt1

Notes You need the Q privilege to use this command. This command starts printing after you issue any of these commands: net queue halt, net queue pause, or net queue stop.

NET QUEUE STATUS

Function Displays the status of one or all shared printers on a server.

Format net queue status *servername printeraddress*

where *servername* is a server name and *printeraddress* is the name of the LPT or COM port of a shared printer. If *printeraddress* is omitted or "all" then all shared printer devices on the server have their status displayed.

Examples net queue status \\server2
net queue status \\server2 lpt1

NET QUEUE STOP

Function Stops despooling on a server or a server's shared printer at the end of the current print job.

Format net queue stop *servername printeraddress*

where *servername* is a server name and *printeraddress* is the name of the LPT or COM port of a shared printer. If *printeraddress* is omitted or "all" then all shared printer devices on the server are stopped.

Examples net queue stop \\server2
net queue stop \\server2 lpt1

Notes You need the Q privilege to use this command. A print job in the middle of despooling when this command is issued completes before despooling is stopped.

NET RECEIVE

Function Displays again the last message you received.

Format net receive *line duration*

where *line* is the screen line number on which to display the message and *duration* is the number of seconds (0 to 65539) to display the message.

Example net receive 8 20

Notes If you omit *line* and *duration*, the message displays on the next available line. If you include both, the message is displayed in a pop-up window in the location and for the time length you specify.

NET RUN

Function Runs a command on a server.

Format net run *servername "command"*
or
net run/nocr *servername "command"*

where *servername* is the server on which you want to run the command and *"command"* is a command to execute on the server. If you include the /nocr parameter, no carriage return is added to the end of the command.

Example net run \\server2 "sortfile infile outfile"

Notes You must have the S privilege to use this command.

NET SEND

Function Sends a one-line message to another workstation.

Format net send *machinename "message" servername username*

where *machinename* is the machine name of the recipient, *"message"* is the message to send, *servername* is the server on which the recipient must be logged in (default is any server), and *username* is the username of the recipient.

Example net send bob "How about lunch today?"

NET SHOW

Function Shows the status of your workstation, including your machine name, username, redirected devices, and some parameter settings.

Format net show
or
net show/batch

where /batch (or /b) changes the format of the output display to look like batch NET commands that you can enter into a batch file to establish your current connections and settings.

Example net show

NET SHUTDOWN

Function Schedules the shutdown or reboot of a server from a remote workstation.

Format net shutdown *servername minutes "message"*
or
net shutdown/*action servername minutes "message"*

where *servername* is the name of the server, *minutes* is the number of minutes before the shutdown occurs (default is zero), and *"message"* is a warning message to send to users logged in to the server (if omitted the default message is "Server is shutting down"). The *action* parameters can be /cancel to cancel a server shutdown that is pending, /halt to halt processing on the server after it shuts down, /reboot to reboot the server computer after the shutdown, and /silent to perform the shutdown without sending a warning message to logged-in users.

Examples net shutdown \\server2
net shutdown/reboot \\srv2 3 "SRV2 reboots in # minute$!"

14

Notes You must have the S privilege to use this command. The # (pound sign) is replaced in messages by the number of minutes, and the $ (dollar sign) is replaced with an "s" (to form plurals in messages) if the number of minutes is two or more.

NET SLOGINS

Function Disables or enables future logins to a server.

Format net slogins/disable *servername*
or
net slogins/enable *servername*

where *servername* is the name of the server, /disable prevents additional logins to the server, and /enable allows future logins to the server. If you disable logins, users already logged in are not affected.

Examples net slogins/disable \\server2
net slogins/enable \\server2

Notes You must have the S privilege to use this command. This command is new in LANtastic 4.1.

NET STREAM

Function Displays or changes server printer streams.

Format net stream *servername streamnum newstream*
or
net stream/*action servername streamnum newstream*

where *servername* is the name of the server, *streamnum* is a stream number (optional), and *newstream* is a new stream name to assign to a stream number. If provided, *action* is either /disable to disable a print stream, or /enable to enable a print stream.

Examples
net stream \\server2
net stream/disable \\server2 3
net stream/enable \\server2 3 @invoice

Notes
The first example displays the stream numbers for all server printer streams. Once you know the numbers, you can use the other example forms to enable or disable any stream you choose. Any changes last until changed again or until the server is rebooted or reset.

14

NET STRING

Function
Manipulates string (text) values in a batch file.

Format
net string *variable string1 string2*
or
net string*/action variable string1 string2*

where *variable* is the name of an environment variable that has previously been set using the DOS SET command, *string1* is a string to replace the environment variable, and *string2* is an optional string to concatenate (attach) to *string1*. If provided, action is either /left=*j* or /right=*k* (or both), which specify substrings of string1 to extract, where *j* and *k* are numbers of characters to extract.

Examples
net string v1 "new v1 value"
net string/left=5 v1 "new v1 value"

Notes
The first example puts the characters "new v1 value" in the environment variable v1. The second example puts "new v" in v1. These commands can be used to manipulate LANtastic's special strings, such as !"date" and !"time". See the *LANtastic Network Operating System Reference Manual* for details.

NET TERMINATE

Function Terminates the logins of one or more workstations on a server.

Format net terminate *servername username machinename minutes*

where *servername* is the name of the server, *username* is the name of a user account (individual or group; wildcards are acceptable) other than yourself, *machinename* is the machine name of the computer being used (wildcards are acceptable; default is *), and *minutes* is the number of minutes before the termination occurs (default is zero, which causes immediate termination).

Example net terminate \\server2 *

Notes You need the S privilege to use this command, which is handy in preparing to reboot a server. New in LANtastic 4.1.

NET UNLINK

Function Unlinks (disconnects) a redirected drive name from a boot server.

Format net unlink

Example net unlink

NET UNUSE

Function Cancels redirection of a device name to a server resource.

Format net unuse *devicename*

where *devicename* is a redirected disk drive name (a: through z:) or a redirected printer name (lpt1, lpt2, lpt3, com1, or com2).

Examples net unuse n:
net unuse lpt2

NET USE

Function Redirects a device name to a server resource.

Format net use *devicename resourcename*

where *devicename* is a redirected disk drive name (a: through z:) or a redirected printer name (lpt1, lpt2, lpt3, com1, or com2), and *resourcename* is a full server and resource name.

Examples net use n: \\server2\c-drive
net use lpt2 \\server2\@printer

NET USER

Function Sets the default username, password, and adapter number to be used for a workstation's automatic login to a server.

Format net user *username password adapter*
or
net user/disable

where *username* is the username to use for automatic logins, *password* is the password to use for automatic logins, and *adapter* is the adapter number to use for automatic logins (if omitted, all adapters will be tried). If specified, the /disable parameter prevents automatic logins.

Examples net user chris
net user/disable

NET_MGR

The NET_MGR program controls a server and the resources it makes available to LANtastic workstations. Starting with LANtastic 4.1, you can use NET_MGR commands on a server from the DOS prompt or in batch files instead of using the NET_MGR menu. Using batch files can simplify a LAN administrator's job of setting up or changing parameters on a large number of servers.

Format

This is the format for NET_MGR,

NET_MGR *subcommand /parameters*

where *subcommand* is one of the subcommands listed after the parameter explanations that follow. In some cases, *subcommand* can be a two-word subcommand.

Parameters

These are the parameters you can specify for NET_MGR:

control=	The control directory you want NET_MGR to use. Default is C:\LANTASTI.NET.
mono	Displays output for a monochrome (black-and-white) screen.

The subcommands you can use with NET_MGR follow.

NET_MGR BACKUP

Function	Makes a backup copy of the server's control directory in the filename supplied.
Format	net_mgr backup *controldir filename* or net_mgr/p=*password* backup *controldir filename*

where *controldir* is the server's control directory and *filename* is a filename for the backup copy you want to create. If you use /p= then *password* is the password for NET_MGR.

Example net_mgr backup c:\lantasti.net ctrlbkup.001

NET_MGR COPY USER

Function Copies a user's account information to another account in the same control directory or to another control directory.

Format net_mgr */parameters* copy user *username1* *username2*

where *username1* is the originating username, *username2* is the target (new) username, and */parameters* is in the following format:

/c=*controldir1* /p=*pw1* /dc=*controldir2* /dp=*pw2*

where *controldir1* is the originating control directory (default is C:\LANTASTI.NET), *pw1* is the password of the originating control directory (default is no password), *controldir2* is the target control directory (default is the same as controldir1), and *pw2* is the password of the target control directory (default is the same as *pw1*).

Example net_mgr copy user bob bonnie

Notes All information for the user is copied, including the description and password. You'll probably want to use the net_mgr menu interface to update these fields if you create a new user's account with this command.

NET_MGR CREATE USER

Function Creates a user account.

Format net_mgr */parameters* create user *username*

where *username* is the name for the new user and */parameters* is in the following format:

/c=*controldir* /p=*pw1*

where *controldir* is the control directory in which you create the user account (default is C:\LANTASTI.NET) and *pw1* is the control directory's password (default is no password).

Example	net_mgr create user whitney
Notes	The user account is created using default settings, including no password.

NET_MGR DELETE

Function	Deletes an individual or group user account.
Format	net_mgr */parameters* delete *accounttype username*

where */parameters* is the same as shown for NET_MGR CREATE USER, *accounttype* is either the word user (for an individual user account) or the word group (for a group account), and *username* is the name of the account to delete.

Example	net_mgr delete user bonnie

NET_MGR RESTORE

Function	Restores a control directory that has previously been backed up using the "backup" option of NET_MGR.
Format	net_mgr restore *filename controldir* or net_mgr/p=*password* restore *filename controldir*

where *filename* is the backup file from which you want to restore and *controldir* is the control directory you want to restore. If you use /p= then *password* is the NET_MGR password.

Example	net_mgr restore ctrlbkup.001 c:\lantasti.net

NET_MGR SET

Function Sets the attributes for an individual or group user account.

Format net_mgr */parameters set accounttype username attrib*

where */parameters* is the same as explained for NET_MGR CREATE USER, *accounttype* is either user or group, *username* is the name of the user account for which you want to change attributes, and *attrib* is one or more attributes you want to change. The possible attributes (followed by an equal sign and a new value) are username, password, logins (the number of logins allowed), privileges (AQMUS and/or none), acct_exp (account expiration date in the form dd-mmm-yyyy), and pw_exp (password expiration date).

Example net_mgr set user whitney pw_exp=27-feb-1993

NET_MGR SHOW

Function Shows the status of a user account.

Format net_mgr */parameters* show *accounttype username*

where */parameters* is the same as explained for NET_MGR CREATE USER, *accounttype* is either user or group, and *username* is the name of the user account for which you want to display status.

Example net_mgr show user kate

Notes You can use an asterisk in the username as a wildcard. For example, the username BO* shows the account status of both BOB and BONNIE. The items displayed are the user name, account description, account privileges, concurrent logins, account expiration date, password expiration date, and last login date.

REDIR

The REDIR program redirects a DOS device name over the LAN.

Format

This is the format for REDIR,

REDIR *machinename /parameters*

where *machinename* is a unique machine name assigned to this computer.

Parameters

You can specify these parameters for REDIR:

beep_cycle=	The number of seconds between warning beeps. Default is 4. Can be 1 to 3600.
beep_delay=	The number of seconds delay before sounding a beep. Default is 4. Can be 0 to 3600.
buffers=	The number of buffers REDIR uses. Default is 1. Can be 1 to 64.
help or ?	See the "Common Parameters" section.
logins=	The number of servers this node can log in to at once. Default is 2. Can be 1 to 255.
mono	Makes pop-up messages appear in monochrome.
nochain	Prevents REDIR from using the NetBIOS "chain send" command, which sends two pieces of data together and which some LAN cards don't implement. The default is that chain sends are enabled.
popup_duration=	The number of seconds pop-up messages remain on the screen. Default is 15 seconds. Can be 0 to 3600.

popup_line=	The screen line number on which pop-up messages appear. Default is 5. Can be 0 to 24.
remove	See the "Common Parameters" section.
size=	The number of bytes in each buffer. Default is 1024. Can be 512 to 32768.
verbose	See the "Common Parameters" section.
@filename	See the "Common Parameters" section.

SERVER

The SERVER program makes server resources available to LANtastic workstations.

Format

This is the format for SERVER,

SERVER *controldirectory /parameters*

where *controldirectory* is the name of the control directory that tracks and limits this server's resources. If omitted, SERVER uses the default control directory named LANTASTI.NET.

Parameters

You can specify these parameters for SERVER:

adapters=	The maximum number of LAN cards installed in this PC. Default is 1. Maximum for AE-x cards is 4. Maximum for 2Mbps cards or the old NE-3 Ethernet cards is 6.

despooler_stopped=	Turns off despooling if set to yes. Default is no. If stopped (yes), you have to enter a net queue start or net queue single command to begin despooling.
files=	Maximum number of files that can be opened simultaneously on this server. Default is 0 , which means the FILES value in CONFIG.SYS is used. To specify over 255 (the maximum in CONFIG.SYS), use this parameter. Can be 0 to 5100.
floppy_direct=	Allows workstations to use the DOS FORMAT and CHKDSK commands on the server's floppy disk drives when set to yes (the default). Can be yes or no.
help or ?	See the "Common Parameters" section.
lock_hold_time=	The number of timer ticks the server waits for a record lock before assuming failure. Default is 9. Heavy database applications may benefit from a higher value. Can be "disabled", 2, 3, 4, 5, 9, 13, 18, 27, 36, 45, 54, 63, 72, 81, 90, 108, 126, 144, 162, or 180. New in LANtastic 4.1.
logins=	The maximum number of workstations that can log in to this server at once. Default is 5. Can be 1 to 300.
network_buffer_size=	The number of bytes in each server task's main communications buffer. Default is 4K. Can be 2K, 4K, 6K, 8K, 10K, 12K, 14K, 16K, 20K, 24K, 28K, 32K, 40K, 48K, or 56K.
network_tasks=	The number of network tasks for the server to handle at once. Each uses a buffer the size of network_buffer_size. Default is 1. Can be 1 to 32.
printer_buffer_size=	The number of bytes in each printer task buffer. Default is 512. Can be 512, 1K, 2K, 3K, 4K, 5K, 6K, 8K, 10K, 12K, 14K, 16K, 18K, 20K, 24K, 28K, or 32K.

printer_tasks=	The number of printer tasks for the server to handle at once. Each uses a printer buffer. Default is 1. Can be 0 to 5. Zero disables despooling.
remove	See the "Common Parameters" section.
request_size=	The number of bytes in the request buffer in which workstation requests are received. Default is 14. Can be 14 to 2048.
resource_cache=	The number of server resources for which user access information is cached. Default is 1. Can be 1 to 50. New in LANtastic 4.1.
rpl=	Set to "read-only" or "read-write" to allow this server to be a remote boot server for diskless workstations. Set to "read-write" to allow you to update the boot image stored on the server. Set to "disable" (the default) if the server is not a boot server.
run_buffer_size=	The number of bytes in a buffer used for net run commands. Default is 127. Can be 0 to 1024.
run_burst=	The number of timer ticks the server processes workstation requests before turning over control of the processor to the local workstation's requests. Default is 2. Can be 1 to 255. Higher values improve server response time but slow down workstation response on the PC itself. New in LANtastic 4.1.
seek_cache=	The number of bytes in a cache buffer that stores random disk access information. Default is "none". Can be none, 1K, 2K, 4K, 8K, 12K, 16K, 20K, 24K, 28K, 32K, 40K, 48K, 56K, or 64K.
send_server_id=	If yes (the default), the server's name appears on workstation menu lists of server names. Can be yes or no.

shutdown_key=	The key, when combined with the CTRL and ALT keys, that starts a server shutdown sequence. Default is the DEL key. If you run software that intercepts the CTRL-ALT-DEL key sequence, you might want to reassign to another key. Can be del or a-z.
verbose	See the "Common Parameters" section.
@filename	See the "Common Parameters" section.

UPS

The UPS program runs on a server and interacts with an uninterruptible power supply (UPS) system. The UPS system sends signals to the server (which runs the LANtastic UPS program) when the commercial power fails and also when the UPS system's backup battery power begins to run low.

Format

This is the format for UPS:

UPS */parameters*

Parameters

You can specify these parameters for UPS:

brownout_seconds=	The number of seconds after the power failure before the shutdown sequence begins. Default is 10. Can be 0 to 1800.
cancel_seconds=	The number of seconds that must pass after power is restored before a pending shutdown is cancelled. Default is 10. Can be 0 to 1800.

device=	The serial port to which the UPS system is connected. Default is COM1. Can be COM1, COM2, COM3, or COM4.
help or ?	See the "Common Parameters" section.
iobase=	An input/output port address if the serial port uses nonstandard addressing. Can be 0000 to FFFF (hexadecimal).
low_battery=	The number of minutes after receiving a "battery low" signal from the UPS system to shut down the server. If specified, this parameter overrides shutdown_minutes. Default is 1. Can be 0, 1, 2, 3, 4, 5, or ignore.
no_cancel	Says not to cancel a scheduled server shutdown even if power returns. Overrides cancel_seconds.
no_power_down	Says not to power down the server computer after the SERVER program ends.
power_down_cycle=	The number of seconds to send the signal to power down to the UPS system. Some UPS systems require a minimum time for this signal or require alternating on-off signals. Default is 5. Can be 0 to 60.
remove	See the "Common Parameters" section.
shutdown_minutes=	The number of minutes until shutdown after the shutdown is scheduled. If zero, the shutdown is immediate. Default is 5. Can be 0 to 300.
warning=	A warning message sent to users periodically after the shutdown is scheduled. Can be up to 79 characters between quotation marks.
@filename	See the "Common Parameters" section.

A

Sample Startup Files

This appendix lists sample startup files for several common LANtastic configurations. You don't have to use files exactly like these, but they should give you some ideas of parameters to try. If not otherwise stated, the files apply to an 80286 or higher PC with at least 640K of RAM. The files are constructed with the assumption that DOS files are in a directory called DOS on the C drive. In all cases, a hardware configuration using LANtastic AE-x Ethernet LAN cards is assumed. Use of LANtastic version 4.1 is also assumed, but most files also work with earlier versions of LANtastic.

The statements in the files are shown using all capital letters because that is the way LANtastic and DOS create the files. (Using all caps also helps avoid confusion between the letter L and the number 1, but you still have to be careful about the letter O versus the number 0.) If you prefer, you can use lowercase letters; DOS and LANtastic accept caps and lowercase interchangeably.

For all the sample configurations, you can use the AUTOEXEC.BAT file shown under the first configuration (the "typical" configuration). When troubleshooting you should use no more than the statements shown in this typical AUTOEXEC.BAT.

If you want to start the LANtastic software automatically whenever you power on your computer, either put all the statements from STARTNET.BAT into the AUTOEXEC.BAT file (at the end) or just add the final statement **startnet** as the last line in AUTOEXEC.BAT.

A "Typical" Configuration

These files configure DOS and LANtastic for a small LAN—a maximum of five computers (the default number of /LOGINS for SERVER). You should find that LANtastic 4.1's INSTALL creates files very similar to these sample files. These files make no attempt to optimize LANtastic for high performance or reduced conventional RAM usage (see subsequent configurations to achieve those goals). Also, some of your application programs such as word processors or databases, as well as utility programs such as memory managers, may require additional parameters or changes to some of the parameters shown here. Think of these files as a starting point for future changes that fit your LAN's and your workgroup's needs.

AUTOEXEC.BAT for a Server or Workstation

```
PROMPT $P$G
PATH C:\LANTASTI;C:\DOS
```

CONFIG.SYS for a Server

```
SHELL=C:\DOS\COMMAND.COM /P
DEVICE=C:\DOS\ANSI.SYS
FILES=50
BUFFERS=32
LASTDRIVE=Z
FCBS=16,8
INSTALL=C:\DOS\SHARE.EXE/L:200/F:2048
```

STARTNET.BAT for a Server Named TOM

```
@ECHO OFF
AEX /IRQ=15 /IOBASE=300 /VERBOSE
AILANBIO
REDIR TOM /LOGINS=3
SERVER
NET LOGIN/WAIT \\TOM TOM
NET LPT TIMEOUT 10
```

CONFIG.SYS for a Workstation

```
SHELL=C:\DOS\COMMAND.COM /P
DEVICE=C:\DOS\ANSI.SYS
FILES=30
BUFFERS=16
LASTDRIVE=Z
FCBS=16,8
```

STARTNET.BAT for a Workstation Named LESLIE

```
@ECHO OFF
AEX /IRQ=15 /IOBASE=300 /VERBOSE
AILANBIO
REDIR LESLIE /LOGINS=2
NET LPT TIMEOUT 10
```


A Troubleshooting Configuration

These files provide a minimum ("stripped-down") configuration to aid in troubleshooting problems with LANtastic, as explained in Chapter 9. Start with files like the ones shown here and then test LANtastic using LANCHECK and, if applicable, an application program or TSR that may be causing you problems. If the tests work, add the other statements you need one by one, testing after each addition. This approach helps to isolate an incompatibility or error that arises from the statements you added last. Remember to load TSR programs after you load the LANtastic software–after the SERVER program on a server or after the REDIR program on a workstation.

Note that the sample STARTNET.BAT files in this section have a PAUSE statement after each LANtastic program. Each PAUSE gives you a chance, before you press a key to continue, to examine the /VERBOSE output from the preceding LANtastic program. You can read any error messages or review the displayed default parameters. Also, you can interrupt the STARTNET.BAT file before all the software is loaded so you can run tests when only some LANtastic programs are active, in case this helps pin down a specific incompatibility.

CONFIG.SYS for a Server

```
FILES=50
BUFFERS=32
LASTDRIVE=Z
FCBS=16,8
INSTALL=C:\DOS\SHARE.EXE/L:200/F:2048
```

STARTNET.BAT for a Server Named TOM

```
@ECHO OFF
AEX /IRQ=15 /IOBASE=300 /VERBOSE
PAUSE
AILANBIO /VERBOSE
PAUSE
REDIR TOM /LOGINS=3 /VERBOSE
PAUSE
SERVER /VERBOSE
NET LOGIN/WAIT \\TOM TOM
NET LPT TIMEOUT 10
```

CONFIG.SYS for a Workstation

```
FILES=30
BUFFERS=16
LASTDRIVE=Z
FCBS=16,8
```

STARTNET.BAT for a Workstation Named LESLIE

```
@ECHO OFF
AEX /IRQ=15 /IOBASE=300 /VERBOSE
PAUSE
AILANBIO /VERBOSE
PAUSE
REDIR LESLIE /LOGINS=2 /VERBOSE
NET LPT TIMEOUT 10
```


A High-Performance LAN Server Configuration

These files show parameters to configure a LANtastic server when you want to provide better-than-default performance for up to ten workstations. The server computer is assumed to have extended memory; if not change TYPE=EXTENDED to TYPE=CONVENTIONAL (or whatever memory type you have) in STARTNET.BAT. The server runs the LANcache program to improve performance and specifies larger-than-default network_buffer_size and network_tasks for the SERVER program. Depending on your environment, you may want to specify additional parameters for SERVER, plus overrides to the defaults for REDIR, AILANBIO, and AEX, as discussed in Chapter 13.

CONFIG.SYS for a Server That Runs LANcache

```
SHELL=C:\DOS\COMMAND.COM /P
DEVICE=C:\DOS\ANSI.SYS
FILES=50
```

```
BUFFERS=8
LASTDRIVE=Z
FCBS=16,8
INSTALL=C:\DOS\SHARE.EXE/L:400/F:4096
```

STARTNET.BAT for a Server Named TOM

```
@ECHO OFF
AEX /IRQ=15 /IOBASE=300 /VERBOSE
AILANBIO
REDIR TOM /LOGINS=3
LANCACHE /TYPE=EXTENDED /VERBOSE
SERVER /NETWORK_BUFFER_SIZE=16K /NETWORK_TASKS=2 /LOGINS=10
NET LOGIN/WAIT \\TOM TOM
NET LPT TIMEOUT 10
```

A "Minimum RAM" Configuration

Well, this configuration doesn't actually use the absolute *minimum* conventional RAM that LANtastic and DOS could. Instead, it uses a slightly smaller amount of RAM than other configurations without totally sacrificing performance. (Most of LANtastic's default parameters are already about as low as you dare go.) This configuration is designed for a computer that needs to free up all it can of its 640K or 512K of RAM. If your computer has more than 640K, use DOS 5 (as the next sample configuration shows) or another memory manager to load DOS and/or LANtastic in the extra RAM. However, the parameters given in this section should be adequate if you

- Have no more than three users on your LAN
- Use a single server with a small workload
- Don't put a high priority on the best possible response time

If you run even a small shared database application, these parameters will probably be insufficient.

CONFIG.SYS for a Server

```
SHELL=C:\DOS\COMMAND.COM /P
DEVICE=C:\DOS\ANSI.SYS
FILES=30
BUFFERS=16
LASTDRIVE=L
FCBS=16,8
INSTALL=C:\DOS\SHARE.EXE/L:60/F:1024
```

STARTNET.BAT for a Server Named TOM

```
@ECHO OFF
AEX /IRQ=15 /IOBASE=300 /VERBOSE
AILANBIO
REDIR TOM /LOGINS=1
SERVER /NETWORK_BUFFER_SIZE=2K /LOGINS=3
NET LOGIN/WAIT \\TOM TOM
NET LPT TIMEOUT 10
```

CONFIG.SYS for a Workstation

```
SHELL=C:\DOS\COMMAND.COM /P
DEVICE=C:\DOS\ANSI.SYS
FILES=20
BUFFERS=12
LASTDRIVE=L
FCBS=16,8
```

STARTNET.BAT for a Workstation Named LESLIE

```
@ECHO OFF
AEX /IRQ=15 /IOBASE=300 /VERBOSE
AILANBIO
REDIR LESLIE /LOGINS=2
NET LPT TIMEOUT 10
```

A DOS 5 Extended Memory Configuration

If your computer runs DOS 5 on a 386 or 486 and has some extended RAM, you can have the best of both worlds: high performance and a large amount of available conventional RAM. Many ways exist to configure such a system, but these sample files show a starting point. This configuration is basically the high-performance configuration listed previously, combined with DOS and LANtastic loaded into high memory. The server configuration leaves available 566,000 bytes of conventional RAM, even though the server runs LANcache and larger-than-default server buffers. The workstation configuration leaves available 626,000 bytes. Depending on how much UMB memory your computer leaves available, you might be able to use LOADHIGH on even more LANtastic programs than are shown here, which would increase the available RAM further.

Two notes about things you may need to change, depending on your computer configuration:

- You may need to add the X= parameter on the CONFIG.SYS EMM386 line to exclude a RAMBASE address for your LAN card or other peripheral device (example: X=D800-DFFF). You do not need to do so for the LANtastic AE-x cards, but you do for the LANtastic 2Mbps cards and some independent Ethernet cards. Check your LAN card manual and jumper settings to see specifically what address range to exclude.
- You will need to adjust the /CACHE_SIZE parameter on the STARTNET.BAT LANCACHE statement to fit your available XMS memory size. Try entering a number that's a little more than one megabyte less than your total RAM. For example, if you have 4 MB (4096K) of RAM, try 3000 or 2900. Of course, if you run an application that needs to use some of your extra memory, give correspondingly less to LANcache.

CONFIG.SYS for a Server

```
DEVICE=C:\DOS\HIMEM.SYS
DEVICE=C:\DOS\EMM386.SYS NOEMS
DOS=HIGH,UMB
SHELL=C:\DOS\COMMAND.COM /P
DEVICE=C:\DOS\ANSI.SYS
FILES=50
BUFFERS=8
LASTDRIVE=Z
FCBS=16,8
INSTALL=C:\DOS\SHARE.EXE/L:400/F:4096
```

STARTNET.BAT for a Server Named TOM

```
@ECHO OFF
LOADHIGH AEX /IRQ=15 /IOBASE=300 /VERBOSE
AILANBIO
LOADHIGH REDIR TOM /LOGINS=3
LANCACHE /TYPE=XMS /CACHE_SIZE=2000 /VERBOSE
LOADHIGH SERVER /NETWORK_BUFFER_SIZE=16K /NETWORK_TASKS=2 /LOGINS=10
NET LOGIN/WAIT \\TOM TOM
NET LPT TIMEOUT 10
```

CONFIG.SYS for a Workstation

```
DEVICE=C:\DOS\HIMEM.SYS
DEVICE=C:\DOS\EMM386.EXE NOEMS
DOS=HIGH,UMB
SHELL=C:\DOS\COMMAND.COM /P
FILES=30
BUFFERS=16
LASTDRIVE=Z
```

A

STARTNET.BAT for a Workstation Named LESLIE

```
@ECHO OFF
LOADHIGH AEX /IRQ=15 /IOBASE=300 /VERBOSE
LOADHIGH AILANBIO
LOADHIGH REDIR LESLIE /LOGINS=2
NET LPT TIMEOUT 10
```

B

LANtastic Support Sources

This appendix shows sources you can draw upon to get support when you need it. Whether you are having a problem with an existing LANtastic LAN or you need answers about a proposed LANtastic LAN, these sources can help.

Artisoft Support

Artisoft takes technical support very seriously and provides several ways to contact them for help. Because of LANtastic's popularity, you may sometimes have a delay getting through. However, Artisoft has repeatedly expanded the number of technical support and sales support people to answer your questions, so your wait is seldom very long.

Before you try any of the sources listed in this appendix, first try to solve the problem yourself by doing the following:

- Read the troubleshooting section in your LANtastic manual and try what it suggests. If LANtastic is displaying any error messages, look up the explanation for the first message in the *LANtastic NOS Reference Manual.*

- Read the other appropriate sections of the LANtastic manuals to make sure you are following directions correctly.
- Read Chapter 9, the troubleshooting chapter of this book.
- Read the other sections of this book that relate to your problem area.

Before calling Artisoft or a dealer for help, have the following information in front of you (if you send a written description of your problem, include this information). Solving your problem is usually not possible unless the exact circumstances and environment are clear.

- The name, model number, and version number of your Artisoft products. Example: LANtastic 4.10 running on AE-2 cards with the default jumper settings, connected by RG58 A/U thin Ethernet cables.
- The version of DOS and/or Windows that you run. Example: MS DOS 5.0 with Windows 3.0.
- A description of your computer. Example: The server is Teltron 386/33 with 2 megabytes of RAM and a 120 megabyte Seagate 1144A disk drive with an IDE controller. The two workstations are (and so on).
- If appropriate, a printed copy of your CONFIG.SYS, AUTO-EXEC.BAT, and STARTNET.BAT files. This is especially true if you are doing anything unusual in these files, such as starting TSR programs, running disk cache software, or using modified LANtastic parameters. (If you haven't yet tried the "Troubleshooting" configurations for these files, shown in Appendix A, do so first.)
- A clear description of your problem, including the exact commands you entered and the exact messages displayed.
- In some cases, you will also need the serial number of your copy of the LANtastic product(s) in question.

Artisoft Voice Telephone Support

You can telephone Artisoft at 602-293-6363, Monday through Friday, 7:00 A.M. to 5:00 P.M. (Mountain Time). From a touch-tone telephone press the number given for Technical Support if you have a technical problem, or for the Sales Department if you want to find a local Artisoft dealer or find out product list prices, features, or other pre-purchase information. Sometimes the lines are crowded and you have a long wait. If so, consider using a fax, Artisoft's BBS, or CompuServe.

Artisoft Fax Support

Telephone 602-293-8065 to submit a fax copy of your problem to Technical Support. Provide the information suggested in the first part of this appendix, or as much of it as possible. Be sure to provide a return telephone number (voice and fax, if you have both).

Telephone 602-293-1397 to use the Artisoft FaxFacts System. You have to call from the phone on which your fax machine is connected. After listening to explanatory messages you can choose several fax documents that you want to have sent to you. These documents include product information, technical bulletins, and other data. The same type of information is also available on the Artisoft BBS.

Artisoft BBS Support

Telephone 602-293-0065 from a computer with a modem set at 1200 to 9600 bps and 8-N-1 (eight data bits, no parity, one stop bit). If you have worked with other computer bulletin board systems (BBS), you will have no trouble logging on and navigating through this one. On this BBS you can do the following:

- Read questions sent in by other users (and Artisoft's answers).
- Download technical bulletin files, product specification files, utility programs, and software demonstrations.

- Leave your own technical questions. Artisoft's objective is to respond to all technical questions within 24 hours. Usually the first response answers the question. Sometimes further investigation is needed, or you are asked for more details about the problem. Address your questions to the sysop (system operator) or to "all."

Some of the most interesting files presently on the BBS for your access include the following:

- NOS.TXT: The current list of independent products compatible with LANtastic.
- CABLE.TXT: Specifications for cable types and lengths supported by various LANtastic products.
- 5STARDL.TXT: A list of Artisoft Five Star dealers. These dealers are experienced with LANtastic and have passed proficiency tests.
- PERFORM.TXT: Tips on improving LANtastic's performance (speed) in your particular environment.
- LANAI41.TXT: A list of the independent LAN cards supported by version 4.1 of LANtastic/AI, the adapter independent version of the LANtastic NOS.
- WIN300.TXT: Notes on running LANtastic under Windows 3.0.

Artisoft Support on CompuServe

If you have access to CompuServe, type **go artisoft** to get access to the Artisoft forum. The capabilities, information, and response time are very much like the Artisoft BBS.

Artisoft Dealers

Artisoft authorizes computer stores and consultants to sell Artisoft products. The best-qualified dealers are called Five Star dealers; these dealers have to pass LAN proficiency tests and promise to stock a full line of Artisoft products. Get the name and number of your nearest Five Star dealer through the Artisoft support channels just mentioned. The Artisoft BBS and the Artisoft CompuServe forum each contain a file, currently called 5STARDL.TXT, which lists these dealers.

Many other dealers are resellers of Artisoft products, too. Check with your local computer store outlets. To find mail-order dealers who sell Artisoft products, look in PC publications, especially the ones that carry the most advertising. Some of the best sources are *Computer Shopper*, *Computer Currents*, *PC Magazine*, *Micro Times*, and *Byte*. By the time you read this, Radio Shack stores may also carry Artisoft products.

Other Support Sources

Support for LANtastic is available from a few companies who are not primarily LANtastic dealers. Of these, your best bet may be to contact one of two catalog vendors who sell either Artisoft products or compatible products (such as IEEE 802.3-compliant repeaters and 10BASE-T hubs).

Catalog Vendors

These are the two leading catalog vendors who sell LAN-related equipment (and have technical support phones to assist you in determining what to buy):

- Black Box Corporation, P.O. Box 12800, Pittsburgh, PA 15241, 412-746-5530. The Black Box Catalog contains a huge assortment of LAN-related products, including LAN cards, cables, connectors, repeaters, and 10BASE-T hubs.
- Inmac, 2465 Augustine Drive, Santa Clara, CA 95054, 800-547-5444. Inmac has a "Networking and Connectivity" catalog that lists a complete selection of LAN products, such as LAN cards, cables, connectors, repeaters, and hubs.

Contact the Author

The author invites your comments on the book. When it's time for a revised edition of the book, your comments may help improve the book so others will benefit. Do you have any favorite tips or traps? Was something in the book unclear? You may not get a response directly (although a self-addressed, stamped envelope greatly improves your chances), but your comments are welcome.

You can reach the author either via the publisher or at this address:

Tom Rugg
LANtastic Made Easy
P.O. Box 24815
Los Angeles, CA 90024

LANtastic Software from the Author

The author has created a series of programs that should benefit any LANtastic administrator or user. One of the programs is the BENCH program mentioned in Chapter 13, which allows you to run your own benchmarks and optimize your LANtastic LAN. Other programs include a variety of utilities to check the status and error statistics for any LAN card (without resorting to running LANCHECK on each computer), to monitor a group of LAN cards, to cancel redirection of all your virtual drives at once, and many others. The list continues to grow.

If you would like a disk with these programs, send $18.00 (U.S. currency) to the author at the address just provided. If you send a formatted floppy disk and a return disk mailer with return postage, the cost is $15.00. California residents, please add sales tax. If you send a check, make it payable to Tom Rugg. You'll get a 5.25-inch, 360K floppy disk unless you request another format. (*Osborne/McGraw-Hill assumes no responsibility for this offer. This is solely an offer of Tom Rugg and not of Osborne/McGraw-Hill.*)

Glossary

10BASE-T An Ethernet LAN standard that uses twisted-pair cabling and RJ-45 modular plugs connected to a central hub in a star or tree topology. Sometimes printed as 10BaseT or 10Base-T.

10BASE2 Thin Ethernet. *See* Ethernet.

10BASE5 Thick Ethernet. *See* Ethernet.

Access Method A logical scheme by which LAN nodes gain access to the communication medium (LAN) to transmit messages to each other without interference. LANtastic Ethernet products use CSMA/CD.

AEX The LANtastic NOS low-level driver software for LANtastic AE-x model Ethernet LAN cards.

AILANBIO The LANtastic NOS high-level driver software that provides the NetBIOS capability for Ethernet and some other LAN cards.

ALONE A LANtastic NOS program that temporarily turns a non-dedicated server into a dedicated server.

Application Software A computer program that accomplishes a particular task for a computer user, such as word processing or accounting.

ARCnet A de facto LAN standard (not accepted by IEEE) that communicates at 2.5 Mbps, usually in a star topology.

AT Bus *See* ISA.

Backup Copy An extra copy of a disk file or entire disk, kept separate from the original (usually on a tape cartridge or floppy disks) in case the original is lost, destroyed, or erroneously changed.

Bandwidth The signal-transfer capacity of a communication channel, such as a LAN or telephone line.

Baseband A signaling method in which a cable carries a single digital signal at a time.

BNC Connector A bayonet-type cable connector used in thin Ethernet LANs.

Bps Either bits per second (usually abbreviated bps) or bytes per second (usually Bps). Dividing your bits per second by either 8, 10, or 11 (depending on the communication method being used) gives approximate bytes per second. *See also* Transfer Rate.

Broadband A signaling method in which a cable's bandwidth is split into several channels, each of which independently carries analog signals.

Bus Topology A physical LAN layout in which all computers are connected to a single length of cable (or a series of cables connected to form one long daisy chain) with a terminator at each end. Thin Ethernet uses a bus topology.

Byte Eight bits of information. Capable of holding either a number from 0 to 255, or one typed character of information.

Cable The most common LAN medium to connect devices together. *See* Coaxial Cable and Twisted-Pair Cable.

Cache *See* Disk Cache.

Character A single typed letter or digit of information, which typically occupies one byte of storage (either in RAM or on disk) in a computer.

Client-Server LAN A LAN software design that typically requires one or more dedicated servers and has clients (workstations) that rely on them for services. Contrast with Peer-to-Peer LAN.

Coaxial Cable Also called co-ax or coax. A cable that consists of a central wire surrounded by insulation material, which in turn is surrounded by electrically protective metal mesh or foil and another layer of insulation. The mesh or foil layer protects the inner wire from electrical interference. Thin coaxial cable is used for thin Ethernet LANs. Thick coaxial cable, used for thick Ethernet LANs, has greater protective characteristics and transmits signals reliably for longer distances, but has become unpopular because it is more expensive and difficult to use.

Collision A garbled message caused by two LAN nodes trying to send a signal at the same time. The IEEE 802.3 standard requires each node to wait a varying length of time before trying to retransmit.

Concentrator A central device to which other devices are connected. Sometimes referred to interchangeably as a hub, but often a concentrator means a hub device with more built-in capabilities for monitoring and troubleshooting. Concentrators and hubs are used in 10BASE-T LANs but not thin Ethernet LANs.

CSMA/CD Carrier Sense Multiple Access with Collision Detection. A LAN access method that is used in IEEE 802.3 LANs (thin Ethernet and 10BASE-T, among others) in which each node listens for availability of the communications channel before transmitting a message, and in which a node can determine if a collision has occurred, making a retransmission necessary.

Database A collection of related information stored on a computer. Examples are a name and address file, a parts inventory, and a magazine article index.

DBMS Database Management System. General purpose software that can create, change, search, sort, and generate reports from a database. Examples are dBASE IV, Paradox, FoxPro, and Q&A. In a LAN environment, many users can simultaneously manipulate the same database on a server's shared disk.

Dedicated Server A LAN-connected computer that acts solely as a server and has no workstation capability. LANtastic permits a server to temporarily act as a dedicated server by using the ALONE program. Stopping the ALONE program turns the server back into a nondedicated server without interrupting the work being performed by the server.

Disk Cache A type of software that uses RAM to store disk information in order to speed up an application's apparent disk access time by reducing physical I/O to a hard disk. The disk cache software provided with LANtastic is called LANcache.

Diskless Workstation A PC with no disk drives. Because the PC has no disks, it has to get its software and data from a server's disk drive. Adding a special ROM chip to the workstation's LAN card gives it this capability.

DTP *See* Twisted-Pair Cable.

Electronic Mail Also called e-mail. A method of exchanging mail-like typed messages over a LAN or other communications medium. LANtastic's NOS has a simple electronic mail capability built into it, which users access using the NET program.

Ethernet An IEEE-accepted standard LAN specification. The most common forms are IEEE 802.3 10BASE2 (usually called thin Ethernet, thin net, or cheapernet, which uses thin coaxial cables), and IEEE 802.3 10BASE-T (usually called 10BASE-T, UTP, or DTP, which uses twisted-pair cables connected to a central hub). An earlier standard, IEEE 802.3 10BASE5 (thick Ethernet), is seldom used for new LANs. All of these Ethernet varieties transmit data at a rate of 10 megabits per second. LANtastic makes products that conform to the thin Ethernet and 10BASE-T standards, and also sells a product called the LANtastic 2Mbps adapter, which does not conform to Ethernet or other standards.

Fiber Optic A newer type of communications cable in which light-beam signals are sent over glass threads rather than electronic impulses being sent over metal wire.

File A collection of information, usually stored on a hard disk or floppy disk.

File Server A server that provides a shared disk on which users can store, retrieve, and manipulate files of information.

Gateway A connection between two unlike systems, such as a LAN and a remote data system (computer or another LAN) of a different type. The gateway typically is a computer (LAN node) with software that performs conversion between the two dissimilar LANs or systems.

Groupware Application software designed to work on a LAN to make a workgroup more effective. Examples are electronic mail and calendar coordination software.

Hub A central device to which other devices are connected. Sometimes referred to interchangeably as a concentrator, although some manufacturers define a concentrator as having additional capabilities. Hubs are used in 10BASE-T LANs but not thin Ethernet LANs.

IEEE Institute of Electrical and Electronics Engineers. An American professional organization that sets standards for LANs, among other things. Best known are the IEEE 802.3 standards for Ethernet and the IEEE 802.5 standards for token ring.

Independent LAN Card For purposes of this book, a LAN card made by a manufacturer other than Artisoft.

ISA Industry Standard Architecture. The name used to describe the standards followed by expansion cards that fit in IBM-compatible personal computers other than IBM Micro Channel PS/2 computers. Also called the AT bus or the PC bus.

LAN *See* Local Area Network.

LAN Adapter *See* LAN Card.

LAN Administrator The person responsible for performing certain regular LAN maintenance and management functions, such as making backup copies of important files, controlling LAN security, establishing user procedures, and managing server disk space.

LAN Card An expansion card that installs in a PC's expansion slot and connects to LAN cables in order to attach a PC to a LAN. LANtastic's most popular LAN cards are the AE-x Ethernet family: the AE-1/T, AE-2, AE-2/T, and AE-3.

LAN Operating System *See* Network Operating System.

LANBIOS The program used by the LANtastic 2Mbps LAN card as a low-level driver and to provide NetBIOS functionality. Different versions of the LANtastic 2Mbps card use different versions of this program, named either LANBIOS, LANBIOS2, or LANBIOS3. Serves the same function as the AEX-AILANBIO combination for LANtastic Ethernet cards.

LANtastic A peer-to-peer network operating system created and sold by Artisoft. *See also* Network Operating System.

LANtastic Z A special version of LANtastic that connects two computers using either serial ports, parallel ports, or two modems and a telephone link.

Local Area Network (LAN) A collection of computers and other devices connected in a relatively small geographic area (usually one building) for high-speed sharing of computer files and peripheral devices.

Local Disk A hard disk physically connected to a computer. Contrast with Shared Disk.

Locking A method of temporarily gaining exclusive control of a shared file or portion of the file to prevent other users from changing or accessing the data at the same time.

Lockup A problem in which a computer stops responding to commands and must be rebooted.

Log In LANtastic's terminology for the act of gaining access from a workstation to a server. If LAN security is in effect, a workstation user must enter a valid username and password in order to log in. Some other vendors call this process "log on."

Log Out The act of terminating access from a workstation to a server. With LANtastic, logging out also terminates redirection of the workstation's device names to a server. Some other vendors call this process "log off."

Logical Topology The combination of LAN card, physical topology, cable, and access method that establishes a standard method by which nodes communicate on a LAN. The three major types are Ethernet, token ring, and ARCnet.

Mail Server A server that supports electronic mail.

Mbps In this book, million bits per second, or megabits per second. Some publications use Mbps to mean million *bytes* per second, but most use a lowercase "b" for bits and an uppercase "B" for bytes.

MB Megabytes (millions of bytes).

MCA Micro Channel Architecture. *See* Micro Channel.

Micro Channel IBM's computer bus architecture on high-end PS/2 computer models. Special expansion cards are necessary for installation in a Micro Channel PS/2. Contrast with ISA.

Modem Modulator-demodulator. A device that converts between digital and analog signals for communication between computers, usually over telephone lines.

MS-DOS Microsoft Disk Operating System. The operating system developed by Microsoft in conjunction with IBM to control internal operation of IBM personal computers. Now sold independently by Microsoft for any IBM-compatible computer. (Often simply called DOS, but other incompatible computer makers sometimes call their operating systems DOS also.) *See also* PC DOS.

NET The LANtastic program a workstation user uses to establish connection to a LAN server and otherwise interact with the LAN.

NET_MGR The LANtastic program a LAN administrator uses to control a server and the access that users are allowed to have to the server.

NetBIOS Network Basic Input/Output System. A de facto standard application-program interface that allows a computer program to communicate over the LAN without regard to the physical or logical topology. LANtastic adheres to NetBIOS standards, which are implemented in either the AILANBIO program (for Ethernet) or the LANBIOS program (for 2Mbps LAN cards).

NetWare A network operating system family sold by Novell. Three versions exist: NetWare 3.x, NetWare 2.x (both client-server LANs), and NetWare Lite (a peer-to-peer LAN).

Network An interconnected system of devices. In a LAN context, the terms LAN and network are used interchangeably.

Network Adapter *See* LAN Card.

Network Administrator *See* LAN Administrator.

Network Operating System (NOS) The system software that runs on each workstation and server in conjunction with MS-DOS to allow computers to communicate and share server resources. The LANtastic product usually refers only to a network operating system, but people often use the name LANtastic to refer to the entire LAN setup, including LAN cards (especially if also bought from Artisoft).

Network Software *See* Network Operating System.

NIC Network Interface Card. *See* LAN Card.

NIU Network Interface Unit. *See* LAN Card.

Node A LAN-connected computer. In some cases, a node can also be a LAN-connected peripheral, such as a printer or terminal. For LANtastic, a node is either a workstation or a server.

Nondedicated Server A server that can also act as a workstation while it simultaneously acts as a server.

Operating System (OS) The internal system software that controls how applications interact with the computer hardware. The most popular operating system used on IBM-compatible computers is MS-DOS.

OS/2 A new operating system jointly developed by IBM and Microsoft to overcome some of the limitations of MS-DOS, for use on newer, high-performance computers. LANtastic is not compatible with OS/2.

Packet A chunk of information sent across a communications channel such as a LAN.

Parallel Port An input/output connection on a computer that sends 8 bits of data at a time between the computer and an external device, usually a printer. The parallel ports on a PC are called LPT1, LPT2, and LPT3. Sometimes referred to as a printer port. Contrast with Serial Port.

PC Personal Computer. In the context of this book, a PC refers to an IBM-compatible personal computer. In some contexts, a PC can refer to any personal computer.

PC Bus *See* ISA.

PC DOS IBM's adaptation of Microsoft's MS-DOS. The same-numbered versions of MS-DOS and PC DOS are essentially the same—that is, MS-DOS 3.3 and PC DOS 3.3 are virtually identical, although some minor internal differences exist. LANtastic works with either.

Peer-to-Peer LAN A LAN on which all nodes can interact with others as equals. In practice, a peer-to-peer LAN has come to mean one that permits nondedicated servers and/or nodes that can switch between server and workstation functionality or support both at once. LANtastic is a peer-to-peer LAN.

Physical Topology The design by which devices are physically connected to a LAN. See also Bus Topology, Ring Topology, and Star Topology.

Print Queue A waiting line of files temporarily stored on a server's hard disk until the server's shared printer is available to print them.

Print Server A server that provides shared printers for workstations to use.

Protocol A standard method of communication. Most often used to refer to the format of data packets exchanged between nodes and the meaning of command codes within those packets. Also sometimes refers to the timing of communication signals.

Read-Only File A file that a user can read but not change.

REDIR The LANtastic program that interacts with MS-DOS to perform redirection of a device name to a server's shared resource. REDIR is what allows a workstation's L drive to really refer to a server's C drive.

Redirected Disk A workstation's disk drive name that refers to a server's shared disk. *See* REDIR.

Repeater A device that amplifies and regenerates LAN signals. A thin Ethernet LAN that exceeds 185 meters total length or 30 nodes needs one or more repeaters.

Ring Topology A physical LAN layout in which all computers are connected in a loop or ring.

Segment A logical section of LAN cable that contains a group of nodes daisy-chained together on thin Ethernet. Each segment cannot exceed 185 meters and 30 nodes. Multiple segments are connected using repeaters.

Serial Port An input/output connection on a computer that sends one bit of data at a time between the computer and an external device, usually a mouse (or other pointing device), modem, plotter, or another computer. The serial ports on a PC are called COM1, COM2, COM3, and COM4. A serial port is sometimes called an RS-232 port. Contrast with Parallel Port.

Server A LAN-connected computer that makes available its shared resources (hard disks, printers, mail, modems, or CD-ROM drives) to other LAN-connected computers.

SERVER The LANtastic NOS program that performs the functions of a server on a LANtastic LAN.

Server-Based LAN *See* Client-Server LAN.

SHARE A DOS program that must be run on a LANtastic server to coordinate multiple users accessing the same files at the same time.

Shared Disk A disk on a server, available for use by workstations.

Shared Printer A printer on a server, available for use by workstations.

Shielded Twisted-Pair Cable *See* Twisted-Pair Cable.

Sneakernet A lighthearted and overused name for exchanging data between computers by means of manually carrying floppy disks instead of using a LAN connection.

G

Stand-Alone Computer A computer not connected to a LAN or any other computer.

Star Topology A physical LAN layout in which all computers are connected to a central hub. *See also* Tree Topology.

Station *See* Node.

System Software A type of software that controls the internal components of a computer. MS-DOS and the LANtastic NOS are two examples. Contrast with Application Software.

Tape Backup System A peripheral device that records data on a tape cartridge for backup purposes.

Terminator A resistor that must be installed at each of the two ends of a bus-type LAN.

Thick Coaxial Cable *See* Coaxial Cable.

Thick Ethernet *See* Ethernet.

Thin Coaxial Cable *See* Coaxial Cable.

Thin Ethernet *See* Ethernet.

Token Ring LAN A type of LAN that keeps track of which node can transmit data by means of a special message called a token. Contrast with CSMA/CD.

Topology *See* Logical Topology or Physical Topology.

Transceiver Transmitter-receiver. A device that connects between a LAN card and a thick Ethernet cable. Transceivers are not necessary on a thin Ethernet LAN. Also a device to connect a LAN card to a fiber optic cable.

Transfer Rate The speed at which data can move from one device to another. Within a computer, such as between a hard disk and a processor, a transfer rate is normally specified in bytes per second. Communications devices such as LANs and phones lines usually specify transfer rates in bits per second.

Tree Topology A physical LAN layout in which all computers are connected to central hubs, and the hubs are connected together in a hierarchy. A series of stars connected together forms a tree. 10BASE-T LANs form a tree topology if more than one hub is used and a star if only one hub is used, even though most people call the topology a star for both cases.

Twisted-Pair Cable A low-cost cable used commonly in 10BASE-T Ethernet LANs to connect each node to a hub. Common types are unshielded twisted-pair (UTP) and shielded twisted-pair, which provides more protection against electrical interference. Either type is also called dual twisted-pair (DTP).

Uninterruptible Power Supply (UPS) A device with battery storage that continues to provide electrical power to connected devices for a limited length of time if regular commercial power fails.

Unshielded Twisted-Pair (UTP) *See* Twisted-Pair Cable.

Wide Area Network (WAN) A series of local area networks in different geographic areas that are connected together using telephone lines or other telecommunications links.

Windows An operating environment from Microsoft Corporation that runs in conjunction with MS-DOS to provide a consistent graphical interface to users who run applications.

Wireless LAN A LAN that makes connections between nodes without cables, by using radio signals or infrared signals. Some wireless LANs are hybrids that connect clusters of wired nodes using wireless methods.

Wiring Closet A building closet or area in which hubs and other cable concentrators are located.

Workgroup A small group of people who work together, generally on the same projects. In a large company, a workgroup is usually a single department. In a small company, the workgroup might be the entire company.

Workstation A LAN-connected computer that uses the shared resources of servers but does not provide shared resources to other computers.

Zero-Slot LAN A LAN that connects computers together without the use of a LAN card. Connection is made instead using serial ports, parallel ports, or modems and telephone lines. LANtastic's zero-slot LAN product is called LANtastic Z.

Index

\\ preceding server name in LANtastic commands, 338
8- and 16-bit expansion slots, 103-104, 217
16-bit enable selection settings, 102-103
386MAX program, 239

A

Access control lists (ACLs), 258, 261-267
Access method, 11
Access rights
- changing, 264-267
- descriptions of, 262-263

Accounting database, 27
- programs, list of, 28

ACOM program, 193-195
ACOM_MGR program, 197-198
AE-1/T card, 42, 47
AE-2/T card, 42, 46
AEX LAN card driver software, 127-129, 148, 211, 246
- command reference, 340-341

AILANBIO program
- command reference, 342-344
- RAM used by, 333
- run_burst parameter setting changed to improve LAN speed, 328
- as variation of NetBIOS, 127-128, 209, 211-212

ALONE program, 41
- benchmark results of, 319
- command reference, 344-345
- to run server as dedicated, 309, 318-319

American Power Conversion, 245

Anti-virus programs, 281-282
Apollo workstation, 21
Apple Macintosh, connecting network with, 62, 70-71, 84
Application software
- dysfunctional, 246
- for LAN, special versions of, 7
- planning for, 82-83, 86
- problems with LAN due to new or incompatible, 233-234, 243
- sharing database, 22

ARCnet (Attached Resource Computing) architecture, 14
ArtiCom Modem Sharing Software, 58, 75, 187-198
- communications software features of, 189
- dialing directory, 196
- installing, 189-193
- purpose of, 188-189
- running, 193-197
- testing, 196-197

ArtiScribe Digital Dictation Starter Kit (ISA), 56
ArtiScribe Station Software, 56
ArtiSoft dealers, 394-395
ArtiSoft Technical Support, 285
- bulletin board of, 285, 393-394
- on CompuServe, 394
- fax, 393
- information to have prior to contacting, 392
- problem solving prior to contacting, 391-392
- voice telephone, 393

ASP Computer Products, 16
AT&T 104, 205, or 315 DTP, 4, 106
Audit trails for LAN security, 250, 271-273, 331
Author, contacting this book's, 396
AUTOEXEC.BAT file, 138, 285
- DOS prompt changed in, 145
- MSCDEX command line in, 182
- SHARE DOS command in, 243
- STARTNET.BAT copied into end of, 238
- troubleshooting by minimizing, 237
- typical, 381-382
- for Windows in a single-user configuration, 295

B

Back-It 4 LAN (Gazelle Systems), 205
Baseband, 12
Belden 1227A DTP, 4, 106
Belden 9880 thick coaxial cable, 44
BENCH program, 316-318
Benchmark suite, 305
Benchmark tests, 286
- ALONE results from, 319
- BENCH program results from, 326-327
- BUFFERS statement results from, 320
- defined, 304
- fundamental problem with running, on a LAN, 305
- LANcache results from, 316-317
- large block, 306
- length of execution time for, 307-308
- possible LAN, 306-308
- recording results from, 308
- repeatability of results from, 307
- small block, 307
- tips for using, 307-308

Black Box Corporation, 16, 72, 395
BLAST PC, 189
BNC T connector for thin co-ax cable, 6, 9, 45-46, 59
- attaching, 89-90, 105-106
- Central Station requirement for, 207
- checking for bad, 241
- removing, from AE-2 or AE-3 card, 104

Boot ROM enable and address selection settings, 101
Broadband, 12
Brooklyn Bridge (Fifth Generation Systems), 17, 68
Bulletin board service, Artisoft, 285, 393-394
Bus topology, 7-9
    recent ARCnet products' use of, 14
Busy token, 13

C

Cabling. *See* LAN cables; individual types
Calendar software for workgroups, 29
Capacity planning, 286
Carbon Copy Plus (Microcom, Inc.), 198
Carrier sense multiple access with collision detection (CSMA/CD), 11-12
Catalog vendors for equipment, 395
cc:Mail, 70
CD Net (Meridian Data, Inc.), 186
CD-ROM disk
    capacity of 600 megabytes, 174
    cost of, 175-176
    index, 175
    response time of, 177
CD-ROM drive, 174-187
    accessed from a workstation, 184-186
    controller card removed during hardware troubleshooting, 237
    installing hardware for, 177-179
    installing software for, 179-184
    prices, 176
    products, 186-187
    sharing, 23, 37-40, 75, 176-177
CD ROM, Inc., 187
CDR-72 CD-ROM drive (NEC), 42
Central Point Anti-Virus (Central Point Software), 284
Central Station Connectivity Processor (Artisoft), 51-52, 68, 206-207
    hardware connections for, 207-208
    software installation for, 208-211
Change file attributes (A) access right, 263
Chinon CDC-431 CD-ROM drive, 177-181
Citrix Multiuser operating system, 17
Client defined, 20
Client-server network, 20
Clipper (Nantucket), 32
Clocks, synchronizing the server's and workstation's, 142-143
Compact Disk Products (CDP), 187
Compressed files for use with Sounding Board, 222
CompuServe, Artisoft technical support on, 394
Computer
    attribute list for LAN planning, 66-67, 73
    backing up data to another, 200
    installing LAN card in, 103-105
    locations, planning, 75-80, 85
    lockup, 238-239, 240, 244
    opening cover of, 103
    portable, 68-69, 206-213
    rebooting, 148
    replacing cover on, 105
    use, analyzing, 66
Computer Select, CD-ROM for, 39
Comspec Communications, 16
Concentrator, 13
Conduit
    floorplan showing, 77
    using existing, 76-78
CONFIG.SYS file
    BUFFERS statement value increased for optimization benchmark tests, 320
    BUFFERS statement value lowered to use disk cache programs, 315
    change to DEVICE statement of, 311-312
    changes to, for CD-ROM disk drive, 181-182

changes to, for Central Station, 209-210
changes to, for LANtastic, 92-94, 118-119, 121, 124, 140
changes to, problems with LAN created by, 233
RAM used by DOS parameters in, 334
for a server, minimum RAM, 387
for a server running LANcache, 385-386
for a server, troubleshooting, 384
for a server, typical, 382
for a server with extended memory, 389
SHARE DOS command in, 243, 322
troubleshooting, 237
for a workstation, minimum RAM, 387
for a workstation, troubleshooting, 385
for a workstation, typical, 383
for a workstation with extended memory, 389
Connectivity of resources
between Macintoshes and PCs, 70
without LANs, 14-17
Connectors, 6
Central Station requirement of, 207
serial and parallel port, 16-17
Consultant
database application created by, 26, 33
non-DBMS programs developed by, 34
Contact management database, 27
programs, list of, 28
Control directory, 120-121
Conventional memory, 310-311
CPBACKUP (Central Point Software), 205
Create File (C) access right, 262
CrossTalk Mark IV, 189
Current Users menu box, 252, 256

D

Data backup
administrator's duty for, 277-278
tape drives for, 199-206
Data space, shared, 22, 24-25
Data transfer speed
2Mbps versus Ethernet, 52-53
benchmark tests for, 304-308
buffer size settings and number of buffers for, 327-328
higher in ring topology, 10
Database
applications, shared, 22, 25-34
applications, specialized, 26-29
business, CD-ROM for, 39
defined, 22
government, CD-ROM for, 39
medical, CD-ROM for, 39
Database management system (DBMS), 26
to design custom databases, 31-32
programs, list of, 32-33
Date, setting, 143
dBASE database application (Borland International), 22
dBASE III Plus, 32
dBASE IV, 32
DE-812TP D-Linke hub, 42
Dedicated server, 20, 67, 309
Default settings, 91
Delete directory (K) access right, 263
Delete file (D) access right, 263
Despooling, 155-156
Dialog Information Services, 175
Dictation product, 56
Digital Products, 16
Direct memory access (DMA) channels, 217, 220-221
Disk buffers, 320
Disk cache, 335
defined, 309

products, independent, 315
Disk cache program, 234
conflicts, 242
creating, 309
Disk drive(s)
CD-ROM, 23, 37-40
connections, 93, 95, 120, 125
floppy, 16
hard, 67, 138-150, 322-323
shared, 22-23, 25
virtual, 24
Disk files
causes of corrupt, 242-245, 321
fragmentation of, LAN speed lowered by, 329, 336
Disk partitions, 322-323
Disk space
for e-mail messages, 164
FAT to track, 322-323
optimizing, 304, 334-336
server, housekeeping for, 278-279, 329-330
DMA channel selection settings, 100
DOS, LANtastic requirement of 3.1 or higher version of, 69, 84, 233
DOS parameters
for RAM optimization, 333-334
for speed optimization, 320-323
DOS prompt
redirection cancellation from, 150
redirection from, 149-150
server login from, 148-149
Drive Connections window, 298
Drive and Printer Connections menu box, 138-139, 143, 151-152, 298
DRM-600 MiniChanger (Pioneer), 187
DrMultiuser DOS, 17
Dual twisted-pair cable (DTP), 4
Dumb terminal defined, 17

E

Electrical interference, 10
Electronic mail (e-mail), 163-171
copied to files, 169
deleting, 169
forwarding, 169
privacy issues, 169, 171
products, 29, 55-56, 70
reading, 169
receiving, 167-170
security for, 169, 171
sending, 165-167
setting up, 163-164
using, 164-171
EMM386 program, 239, 388
Enterprise (Chronos Software), 30-31
Error messages, procedure for interpreting LANtastic, 235
Ethernet, 11-13
10BASE2: thin cable, 12-13, 44, 71, 76, 78-79, 88, 207, 233
10BASE5: thick cable, 12, 44
10BASE-T: twisted-pair cable, 13, 48, 71, 76, 79-80, 207
IEEE 802.3, 11-12, 44
LAN products from Artisoft, 43-51, 98
Ethernet type selection, 100-101
Execute program (E) access right, 263
Expanded memory, 182, 239, 310-311
Extended memory, 310-311
configuration providing high performance and large available conventional, 388-390
management, 332, 334-336

F

FASTOPEN DOS command
for database applications, 320
disk file problems associated with, 243, 321
Fax cards, 58
Fifth Generation Systems, 16-17
File allocation table (FAT), 322-323
File, loading and saving, 25
File lookups (L) access right, 263

File server, 20
File-transfer programs, 16-17
"Five Star" dealers, Artisoft, 81
Floor plan for LAN, 77-78, 85
Floppy disk drives, data exchange between systems with unlike, 16
Floppy disks for data backups, 200, 205
Font cartridges for laser printers, 161-163
Forms design database, 27
FoxBASE database application (Fox Software), 22
    FoxBASE+, 32
    FoxPro, 32
Fragmented disk files, 329, 336
Free token, 13

G

Gateway defined, 70
Glossary, 397-409
Group user account, 258-261
    adding, 260-261
    common rights for everyone in, 251
    concurrent logins within, limiting, 259
    created for each server, 250
    default maximum users per, 246
    defined, 259
    deleting the unrestricted, 260
    password shared within, 260
Group Users menu box, 260
Groupware, 7
    database software, 26, 29-31

H

Half-cards, 104
Hardware
    conflicts, eliminating, 237
    problems, isolating, 236-237
    upgrades to improve speed, 330
HP LaserJet III or IIID laser printer, 160-161
HP LaserJet IIIP laser printer, 160
HP LaserJet IIISi laser printer, 159-161
HTEST program, 220
Hub(s)
    2Mbps, 54
    10BASE-T, 48, 51, 233
    checking for bad, 235, 242
    defined, 9, 13
    D-Link, 42
    failure of, 10
    manufacturers of, 72
    maximum of 100 meters (328 feet) between UTP cable's node and star topology's, 13, 106
    network's size and number of, 71-72
    planning, 79-80

I

IBM LAN Server (IBM), 63
IBM PC, announcement in 1981 of, 2
IBM, token ring LANs advocated by, 14
Incremental backups, 202-203
Indirect file (I) access right, 263
Industry standard architecture (ISA) defined, 44
Inmac, 395
INSTALL program, LANtastic, 91-95, 111-126, 140
    buffer values in, 320
    for Central Station installation, 208-211
    default resources set up by, 264
    ending, 121, 125
    opening screen, 113
    options, selecting, 112
    for portable LAN adapter, 212
    rebooting system after running, 232
    starting, 91, 112, 123
Installation directory

changing, 115
default, 92, 123
Installation disk, making, 110
Installation, LANtastic, 87-135
detailed hardware, 96-108
detailed server software, 109-122
detailed workstation software, 122-125
quick, 88-95
Institute of Electrical and Electronics Engineers (IEEE), 11
INT 14h standard, 189
Interface card for CD-ROM disk drive, 177
Interleave factor, LAN speed and, 328-329, 336
Interrupt selection settings, 99-100
I/O card removed during hardware troubleshooting, 237
I/O port address
conflict of LAN card with CD-ROM disk drive's, 178
conflicts, LAN problems caused by, 234, 237
selection settings, 100
IOBASE
conflict, 239
setting, 178
IQ Engineering, font cartridges from, 162-163
IRQ
CD-ROM card's settings for, 178
conflict, 234, 239
jumper settings for, 126, 129

J

Jumper
defined, 98
settings for IRQ or IOBASE, 126, 129
settings on the AE-2 LAN card, 98-103
Justis Weekly Law Reports, 39

L

LAN (local area network)
administration, 83, 86, 275-286
background, 1-17
budget restrictions, 61, 83
components, 3-7
configuration management, 276, 285-286
equipment sources, 81-82, 85, 96-97
hazards to, 81, 85, 241
large, configuration issues for, 63, 71, 85
objectives of, 65, 84
optimization, 276-277, 286, 303-336
planning for, 59-86
products, LANtastic, 43-58
proprietary designs of early, 3
starting software for, 96
steps prior to installing, 84-86
testing, 96, 109
throughput, 303
usage and policies, training users for, 86
wireless, 4, 77
zero-slot, 17, 57
LAN administrator, 275-286
M (Super Mail) privilege for, 171
planning for, 83, 86
role and duties of, 251-252, 276-277, 279, 281-282, 284-286
selecting, 276
LAN cables, 4-5. *See also individual types*
attaching, 105-106
checking for bad, 235, 241, 330-331
connecting, 76-77
floor plan for, 77-78, 85
integrity of, testing, 107
jumbles of, 75-76
lengths of, planning, 78-79, 85
nonstandard, 241
routing, 106
using existing, 77
LAN card(s), 4

2Mbps, 52-53, 82-83, 148, 293, 330
AE-1/T, 64, 83, 97, 104
AE-2, 41, 59, 64, 83, 88-89, 98, 178, 181, 330
AE-3, 64, 83, 97, 178, 330
AEX driver program that won't work with, 246
ARCnet, 82, 330
available card (expansion) slot for, 69-70, 84, 103-105
checking for bad, 242, 330-331
default settings, 98-103
driver software, AEX, 127-129
Ethernet, 64
EtherTalk, 70
IMC, 64
installing, 103-105, 123
LocalTalk, 70
node number of, 132
non-Artisoft, 82, 147-148
problem with, 236
selecting, 85
situations inappropriate for using, 62-63, 83-84
software drivers, 118, 134
sources, 82
in starter kit, 97
TokenTalk, 70
LAN Manager NOS (Microsoft), 7, 63
LAN+Modem NetBIOS (Cross Communications Company), 198
LANcache disk cache program, 242, 309-318, 335
benchmark results with and without running, 316-318
checking performance of, 314
command reference, 345-347
parameters for data output, 313
speed optimization for LAN by using, 308
startup files for configuration running, 385-386, 388-390
using, 312-316
writing caching problems with, 313-314
LANCHECK program, 131-133, 235-236
command reference, 347-348
inability to communicate analyzed by running, 240-242
startup file configurations to use when you run, 383-385
LANPUP program command reference, 348-349
LANspan/NBP (IMC Networks Corporation), 64
LANtastic 2Mbps Adapter
ISA, 54-55
Micro Channel, 54
not widely used in new LAN installations, 98
LANtastic 2Mbps Hub, 54
LANtastic 2Mbps Starter Kit
ISA, 53-54
Micro Channel, 53-54
LANtastic 8-Bit AE-1/T 10BASE-T Ethernet Adapter, 48, 50
LANtastic 10BASE-T Starter Kit, 40, 47
LANtastic AE-1/T LAN card, 64, 83, 97, 104
LANtastic AE-2 Ethernet Adapter, 4-5
default, 116
ISA, 48
Micro Channel, 48
LANtastic AE-2 Ethernet Starter Kit, 59, 81
hardware installation for, 89-90, 95, 96-108
ISA, 44-46, 48
Micro Channel, 46-47
quick installation of, 88-95
software installation for, 90-96, 109-125
LANtastic AE-2 LAN cards, 41, 59, 64, 83, 88-89, 98, 178, 181, 330
LANtastic AE-2/T 16-Bit Ethernet Adapter, 48-49

LANtastic AE-3 Ethernet Adapter (ISA), 48-49
  default, 116
LANtastic AE-3 Ethernet Starter Kit (ISA), 46
LANtastic AE-3 LAN card, 64, 83, 97, 178, 330
LANtastic (Artisoft)
  automatic startup of, 138
  broadband signaling used for, 12
  case studies of users of, 40-42
  command reference, 337-379
  defaults, changing, 112-125
  DOS parameters and, 332-334
  installation and testing, 87-135, 289-296
  multiple layers of, 127
  as network operating system, 7
  planning for installation of, 59-86
  product line, 2Mbps, 52-56
  product line, Ethernet, 43-52
  software from the author, 396
  starting, 125-130
  stopping, 146-148
  support sources, 391-396
  tape backup systems used with, 203-204
  testing, 130-133
  troubleshooting procedures, 231-247
  uses of, 19-42
  voice mail with, 225-229
  Windows and, 287-301
LANtastic NOS
  upgrading, 330
  version 4.0, 210-211
  version 4.1, 88
LANtastic for Windows, 58, 288, 296-301
LANtastic Z Two Station Kit (Artisoft), 17
  connecting portable and LAN computers using, 68-69
  connecting two computers using, 57-58, 83
  installing, 134
  remote access to modem using, 74
  starting, 135
  testing, 135
LANtastic/AI, 57
  adapter drivers, 124
  copy of, required for each node of non-Artisoft hardware, 97
  copy of, required for each non-Artisoft LAN card, 82, 111, 123
  driver software compatibility with, 108
  installation, 111
LANtastic/AI Network Adapter, 117
LANVOICE.EXE software driver program, 219-220
LapLink (Traveling Software), 17, 68
Locking files, 243, 322
LTEST program, 220-221

M

M privilege for network administrator, 171
Machine name, 92, 94, 112-114, 123
  username same as, 142-143
Machine type, 92, 94, 115, 123
MACLAN Connect (Miramar Systems, Inc.), 70
Mail Options menu box, 168-169
Main Functions menu box
  ACOM, 193-194
  LANtastic, 138-139, 146, 155, 164, 183
  LANtastic Net's equivalent to, 299
Make directory (M) access right, 263
Memory. *See* RAM
Memory addresses, 234
Memory management programs, 239
Memory usage, measuring, 332
Microsoft Bookshelf Reference Library (Microsoft), 38

Microsoft CD Extensions (MSCDEX), 179, 181-182
Microsoft Mail, 70
Mirror III, 189
Modem(s)
  installing, 134-135
  pool, 58
  products, 198
  remote access to, 74
  sharing, 23, 40, 74-75, 187-198
  single-workstation, 74
Modem Protocall NetBIOS (Protocall Communications), 198
MS-DOS, LANtastic requirement of 3.1 or higher version of, 69, 84, 233
Multiport serial adapters, 188
Multiuser operating systems, 17

N

NE2000 driver software (Novell), 44
NE2000 emulation mode settings, 103
NET ATTACH command reference, 350
NET AUDIT command reference, 350-351
NET CHANGEPW command reference, 351
NET CHAT command, 223-225
  command reference, 351
NET CLOCK command reference, 351
NET COPY command reference, 352
NET DETACH command reference, 352
NET DIR command reference, 352-353
NET DISABLEA command reference, 353
NET ECHO command reference, 353-354
NET EXPAND command reference, 354
NET FLUSH command reference, 354
NET HELP command reference, 355
NET INDIRECT command reference, 355
NET LOGIN command to log in to LANtastic from the DOS prompt, 148-149, 171
  command reference, 355-356
NET LOGOUT command to log a workstation out from a server, 150
  command reference, 356
NET LPT COMBINE command reference, 356-357
NET LPT NOTIFY command reference, 357
NET LPT SEPARATE command reference, 357
NET LPT TIMEOUT command reference, 357-358
NET MAIL command reference, 358
NET menu, 138-148
  canceling redirection from, 145-146
  e-mail from, 164-165
  printer control and queuing from, 155-159
  printer redirection from, 151-153
  redirection from, 138-146
  to share resources, 137, 150-151, 153-154
NET MESSAGE command reference, 358
NET PAUSE command reference, 359
NET POSTBOX command to see summary of mail waiting, 168
  command reference, 359
NET PRINT command reference, 359-360
NET program, 298
  command reference, 349-350
  to display NET menu, 138
  run before WIN to use Windows, 295
  text editor of, 157, 165-166
NET QUEUE HALT command reference, 360-361
NET QUEUE PAUSE command reference, 361

NET QUEUE RESTART command reference, 361-362
NET QUEUE SINGLE command reference, 362
NET QUEUE START command reference, 362-363
NET QUEUE STATUS command reference, 363
NET QUEUE STOP command reference, 363
NET RECEIVE command reference, 364
NET RUN command reference, 364
NET SEND command reference, 364-365
NET SHOW command to list LAN resources and status, 133
    command reference, 365
NET SHUTDOWN command reference, 365-366
NET SLOGINS command reference, 366
NET STREAM command reference, 366-367
NET STRING command reference, 367
NET TERMINATE command reference, 368
NET UNLINK command reference, 368
NET UNUSE command to cancel disk drive redirection, 150, 154
    command reference, 368
NET USE command to redirect a disk drive from the DOS prompt, 149-150, 154
    command reference, 369
NET USER command reference, 369
NET_MGR BACKUP command reference, 370-371
NET_MGR COPY USER command reference, 371
NET_MGR CREATE USER command reference, 371-372
NET_MGR DELETE command reference, 372
NET_MGR program, 182-184
    to change the server startup parameters, 323-327
    command reference, 369-373
    to control access rights of LAN users, 264-267
    to control security of LAN, 246, 252, 272
    to control server resource access, 267-271
    ending, 256, 265, 271
    graphical user interface for, 296, 298
    protecting, 273-274
    starting, 252, 264, 268
NET_MGR RESTORE command reference, 372
NET_MGR SET command reference, 373
NET_MGR SHOW command reference, 373
NetBIOS software, 53
    LAN cards that run, 191
    time elapsed since you started, 132-133
NetWare Lite, 63-64
NetWare NOS (Novell), 7, 20
    connecting Apple Macintoshes with PCs using, 70-71
    connecting LANtastic network to, 62-64
Network. *See* LAN (local area network)
Network buffer, 324-325, 333
Network Eye, The (TNE), 58
Network interface card (NIC), 4
Network interface unit (NIU), 4
Network operating system (NOS), 7, 45
Network productivity software, 29
Network software. *See* Network operating system (NOS)
Network startup batch file, 92, 116, 381-390. *See also* STARTNET.BAT file
    DOS 5 extended memory configuration's, 388-390

high-performance LAN server configuration's, 385-386
minimum RAM configuration's, 386-387
troubleshooting configuration's, 383-385
typical configuration's, 382-383
Network tasks, 324-325, 333
Newspaper archives on CD-ROM, 39
Node defined, 7, 19
Nondedicated server, 20, 67
Nonstandard bus selection settings, 102
Norton AntiVirus (Symantec Corporation), 284
Norton pcANYWHERE/LAN (Symantec Corporation), 198
Norton Utilities, 279, 306, 329
Null modem cable, 16-17

O

OEMSETUP.INF file, 290, 292
Office automation
checklists for, 83-86
planning for, 59-83
Office environment of workgroup, 80-81, 85
Office Works (Data Access Corporation), 31
Off-site backups, 202, 278
ONDISC (Dialog Information Services), 186
Operating systems
multiuser, 17
network, 7, 82. *See also individual types*
Optimization, 303-336
administrator's role in network, 276-277, 286
areas addressed by, 303-304
defined, 303
methodology, 304-308
for speed, 308-331
OS/2, no LANtastic version for, 62

P

Pacific Data Products, font cartridges from, 162
PARA Systems, 245
Paradox database application, 22
Parameter(s), LANtastic command
@filename, 340
/help (/?), 339
/remove, 339-340
/verbose, 340
common, 339-340
defined, 147
general format of, 338
NET_MGR program, 370
Part swapping to isolate hardware problems, 236-237, 241
Password
automatic encryption of, 256
case insensitivity of, 254-255
changed by user, 254
for e-mail security, 169, 171
expiration date to force assignment of new, 257
group account, 260
naming rules for, 252-253
for NET_MGR program, 273-274
for network security, 143, 149, 165, 251
renewing, 258
PC Tools, 279, 329, 335
Peer-Hub 10BASE-T Concentrator (Artisoft), 71
configuring, 106
planning for use of, 79-80
product details and price of, 47-48, 50-51
in starter kit, 97
Peer-Hub AUI Interface Kit, 50-51
Peer-to-peer network, 20, 64
Peripheral devices, access to, 3, 85
PhoneDisc U.S.A. Corp., 187
Physical (P) access right, 263
Plotters, shared, 58, 75

Pocket Ethernet Adapter model PE10B2 (Xircom), 211-212
Pocket Ethernet Adapter model PE10BT (Xircom), 211-212
Port connectors, serial and parallel, 16-17
Port, parallel
 Central Station requirement of, 206-207
 LANtastic Z installation on, 134-135
 printer, 22, 92, 119
Port, serial
 for ArtiCom use, 188
 LANtastic Z installation on, 134-135
 plotter's use of, 75
Portable LAN adapter, 211-213
Power failures, UPS for use during, 81
 features of, 244-245
 suppliers of, 245
Power problems, disk file problems caused by, 243-244
Print buffers to share printer among multiple PCs, 15-16, 23
Print server, 20
Print spool, 155, 278
Print stream names, 156
Printer(s)
 access from a server, 153
 access from a workstation, 151-153
 buffer, 325, 333
 color, 24
 conflicts between use of, by Windows and LANtastic, 293-294
 connections for, 119-120, 124
 dot matrix, 24, 73
 laser, 15, 22, 24, 73-74, 159-163
 locations of, 75-80
 redirection, canceling, 153-154
 redirection from the DOS prompt, 154
 redirection from the NET menu, 151-153
 shared. *See* Shared printers
 tasks, 325, 333
Printer queue control, 154-159
Procomm Plus Network, 189
Protocol, selecting communications, 197
PS/2 Micro Channel computer (IBM), 46

Q

Q&A database application (Symantec Corporation), 22, 33
Q-DOS (Gazelle Systems), 335
Q-DOS LAN, 279
QEMM program, 239

R

R:BASE (Microrim, Inc.), 33
RAM
 accessing data in, 308
 added to run disk cache program, 316
 added to speed network performance, 330
 chips, price of, 313
 disks, 321-322
 optimizing, 331-334
 startup files that minimize use of, 386-387
 types of, 310-311
 use, trade-offs between speed and, 324, 332
RAMBASE conflicts, 239-240
RAMDRIVE.SYS program, 321
Read (R) access right, 262
README.DOC file
 for LANtastic, 91, 94, 110-112, 130, 218
 for the Sounding Board, 218
Real estate management database, 27
RECORD program, 221-222
REDIR redirector program, 128, 327-328, 333, 335

command reference, 374-375
Redirection
cancellation from the DOS prompt, 150
from the DOS prompt, 149-150
from the NET menu, 138-146
Rename file (N) access right, 263
Repeater to amplify and regenerate LAN signals, 13
Request size for buffer, 325, 333
Resource Name menu box, 183
Resource scheduling groupware products, 30
Retail store management database, 27
RG58A/U and RG58C/U thin coaxial cable, 4, 45, 105-106
RG62 coaxial cable, 14
Right Hand Man II (Futurus Inc.), 30
Ring topology, 7-8, 10
RJ45 modular plugs for twisted-pair cable, 6, 47, 106
ROM BIOS chip, 69, 84
Rotation method of data backup, 202
Run burst, 326

S

SAY program, 221-222
Scalable fonts, 162
SCSI interface card, 177-179
Security, 249-274
administrator's role in, 276-284
backups of data for additional, 199-200
features of LANtastic, 140-143
four methods of imposing, 249-250
office, 284
Seek cache size, 326, 333
Segment(s)
defined, 13
length selection settings, 102
maximum cable length of 185 meters (607 feet) per, 13, 106
thin Ethernet's connection of up to four, 71
Selective backups, 204
Send Mail Options menu box, 165, 226
Server(s)
access from various workstations, controlling, 251
access times, limiting, 251, 258-259
access type, controlling, 250
accessing three or more, 145
activity level, LANtastic for Windows to monitor, 300-301
backing up files from, 72, 203
choosing between a dedicated and nondedicated, 67-68
configuring, 93
data lost by rebooting, 148
defined, 19-20
disk space, housekeeping for, 278-279, 329-330
displaying available, 140
hard disk, accessing, 138
inaccessible, 245-246
logging in to, 140, 142, 148-149, 165, 249-261
logging out from, 150
mail, 163-164
modem, 189-192, 194-197
multiple, large LAN's use of, 71
name, entering custom, 119. *See also* Machine name
powered off ungracefully, file problems caused by, 243
primary, 164
printer access from, 153
removing LANtastic from, 146-148
resources, limiting offerings of, 250, 267-271
response time, 303
SHARE DOS command required to run on, 243
shared between LANs, 71
sharing violation of program run on, 247

software installation, 90-93, 109-122
special access privileges and restrictions for, 251
splitting file sharing and printer sharing among different, 331
starting, 125-127
usage, audit trails for, 250, 271-273, 331

Server Connections menu box, 140, 151, 164
SERVER server program, 128, 323-327, 335
command reference, 375-378
Server Startup Parameters menu, 324
SHARE DOS command required to run on server, 243
Shared CD-ROM drives, 23, 37-40, 75, 174-187
Shared data files, 3, 268
Shared directory, 268-271
Shared disk space, 22-23, 25
Shared fax cards, 58
Shared hard disks, 138-150
Shared modems, 23, 40, 58, 74-75, 187-198
Shared peripherals, number and type of, 72-75
Shared plotters, 58, 75
Shared printers, 15-16, 150-163
avoiding LPT1 port for output with Windows and LANtastic for, 293-294
foot traffic generated by, 77-78, 85
planning for, 73-74
printer port number for, 92-93
products for, 159-163
as reason to purchase a LAN, 22-24
Shared servers, 71
Shared software, 23, 34-37
products list of LAN editions for, 36-37
Sharing primary resources, 137-171
Signaling methods on LANs, 10-14
Silver satin telephone extension cable, 4, 13
SMARTDRV.SYS, 315
SmarTerm, 189
Sneakernet joke, 15
Softerm, 189
Software
from the author, 396
legal restrictions for, 35-36
sharing, 23, 34-37
SOLA Electric, 245
Sounding Board Adapter (ISA and Micro Channel) (Artisoft), 55-56, 215-229
components of, 216
custom message, creating and playing, 221-222
expansion slot for, 217-218
hardware installation for, 217-218
prerecorded message with, playing, 221
price of, 215
programs, 220-222
software installation for, 218
starting, 219-220
testing, 220-222
voice message file size with, 216
Specialties database products, list of, 28-29
SpinRite II, 329
Spooling print jobs, 155
Stacker (Stac Electronics), 335-336
Stand-alone computers, 2-3
Star topology, 7-10
ARCnet use of, 14
token ring LAN use of, 13
STARTNET.BAT file
batch file commands added to, 148
changed for less erratic printing speed, 247
changed for more than five users per server, 246
changed for more than ten users per server, 246

changed to make LPT2 available on the workstation, 293-294
changed to run Central Station, 208-211
changed to run high-level MSCDEX driver software, 181-182, 185
changed to run LANcache, 309-310, 312-314
changed to run portable LAN adapter, 212
changed to run Sounding Board, 219-220
changing IRQ or IOBASE parameter in, 129
customized, 285
executing, 127-130
installing, 93, 95, 118, 121, 123
RAMBASE parameter in, 293
run before WIN, 295, 297
for a server, minimum RAM, 387
server parameters in, 323-327
for a server running LANcache, 386
for a server, troubleshooting, 384
for a server, typical, 383
for a server with extended memory, 389
to start LANtastic used with Windows, 290
troubleshooting, 232, 234, 237-238
for a workstation, minimum RAM, 387
for a workstation, troubleshooting, 385
for a workstation, typical, 383
for a workstation with extended memory, 390
Static electricity, discharging, 98
Station or node defined, 7, 19
Sun workstation, 21
Super ACL (A) privilege, 258
Super Mail (M) privilege, 258
for network administrator, 171
Super PC-Kwik (Multisoft Corporation), 315-316
Super Queue (Q) privilege, 258
SuperTime (SuperTime Inc.), 31
Surge suppressors/filters, 80, 85, 244
Switch file, 323
Switch (parameter) defined, 147, 338
System crash, 238-239
System Manager's (S) privilege, 258
SY-TOS (Sytos Plus, Sytron Corporation), 203-205

T

Tape backup devices, 72, 199-206
for archiving files, 335
capacity and cost of, 201
components, 201
reasons to use, 199-200
strategies for using, 201-203
suppliers and products, 205-206
used with LANtastic, 203-204
Tapemaster 250 (CMS Enhancements), 203-204
Telephone lists on CD-ROM, 39
Terminal Emulator menu box, 197
Terminate-and-stay-resident (TSR) programs, 348
troubleshooting, 234, 238, 240
Terminators, 6, 90
attaching LAN, 106-107
checking for bad, 235-236, 242
required for SCSI daisy chain, 179
spare, maintaining, 237
for thin Ethernet, 233
Texas Instruments microLaser XL PS35 laser printer, 161
Thick coaxial cable, 46
Thin coaxial cable, 4-5, 45-46
BNC connector for, 6
bus topology with, 8
terminators for, 6
Thin Ethernet segment length selection settings, 102

Thomas Conrad (hub manufacturer), 72
Tiara Computer Systems, 72
Time and billing database, 27
Time, setting, 143
Timer tick defined, 337
Token Ring, IEEE 802.5, 13-14
Topologies of LANs, 7-10
Toshiba TXM-3301A4 CD-ROM drives, 187
Toshiba XM-3300 internal and TXM3300 external CD-ROM drives, 177-182
Tree of multiple hubs, 9
Tripp Lite, 245
Troubleshooting for LANtastic networks, 231-247
    examining recent LAN changes during, 233-234
    general, 232-238
    isolating the problem for, 235-238
    questions to start with in, 233
    specific, 238-247
    startup file configurations for, 383-385
Twisted pair cable. *See also* Unshielded twisted-pair (UTP) cable
    Artisoft's specifications for, 106
    dual, 53

U

Uninterruptible power system (UPS), 81, 85, 244-245
Unix, 17
Unshielded twisted-pair (UTP) cable, 4-5
    buildings prewired with, 9
    electrical interference on, 10, 80
    installing, 106
    LAN products using, 46-47
    RJ-45 modular plugs and jacks for, 6
Updata Publications, Inc., 187
UPS program, 245
    command reference, 378-379
User accounts
    defined, 250-251
    for e-mail, 164, 167, 169, 171
    establishing, 252-261
    expiration date of, 251, 257
    group. *See* Group user account
    privileges for, 258
    restrictions possible for, 251
    for security on LAN, 249
User Auditing (U) privilege, 258
User description, 254-255
User error as cause of corrupt disk files, 242
User Information menu box, 256-257
User support, 276, 284-285
Username
    changes to access rights performed using, 264, 266-267
    entering e-mail recipient's, 165, 167
    entering your, 140-143, 165
    maximum of 16 characters for, 252-253
    required to access server, 251
Utility software, LAN
    groupware, 30
    LANCHECK, 131-133
    purpose of, 7

V

Vertical market software, 26
VGA video card, hardware problems from, 239-240
VINES NOS (Banyan), 7, 63
Virex-PC (Microcom, Inc.), 283
Virtual disk drive, 24, 321
Virus, computer
    author of, 279-280
    contagious and destructive stages of, 280-281
    checking for, 234, 240
    defined, 279
    sources of, 280-281
    treatment, 281-282

"trigger" logic of, 281
ViruSafe/LAN (XTree Company), 283
VIRUSCAN Series (McAfee Associates), 283
Virus-checker program, 281-282
Virus-cleanup program, 282
Virus-protection products, 282-284
Voice board. *See* Sounding Board Adapter (ISA and Micro Channel) (Artisoft)
Voice chat to connect two users who have Sounding Board, 222-225
Voice mail, 225-229
Voice Message Recorder menu box, 226-229
Voice products by Artisoft, 55-56

W

Western Digital Ethernet cards, 41
WIN300.TXT document, 289, 296
Windows
changes to, for use with LANtastic, 294
disk cache to use with LANtastic and, 315
installing, 290
LANtastic and, 287-301
LANtastic configuration for, 288
multiuser configuration for, 288
new version of Sounding Board for, 216
overhead of, performance degradation due to, 331
reasons for popularity of, 287
shortcomings of, 288
single-user configuration for, 288-296
Wireless LAN, 4
WordPerfect Office LAN (WordPerfect Corporation), 30, 70
Workgroup
calendar software to arrange meetings for, 29
defined, 21
electronic mail within, 29
functions of, learning about, 61
needs and wants, assessing 65-84
office environment of, 80-81, 85
user account. *See* Group user account
Workstation
concurrent logins, 254, 256
defined, 20
engineering workstation versus, 21
hardware problems, 236
login problems between server and, 247
modem, 189, 192-193
printer access from, 151-153
redirecting drive of, 247, 296
resources offered automatically to, 120
software installation, 94-95, 122-125
starting, 130-131
tape backup system installed on, 203
Write (W) access right, 262

X

Xenix, 17
Xircom Pocket Ethernet Adapter, 68
XMS (extended memory specification) standard, 311
XMS memory, 311-312, 316
XTree Pro Gold (XTree Company), 279, 335

Z

Zero-slot LAN, 17, 57

PLEASE
AFFIX
CORRECT
POSTAGE

LAN TIMES BUYERS DIRECTORY
7050 Union Park Center
Suite 240
Midvale, UT 84047

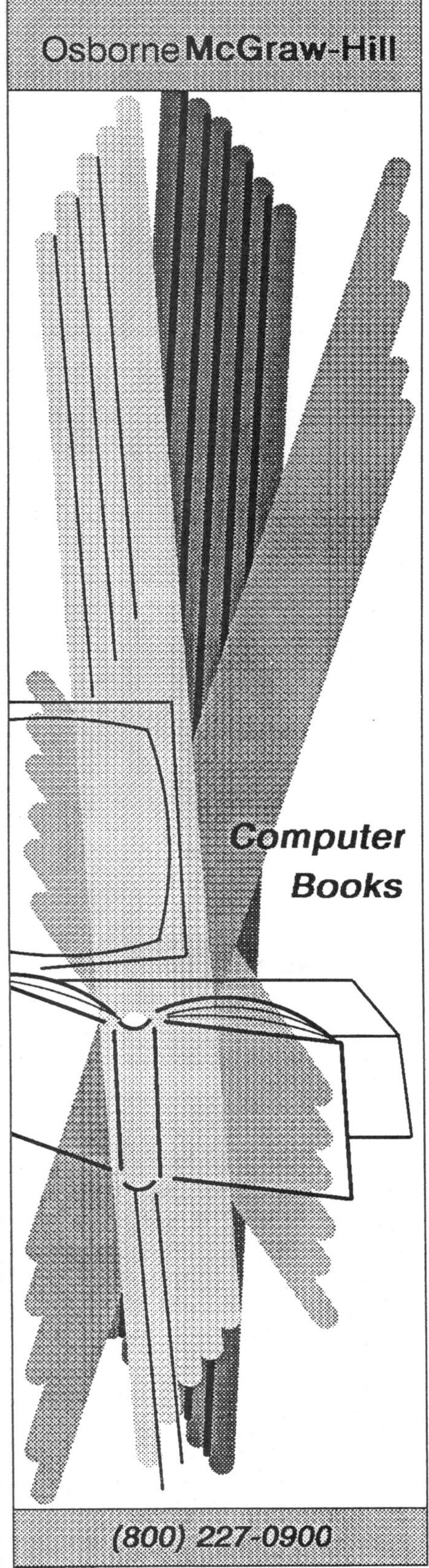

Bookmarker Design — Lance Ravella

Tear off for Bookmark

You're important to us...

We'd like to know what you're interested in, what kinds of books you're looking for, and what you thought about this book in particular.

Please fill out the attached card and mail it in. We'll do our best to keep you informed about Osborne's newest books and special offers.

YES, Send Me a FREE Color Catalog of all Osborne computer books
To Receive Catalog, Fill in Last 4 Digits of ISBN Number from Back of Book (see below bar code) 0-07-881 _ _ _ – _

Name: ______________________ Title: ______________

Company: ______________________________________

Address: ______________________________________

City: ______________ State: __________ Zip: __________

I'M PARTICULARLY INTERESTED IN THE FOLLOWING *(Check all that apply)*

I use this software
- ☐ WordPerfect
- ☐ Microsoft Word
- ☐ WordStar
- ☐ Lotus 1-2-3
- ☐ Quattro
- ☐ Others ______________

I use this operating system
- ☐ DOS
- ☐ Windows
- ☐ UNIX
- ☐ Macintosh
- ☐ Others ______________

I rate this book:
☐ Excellent ☐ Good ☐ Poor

I program in
- ☐ C or C++
- ☐ Pascal
- ☐ BASIC
- ☐ Others ______________

I chose this book because
- ☐ Recognized author's name
- ☐ Osborne/McGraw-Hill's reputation
- ☐ Read book review
- ☐ Read Osborne catalog
- ☐ Saw advertisement in store
- ☐ Found/recommended in library
- ☐ Required textbook
- ☐ Price
- ☐ Other ______________

Comments ______________________________________

Topics I would like to see covered in future books by Osborne/McGraw-Hill include:

____

IMPORTANT REMINDER
To get your FREE catalog, write in the last 4 digits of the ISBN number printed on the back cover (see below bar code) 0-07-881 _ _ _ – _

NO POSTAGE
NECESSARY
IF MAILED
IN THE
UNITED STATES

BUSINESS REPLY MAIL
First Class Permit NO. 3111 Berkeley, CA

Postage will be paid by addressee

Osborne **McGraw-Hill**
2600 Tenth Street
Berkeley, California 94710–9938

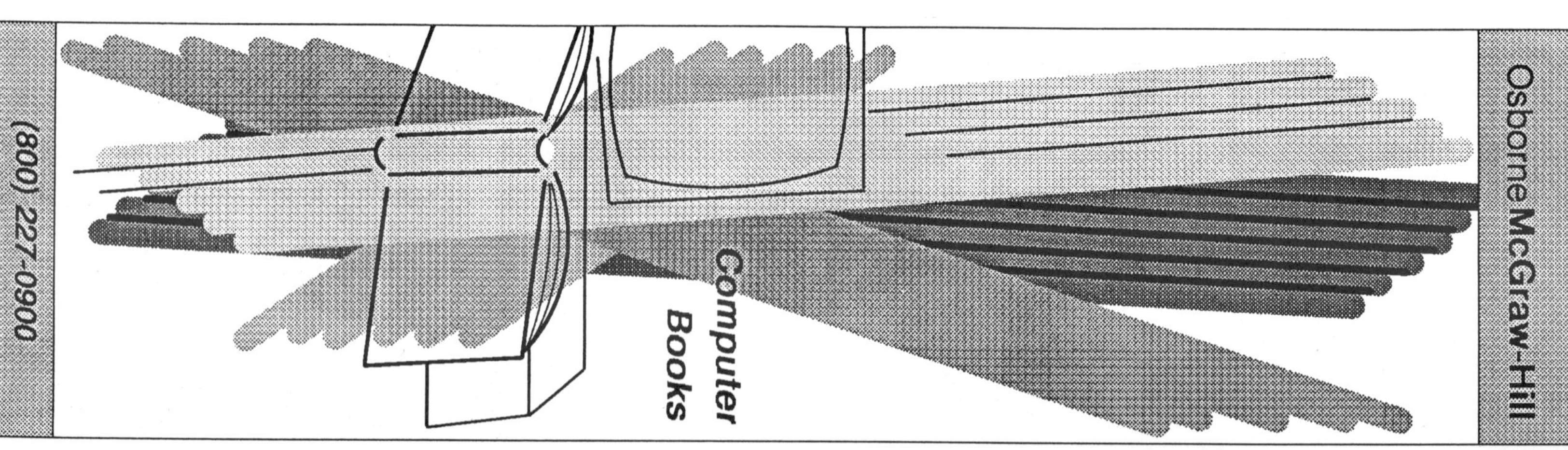